Tourism

5

35

BY PROFESSOR S. MEDLIK

Published by Pitman:
The British Hotel and Catering Industry

Published by Butterworth-Heinemann:
A Manual of Hotel Reception (with J. R. S. Beavis)
Profile of the Hotel and Catering Industry
The Management of Tourism: A Selection of Readings (with A. J. Burkart)
The Business of Hotels

Tourism

Past, Present and Future

A. J. BURKART
M.A. (Oxon), F.T.S.
Reader in Tourism
Department of Hotel, Catering and Tourism Management
University of Surrey

and

S. MEDLIK
M.A., B.Com., F.H.C.I.M.A., F.T.S.
Formerly Professor and Head of Department
of Hotel, Catering and Tourism Management
University of Surrey
Currently Visiting Professor and
Director Horwath & Horwath (UK) Ltd.

SECOND EDITION

BUTTERWORTH
HEINEMANN

Butterworth-Heinemann Ltd
Linacre House, Jordan Hill, Oxford OX2 8DP

 PART OF REED INTERNATIONAL BOOKS

OXFORD   LONDON   BOSTON
MUNICH   NEW DELHI   SINGAPORE   SYDNEY
TOKYO   TORONTO   WELLINGTON

First published 1974
Reprinted 1976
Second edition 1981
Reprinted 1982, 1984, 1986, 1987, 1989, 1990, 1992

ISBN 0 7506 0649 5

Printed and bound in Great Britain by
Redwood Press Limited, Melksham, Wiltshire

Preface

Tourism denotes the temporary, short-term movement of people to destinations outside the places where they normally live and work and their activities during the stay at these destinations. Much of this movement is international in character and much of it is a leisure activity. In recent years it has become an important factor in world trade and a major element in the balance of payments of many countries, which has grown faster than the trade in goods. For countries, regions, towns, and villages, which attract tourists in large numbers, tourism can be a significant element in their prosperity. Tourism generates wealth and employment. It is a major source of income and employment for individuals in many places deficient in natural resources other than climate and scenery. It makes use of resources, which may not be used otherwise, in particular of unemployed labour in developing countries and regions with few or no alternative sources of employment. Beaches, moors, and snowfields are examples of natural resources, which cannot readily contribute to the economic well-being of the area, except through the medium of tourism. It is also a major source of income to many transport operators, providers of accommodation and entertainment, shops, and other businesses. For residents of an area tourism often provides amenities which the resident population would not be able to support otherwise. But if not skilfully managed, the injection of a large alien population into a society may also give rise to social and political tensions, which may vitiate the economic benefits the tourists bring.

By its very nature, tourism is a conspicuous phenomenon. The incidence of a mobile population visiting places outside their normal domicile is an expression of living standards and of quality of life. It can also decisively influence living standards and the quality of life in places visited; it is one of the visible pressures, which modern civilizations exert on the environment. Tourism is also a highly complex phenomenon. It involves the activities and interests not only of large transport undertakings, owners of tourist sites and attractions, and of various tourist services at the destination, but also of central and local government. Each of these serve both the resident population and visitors, and their management must reconcile the needs of tourists with the needs of the resident population.

Tourism is in short an important human activity not only of economic significance, but also of social, political, cultural, and educational significance. As such it is interesting and deserving of study for its own sake, for greater understanding of the economy and society, quite apart from any vocational or other utilitarian purposes. But tourism is also an important economic and industrial activity, in which many individuals, firms, and other organizations are engaged, and which is of direct and indirect concern to many others. To them the study of tourism is of practical necessity and usefulness.

The complex nature of tourism implies that many academic disciplines are involved in its study. Basic disciplines such as economics, geography, psychology, and sociology, as well as the newer disciplines of politics, management, and marketing, all have a contribution to make, in addition to such tools and techniques as market research, planning, and statistics. The need is for a systematic framework to explain the tourism phenomenon in its various manifestations. In this search for a systematic framework, two alternative approaches may be distinguished. One is to use a basic discipline as a starting point; thus we may study the economics of tourism, the geography of tourism, the sociology of tourism. The other is to conceive of tourism as a study of its own, in which a body of knowledge is formulated and examined systematically, with its own boundaries and relationships. This book endeavours the latter approach and is based on the authors' work at the University of Surrey. It is not the first such attempt and the authors readily acknowledge the influence of earlier works in this field.* But it is different in its structure and approach in attempting to draw a synthesis between theory and practice and to reflect the dynamic nature of tourism in the second half of the twentieth century.

The basic concepts, determinants, and significance are examined as the anatomy of tourism in Part II and statistics of tourism in Part III. Parts IV, V, and VI provide an analysis of the role of the major industries involved in tourism — passenger transportation, accommodation, tour operations, and travel agencies. Parts VII and VIII are concerned with the two main functions of marketing and of physical planning and development in tourism, and Part IX with organization and finance. Corresponding to Part I, which traces the historical development of tourism over the last few centuries to the present day, Part X looks ahead and discusses the future.

The book is intended as a text for the student of tourism, and to be helpful to all those with an interest and involvement in tourism: official tourist organizations at national, regional, and local levels; transportation, hotel, tour-operating, and travel agent companies; central and local government, and other organizations in which specialist knowledge of tourism is important.

The approach has been to provide a simple and reasonably comprehensive outline, rather than a detailed and exhaustive treatment of some or all aspects of tourism in depth. Suggestions for further reading on particular aspects are made at the beginning of each of the ten main parts of the book; material used in writing the book and much other relevant literature are listed in the bibliography. The planned extension of this outline is the companion volume, *The Management of Tourism: A Selection of Readings,* also published by Heinemann.

Although tourism is seen here from the British viewpoint, the book is not merely about British tourism. Historically tourism has been a British pheno-menon; the propensity to take holidays in the British population is among the highest in the world; Britain continues to be an important tourist-generating country and in recent years has become one of the principal destinations for tour-

*In particular Hunziker, W. and Krapf, K., *Grundriss der Allgemeinen Fremdenverkehrslehre,* and Lickorish, L. J. and Kershaw, A. G., *The Travel Trade.*

ists from other countries. Much innovation in tourism continues to originate in Britain, which also exercises a leading influence in international organizations concerned with tourism. For these reasons, and because British tourism has so far been better documented than that of other major industrial countries, much material in this book is about the British and about their approach to tourism, and many examples are drawn from British practice. But the concepts and methods are described in a wider context, comparisons are drawn with other countries and with their approaches as appropriate, and the outline of tourism drawn in this book should have a universal interest and validity.

As far as possible, statistical and other data are included to 1970; the writing of the book was completed in the autumn of 1972 and, wherever possible, the manuscript was revised in the summer of 1973. At that time the dynamic progress of tourism continued and when describing this rapidly developing field, the risk was that of being overtaken by events. Although the book does not stop in 1970, and a conscious attempt has been made to look into the future, particularly in Part X, it is perhaps most appropriate to view this text as establishing a set of benchmarks which tourism has reached on the threshold of the 1970s, and from which the future may be contemplated. But above all, it provides a framework in which tourism can be examined now and in the future.

We cannot hope to record our gratitude to all the people concerned with tourism who have contributed to our thinking and writing, but at the risk of appearing invidious, we must refer to several, as well as make a more general acknowledgement.

Anyone with any knowledge of tourism must be profoundly influenced by the work and writing of Professor W. Hunziker, President of the International Association of Scientific Experts in Tourism, Mr L. J. Lickorish, Director-General, British Tourist Authority, and of Mr S. F. Wheatcroft, member and Group Planning Director, British Airways Board. We have been so influenced and additionally enjoyed many hours of discussion with them, before and during the writing of this book. Our colleague Mr V. T. C. Middleton painstakingly read and commented on the entire manuscript and earned our thanks for numerous improvements both of content and style. We have endeavoured to acknowledge our debt to many others in the references to individual chapters and would ask to be forgiven by those whose contribution has gone unrecorded. Errors and omissions are, of course, our own responsibility.

We owe a debt of gratitude to Miss F. Hathaway, Mrs B. Hill, Mrs J. Smith, and Miss E. Westley, secretaries in the Department of Hotel and Catering Management, University of Surrey, who have typed so much of the material in its early stages as teaching aids for our work at the University.

Finally we place on record our gratitude to our past and present students who have been the patient first recipients of many of our thoughts and who have contributed to their formulation by their demands on us and by their response.

University of Surrey   A. J. BURKART
Guildford, Surrey   S. MEDLIK

Preface to Second Edition

The first edition of this book was completed in the autumn of 1972 and, wherever possible, included revisions up to the summer of 1973. It established a set of benchmarks, which tourism reached in the early 1970s, but excluded such major happenings of that decade as the onset of the energy crisis and worldwide recession, the collapse of some of the world's largest tour operators, and major developments in the fields of transport, accommodation, and travel organization.

Much of the 1970s was a period of uncertain disposable incomes, growing unemployment, and unprecedented inflation in many countries, including Britain. But it was also a period of much innovation and development in tourism, with an increasing involvement of governments, and in face of the many problems and challenges, tourism continued its growth in most parts of the world.

The new edition of this book was prompted by the need to record the eventful 1970s, to see where tourism stood at the turn of the decade, and from there to contemplate its future. The basic structure of the book of ten main Parts and thirty chapters with a similar coverage has been retained. As far as possible, statistical and other data have been included to the end of the 1970s and the text has been thoroughly revised to reflect what has changed since we first wrote, which seems like many years ago.

Again we wish to record our appreciation to those who in various ways influenced our thinking about tourism generally and the new edition of this book in particular, and to express our hope that it may continue to serve the needs of students, teachers and practitioners of tourism as well as the first edition appears to have done.

Guildford 1980   A. J. BURKART
                                                                     S. MEDLIK

Contents

Appendixes

Tables

Part I

Historical Development

Further Reading for Part I

Burkart, A. J. and Medlik, S. (editors): *The Management of Tourism,* Part I
Dyos, H. J. and Aldcroft, D. H.: *British Transport*
Lickorish, L. J., and Kershaw, A. G.: *The Travel Trade,* Chapter 2
Mathias, P.: *The First Industrial Nation*
Medlik, S.: *Profile of the Hotel and Catering Industry,* Part I

References to Part I

1 *Boswell's Life of Johnson*
2 Dyos, H. J., and Aldcroft, D. H.: *British Transport*
3 Gilbert, E. W.: *Brighton*
4 Quoted in Rae, W. Fraser: *The Business of Travel*
5 Smart, Eynon: 'The Holiday You Can Bank On', *The Times,* 28 August 1971

1   *The Beginnings of Tourism to 1840*

Tourism is a recent phenomenon. Even if business travel is included as tourism, as it is in some definitions (*see* Parts II and III), it is still of comparatively recent origin. The word *tourism* did not appear in the English language until the early nineteenth century, and the word *tour* was more closely associated with the idea of a voyage or peregrination or a circuit, as in the case of a theatrical tour, than with the idea of an individual being temporarily away from home for pleasure purposes which is such a significant feature of the use of the word *tourist* today.

Three principal epochs of tourism may be distinguished. The first, which is discussed in this chapter, takes the story to the early days of the railway age, that is, to about 1840 in Britain, a little later elsewhere. The second epoch covers the railway age itself. The years between the two world wars, which witnessed the significant development of the private motor car and of the bus and coach, and the period after the Second World War, when civil aviation came to share with the private car the principal transport role in tourism, form together the third epoch.

Transport is the necessary pre-condition of tourism, and the three epochs are to be identified with particular modes of transport. For tourism is a matter of being elsewhere, and to be elsewhere implies the use of transport. Mechanized transport has made travel possible for a significant part of the populations of the developed countries at least, and thus tourism has become a matter of interest and concern to governments and governed alike. Much of the historical study of tourism will be concerned with the development of modern transport, and other aspects of tourism have followed the evolution of the various modes of transport. Tourism in the modern sense has its antecedents historically, but it will be argued that the difference between the world of the eighteenth century and earlier, and more recent times is not merely a matter of degree, but that the world of 1850, for example, differs structurally from the world of 1750 in tourism, as in everything else.

Travel Before the Industrial Revolution

Travel before the Industrial Revolution was largely a matter of pilgrimages, and of travel for business or official purposes, and there is little evidence of the extent and volume of private travel in the medieval period. However, from the end of the sixteenth century some growth in private travel can be detected, initially for educational purposes, and later as satisfying a new curiosity about the way in which the inhabitants of other parts of this country, and indeed foreign countries, lived.

Samuel Johnson contemplated a journey to Italy in 1776, and Boswell records him as saying '. . . A man who has not been in Italy, is always conscious of an inferiority, from his not having seen what it is expected a man should see. The grand object of travelling is to see the shores of the Mediterranean. . . . All our religion, almost all our law, almost all our arts, almost all that sets us above savages, has come to us from the shores of the Mediterranean.'[1] In this sentence lies the concept of the Grand Tour, the peregrination through Europe, by which the wealthy young might become civilized by exposure to European art, architecture, and manners, and by which they might also enrich their country houses at home.

Foreign travel was a part of an aristocratic man's education. Domestic travel for pleasure began in the eighteenth century with the emergence into the fashionable era of spas and seaside resorts. Originally owing their existence to the supposed medicinal benefits of mineral and sea water, they became places of entertainment. Only in the very last years of the period under examination does anything like the concept of leisure in a modern sense appear, and only a small number of towns enjoyed a reputation as a destination for visitor traffic on a national scale. The legends associated with the Prince Regent obscure the small scale of resort activity; only a small fraction of the population was affected by their development.

The Idea of Leisure in the Eighteenth Century

Travel in the eighteenth century was an activity undertaken by a small, wealthy, and mostly landed *élite*. This *élite* travelled chiefly for educational and for official purposes. Other travel took place for what would now be called business purposes by merchants and the like. The vast majority of the population hardly travelled beyond their village and the nearest market town. For this majority, the idea of leisure and of holiday in a modern sense did not exist: life was not to be divided into work and leisure, and this modern dichotomy would have seemed artificial. Nor would the landed *élite* have understood the distinction between work and leisure; the members of the *élite* did not see themselves as working, nor work as an activity in life from which respite was needed.

Leisure in the eighteenth century was an attribute of social class, not a division of the working day or of one's lifetime. Either a man belonged to a stratum of society where he had to labour all day and every day, though not without rest, or he belonged to a stratum of society where he was at liberty to order his life as he wished. To peer and peasant alike, the idea of dividing life into work and leisure would have seemed very strange. The reason for this unpunctuated existence must be sought in the extremely localized life of a predominantly agricultural society. Both the landowner and his tenants and employees lived the major part of their life in one place, bound to it by the ties of the land, and in these circumstances life was readily viewed as a continuum. Only when the place of earning one's living began to be separated from the place where one reared one's family, could the modern separation of work and leisure be valid.

Changes in the Structure of Society

In the later eighteenth century occurred the phenomenon we now call the Industrial Revolution. It brought about changes in the economy of Britain which had marked effects in laying the foundations of modern tourism.

The most dramatic feature of the hundred years from 1750 to 1850 was the increase in the absolute size of the population. At the end of the seventeenth century, Gregory King's estimate of the population of the kingdom at $5 \cdot 5$ million is thought to be reasonable, but by the time of the first Census of 1801 (itself rather imperfect), the population exceeded 15 million, and by the mid-nineteenth century it exceeded 25 million. Such an increase could only be supported by the increasing industrialization of the economy: countries such as Ireland, where similar increases had to be supported by a merely agricultural economy, saw a subsequent reduction in the absolute number of the population brought about by famine and emigration. (*See* Mathias, P., op. cit. in Further Reading at the beginning of this Part for general discussion of these points.)

More significant in the present context than the increase in the absolute size of the population, is the considerable internal migration which took place in the eighteenth century. The increase in the population was accompanied by a steady drift of population from the rural areas to the newly emerging industrial towns of the North and of the Midlands, because only in these towns did sufficient employment opportunities exist; indeed, there seems to have been little migration from the agricultural South into the industrial towns of the North which attracted their own hinterland population.

The migration to the towns led to the creation of new households and new purchasing power, stimulating internal consumer demand in a way that the more self-sufficient peasant communities of the rural areas could not do. The effect was to create an urban population with its family roots elsewhere than in the towns in which it now resided, and with a rising *per capita* income higher than that of the rural areas whence it came. It may not be fanciful to see a connection between this internal mgration and the emergence of modern tourism in the North and Midlands rather than in the South.

The point can be illustrated by comparing the growth of several large towns between 1801 and 1841. In the South, for example, Oxford only just doubled its size from 12,000 to 24,000, Norwich not even that, from 36,000 to 62,000, and Bath from 33,000 to 53,000. Contrast this with the growth of Birmingham from 71,000 to 202,000, of Manchester from 75,000 to 252,000, or of Bradford from 13,000 to 67,000.

In the eighteenth and early nineteenth centuries, there must have been a marked increase in national income to support the rapidly increasing population, but more telling for present purposes are the changes which took place in the shares of the national income taken by various sectors of the economy. The contraction of the share attributable to agriculture and the expansion of the share taken by manufacturing industry had already begun by the end of the eighteenth century: in 1801 a third of the national income was attributable to agriculture; by 1851 that share fell to 20 per cent. In 1801 the proportion of national income accounted for by manufacturing industry was scarcely higher than in Gregory King's day, but the value of that share was five times higher, and the greatest decline in the share of national income accounted for by agriculture awaited the end of the nineteenth century. *(See* Mathias, P., op. cit.)

The proportion of the national income accounted for by government, by the professions, by the armed services, and by what may be broadly termed the white-collar sector, remained more or less constant, at about 30 per cent. But this constant share conceals other changes. With a rising population, there was an absolute increase in the numbers of government officials, of the professions, and of the managerial occupations. The increasing complexity of industrialization has probably concealed the true size of this class. At the same time, especially at the end of the eighteenth century, the need to expand the national debt to finance the war with France created a large body of 'fundholders', a *rentier* class whose wealth for the first time was not locked up in land. Settlements on children, spouses, and widows could now be made in the marketable medium of consols rather than in land. The size of the national debt created new financial intermediaries, bankers, brokers, jobbers, and the like to handle it – again a new class of non-landed wealth owners.

The way in which tourism emerged was influenced by a dramatic shift in the country's foreign trade. Until the third quarter of the eighteenth century, the major part of Britain's foreign trade had been with North-West Europe and the Mediterranean. But the export trade to North America expanded very rapidly after the American War of Independence. A considerable fleet was required to handle it, and the upsurge in this trade led to the expansion of the Atlantic ports of, notably, Bristol, Liverpool, and Glasgow.

Industrialization, therefore, created two new sectors of society. First, an urban population, chiefly in the Northern and Midland cities, which was to become the principal market for the passenger railway and for the popular excursions associated with it. It is not coincidental that the earliest railways had their origins in the Northern industrial cities or that Thomas Cook laid the foundations of his enterprise in the Midlands. Secondly, the new classes of fundholders and financial intermediaries, with wealth not committed to land, formed the market for travel and tourism as soon as the supply of transport made travel possible. At the same time the influence of the North Atlantic foreign trade played a decisive part in the development of the transatlantic passenger shipping industry, and in the far-seeing concept of the Great Western Railway of an integrated railway and liner service to link London and New York via the port of Bristol.

The Pattern of Transport Before the Railway

Before the railway, passengers and most freight travelled by road. Until the middle of the seventeenth century, such roads as existed were maintained from local funds, but the subsequent growth of trade, involving long-distance traffic rather than local, began to place burdens on the road system it was never intended to bear. The provision of better roads was left to the device of the turnpike, rather than to the creation of a national road authority. European countries with land frontiers adopted a more centralized system, in order that military movements could be rapidly effected. In Britain, the turnpike system evolved as a business enterprise rather than as a charge on local or national tax funds. The required capital to construct or to improve roads to turnpike standards was subscribed by the trustees, usually local landowners, who were empowered to levy tolls on traffic using the turnpike. The turnpike concept has found favour again today, especially in the USA, and it remains one solution to the problem of transferring the cost of using a road or a bridge from the local population, in whose locality it lies, to the actual user.

The first turnpike road appeared in Hertfordshire in 1663. New turnpikes followed sporadically, and Defoe writing sixty years later speaks with approval of the system. But the rapid expansion of the economy placed further burdens on the turnpikes, and after a huge increase in the number of turnpike Acts brought before Parliament, the General Turnpike Act 1773 consolidated the governance and regulation of the turnpike system. Fifty years later, after a further series of inquiries, the Turnpike Act 1822 was passed. All this legislative activity reflected the growing pressure of demand for efficient transport in an expanding economy on an essentially local road system. By 1838 there were 22,000 miles of turnpike roads open, representing a fifth of the public roads of the country.

Contemporary writers deplored the state of the roads. In fairness it must be said that, however much it was improved, the road system had demands placed upon it which outstripped the feasible performance of an essentially local enterprise. At a time when the economy as a whole was becoming nationwide in scale and in interdependence, the road system lacked any kind of national planning, despite the work of the three great engineers, Metcalfe, McAdam, and Telford. Consequently, effort was devoted to mitigating the worst effects of the pressure of demand for better roads. Characteristically, improved transportation generates more traffic than the system can bear, and this was as true of the early road system as it has been of modes of transport developed subsequently.

Stage-coaches and Mail-coaches

Until the eighteenth century the most usual form of transport was the horse, and on horseback nearly all individual travel was performed. Today, when public transport in large vehicles is perfectly familiar, it is easy to overlook the fact that historically the one-man one-vehicle principle predominates. The multi-passenger vehicle is one of the ways in which the modern world differs structurally from its predecessors. With the widespread ownership of cars, there is now a return to the historical norm of individual transport. What needs explaining is not the private car, but the train, the coach, and the aircraft.

The increasing demand for travel and the improvement of the road system in the eighteenth century were associated with an increase in coach services. By the advent of the passenger railway, coaching constituted something like a national network of public passenger transport. But in the seventeenth and early eighteenth centuries the coach services were seasonal, rudimentary, and offered a speed rarely in excess of three or four miles an hour. The state of the roads saw to that. Around London and the larger cities short-distance services operated to towns and hamlets within thirty miles or so. The first attempt to offer a relatively fast service may be dated to 1669, when Oxford was connected to London by a one-day service in summer and a two-day service in winter. However, by the beginning of the nineteenth century, all the major cities were connected to the capital by as many as twenty or thirty services a day, and journeys of up to 200 miles could be completed by a coach within a long day.

The number of passengers using these services remained a small fraction of the population. The coach as a vehicle was small and capable of carrying perhaps a dozen people. In 1831, the population of Portsmouth was 30,000 and the daily coach capacity to London scarcely more than 200 seats. The increased demand for travel by coach was more an expression of a growing population than of the extension of travel to sections of the population which had hitherto been denied it.

Increasing business activity in the eighteenth century led to a vigorous demand for better postal services. At the beginning of the century, Her Majesty's mail was largely conducted by mounted post-boys, a service both vulnerable and slow. In 1784 the possibility of improvement was demonstrated by John Palmer with the introduction, initially at his own expense, of a fast service by diligence between Bristol and London. Palmer's enterprise was rewarded by an appointment to the Post Office, and by 1791 there were more than 17,000 miles of mail coach route in operation. In addition to the mail box, a small number of passengers were carried, as well as armed guards. The change of horses at each stage was effected by innkeepers acting as contractors to the Post Office: these horsing contracts were valuable and sought after, not only for the fees paid by the Post Office, but also for the sake of the custom of travellers travelling by coach. Thus began the long history which has linked the carriage of mail to the carriage of passengers, and which is still a factor in transport.

Shipping and Sea Travel

The long indented coastline of Britain, pierced by numerous rivers, has made water transport important for the carriage of goods. But its slow pace has mitigated its exploitation for passengers. Then as now the passenger has been prepared to pay a premium for speed. Some coastal passenger traffic existed in the seventeenth and eighteenth centuries, and Defoe in his classic *Robinson Crusoe* has given a graphic account of the perils of an East Coast journey from Hull to London.

Overseas travel had to be by sea across the English Channel and the North and Irish Seas. The significance of the growth of sea services lies in the effect it had on the growth of ports, particularly those on the West Coast. The route to Ireland lay via Holyhead, Liverpool, and Bristol and thus the Great West Road and the Holyhead Road received more attention from government than would otherwise have been the case. Further, the proportion of Britain's trade that passed through London (trade with Europe and the Baltic) steadily declined as the North American and West Indian trade expanded through the West Coast ports of Bristol and Liverpool and Glasgow. The growth of shipping in the early nineteenth century was almost exclusively transatlantic in orientation.

Inns and Hotels

Accommodation for travellers may be conveniently viewed in two ways. The traveller requires accommodation at his destination and for journeys which cannot be concluded in a single day, he will require overnight accommodation. The distinction between terminal and transit accommodation is not absolute, but it serves as a tool for discussing the provision of accommodation in the eighteenth century.

Those who travelled were wealthy for the most part, and before embarking on a journey would equip themselves with letters of introduction for use at their destination. There the traveller would expect to stay in a private house. If this solution were not available to him, he would expect to hire lodgings or chambers. He would not expect usually to stay at an inn, except for transit purposes. With the growth of travel in the eighteenth century, there appeared in London the prototype of the modern hotel with the opening by one David Low in 1774 of the 'first family hotel' in Lord Archer's former house in Covent Garden. The next sixty years saw a gradual increase in the recognizable ancestors of the modern hotel in London and in resorts such as Brighton and Buxton. However, the substantial development of the terminal hotel awaited the volume and type of traffic only the railway could bring.

The staging inn where the traveller in transit might spend a night, had reached a high level of development by the culmination of the stage-coach era. In England at least, the traveller could reasonably expect at most inns a clean and comfortable welcome when he wished to eat or spend the night. The volume of travel at the beginning of the nineteenth century on the improved roads by the considerable network of stage-coach services was sufficient to keep the staging inn in business, so that by the time the inn reached the peak of its prosperity, it provided the bulk of accommodation *en route*; at the destination it began to give way to the hotel, but only very gradually.

Spas and Resorts

Some have seen the beginnings of tourism in the development of the specialized resort in the seventeenth and eighteenth centuries. It is as well to consider the origins of resorts and the people who frequented them at this period. The inland spa had its origins (often of respectable antiquity) in a belief in the efficacy of its mineral waters for medicinal purposes, either by drinking the water or by immersing in it. The patients would require diversions, and gradually the spa resorts added facilities for pleasure and entertainment to their medical facilities. But the curative mission of the spa lingered on for many years and only recently has spa treatment been finally disallowed in Britain under the National Health Service. In contrast continental Europe has continued to value spa treatment and the great spas of Baden-Baden in Germany and Marianske Lazne (Marienbad) and Karlovy Vary (Carlsbad) in Czechoslovakia are still thronged with patients rather than tourists.

By the middle of the eighteenth century, attention began to be paid to the possible curative effects of sea water and sea bathing. A Dr Russell[3] was the principal protagonist of the merits of sea bathing, and the seaside resort began to appear as an alternative to the inland spa. But even so no considerable fraction of the population could enjoy either seaside resort or inland spa. The use of both was still confined to a leisured class. To go to Brighton was a matter of being leisured, not a matter of being on holiday. Nor should one exaggerate the influence of royal patronage on the popularity of a resort at this time. It took the railway, and the national newspaper, and photography to make the Royal Family a model and an example to its subjects. Nevertheless, both the spas and the seaside resorts were embryonic tourist destinations, and some of them, with the railway age, built magnificently upon their early experience of catering for the visitor.

Concern for the Environment

At no point is the contrast between the eighteenth century and the modern world clearer than in society's attitude to the natural environment. For the eighteenth century and earlier, nature was seen as unkempt and fit to be tamed. Nature was at worst dangerous and at best uncomfortable, and man's duty was to improve nature. The greatest feat of improvement was the enclosure of common land that has given us the landscape of the English countryside with its hedges, fields, and copses. On a lesser scale, the landscape architects such as Lancelot 'Capability' Brown and Humphrey Repton moulded the raw landscape to a more civilized pattern of park and demesne. To the eighteenth-century observer, nature was raw material to be moulded by man, not a resource to be conserved.

The eighteenth century did not deplore the impact of man on the environment. (Blake's 'dark satanic mills' refer not to the factories of the Industrial Revolution but to the churches of the Established Church of England.) The building of railways in the nineteenth century was seen to enhance the landscape. J.W.M. Turner and the French Impressionists (as late as the Pissaros) celebrate the railway in their painting, not deplore it. In much of the nineteenth century, railways and their attendant works were perceived as an expression of man's endeavours to overcome the savagery of nature. The idea of a conflict between man and his environment is largely a late nineteenth- and a twentieth-century concept, which would not have occurred to eighteenth-century man at all.

2   The Age of Coal and Steam to 1914

Travel and tourism in the nineteenth century were dominated by the railway inland and by the steamship internationally. For not only were these two technological changes in the available means of transport to become the chief vehicles for travellers, but at least as importantly the advent of the railway and the steamship brought with it profound effects in the financing of large capital projects, in the pattern of trade and in the development of new service industries, generated by, and closely associated with, the operations of the railways and the steamship lines. The Victorians (and the term may be usefully extended to embrace contemporaries in countries other than the United Kingdom) were themselves aware of the dramatic change that steampower was making and were themselves fascinated by this drama.

The population continued to grow, from some 25 million in the United Kingdom in the 1830s to some 45 million in 1914. But the most significant feature of the population growth was the change in its occupational structure. Over the period, agriculture gradually employed a smaller and smaller fraction of the working population, labour moved first of all into manufacturing industries, then into transportation, especially the railways, and later still into the tertiary service sector of new and enlarged services required by the growth of shipping services in particular. As British shipping increased its share of the world market to something like 40 per cent of world trade, it was serviced as to financing, insurance, bill discounting, and so on from London. Goods carried in British hulls were supported financially by British insurers, brokers, and bankers, and the growth of London as a major financial centre owes much to the dominant role of British shipping in world trade in the nineteenth century. In the later part of the century, the income derived from services was paralleled by income from capital investment abroad. During the century there was nearly always a deficit in the commodity balance of payments account, made good first by income from services and later by interest and dividends resulting from investment abroad.

The extension of railway services encouraged the urbanization of the population which had already begun after the Napoleonic War. During the nineteenth century, London more than trebled its size and became the major trading centre in the country. Other major cities grew as well, particularly ports with large industrial hinterlands. To London and other large towns gravitated a relatively prosperous middle-class population engaged in the service industries. Outside the professional middle class real wages increased, though not without interruptions, for the whole employed population. Increasing prosperity in real terms brought sufficient income to match leisure, and the first manifestations of an entertainment industry began to appear. Blackpool, Southend, Brighton, and Bournemouth began to develop their characteristic attractions. Professional football, betting on horse races, and attendance at the big race meetings were by the end of the century evidence of widespread prosperity and mobility.

Much of Britain's trade was with the United States and Canada, and much of the emigration was in the same direction. By the end of the century American visitors to London were a familiar group of travellers. Perhaps because there were fewer political disturbances across the Atlantic than there were in India and Africa, it is too easy to overlook the tranquil development of transatlantic trade, only punctuated by the American Civil War. Politically, the United Kingdom was facing eastward, and the American influence on Britain passed unremarked.

The Development of the Railway System

The success of the Liverpool and Manchester Railway, opened in 1830, heralded a period in which the great trunk lines were inaugurated. By 1845, the railway linked many of the larger cities to London; for example, Bristol, Birmingham, Manchester, Leeds, and York. By the same year, something like 2,500 miles of line had been opened, more than twice that mileage had been authorized, and by the mid-century nearly 7,000 miles had been laid. By the end of the period under discussion the railway system sprawled over nearly 22,000 miles of line, linking every place of consequence to the main lines.

In 1881, the railways carried 623 million passengers over lines operated by a hundred-odd companies. This feat was facilitated by the Railway Clearing House, which had been established in 1842, as a means of recording and paying for traffic that used several companies' lines. Without the clearing house, travel by railway would have been a complex journey with many tickets.

By the 1870s the railways were to keen to stimulate travel and to improve their carryings. Competition took the form of service competition rather than price reduction. A notable exception was the introduction by the Midland Railway of third-class carriages on all its trains, but the same company also first introduced from the USA the Pullman cars. The longer distances in America made greater comfort for the passenger important and by 1872 the Pullman Company had 700 cars working over 30,000 miles of railway under contracts with 150 different companies. It was to Brighton in the 1880s that the first all-Pullman trains ran in Britain, and continued to do so for ninety years. In the same period arrangements were being made to run sleeping cars and Pullmans from Paris to Vienna and thence to Constantinople (Istanbul).

Until the 1860s, the cross-Channel shipping services were not directly operated by the railways, but from that decade the railway companies came to dominate cross-Channel shipping, to France and Belgium and also to Ireland. Towns such as Folkestone, Dover, and Southampton owe a debt to the railways, which made them important ports for passenger traffic.

The growth of the railway system can be seen to have taken place in three stages. First, the initial development of the 1830s embraces the years when the main framework was laid out. Secondly, there is the period of the 'railway mania' of the 1840s and its aftermath, during which time capital formation by railways may have reached 6 per cent of the national income. Thirdly, a long period of gradual extension and much consolidation from the middle of the nineteenth century onwards saw the extension of the railway system throughout the country.

The Growth of Deep-sea Shipping

The technology of shipping made a number of strides in the nineteenth century. During the early decades steam was introduced as the motive power, applied by reciprocating engines to paddle wheels, but traditional sailing ships persisted in large numbers until half-way through the century. The best of these sailing ships were American, and the plentiful supply of timber in the New world gave the American owner a cost advantage over his British competitor. British ship-owners have to their credit the introduction of steam and of iron hulls. Screw propulsion superseded the paddle wheels, and compound reciprocating engines and later the steam turbines further increased the British technological lead. British shipping came to dominate world trade.

The need for improved communication with the USA played an important role in the development of deep-sea shipping. An example is to be found in the history of the Cunard Steamship Company which demonstrates important features in the growth of North Atlantic shipping. First, the award of a mail contract, in effect a subsidy, represents a recurring theme in the development of passenger transport; payment for the carriage of mail has frequently been used as a form of government support to fast passenger transportation. It has per-sisted to this day, not only in shipping, but in airlines, notably in the USA, and in rural bus services. Secondly, it is to be observed that the Cunard Company owes its origin in the 1830s and 1840s to the enterprise of Glasgow and Liverpool businessmen rather than to Londoners — again we see significant developments in travel owing much to the foresight of Northerners. Thirdly, as the century advanced, emigrant traffic became an important factor in North Atlantic travel, with Britain and later Germany as the principal generators of emigrants to the New World.

The transfer of the interests of the East India Company in 1858, the American Civil War in the early 1860s, and the opening of the Suez Canal in 1869 produced a re-orientation towards the East in government and in the public mind. The possibility of a much shortened route to an India which was now the government's direct concern stimulated the introduction of better steamship carriage to the Far East. But the transatlantic trade remained the most vigorous and soon faced competition from the lines of other countries.

In the final decades of the century, cartel-like agreements between passenger shipping lines began to appear, at least in part inspired by the desires of European lines to win from British lines a larger share of the transatlantic trade. These agreements, euphemistically called conference agreements, sought to secure the agreement of the conference members to offer common fares and conditions of service and even to share revenue between them. The conference agreements tried to solve the problems of scheduled transport operators, chief of which can be identified as how to maintain the profitability of a scheduled service operating to a published timetable, which can result in uneconomic loads presenting themselves from time to time. By the beginning of the twentieth century, the cartel-like features of the shipping conferences were beginning to create suspicions that higher than necessary fares were being charged, and a Royal Commission was appointed to look into the operation of conferences. A moderate conclusion was reached by the Royal Commission, neither approving wholly nor condemning wholly the effects of the conference system in the public interest. (*See* Part IV below for contemporary conferences.)

Mention must be made at this point of the use of ships in the cruising mode, for the charter and operation of cruises, albeit on a limited scale, dates from the mid-nineteenth century. Certainly one of the earliest cruises was that described by Mark Twain in his first major book *The Innocents Abroad,* published in 1869. But cruising did not play a significant part in the shipping world until a later period. The heyday of liner passenger service was the period just before the First World War. It was an era of large, fast ships operated by a relatively small number of companies (and countries), and of considerable competition for first-class passengers. However, the biggest volume of transatlantic passenger trade was the emigrant steerage traffic. The glamour of deep-sea travel was reserved for the wealthy American or European, but in a period of low profits and brisk competition, that glamour would not have been possible without the steerage passenger. The descendants of those migrants must have formed a large part of the transatlantic tourist movement in the first half of the twentieth century.

The Travel Organizer

When travel was a relatively limited activity, both in the sense that complex journeys were not common and in the sense that the total volume of travel was still small, the traveller could make his own arrangements and, for example, pay for his conveyance directly to the railway or shipping company's office. However, when there were sufficient transport undertakings, a need arose for a specialist travel organizer who could assemble the traveller's more complex journeys on his behalf, issuing tickets to cover the whole journey as an agent for the transport companies. At the same time, the evolution of travel and the growing complexity of commercial and industrial life called for improved accommodation, and the travel organizer could make arrangements for the traveller's stay at hotels.

From these developing needs the retail travel agent was born. There also emerged a different sort of travel organizer. The large part of the population now able to enjoy the benefits of travel came to look to a travel organizer to compile their whole excursion. From the transport undertaking's point of view, this practice offered the prospect of tapping a new market. Few industrial systems are capable of producing so much potentially wasted capacity as transport systems. The effect of this is that the managers of transport can sell the last 40 per cent or so of their capacity at very low prices; having covered their inescapable costs first, they can price the last part of their production at a level which will cover direct operating costs only plus a desired profit. The direct operating costs can usually be very low for the last part of the capacity, and the revenue taken can be nearly all profit. From this feature of transport, the excursion derived and the kind of travel organizer we now describe as a tour operator. Such a tour operator buys bulk capacity from the transport undertaking at low rates and offers it to the public at lower fares than they would be able to obtain otherwise (*see* Part VI below).

Thomas Cook was first such a tour operator and only later a retail travel agent. A zealous temperance speaker and publisher, he conceived the idea of chartering trains to bring supporters to temperance meetings in the Midlands. His first excursion train ran from Leicester to Loughborough and back on 5 July 1841 with 570 passengers at a round trip fare of one shilling.

His services were soon sought by others interested in bulk travel of this kind, and by 1845 he was organizing relatively complex excursions comprising travel over several companies' lines, a feat made possible by the earlier establishment of the Railway Clearing House. By the end of 1850, Cook began to 'contemplate foreign trips including the Continent of Europe, the United States and the Eastern Lands of the Bible'. This idea was temporarily abandoned in favour of operating excursions to the Exhibition of 1851 in London, and subsequently to exhibitions on the continent of Europe. Despite the increasing range of his travel activities, they occupied only a part of his time, and in some of his posters and literature dating from 1866, Cook describes himself as either 'Thomas Cook, Tourist Manager' or as 'T. Cook Printer &c'. By 1865 he had opened offices in London which could also provide or arrange accommodation for his excursionists: guide-books were also available and his periodical, *Cook's Excursionist and Tourist Advertiser*. In the following year Cook's first American tour was made, although with somewhat disappointing results both in numbers and in the adequacy of the arrangements in the United States. Thomas Cook also devised in 1867 the now familiar hotel coupon. Banking and foreign currency exchange was added to the business in 1879. The business grew rapidly and by the end of the century offices had been opened in most parts of the world and Thos Cook & Son became a household name.

The significance of Thomas Cook's life work (he died in 1892 at the age of 84) lies in the origination of the excursion or holiday as a single transaction or package, rather than in his establishment of a retail agency. His concept perfectly complemented the growth of the railways and later of passenger shipping, and brought organized travel to an increasingly large section of the public. Two contemporary quotations are illuminating: a writer in *Blackwood's Magazine* in 1869 writes of 'tribes of unlettered British over the cities of Europe', an early manifestation of the obtrusiveness of tourists in their host countries. More perceptive perhaps is the article in Charles Dickens's magazine *All the Year Round* in 1864: 'the trip to Edinburgh and the short excursions in England attract tradesmen and their wives, merchants, clerks away for a week's holiday . . . In the return trips from Scotland to England come many students of the schools and universities. . . . As to Swiss excursions the company is of a very different order; the Whitsuntide trip has a good deal of the Cockney element in it and is mostly composed of very high-spirited people. . . . From these roysterers the July and August excursionists differ greatly: ushers and governesses, practical people from the provinces, and representatives of the better style of the London mercantile community . . . many of them carry books of reference with them and nearly all take notes.'[4]

Thos Cook & Son had its origin in the inspiration of its founder, the first organizer of bulk travel. The story of the American Express Company's entry into the travel business via the transport of valuables and of money is perhaps more typical. Cook's invention was a brilliant insight, the American Express has been a natural evolution. Founded in 1841 by Henry Wells, and not at once trading under its present name, the business began its life as a carrier. It merged in 1850 with two similar firms (one of whose principals was James G. Fargo, hence the firm of Wells Fargo familiar to readers of 'Westerns') and specialized in the carriage of valuables and of bullion. After the American Civil War, the business (now known as American Express) suffered from the introduction of the money order which gradually reduced the demand for currency tranship-ments. The American Express introduced its own money order in 1882, and nine years later the traveller's cheque. This device proved a popular innovation replacing the circular letter of credit. Thus the evolution of the American Express was founded on the carriage of goods and of bullion, and by the end of the century on various instruments of transmitting money. The development of the business overseas came in the two decades prior to the First World War with offices being opened in Paris in 1895 and in London in 1896, still dealing mostly in baggage and banking business. It seems probable that the overseas offices were by this time developing a true travel business in assisting visiting Americans to find accommodation and to make transport bookings, for the company began to enter the travel business in London in 1909 (in the USA only in 1915). The American Express thus grew out of its business as a carrier, and so too did some of the older firms in travel today; Pickfords and Cox & Kings are two examples in the travel business of the firm growing out of carriers or bankers rather than having their origin in travel *per se.*

The enterprise of Sir Henry Lunn created modern winter sports. A doctor, he first visited Switzerland in 1883, and realized the possibilities of introducing the Norwegian practice of skiing to Switzerland. By the beginning of the twentieth century the first English ski club in Switzerland had been founded, to be followed by the Ski Club of Great Britain, and for the purposes of marketing the new winter sport, the Public Schools Alpine Sports Club. Resorts such as Wengen and Murren were in effect created by Lunn and his colleagues E. C. Richardson and S. C. Dobbs. The appeal of skiing was essentially to a middle-class market, and the operation of the Public Schools Alpine Sports Club was geared to ensure that the winter sports enthusiast would find compatible companions in his hotel and in his resort. Like that of Cook's, Lunn's achievement was that of a tour operator, and he created a new form of tourism in the process.

Travel Literature

With the increase of travel came a desire to know more about the places visited; for throughout the early part of the period at least, the main motivation of much travel was educational. A flourishing section of the publishing industry grew up to meet visitors' demands for guide-books, handbooks, and maps.

It is interesting to compare the guide-books available in the 1840s, at the very beginning of the modern tourist movement, with those at the end of the period available to the Edwardian traveller. John Murray's *Handbook for London* was published in 1849 in two fairly substantial volumes, each of about four hundred pages, with a wealth of quotations from earlier historians and geographers of London − it was a book for planning daily excursions from the privacy of one's room; the two volumes were hardly designed for carrying around crowded London streets. The most famous of all guide-book publishers, Baedeker, only published a handbook for London in 1878, alleging that there were sufficient guide-books already available. In fact it was the increasing number of American visitors to London that spurred Baedeker on to produce his handbook. At the end of the nineteenth century, Baedeker was no less lengthy than Murray, running to over 400 pages, but of much smaller format and printed on thinner paper, with the result that it was a volume that fitted the pocket and was admirably suited to being carried by the visitor on his perambulations. It is note-worthy that Baedeker devoted three pages to information about routes to and from North America and less than a page to routes to the Continent. In the early 1900s, to judge from contemporary advertisements, practically every place a tourist might visit boasted a guide-book; most of these were designed for the domestic tourist, travelling in the main by train, but also by bicycle and by private car.

By the turn of the century, travel for pleasure had become well-established and an idea of its scope is obtained from advertisements in the guide-books them-selves. Henry Lunn advertised world travel (specifically cruises to Palestine, Egypt, and the Near East) and six-guinea weeks all-in to Geneva and Lucerne. Ernest Suffling offered yachts on the Norfolk Broads and the Cambrian Railway special tourist tickets (*sic*) to North Wales; hotels included establishments in Cairo and Madeira, as well as in the principal British resorts.

The Rise of an Hotel Industry

The evolution of the railway system profoundly affected the kind and the quantity of the accommodation used in conjunction with travel. The growth of the railway brought to a speedy end the intricate network of stage-coach services, and by the mid-nineteenth century, the use of the stage-coach as a means of travel had virtually ceased along with the turnpike roads. The staging inn was a victim of the railway as much as the stage-coach, for the volume of passenger travel was no longer using the roads. The return of the transit hotel had to wait for the arrival of the motor car. Nevertheless, the increased urbanization of the population and the growth of towns generally, enabled hotels and inns in many towns to cater for an increasingly local market, and to learn to serve the greater number of travellers carried by the railways. Thus, in important county towns the former staging inns came to survive the disappearance of their stage-coach passengers, and to align themselves with the needs of the railway passenger. As the stage-coach proprietors adapted themselves to the railways by offering feeder services, so did the hotels adapt and the greater volume of travel generated by the railways produced an expanding demand for accommodation.

However, there were other types of market to be served by the hotel industry. The railways themselves were protagonists in stimulating a type of hotel, a terminus hotel, for the same reasons that later the airlines recognized in building airport hotels. A train was capable of carrying a hitherto unprecedented number of passengers, and the railways feared that their own traffic might be depressed if sufficient accommodation was not available at the destination. During the period a significant number of railway-inspired (and sometimes railway-owned) hotels grew up at important destinations. The hotel at Euston was opened in 1838, and in 1873 that at St Pancras. In the provinces the South Western Hotel at Southampton Docks served as the terminus for the railway, as well as for the shipping companies which came to use the double tides of the Solent for passenger shipping. The two hotels at either end of Princes Street in Edinburgh, actually built over the railway, are further examples of the growing interdependence between the mode of transport and the provider of accommodation.

The other area which saw an expansion of accommodation during the nineteenth century was the resort. Rail travel brought within reach the coastal resorts, principally the South coast drawing on London, and the Lancashire and Yorkshire coasts serving the industrial North. Some of these resorts were in effect created by the railway, other simply benefited from them. Brighton and Scarborough already flourished before the railway and much benefited by this improved method of travel. But Bournemouth was literally nothing, not even a fishing village, until the extension of the railway beyond Southampton. Blackpool in the Census of 1841 registered as a town of 2,000 souls, but by the Census of 1901 was reporting a population of 47,000, which in turn doubled twenty years later.

The interdependence of the railways and hotels deserves a further comment. There is a sense in which it is true to say that the ownership of an hotel was more valuable to the railway than to another owner; for the revenue from the hotel bed is backed by the purchase of a ticket on the railway. Further, the advantage to a railway of extending its route mileage stems from the same point mentioned above (p.14) about incremental costs in extended mileage. But the railways feared that shortage of accommodation would reduce the amount of travel by rail, and the addition of large units of accommodation in London and particularly in the provinces was achieved by and for the railways.

London was, as so often, a special case. Hotel development was influenced by the greater volume of internal travel in Britain, but the growth of London as a world centre of power and trade contributed as much as the railways to the evolution of hotel accommodation. The position of London as the capital and centre of administration attracted far more visitors than could be accommodated privately. Thus by the end of the nineteenth century the pressure of demand for hotel accommodation had prompted a considerable hotel development in the West End of London, lying significantly in a crescent with its focus in Whitehall, and stretching from the Strand to Hyde Park Corner.

The progressive urbanization witnessed in the nineteenth century gave rise to the practice of eating out. As a major part of the population came to live in suburbs, there was an increase in the number of modest restaurants and tea-rooms in city centres to cater for those who could no longer go home for lunch, and for visitors from the suburbs intent on a day's shopping. There were always, to be sure, coffee-houses and taverns, but by the end of the century the popular catering multiples had appeared such as J. Lyons & Co., Slater, and the Aerated Bread Company. The main clientele of such establishments was the working population, but they were also commended to tourists in the guide-books of the time.

Tastes and practices in catering changed. At the beginning of Queen Victoria's reign in 1837 tastes might fairly be described as native English. By the 1860s, an American taste especially in beverages began to be catered for, reflecting in part the growing importance of the American visitor. Almost at the same time, culinary practice began to reflect the French taste, and the great French masters began to influence at least the higher class of establishment.

In the second half of the nineteenth century, in London and in other large cities in Europe and in America, the management of the larger hotels began to pass from the hands of a sole or family proprietor to some form of company organization. In this the hotel industry was merely taking advantage of the limited liability provisions of early company legislation. But also the capital required for the operation of large hotel enterprises was beyond the reach of a personal proprietor, again reflecting the increasing scale of operation. The hotel company appeared on the scene and with it the hotel chain with several establishments enjoying common management and often a common name, such as Ritz.

The Edwardian period was the zenith of development of the luxury hotel catering for a minority of wealthy families demanding great comfort and style. Popular travel was still to come, but the seeds of future changes were being sown. The car was still a plaything for the rich but the bicycle was a practical vehicle. A return to road travel from the railway was getting under way. To guide the traveller by road, Michelin published its first guide to hotels – in France – in 1900 and the Automobile Association produced its first hotel guide in 1911. Attempts were made to improve the facilities for travellers which were offered by the transit hotel and inn; notably the formation of Trust Houses, originally in Hertfordshire, recognized a new mobility of the traveller and anticipated an era when travel and accommodation were to be enjoyed by a much larger part of the population than the wealthy *élite* of the luxury hotel.

Resorts, Spas, and Other Places

As indicated in Chapter 1, the inland resort has a long history usually associated with a spring of mineral water. The use made of it remained medicinal rather than recreational during the nineteenth century even though the taking of the waters was accompanied by considerable entertainment. This remained true until fairly recent times, and the seaside resort no less than the inland spa owes its emergence to a belief in the efficacy of sea-water drinking or sea bathing. Not until the latter half of the nineteenth century did the concept of relaxation begin to appear, and the curative properties of the resort were still seen in physiological, terms rather than in psychological ones. The possible psychological disturbances which urban life might inflict, were not even a matter for speculation until towards the end of the century. But as part of more widely based efforts to make life less grim for the working population, Sir John Lubbock brought to the statute book an Act which created the August Bank Holiday, and himself recalled the first Bank Holiday on 7 August 1871 as 'a great success – the day was splendid and the holiday very generally kept. Every seaside place near London, every railway and place of amusement was chock full. Eight excursion trains went to Margate alone. The South Eastern Railway had only prepared for two. Indeed the railways and hotel keepers were altogether taken by surprise.'[5]

The medicinal properties of resorts influenced their development in other ways. In particular, the treatment of tuberculosis was a principal factor in the creation of the French Riviera resorts favoured by the British. The intention was to treat the terminal patient in conditions which would ensure his comfort if not his cure, and it was a Dr H. G. Bennett who first established Menton as a resort with this purpose in mind. Later, when the effects of a high altitude were thought to be curative, many sanatoria were established in Switzerland, again chiefly for the treatment of tuberculosis.

Resorts were not the only destination of the tourist. Those wealthy enough (and we are talking of a tiny fraction of the population) also began to visit the Holy Land, Egypt and, of course, Italy and Greece. Thomas Cook organized his first tour to Egypt and the Holy Land in 1869, two years after the visit by Mark Twain in *Quaker City,* and it was in the end the Middle Eastern business that gave Cook's an entry to the American market for travel. Nearer home, Switzerland may be thought to have founded its tourist industry on the British visitor. Thomas Cook quite early on conducted parties to Switzerland, but the distinctive character of tourism to Switzerland was conveyed first by the mountaineers, such as Whymper, and later by Henry and Arnold Lunn and their introduction of skiing to that country.

Concern for the Quality of Life

The Victorian age saw a new attitude to the physical environment emerge. It is best described perhaps by saying that the Victorians began to be apprehensive about the effect their material prosperity was having on the quality of life and on the environment in particular. Many threads make up this concern. The Romantic Movement, which may be characterized by, say, Wordsworth as a poet and J.M.W. Turner as a painter, encouraged people to see in Nature something to be enjoyed as it stood. The landscape could then be seen not as a raw material for the ingenious labours of man to refashion, but rather as evidence of a natural state in which man could refresh himself. This realignment of attitudes to the environment was paralled by, in this country at least, a religious revival in the Oxford Movement which consciously saw the medieval as good and the eighteenth century as bad. At first, and until about the middle of the century, the effects of the railway on the landscape were seen through eighteenth-century eyes. The railway was not seen as scarring the landscape, but improving it. Its progress was celebrated as improving the landscape and the banks and tunnels and cuttings were seen as part of the excitement of progress.

By the end of the nineteenth century, concern was felt about what man was doing to his environment and to his heritage. This concern in part arose as a by-product of the urbanization of the country and given some urgency by the depression which afflicted British agriculture in the mid-1870s. There set in an intellectual reaction to the material benefits of the Industrial Revolution and a conscious desire to preserve the visible remains of the past which was inevitably largely rural in its nature. There was a conscious nostalgia for the past which could be represented as a better and above all a non-industrial society, in the sense that Ruskin and William Morris described it and tried to recreate it. One effect of this changing attitude was the formation in 1895 of the National Trust, to look after 'places of historic interest or natural beauty'. A charitable body, the National Trust was given power by an Act of 1907 to declare its land inalienable, thus securing that only an Act of Parliament could deprive it of the properties it held in trust for the nation. The founders of the National Trust were performing a rescue operation, but there existed at the time hardly any town-planning legislation to control or regulate the growth of towns into suburbs, nor was much deliberate town planning possible.

The Progress of Society in Relation to Travel

Reasonable safety for the traveller is a prerequisite of tourism, both in his own country and abroad. The political and naval supremacy of the UK did much to ensure that her citizens were treated with respect abroad. Passports to at least the Western European countries were not needed except, for example, for France at the time of the Franco-Prussian War. War in any event was still largely a matter for professional armies.

At home, the establishment of an effective police force in the early days of the period under consideration had removed many of the dangers of travel. The stage-coach carrying a few passengers might have been the victim of a highwayman, but a whole trainload of passengers would be too big a target at least in this country. The essentially civilian nature of the police force as it developed was enhanced by the removal of the main military garrison to Aldershot, still easily within the reach of both London and Windsor by train, should the need arise.

Successive improvements in public health removed another hazard from the tourist. The construction of main drainage in London and in most of the larger European cities reduced the risk of cholera and typhoid, and a supply of chlorinated water in the northern cities of Europe began to reduce the risks attendant on drinking untreated water.

Throughout the century, primary education was developing in denominational schools. The Education Act of 1870 (and later that of 1902) ensured a high degree of literacy in the population by the time of the First World War. Newspaper readership increased and was boosted by the arrival in 1895 of the first popular newspaper, the *Daily Mail.* By the closing years of Queen Victoria's long reign, photography was a widely practised hobby, and with the invention of the daylight loading film, the camera became a part of every tourist's equipment. Picture journalism could stimulate the desire to travel, both at home and abroad.

The Nineteenth-century Transformation − a Summary

The change in so much of national and everyday life that occurred in the nineteenth century was so great that an attempt must be made to summarize the principal facets of the change, as they have affected the growth of tourism. First among these changes must be identified the urbanization of the population. In the early years of the railway a large part of the urban population was not more than a single generation away from rural life. By the end of the century, two or three generations of urban dwellers had become commonplace. Urbanization produced a rapid expansion of middle-class activity at work, professional services, government, banking and so on, that created the market for travel by generating a literate and relatively wealthy *élite.*

The capacity and desire of this new middle class to travel was satisfied by the development of travel at a speed and with a comfort never before known. In company with the expansion of the means of travel inland, the development of large steam-driven ocean-going passenger liners brought the USA within five or six days' reach of Europe. After the American Civil War, in particular, American visitors to this country and to the rest of Western Europe began to play a significant role in tourism. The political stability of both the United States and of the United Kingdom made the growth of tourism between them more certain, even though the common heritage and language formed a natural link.

Throughout the century, the idea of leisure took hold on the minds of urban man. The railways by making it possible to live at some distance from one's work, to commute in fact, had underlined the distinction between work and leisure; once this distinction had been made on a daily basis, it soon came to be applied to the working year, and the concept of an annual holiday began to be formulated as a condition of work. By the end of the century, the idea was a perfectly understood one, whether it eventuated in a Wakes Week, as in the North, or in less dramatic forms in the South. Town dwellers sought escape from the towns, at least occasionally.

As the railway and the steamship provided the transport, so the emergence of the modern hotel in resorts (London too and Paris were resorts) altered the accommodation picture. In Europe, the influence of the British visitor is seen in the names d'Angleterre, Bristol, and so on. The modern hotel even by the early twentieth century was more than a place in which to sleep, and had become an element in the attractions of the resort.

3   *The Modern World 1919-1979*

The First World War (1914-18) directly affected the development of tourism in that it confirmed the coming importance of the motor car. In the same way, the Second World War (1939-45) confirmed the position of aircraft for civil use. In neither case were the military actions, of course, responsible for either vehicle, but their military use gave large numbers of people experience of them. Indirectly, the two wars were significant for our study in the sense that they involved for the first time the whole population, which was persuaded that a better material life would be the prize of victory. Moreover, both wars were fought over many countries and a significant proportion of the populations of all the combatants gained direct experience of countries other than their own.

The inter-war period was a period of fluctuating prosperity, depression, and recovery, two periods of some prosperity being separated by the Great Depression of 1929-31. The appalling effects of the Great Depression resulted in governments becoming resolved to master this kind of economic catastrophe and the period witnessed increasing intervention by the State in matters which an earlier period would have regarded as outside the competence of government. After the Second World War, government intervention became even more pronounced especially in Europe in order to speed up recovery and to administer effectively the massive aid of the Marshall Plan. In the UK the immediate post-war period was the time of the great nationalizations which placed most of the country's transport undertakings in public ownership. The twenty-five years immediately after the Second World War did not experience the depressions which the gloomy had forecast, and increased wealth and prosperity generated in the developed countries a society with increasing capacity to consume. With this came inflationary pressures and the erosion of the purchasing power of most currencies, but also a widespread desire to travel; and today tourism has become the world's largest and fastest growing economic activity, with something like 80 per cent of international tourist movement originating from just twelve rich countries.

By 1970 tourism had become no longer the preserve of the wealthy and the leisured, but rather a mass market. The populations of the developed countries had the level of education and the disposable income to regard a holiday as an essential feature of their life, and even in those years when economic growth slackened a little, demand for leisure travel experienced only a slower rate of growth and not a decline. The increasing volume of world trade ensured the growth of business travel in line with it; the air services covering the whole world and the steady reduction in the real cost of air travel extended business travel to echelons in companies which would not have envisaged travelling on business in an earlier period. The fifty years following the First World War were marked by substantial migration. The westward flow of European emigrants to the USA was checked from 1921 onwards by the introduction of quotas, but the events preceding the Second World War and immediately after it, the Third Reich in Germany and the Russian domination of Eastern Europe, stimulated migration from Central Europe to Western Europe. As the Western countries regained their prosperity in the 1950s and 1960s, they attracted further immigrants from relatively undeveloped countries; to the United Kingdom, from firstly the Caribbean and subsequently from India, Pakistan, and East Africa; to Germany and Switzerland from Southern Italy, Spain, and Turkey; to France from North Africa, and to mainland USA from Puerto Rico.

The annual holiday was established during the inter-war years as a reality for a considerable part of the population and as a realizable goal for all. Entertainment and leisure pursuits and the industries serving them all grew steadily. By 1939, in the UK, some 11 million people were covered by the Holidays with Pay Act (1938), and an estimated half-a-million foreign visitors came to this country. Tourism in its modern connotation had arrived and was identified as a phenomenon to be taken seriously. In 1924 the International Union of Official Organizations for Tourist Propaganda was formed, later to become the International Union of Official Travel Organisations, as the world body concerned with tourism. In the UK, by the outbreak of war in 1939, the precursor to the British Tourist Authority had been in operation for ten years with the object of encouraging visitors to Britain.

During the inter-war years of increasing international tension, travel abroad was felt to be a valuable instrument to international peace. The underlying assumption was that if people of one country had the opportunity to see how other countries lived and conducted themselves, greater international understanding would flow. Travel was often endowed with a moral purpose and particularly for the young, the traveller abroad was seen as an ambassador for his country's political stance; Germany, in particular, saw travel abroad in that light. It was not until after the Second World War that mass travel was seen as merely one facet of the good life, to which anyone might aspire, in the same sense that a refrigerator, a car, or other durable consumer goods are seen as desirable concomitants of affluence.

The Slow Decline of the Railways

Throughout the history of the railways, doubts were frequently aired in Britain about the monopoly they enjoyed. With the outbreak of war in 1914, the way was clear to bring the railways under state control. It was felt that greater efficiency had been achieved by the process and in pursuance of economies of scale the amalgamation of the hundred or so individual companies into four groups was carried out in 1921. In the event this amalgamation did little to shore up the growing strains on the railways, strains caused by a decline in the bulk freight volumes such as coal, and by the rapid onset of motorization for both freight and passengers. By the outbreak of the Second World War, the railways were in some financial disarray, and then once again came under state control. Years of financial stringency and neglect of all but the most necessary maintenance during the war left the railways with the prospect of an enormous modernization. The Transport Act 1947 effected the nationalization of the railways. Successive long-term plans and a number of changes in organization, the replacement of steam traction first by diesels and later by electrification, did not stop the accumulating losses of the railway system. By 1962, a further reorganization was carried out under Dr Beeching (whose report was published in 1963). This envisaged the drastic reduction of unprofitable lines and further technical modernization. Another Transport Act was passed in 1968, which made an attempt to secure an integrated transport system, providing for the creation of Passenger Transport Authorities for the conurbations and for the financial support of socially desirable but commercially unprofitable lines.

American experience closely paralleled that of the United Kingdom. Control by regulatory bodies was preferred to outright state control. But the railway system continued to operate uneconomically and in 1970 the passenger content of the American railroads was handed over to a Federal organization called Amtrak. European railways have been similarly faced with the problem of uneconomic operations and the need for support from the state.

If the main causes of the decline of the railways are to be sought, the growth of the private car must be identified as a major cause. In both the USA and in the UK, passenger rail traffic halved in the first ten years or so after the First World War. The car gradually came to be the alternative means of transport for short and medium-length journeys. After the Second World War, further competition was faced from the airlines for the longer journey, where speed of travel was important. This left the railways competing with the car and with the airlines. A good example of the railways' dilemma is to be found in a journey such as London to Manchester, rather under 200 miles. In the pre-electrification era of the 1950s, the airlines severely cut into the rail traffic on that route. The position was reversed by electrified fast inter-city rail services, which made the city centre to city centre journey time by rail comparable with that of flying. With the completion of the motorway in 1972, it may be anticipated that the private car will reassert itself as the preferred means of travel for such journeys. For holiday purposes, in the last twenty years the railway has largely been displaced by the car; in the 1950s two-thirds of holidays used the railway as the means of transport and by 1970 this had fallen to only one-seventh, although it must be remembered that the capacity of the railways had been much reduced under the modernization plans.

The railways have been also burdened by the development of commuter services in the conurbations especially London. Indeed the railways themselves promoted consciously the development of the outer suburbs. But commuter services involve long periods of idleness for the rolling stock which has to be provided for the peak load, and attempts to recover in fares the inherent losses of commuter services have been found merely to promote a further switch to the private car.

Nevertheless the inter-war period was in some ways the zenith of the railway achievement. At home fast and comfortable trains were run at high speed to Scotland and the West Country, and such trains as the Flying Scotsman or the Brighton Belle enjoyed both good loads and a high reputation. Internationally, the period between the wars was the heyday of the railway, with named trains again, such as the Golden Arrow, the Rheingold Express, the Blue Train, and above all the Orient Express to Istanbul, which provided the *mise en scène* for the novelist, for example Graham Greene's *Stamboul Train* or Agatha Christie's *Murder on the Orient Express*.

The Great Leviathans
The post-war period also saw the virtual extinction of the great passenger liners. In the decade after the First World War, the victorious countries re-equipped their merchant navies from tonnage exacted as reparations from Germany, and competition entered the field from countries not hitherto seen as operating a substantial merchant marine. British shipping stagnated, and most of the passenger ships of the 1920s were relatively old. Many of Britain's competitors received subsidies either for shipbuilding or even for operating. During this period there was a marked reduction in emigration to the USA, and such as there was originated in Southern Europe.

The most significant technical development in passenger shipping was the construction of the *Queen Mary* and later the *Queen Elizabeth,* both with the aid of government loans, and of similar if smaller ships by the UK's competitors. The *Queen Mary* launched in the mid 1930s and of more than 80,000 gross registered tons was a highly specialized vehicle, designed to perform the trip from Southampton to New York in five days carrying up to 2,000 passengers. In her first few years she justified the expectations of her owners. Her sister ship the *Queen Elizabeth* entered commercial service after the Second World War, both being used as troopships during the war. The writing was already on the wall, however, for in 1957 the volume of transatlantic passenger trade by air first exceeded that carried by sea, and the successive reduction in the real cost of flying initiated by the introduction of, first, tourist fares and, later, economy fares dramatically cut passenger traffic by sea. The superior speed of the pure jet aircraft hastened the decline of passenger shipping.

If we look at the picture in, say, 1965, there were four large ships offering regular scheduled services across the Atlantic, the two *Queens*, the *France* and the *United States*, the last with the aid of a subsidy; on the Mediterranean route, the ships of the Italian Line, and several smaller operators, American, Greek, and Italian. P. & O. were operating to India and the Far East and to Australia, Union Castle to South Africa, and a new *Queen* was about to be launched. Five years later, the picture had completely changed; P. & O. had ceased regular service to India, the two *Queens* had been sold, the *United States* withdrawn from service, and there was only a very limited service across the Atlantic, confined to the summer months. The shipping companies tried to compensate for the loss of their liner services by cruise employment. A ship with hull and engines required for fast liner service is not economic to run in cruising, nor is it necessarily navigable in the confines of the Caribbean and the Mediterranean. In the USA, the cruise market to the Caribbean became fiercely competitive as liner owners sought to offer cruises to the rewarding American market.

If deep-sea passenger liner shipping is on the edge of extinction, the ferry and car ferry industry shows every sign of prosperity. There are several hundred car ferry operations in Europe, connecting the UK with continental ports and with Ireland, connecting the North African coast with Europe, Italy with Greece, and so on. The car ferry is perhaps best seen as an extension of the road, as a bridge and it is the growth of car traffic that has brought out the car ferry and made it worthwhile to build specialized vessels. It is noteworthy that Dover for that reason is Britain's largest passenger port with some 70 per cent or more of total seaborne passenger traffic in and out of the country.

The hovercraft was introduced to ferry service in the late 1960s. These services and those of the conventional ferries help to make the prospect of a tunnel under the Channel controversial.

Motorization

The internal combustion engine was invented well before the end of the nineteenth century; by the outbreak of the First World War there were some 132,000 private cars in use in the UK and an estimated 2 million in the USA. The internal combustion engine was also applied to taxis and coaches and buses. The refinement of systems of mass-production during the 1920s brought down the real price of car ownership so that by 1938 there were nearly 2 million private cars in use in Britain, and the post-war extension of car ownership has risen from that figure in 1949 to 11 million in 1969. Put the matter another way — in 1949, 140 households in every thousand had access to a car, while by 1969 600 households in every thousand had access to a car, and a large part of the non-car-owning households were single person households, often elderly persons on low fixed incomes.

The growth of car-ownership made imperative the proper provision of roads the car could efficiently use. The road system in the early twentieth century was inadequately prepared for fast-moving vehicles, which produced clouds of dust from unmetalled roads. The control of the road system and responsibility for it still rested with the local authorities. Accordingly, a series of attempts were made rather in a piecemeal way to improve the road system, chiefly by securing a proper surface to the existing alignment. Critics of the parsimonious expenditure on roads in the inter-war period must, however, remember that this country probably still has the best-made roads of any country — there are practically no unmade roads left. By the 1930s it began to be recognized that the car called for motorways, if its advantages were to be exploited properly. In Germany (no doubt for defence reasons) a major programme of constructing autobahnen was realized, and the expressway, thruway, and other variations of American nomenclature began to be built. In the 1950s and the 1960s, the UK embarked upon a national motorway policy, which resulted in some thousand miles of new construction by 1975.

The car has profoundly changed the nature of domestic tourism. It has engineered the abandonment for most families of the coach and the railway as the preferred means of transport for holiday purposes, and it has enabled its owner to extend his leisure by short holidays and day trips in a way which would be impracticable by public service transport. Here as in other countries, the transit hotel has returned: in the UK this has meant a new life for many old coaching inns, and throughout the motorized world the creation of new kinds of accommodation, the motel, the motor hotel, and the post-house. The car has also brought the towed caravan and in the USA a range of sophisticated self-propelled caravans.

Motor buses had already made their appearance in large numbers by 1914. But the post-war years were the years of very rapid expansion of bus and coach services. The war had produced a number of returning soldiers with the ability to drive and also a number of ex-military vehicles capable of initiating bus services, some of the vehicles justifying the literal translation of charabanc. Besides municipal bus undertakings, and the larger territorial companies, there were a large number of independent coach and bus operators. In circumstances of extremely vigorous competition during the 1920s, many of these independent operators resorted to tactics of competition which both endangered life and ensured that regular services to the public could not be offered. Racing, chasing, creaming, hanging back are the contemporary phrases to describe this form of competitive rivalry, and it was not unknown that a competitor would physically ram his rival's vehicle.

Considerable public disquiet was felt about unbridled competition, which was failing to produce adequate public services. First in London in 1924 and later in 1930 in the shape of the Road Traffic Act, a system of licensing coach and bus operators was introduced, the device being the setting up of quasi-judicial bodies, the Area Traffic Commissioners, with wide powers not only to license the operators, but also to impose conditions on their manner of operation in the public interest. Although the impact of the Act was primarily on non-tourist services, it was a seminal attempt at public regulation of transport which remained virtually unaltered until the Transport Act 1968, and set a pattern whereby air services were to be regulated after the Second World War.

After the war, there was a marked reduction in public service vehicle usage. The high point of bus and coach services was reached in 1948, when the network of bus and coach services had penetrated into the remotest villages as the railway had done fifty years earlier. The private car from that date on rapidly displaced the coach and the bus. Today the bus and coach system is undergoing the same kind of agonizing reappraisal that Beeching brought to the railways, and it seems reasonable to think that in a few years' time the motor vehicle, as a public transport system, may virtually disappear from long-distance transport, remaining residually in feeder and suburban uses.

Motorization has brought a new problem; the problem of the terminal has not been solved. The road is not merely a track but must also be a terminal. There is the need for parking. Tourist attractions and facilities require parking space — Disneyland in California attracts 10 million visitors annually, occupies 83 acres, and has car parking of 110 acres. This is the scale of the parking problem. Congestion on the track is not so burdensome as congestion at the terminal.

The Mastery of the Air

The years immediately after the First World War witnessed the first stumbling attempts to create commercial airlines in Europe. The French airlines in particular were heavily subsidized, and competition from France and from KLM and Lufthansa (the Netherlands and Germany respectively) ensured that British airlines operated very perilously in a financial sense. The British Government's policy had been that civil aviation must fly by itself (the phrase was Winston Churchill's). By the early 1920s, foreign competition and defence considerations (the need to maintain a pool of pilots as a reserve for the RAF, the need to keep design teams together and so on) led to the formation in 1924 of Imperial Airways as the chosen instrument of British aviation supported by a substantial subsidy.

There developed during the 1920s and early 1930s what we may call the imperial concept in civil aviation. In a nutshell, this asserts that it is more important to carry the mail to India than any other task, and perhaps reflects the continued preoccupation with the Commonwealth and with the Colonies, which was a constant engagement of the British Government. In various ways, this pre-occupation with a Far East route coloured aviation thinking well into the period after the Second World War. It led to the ill-fated airship ventures, to the development of flying-boats, and to a concentration on relatively short-range aircraft. The primitive navigational resources of the period, and the solely fine weather capability of the aircraft meant that much flying pioneering was best conducted in or near the Arabian peninsula and, from routes across the desert, developed linking services east and west of a core of operations in the Middle East.

By the mid-1930s, a second chosen instrument appeared in the shape of British Airways with routes to Northern Europe and proposed routes to West Africa and South America. This broke the monopoly of Imperial Airways, and its continuing difficulties of finance and labour relations led in 1940 to the nationalization of British airlines into BOAC.

The early development of British aviation is of interest because many of the people engaged in it then are still within the management of the principal airlines today, and the earlier history must have affected their contemporary policy-making. But the number of passengers carried annually by British airlines before the Second World War was only some 250,000, and by US airlines some 3 million.

After the Second World War, British air services were placed in the hands of

State-owned public corporations, BOAC, BEA, and British South American Airways, the latter being amalgamated with BOAC after the loss of several aircraft in the Atlantic.

The post-war period in British civil aviation is thus initially a record of the activities of the State-owned corporations, and latterly of the appearance of privately owned airlines, both on scheduled routes and also in the development of charter operations. Until the 1960s that record is one of continuing difficulties experienced by BOAC, facing in many years substantial losses, and relying on American aircraft to operate. Part of the blame for these difficulties must rest with successive Governments, who failed to give BOAC clear directions, or did so in an exhortatory manner which lacked clarity. However that may be, the operations of BOAC were often consistent with the hypothesis that the airline saw itself as part of the Foreign Office and thus obliged to operate some of its routes non-commercially. In 1963 a major reconstruction of BOAC management was effected, and the airline was given fairly explicit instructions to fly commercially.

BEA, on the other hand, with the European routes, was able to develop a consistently profitable operation and to use almost exclusively British manufactured aircraft of relatively advanced design. In the 1960s BEA faced competition not only from its European competitors (with whom it had pool agreements (*see* Chapter 21 below), but from a development of charter services operated in conjunction with inclusive tours. The disparate operations and fleets of the two State airlines led many critics to ask whether there would not be an advantage in combining the two, and the Civil Aviation Act 1971 explicitly envisaged this, and created a super-Board — British Airways Board — to control the two State airlines. The same Act lays down civil aviation policy, part of which is to secure the operation of at least one privately owned airline of substantial size.

The introduction of successively larger aircraft to both long-haul and short-haul routes has meant successively lower air fares in real terms. The steady fall in the real cost of flying has been chiefly productive of traffic across the Atlantic and within the USA, stimulated first by the introduction of tourist fares in 1952 and followed by economy class fares in 1958. In Europe with the complexities of national states, the development has been the creation of a wide range of promotional fares with specific validities attached to them. Both types of fare have been instrumental in promoting the growth of tourism, particularly holiday tourism.

Regulation of Transport

The enormous upsurge in travel created first by the private car and later by the airlines led to increasing governmental control of transportation. By the 1960s the private car was giving rise to congestion on the roads and at parking sites. It is fair to say that as yet no way has been found to regulate the use of the car. In civil aviation, a complex and elaborate system exists. The stage was set in 1919 when the doctrine of national air space above sovereign territory was established. By the time of the Chicago Convention 1944, it was evident that the regulation of international air services was to be a matter of bilateral treaties between governments. In the crucial question of the fares to be charged, the matter was left in the hands of the airlines' trade association, the International Air Transport Association, subject always to Government approval. In these matters the USA through its domestic regulatory tribunal, the Civil Aeronautics Board, has generally been liberal in the matter of fares, pressing generally in favour of lower fares. The huge market represented by travel to and from the USA has meant that no large airline can opt out of it, and consequently the *de facto* power of the CAB in regulating international aviation has grown to substantial proportions.

The regulation of the railways has been effected directly by the appropriate Government department, except in the case of rates and fares which were matters for a quasi-judicial tribunal, and it was not until the early 1960s that the railways were free to fix their own charges on commercial criteria.

Tour Operation

In the 1960s tour operation led to the extensive use of package holidays, particularly in Europe and from the northern industrial countries, Scandinavia, West Germany, and the United Kingdom, to the resorts of the Mediterranean. The development of package holidays or inclusive tours has been substantially a British contribution. It originated in the post-war era when scheduled air services were reserved in the United Kingdom to the two State airlines. The independent operator was thereby compelled to rely on non-scheduled services, at first trooping, but later on charter services in conjunction with a tour operator (*see* Chapter 17 below).

The late 1960s saw the emergence of the inclusive tour as the principal medium of holiday travel. In 1965, just over 1 million holiday visits to Western Europe from the United Kingdom were inclusive tours by charter, already twice the number of air independent holidays. By 1970, while the number of independent holidays by air remained at just over half a million, inclusive tours by air had doubled to 2 million in number. During the five years, the British tour operation had concentrated into ten large concerns, and these offered not only holidays priced at a figure hardly more than the lowest scheduled air fare, but introduced extremely cheap winter holidays as well.

The rate of growth of tour operation has been threefold that of scheduled services, and tour operation has become the most vigorous sector of the holiday market. In doing so, the tour operators have penetrated markets untapped by the scheduled airlines, and in a real sense have offered to the holiday tourist a true and complete tourist product, making a holiday abroad part of the good life, as much as television or the car are.

Travel Agents

The growth of the airlines has done much to promote the retail travel agents. Retail travel agents began to appear in any numbers rather hesitantly at the turn of the century, but the principal transport carriers, the railways and the shipping lines, had already established their own retail outlets. The emergent airlines were in no position to build an adequate chain of retail outlets of their own, and preferred to sell tickets through the travel agent. In 1950s and 1960s, the travel agent could expect that at least 75 per cent and often more of his turnover would be represented by airline tickets. With the decline of rail travel and of sea travel, the retail agent has come to depend on the airlines and more recently on the tour operators for his existence. This remains true of most developed countries with the exception of the USA, where the airlines have felt more able to open their own retail offices, the greater volume of air transport making this possible.

The Accommodation Industry

The conventional large city centre hotel in the inter-war years remained much as it was in the Edwardian period. The depression of the early 1930s saw the extinction of some well-known establishments, and the shift in the centre of large cities brought the closure or conversion of others. In London the hotel centre of gravity, as it were, shifted from the Strand to Mayfair and Piccadilly, and in New York a similar shift up-town took place. After the Second World War, the airlines, concerned that the supply of aircraft seats might outstrip the supply of hotel beds, entered the hotel field, notably Pan American and the Intercontinental Hotel chain. Later, TWA acquired the Hilton International, and both BEA and BOAC, as well as the European airlines, developed interests in hotels, At first, these interests were chiefly in the provision of Western-standard hotels in the developing countries, but increasingly the emphasis has been on city centre hotels in Europe. The growth of tour operation in the 1960s has lead to the closer association of airline and resort hotel, often in common ownership, and some tour operators have built purpose-designed hotels exclusively for their own use.

The growth of private motoring has given a new importance to existing transit hotels. But additionally there have come into existence special forms of accommodation for the motorist, the motel and the motor hotel. Caravanning represents a new form of accommodation, firstly as a genuinely mobile home for holiday use, but more recently as a static holiday home which, being wheeled, escapes the standards of accommodation which would be legally enforced for a holiday cottage of conventional construction. The typical boarding-house in British resorts is yielding steadily to the newer forms of accommodation, after reaching a peak of popularity in the inter-war years.

The increase use of the car for holiday purposes and a rising real standard of living have together brought about the decline in popularity of the traditional boarding-house. The simple standards of accommodation offered and the 'family atmosphere' are no longer in keeping with the tastes of today's holidaymakers. Even in traditional resorts their hold on a traditional market has been eroded by conventional holiday camps and by static caravan sites.

At the end of the 1960s and the beginning of the 1970s, much attention both official and private was given to the needs of modernizing the accommodation industry. After an experimental Government scheme of hotel loans and grants, the Development of Tourism Act 1969 established a three-year programme of hotel development grants and loans, which added substantially to conventional hotel room stock, although this increase has mostly taken place in London and other large centres.

In the Mediterranean and in the Caribbean, the first twenty-five years after the end of the Second World War witnessed a major expansion of hotel accommodation, particularly on the east coast of Spain and in Florida. From the mouth of the Tagus in Portugal to the mouth of the Danube, almost the entire coastline serves as a resort for Europe. The relative cheapness of the Mediterranean countries and the relative wealth of the population of Northern Europe has made a Mediterranean holiday very attractive to the residents of the cooler northern countries.

Resorts and Spas in mid-twentieth Century

The factors that have led to changes in the demand for traditional holiday accommodation, particularly increasing motorization, have had an effect on demand for traditional resorts as well. The curative powers of mineral springs have lost some credibility in the mid-twentieth century, and the traditional spa is either disappearing or changing its nature. Improving mobility by car has turned resorts close to large centres of population into dormitory suburbs. Brighton now serves as a suburb of Greater London, and in Europe the resorts of the Belgian coast such as Knocke le Zoute serve Brussels and the manufacturing belt of Belgium in a similar way.

An alternative use made of some resorts and other towns in resort areas is as retirement enclaves. St Petersburg, Florida, for example, is such an enclave for American senior citizens, and in the United Kingdom, Worthing enjoys the distinction of having the highest average age of any town in the country.

Concern for the Tourist Environment

A prominent feature of the climate of opinion in the 1960s was an increasing concern for the impact of man's economic life on the quality of his environment. Stemming from the horror felt at the prospect of dangerous irradiation becoming widespread as a result of uncontrolled atmospheric nuclear explosions, this concern was stimulated by the discovery of the world-wide contamination of all living creatures by residual DDT insecticide. Several incidents occurred of a local nature, such as the wreck of an oil tanker off the Scilly Isles and the uncontrolled discharge of an oil well off the Californian coast, which served to stimulate awareness that the natural environment needed protection from pollution caused by the very economic activity which made the enjoyment of the environment accessible to so many people.

Also by the early 1970s an apprehension about the effects of tourist demand itself began to appear. Resident populations in resort areas (including London as well as Florence and Venice) began to question the claims of tourism to benefit the resort and the reception areas, and phrases like 'pollution by tourism' began to be current.

As a result of these considerations, not only was the natural environment conceived of as of clearly finite extent, to be conserved and managed by man for his enjoyment, but also pleas were made for the more positive management of tourism flows themselves. It was recognized that a tourist attraction itself might be destroyed by the very tourists visiting it, that Westminster Abbey might be literally trodden into the ground by its visitors.

The Interests of Governments in Tourism

In the inter-war years, governments began to recognize the importance of tourism to the economy, particularly as an item in the balance of payments. This recognition of the importance of tourism was stimulated in the period of post-war reconstruction in the 1950s. The promotional activities of European national tourist organizations were at first directed chiefly towards the North American markets. However, by the early 1960s the pattern of tourist movements became more complex, and today most Western European countries are both substantial generators and recipients of tourism. These countries have established networks of tourist offices throughout the main generating countries, and have invested massively in advertising and in the production of tourist literature and its dissemination.

In the United Kingdom, after the Second World War, the British Travel and Holidays Association (later to become the British Travel Association, and in 1969 the British Tourist Authority) was selected as the chosen instrument for the overseas promotion of the country as a tourist destination. An annual grant-in-aid was made for this purpose. Recurring balance of payments crises led to the identification of Britain's profit and loss account from tourism, and the Development of Tourism Act 1969 created four statutory bodies charged with responsibility for the promotion and development of tourism. Overseas promotion was reserved to the British Tourist Authority while the three national boards for England, Scotland and Wales were charged with the promotion of their countries within the United Kingdom and with the development of tourist attractions and facilities. The same Act also made provision for a temporary scheme of grants and loans for new hotel buildings, extensions and modernizations of existing ones, and for ongoing development assistance to tourism projects.

Part II
Anatomy of Tourism

Further Reading for Part II

British Tourist Authority: *Digest of Tourist Statistics,* annual
British Tourist Boards: *Annual Reports*
Burkart, A. J., and Medlik, S. (editors): *The Management of Tourism,* Part II
English Tourist Board: *Tourism Multipliers in Britain*
Gray, H.P. *International Travel — International Trade*
Middleton, V.T.C. *Tourism in Context*
Organization of Economic Co-operation and Development: *International Tourism and Tourism Policy in OECD Members Countries,* annual
Working Group of National Tourist Organizations of the EEC: *The Economic Significance of Tourism within the European Economic Community,* 1975, 1977, 1978
World Tourism Organization: *Economic Reviews of World Tourism,* biennial
World Tourism Organization: *Tourism Compendium,* biennial

References to Part II

1 World Tourism Organizations: *Tourism Compendium*
2 Department of Industry: International Passenger Survey
3 British Tourist Boards: British Home Tourism Survey
4 Hunziker, W. *Grundriss der Allgemeinen Fremdenverkehrslehre*
5 Hunziker, W.: *Social Tourism, Its Nature and Problems*
6 English Tourist Board: *Holidays: The Social Need*
7 OECD: *International Tourism and Tourism Policy*
8 Central Statistical Office: *Social Trends No. 10*
9 Gray, H.P. *International Travel — International Trade*
10 South East England Tourist Board: *Tourism in South East England*
11 English Tourist Board: *Woodspring Tourism Study*
12 International Union of Official Travel Organizations: *Travel Research Journal,* 1966, 1968, 1970
13 Working Group of National Tourist Organizations of the EEC; *The Economic Significance of Tourism within the European Economic Community,* 1975
14 Henley Centre for Forecasting: The Employment Generating Effects of Tourism, *British Travel News* No.61
15 Medlik, S. Tourism Employment in the Economy, in *Manpower in Tourism,* AIEST Publications No.20
16 Richards, G: *Tourism and the Economy*
17 WTO: *Economic Reviews of World Tourism*
18 OECD: *International Tourism and Tourism Policy*

4   *The Meaning and Nature of Tourism*

The World Tourism Organization estimated that by the end of the 1970s some 270 million journeys were made throughout the world by people travelling to other countries and that they spent some $75 million in the countries they visited.[1] The United Kingdom alone received some 12½ million visits from other countries with an expenditure of about £2,750 million in the country; British residents made some 15½ million visits abroad and spent more than £2,000 million in the countries they visited.[2] Still larger numbers travelled and spent still larger amounts in their own countries. For example, British residents made well over 100 million trips in Britain involving an overnight stay, on which they spent well over £3,000 million each year.[3]

All this activity may be described as tourism. However, a clearer concept and a more precise definition of tourism is required for various purposes. First, for purposes of study: in order to examine any phenomenon systematically, it is necessary to define what it covers. Secondly, for statistical purposes: when a phenomenon is to be measured, it must be defined; in practice available techniques of measurement frequently determine what is possible to measure and in turn tend to define tourism for particular purposes. Thirdly, for legislative and administrative purposes: legislation may apply to some activities and not to others. Fourthly, for industrial purposes: particular economic activities give rise to market studies and provide the basis for the formation of industrial organizations.

In endeavouring to define tourism it is helpful to distinguish between the *concept* and the *technical definitions.* The concept of tourism provides a broad notional framework, which identifies the essential characteristics, and which distinguishes tourism from similar, often related, but different phenomena. Technical definitions, evolved through experience over time, provide instruments for particular study, statistical, legislative and administrative, and industrial purposes; there are different technical definitions appropriate for different purposes.

The Concept of Tourism

The concept of tourism was first formulated in the period between the two World Wars and the definition put forward by the Swiss Professors Hunziker and Krapf was subsequently adopted by the International Association of Scientific Experts in Tourism (AIEST):

> Tourism is the sum of the phenomena and relationships arising from the travel and stay of non-residents, in so far as they do not lead to permanent residence and are not connected with any earning activity.[4]

Since then the basic concept has been broadened to include various forms of business and vocational travel, because as long as they do not lead to permanent residence or to employment remunerated from within the destination visited, their economic significance is the same—the traveller is a pure consumer, and because it is often difficult or impossible to distinguish sharply between business and vocational and other travel in practice.

Five main characteristics of tourism may be identified conceptually:

(a) Tourism arises from a movement of people to, and their stay in, various destinations.

(b) There are two elements in all tourism: the journey to the destination and the stay including activities at the destination.

(c) The journey and the stay take place outside the normal place of residence and work, so that tourism gives rise to activities, which are distinct from those of the resident and working populations of the places, through which tourists travel and in which they stay.

(d) The movement to destinations is of a temporary, short-term character, with intention to return within a few days, weeks or months.

(e) Destinations are visited for purposes other than taking up permanent residence or employment remunerated from within the places visited.

Much tourism is a leisure activity, which involves a discretionary use of time and money, and recreation is often the main purpose for participation in tourism. But this is no reason for restricting the total concept in this way and the essential characteristics of tourism can best be interpreted to embrace a wider concept. Tourism denotes the incidence of a mobile population of travellers who are strangers to the places they visit and where they represent a distinct element from the resident and working population. All tourism includes some travel but not all travel is tourism. The temporary short-term character of tourism distinguishes it from migration, which represents a long-term population movement with a view to taking up permanent residence; tourism is also distinguished from short-term migration, as exemplified by movements of seasonal and temporary labour. In tourism money earned in one's normal domicile is spent in the places visited and on the way to these places.

Technical Definitions of Tourism

Within the broad concept outlined above, tourism is variously interpreted for particular purposes and there are at least three particular aspects, which usually need to be defined.

The first is the *purpose* of travel or visit, which expresses a particular motivation. This has important implications for marketing in general and for promotion in particular, as between different types of traffic to particular destinations. Different considerations obtain in the case of business and holiday travel, visits to friends and relatives, and in travel for other reasons. A technical definition of tourism must, therefore, first define the categories of travel and visits which are, and those which are not included for a particular purpose.

Secondly, it is usually necesary to define the *time element.* The minimum and maximum period, in terms of length of stay away from home or in terms of length of stay at a particular destination may have to be established for a particular purpose. Thus travel or stay for a period shorter than a postulated minimum, for example less than twenty-four hours, may be excluded. Similarly, a person may be away from home or resident at a particular destination for so long that he loses the character of a tourist and this is normally recognized in postulating a maximum period, for example a year.

Thirdly, a technical definition has to recognize *particular situations* which may obtain for particular purposes and it has to be determined whether they are or not regarded as tourism, for example sea cruises and transit traffic.

Various technical definitions are considered in greater detail in Chapters 7, 8 and 9, in connection with statistics of tourism, and elsewhere in this book. A glossary of basic terms and concepts discussed in this Chapter is included in Appendix D.

Some Basic Distinctions

As in trade, so in tourism, a distinction is drawn between domestic or internal and foreign or international tourism. In *domestic tourism* people travel outside their normal domicile to other areas within the country. They normally find it easy to do so, because there are neither language nor currency nor document-ation barriers. Their own language serves as a medium of communication; the currency which they use in everyday life continues to be the medium of exchange; there is no need to meet particular requirements of documentation. It follows that domestic tourism has no balance of payments implications, except that it may be a substitute for foreign tourism and, therefore, result in a saving of foreign currency for the country of residence and a reduction of income for countries which would have been visited.

When people travel to a country other than that in which they normally live, and which is a separate national unit with its own political and economic system, they are involved in *international tourism*. The difference between domestic and foreign tourism depends on the extent to which the country visited has a different language, a different currency, and to which obstacles to free movement exist between the country of residence and the country visited. Of these differences the latter two are the most significant. Where different currencies are involved, tourism has repercussions on the balance of payments because each country has to balance its transactions with the rest of the world. Where in the crossing of national frontiers obstacles are put in the way of tourists by the authorities, the requisite documentation may restrict and regulate the flow by means of pass-ports, visas, and other conditions of entry and movement to be met by tourists.

However, for the true understanding of tourism the distinction between dom-estic and foreign tourism is better regarded as one of degree rather than one of substance. If tourism is viewed in this way, aspects of common significance can be recognized and evaluated. Moreover, the distinction is diminishing, as language barriers are being lowered with improving language skills, especially on the part of the population of host countries, as currency and customs unions are developing in number and intensity, and as the free movement of people between countries is growing.

We have seen earlier that tourism may be classified for various reasons according to *purpose of visit*. A broad distinction based on purpose is between holiday, business, and common interest tourism; the third category includes tourists with other specific purposes for their journeys and is sometimes sub-divided further into visits to friends and relatives, or for study, health, religious, and other miscellaneous purposes.* This distinction is of relevance for marketing and for the physical development of facilities, as well as for other aspects of visits.

According to the *duration*, short trips which do not involve an overnight stay are usually described as day trips or excursions both internally and internationally, and should be differentiated from journeys and stays at destinations of at least twenty-four hours, which are described as tourism, and which involve an overnight stay. Apart from its obvious statistical significance, the distinction between excursions and tourism is of particular significance for the provision of accommodation facilities.

Another distinction of growing importance is between *individual and group travel* and, quite separately, between independent travel and inclusive tours. In the former case the terms denote no more and no less than that the tourist moves about individually or as a member of a group, irrespective of the way the travel and stay is arranged. The distinction is of some significance in the handling of traffic and in the reception of tourists at destinations.

The classification of travel and tourism into *independent travel and inclusive tour* is based on how the individual elements of a trip are bought by the tourist. In the former case transport, accommodation, and possibly other elements are arranged separately either by the tourist himself directly with the carrier, hotel, or another supplier, or through a travel agent. In the latter case the tourist buys a trip, for which he is unable to distinguish the pre-paid cost of his fare from the cost of accommodation and other elements; this arrangement is also known as the package tour. The tourist may then move about as an individual or as a member of a group, according to the particular arrangement entered into; the terms 'group, and 'inclusive' may, therefore, coincide in specific instances, but they describe two distinct forms of holiday or trip.

Some other terms have been often applied more or less discriminately to tourism, in particular mass, popular, and social tourism, to which it is desirable to attach more precise meanings at the outset.[5]

Mass tourism refers to the participation of large numbers of people in tourism, a general characteristic of developed countries in the twentieth century. In this sense the term is used in contrast to the limited participation of people in some

*This classification gives expression to the intensity of the link between the tourist and his receiving country or locality. The holiday tourist is a stranger; the businessman less so in having his customers or suppliers at the destination; the common interest tourist has even closer hosts: friends or relatives, ethnic or religious groups, educational institutions, who may share with him a common interest in his visit to a still higher degree.

specialist forms of tourist activity, such as yachting, or in contrast to the situation in developing countries or in countries with extreme inequalities of income and wealth or, indeed, to the limited extent of tourist activity everywhere until a few decades ago. Mass tourism is essentially a quantitative notion, based on the proportion of the population participating in tourism or on the volume of tourist activity.

Popular tourism denotes tourist activities meeting with a wide acceptance by people, because of their attractiveness and availability. The acceptance may be due to meeting the needs or tastes of people or more particularly to being available at a low price. Popular tourism is, therefore, essentially a qualitative notion, although by its nature it may give rise to mass tourism.

As distinct from the two, *social tourism* is concerned specifically with the participation in tourism of people of limited means and others disadvantaged through age, disability or family circumstances, and with the measures to encourage this participation and to make it possible. Although many individuals and groups with whom social tourism is concerned are often identified with manual workers, and social tourism is often identified with workers' travel (tourisme ouvrier, Arbeitertourismus, turismo dei lavoratori), it is neither exclusive to them nor confined to them. Action in social tourism is concerned in practice with subsidies, special facilities, and other measures, sometimes of a co-operative nature, sometimes by the State or another third party, to make participation in tourism possible in the interests of society and the well-being of those covered by the term 'social tourism'.[6]

These and related distinctions are considered further in Chapters 5, 7, 8, and 9 in connection with the determinants and the statistics of tourism.

The Tourist Destination

We have seen in the historical outline (*see* Chapters 1—3) that the evolution of tourism has been closely identified with the beginnings and subsequent development of *resorts*. Indeed, historically resorts have been the main centres of tourism and this is still the case today. From the original spas of the eighteenth century various types of inland and coastal resorts have grown up, including mountain and other centres. Gradually the term resort has come to acquire its literal meaning to denote any visitor centre to which people resort in large numbers. Capital cities as centres of commerce and government, often with strong historical and cultural associations, good communications, as well as accommodation, catering, entertainment, and shopping facilities, have become the largest and most prosperous resorts in their countries, especially for international tourists.

Two recent developments have been changing the nature of resorts. As a result of the rapid growth of individual means of transport, most resorts have lost their local character; many have become bases for touring within their districts and regions; many are stopping places for holidays, which include several stays in different places within a region. In contrast, many hotels have greatly extended the range of their amenities to cater for all or most requirements of their guests and become resorts in themselves; elsewhere comprehensive recreation centres ranging from holiday camps to holiday villages have been created.

In these circumstances much marketing and development in tourism ceases to be confined or even directly related to the traditional inland or coastal resort. It is, therefore, desirable to adopt a different focus in examining the location of tourist activity, of the whole pattern and of the characteristics of tourism. The geographical unit visited by a tourist may be a self-contained centre, a village or a town or a city, a district or a region, an island, a country or a continent. This geographical unit may be described as *the tourist destination*. Throughout the year its amenities serve its resident and working populations. But at some or all times of the year there are also temporary users — tourists, who are away from their normal place of residence and work, to which they return after a short time. The tourist destination, however defined geographically, provides a convenient focus for the examination of the tourist movement and of its manifold impact and significance.

How important any geographical unit is as a tourist destination, or how important it is potentially, is determined by three prime factors: attractions, accessibility, and amenities which may be termed *the tourist qualities of a destination*.

The *attractions* may be site attractions (for example, climatic, scenic, historical), or event attractions (for example, congresses, exhibitions and sporting events), both of which exercise a gravitational influence on non-residents. The site attractions have clearly determined the tourist importance of such destinations as the Mediterranean, the Alps, Athens, and Rome, as well of the Channel Islands, the Lake District, and towns like Edinburgh, Oxford, and Stratford-on-Avon. By contrast deserts, centres of heavy industry, and new towns rarely attract significant numbers of visitors. Trade fairs and Olympic Games are attractions in themselves; they may also enhance the site attractions of a destination, or be enhanced by them.

Accessibility is a function of distance from centres of population, which constitute tourist markets, and of external transport and communications, which enable a destination to be reached. Accessibility provides another explanation of the importance of Britain and of much of Western Europe as tourist destinations, in contrast to the many attractive parts of Africa and Asia.

Amenities at the destination comprise accommodation, catering, entertainment, as well as internal transport and communications, which enable the tourist to move round during his stay. It is clear that amenities contribute much to many established resorts as tourist destinations, in contrast to areas which lack in particular adequate accommodation for visitors.

What the three qualities are and in what measure they are present in a particular place determines not only its importance but also its likely success as a tourist destination. But in order to maximize the opportunities from tourism, a tourist destination must also have a *tourist organization*, in order to provide the framework in which tourism can operate to develop the tourist product and to promote it in appropriate tourist markets. In that sense, organization constitutes a fourth factor which determines the importance and success of a destination. This aspect is developed further in Chapter 25 in connection with the organization of tourism.

Tourist Services

The journeys and stay of tourists give rise to a demand for a wide range of services in the course of the journey and stay at destinations, each of which may occur more than once during a single trip away from home.

The principal tourist services required during the journey in tourism are supplied by *passenger transport*, which provides the means to reach the destination and also the means of movement at the destination. The most significant distinctions in transport are between public and private, inland and international, air and surface and, of course, between the various modes. Of these in recent years by far the fastest growing means of long-distance tourist transport has been the aircraft, which now constitutes the primary means of transport on many routes. By contrast shipping, which provides transport coverage for all distances including movement at the destination, has come to play a more prominent role on short sea routes and waterways and also for cruises. Rail represents short- and medium-distance transport within and between countries, both for reaching a destination and for movement at the destination; in some mountain locations it forms the only means of access. Road transport by bus and coach provides regular direct route services for short and medium distances to the destination, means of transport at the destination and, on many routes, alternative facilities to rail. But one of the most significant developments of recent years has been the replacement of travel by public road and rail transport by the motor car, which has become the principal means of tourist transport in most countries. Concurrently the combined uses of motoring with rail and shipping services and air car ferries have grown into significant new forms of tourist transportation to destinations. Transport is a necessary but not sufficient condition of tourism by itself.

At the destination *accommodation, catering, and entertainment* constitute the primary tourist services. Although transport is the key factor in the tourist growth of many destinations, hotels are of vital concern to a large proportion of tourists. However, many stay with friends and relatives and in other private accommodation, others take their own means of accommodation with them in the form of caravans and tents.

The growing popularity of self-catering holidays is a further manifestation of the trend to individual independence, which reduces the reliance on tourist services at the destination in a way analogous to that in which the motor car is a preferred substitute to public transport to the destination. The outcome has been a decrease in the relative importance of the two traditional backbones of domestic tourism — hotels and public transport. But as a result of the rapid growth of inclusive tours, they have increased in importance in international tourism.

The growth of international tourism has been accompanied and often brought about by the increasingly important role of a third group of tourist services — those provided by *the travel agent* and even more so by *the tour operator*. The former fulfils an intermediary function between the tourist and the providers of transport and accommodation in particular, the latter an organizing function in which he combines the individual components of a holiday into a product, which is then marketed on his own account and risk.

Apart from the above three principal groups of providers of tourist services, many others meet the tourists' requirements ranging from currency and documentation to information services, sightseeing, and shopping. From a marketing point of view, if tourists constitute the demand, tourist services represent the supply in the market. Although it is difficult to apply to these services the normal concept of an industry — in view of the special nature and complexity of their respective contributions to the tourist product — they may be described as *the tourist industry*: they include that part of the economy which has a common function of supplying tourist needs. This enables us to link demand and supply in tourism and to analyse the impact of tourism on the economy.

The concept of the tourist industry is developed further in Chapter 6 which is devoted to the examination of the significance of tourism; individual tourist services are described and analysed in Parts IV, V, and VI.

Tourist Products and Markets

A tourist may use individual tourist services with or without advance arrangement or he may arrange some in advance, for example his transport, and some, for example his accommodation, on arrival at the destination. He may also purchase them in advance as a package. The elements of his trip, consisting of what he does on the way to the destination and when staying there, comprise the *tourist product*.

In a narrow sense the tourist product consists of what the tourist buys. In a wider sense the tourist product is an amalgam of what he does at the destination and of the services he uses to make it possible. Therefore, each destination has a particular product or products to offer. Switzerland offers an environment of mountains and lakes, which may be used for skiing in winter and for walking, climbing, and relaxation in the summer; the Riviera offers an environment of Mediterranean sea and sun; Blackpool offers an environment of breezy beaches. In each of these destinations the tourist selects an activity or activities in which he engages, and the services which he uses during his stay. In this sense the destination product is analogous to a selection of articles in a shop, to which the buyer goes to make his purchases. If the buyer has the articles delivered to his home, the delivery forms part of the purchase, for which he pays directly or indirectly. In an analogous way transport to a tourist destination may be viewed as an essential part of the tourist product.

The tourist product at the destination may be developed consciously to appeal to particular people or it may develop without any conscious effort. In the former case certain features of the destination are selected and developed in the physical sense — swimming pools, parks, or large-scale indoor entertainment facilities are examples; they are also developed in the minds of potential tourists, through the creation of a particular image of the destination, by promotion. The conscious development of the tourist product is usually determined after a study of the potential market. When the tourist product develops without any conscious effort, the market tends to shape itself to the product.

In the formal study of economics, the economist views *the market* as a network of dealings between the sellers and buyers of a product; a particular market is defined by reference to the product, the sellers who supply it, and the buyers who exercise the demand for it. In this sense the tourist market is defined by reference to the tourist product, which is as we have seen a composite product, the providers of tourist services which enter into the composite product, and the tourists who buy it.

In normal business usage buyers are seen to constitute the market and a common distinction is drawn between the actual (existing) market, which comprises those who currently buy the production in question, and the potential market, which includes those who do not buy currently but may do so in the future. Correspondingly, the tourist market focuses on existing and potential tourists.

The two uses of the concept of the market are not mutually exclusive, but represent two different viewpoints: the former is the total view, the latter is the viewpoint of the seller. Any seller may supply more than one market. In the tourist market a transport operator or an hotelier may be providing respectively transport and hotel services to various travellers, some of whom may be and others who need not be tourists. But any particular operator rarely supplies the whole tourist product himself. We have seen that the composite nature of the tourist product is an important characteristic. Individual elements may be bought in separate parts or all together, but they are usually supplied by different operators.

Corresponding to each tourist product there is a tourist market. Whether seen as a network of dealings or as the sum total of tourists, as there is a multiplicity of tourist products so there is a corresponding multiplicity of tourist markets. In these there are more or less homogeneous groups of tourists who behave more or less similarly and who buy more or less similar tourist products. It is the function of marketing in tourism to identify these groups, to influence the development of tourist products, and to bring the information about products to the potential tourists.

An important consequence follows from the composite nature of the tourist product: marketing and development in tourism are at two levels: at the level of the individual operators and at the level of the tourist destination. This distinction, the nature of tourist products and markets, and marketing and development in tourism are considered in some detail in Parts VII and VIII.

5 *Determinants and Motivations*

In the nineteenth century the growth of tourism was the result of three main sets of influences in the Western World. First, following the Industrial Revolution a large and prosperous middle class came into being and a general increase in material wealth followed industrialization and development in trade; the population came to be increasingly concentrated in towns and cities. Second, the rapid spread of railways provided the means of quick and cheap inland travel; soon after, the steamship met the need for improved inter-continental travel. Third, large hotels were built to accommodate the increasing traffic and advances were made in the organization of travel with the emergence of the first travel organizers, guide-books, and other travel services. (*See* Chapters 1 and 2).

The three major stimuli — the wealth of the industrial society, developments in transport, and organization and servicing of travel — were first discernible on any scale in Britain and in America. But their influence soon spread across most of Western Europe. So also did the basic motives to engage in tourism, which had been apparent particularly in Britain even before the middle of the nineteenth century — curiosity and education, health and recreation.

In the twentieth century the growth of tourism continued to be determined by the living standards in the developed countries, but its major impact on the lower income groups had to await the widespread introduction of holidays with pay after the Second World War. The motor car and the aircraft superseded the railway and the steamship as the main transport modes soon after the middle of the century. New forms of accommodation, the emergence of the tour operating industry, the marketing efforts of individual providers of tourist services and of tourist organizations, all found a ready response in a rapidly growing travel market with its increasing complexity of motivations and reasons for travel. (*See* Chapter 3.)

Historically the development of tourism can thus be seen to have been determined by economic and social factors on the one hand and by the providers of tourist services on the other hand; these factors explain the conditions which have made it possible for people to engage in tourism. When these conditions are created, it is necessary to consider why people wish to become tourists, that is, what are the motivations to tourism.

Propensities to Holidays

An indication of the extent of participation in tourism by residents of various countries is available from national holiday surveys. An increasing number of countries measure the holiday volume, characteristics, and behaviour of the resident populations systematically through such surveys and recent data for countries of the European Economic Community are shown in Appendix E.

In late 1970s in most EEC countries a half or more of the population took at least one holiday away from home each year, giving a net holiday propensity of 50 per cent or more. An increasing proportion of the populations of EEC countries took more than one holiday away from home annually and this is expressed as gross holiday propensity. The ratio between the two gives holiday frequency, i.e. the average number of holidays taken by those who do go away on holiday in any year. When holidays abroad are related to population, the proportions express propensities to holidays abroad.

Caution has to be exercised in interpreting the results of the surveys and particularly in inter-country comparisons. Although a common framework for national holiday surveys has been recommended by the Tourism Committee of the Organisation for Economic Co-operation and Development (OECD)[7], surveys of individual countries tend to differ in their definitions, scope, and methods.

However, most holiday surveys demonstrate some variation in holiday propensities according to income, both for countries as a whole, and more particularly for different income groups within countries. Another significant variation in holiday propensities emerges from the surveys between those living in urban areas and those living in rural areas, and also according to such characteristics as occupation, age, and size of household. Highest participation in tourism has been found among residents of large urban areas; those with high incomes; administrative, managerial, and professional groups; younger age groups and members of small households. Residents of rural areas, low income groups, agricultural semi-skilled and unskilled occupations, families with small children, the retired, and members of large households tend to display low participation.

Sources of International Tourist Traffic

An indication of the countries of origin of international tourists is available from studies of the World Tourism Organization (WTO) and the Organisation for Economic Co-operation and Development (OECD). Data for 1965 and 1975 are compared in Table 1.

In the mid 1960s the arrivals from twelve leading generating countries accounted for three-quarters of all international tourist arrivals in the world, and all other countries contributed only a quarter of the total. Ten years later, in the mid 1970s, the share of twelve leading countries increased to four-fifths and there were two significant changes in 1975 compared with 1965. In 1965 the first two countries, the United States and Germany, contributed over 20 million arrivals each, and all the leading generators of international tourism were in Europe and in North America. By 1975 Germany became unmistakably the leading generator, producing twice as many world tourist arrivals as the United States and over a quarter of the world total. The second major change was the inclusion of Japan in the top twelve.

The position has not changed significantly in the late 1970s. Twelve countries generate some 80 per cent of world tourist arrivals and some 80 per cent of world tourist expenditure: of this the top five account for almost two-thirds, the top two for over a third, the top one for over a quarter of the total.

In terms of tourist flows, the developed world is competing for the great majority of international tourists from developed countries; the whole of the developing world is competing for a small, mainly long-haul market from the developed world. The developing world is generating few international tourists either for the developed world or for its own destinations. The dominant international tourist flows are, first, north to north, and second, north to south.

In the assessment of the generation of international tourist flows it is often more meaningful to relate the tourist arrivals generated by individual countries to the size of their population; a coefficient then expresses the propensity to travel abroad. This is, of course, influenced by such factors as the size of the country and its geographical position in relation to the rest of the world, which tend to affect negatively the coefficient for a large country such as the United States with a large colume of internal travel; for most US residents foreign travel involves long journeys, as compared with many European countries where a short journey takes the resident abroad. Smaller countries such as Belgium, the Netherlands, and Switzerland, generate several hundred international tourist arrivals per thousand population and show particularly high coefficients.

Table 1
Leading Generators of World Tourism 1965 and 1975

		1965		1975	
		Million	Rank	Million	Rank
Europe	Austria	2·1	10	3·0	12
	Belgium	3·8	7	5·7	8
	Denmark	1·4	12		
	France	10·0	3	23·2	3
	Germany F R	21·6	2	55·4	1
	Italy	3·1	8	7·3	7
	Netherlands	4·1	6	9·9	6
	Sweden	1·4	11	3·2	11
	Switzerland	2·2	9	3·8	9
	United Kingdom	7·5	4	13·9	4
North America	Canada	6·7	5	12·3	5
	United States	21·7	1	28·4	2
Asia	Japan			3·6	10
12 main countries		85·6		169·9	
Total world tourist arrivals		115·5		206·9	

Source: International Union of Official Travel Organizations,
World Tourism Organization, *Reviews of World Tourism 1968-1978*;
World Tourism Organization, *Tourism Compendium*, 1979 edition

Britain as a Generator of Tourism

During the 1970s the population of the United Kingdom increased very little, only 0·1 per cent p.a., and reached 55·9 million by mid 1978. The UK Gross National Product and consumer expenditure at market prices more than trebled between 1970 and 1978; consumer expenditure moved broadly in line with the Gross National Product, as shown in Table 2.

Table 2
UK Gross National Product and Consumer Expenditure 1970-78

	1970	1971	1972	1973	1974	1975	1976	1977	1978
GNP[a] (£ 000 million)	51·6	57·8	63·8	74·1	84·0	104·7	124·6	142·3	162·5
Change (% p.a.)		12·1	10·4	16·1	13·3	24·7	19·0	14·2	14·2
Consumer exp'ture[a] (£ 000 million)	31·7	35·5	40·0	45·5	52·1	63·7	73·8	84·1	96·1
Change (% p.a.)		11·9	12·7	13·6	14·5	22·3	15·8	14·1	13.5

[a]at market prices

Source: Central Statistical Office, *National Income and Expenditure*, 1979 edition

In real terms the Gross National Product increased only by an average of 1·6 per cent p.a. and reached £2,900 per head of population by 1978. Private car ownership increased from 11·5 million to 14·1 million or from over 200 to over 250 cars per thousand population. In 1970 about a half of manual workers had a basic holiday entitlement of three weeks or more; by 1978 all manual workers were entitled to annual holidays of three weeks or more and over a third of them to four weeks or more. During the 1970s almost a half of the population lived in conurbations, cities and large towns; over three-quarters were urban and less than a quarter rural dwellers.[8] British residents' participation in tourism between 1970 and 1978 is summarized in terms of volume and expenditure in Table 3.

The volume of British residents' tourism for all purposes, which includes holidays, business, and other travel, in Britain declined and tourism abroad remained static during the period, until a significant increase occurred in 1978. Growth in total expenditure, which represents in the region of 5 per cent of total consumer expenditure, did not follow closely changes in the GNP or total consumer expenditure.

British holidays of four nights or more away from home increased in the early years of the decade but declined subsequently, until a significant increase occurred in 1978. In most years holiday expenditure, which represents between 3 and 4 per cent of total consumer expenditure, followed more closely changes in the GNP and in consumer expenditure, reflecting the discretionary nature of holiday spending.

Table 3

British Residents' Tourism 1970-78

	1970	1971	1972	1973	1974	1975	1976	1977	1978
Trips in Britain (m)			132	132	114	117	121	121	119
abroad (m)			11	11	10	11	11	11	13
total (m)			143	143	124	127	132	131	130
Nights in Britain (m)			605	590	535	550	545	545	530
abroad (m)			120	120	110	115	110	115	135
total (m)			725	705	640	665	655	655	660
Spending in Britain (£m)			1,375	1,450	1,800	2,150	2,400	2,625	3,100
abroad (£m)			775	825	975	1,150	1,325	1,500	2,075
total (£m)			2,150	2,275	2,775	3,300	3,725	4,125	5,175
Change in spending (% p.a)				+6	+22	+19	+13	+11	+26
Holidays[b]									
Number in Britain (m)	34·5	34·0	37·5	40·5	40·5	40·0	37·5	36·0	39·0
abroad (m)	5·75	7·25	8·5	8·25	6·75	8·0	7·25	7·75	9·0
total (m)	40·25	41·25	46·0	48·75	47·25	48·0	44·75	43·75	48·0
Spending in Britain (£m)	790	810	920	n.a.	1,100	1,270	1,460	1,570	1,700
abroad (£m)	470	630	830	870	740	1,080	1,210	1,360	1,860
total (£m)	1,260	1,440	1,750	n.a.	1,840	2,350	2,670	2,930	3,560
Change in spending (% pa)		+14	+22	n.a.	n.a.	+28	+14	+10	+22

[a] Tourism for all purposes for one night or more away from home.
[b] Holidays of four nights or more away from home.
[c] Some totals may not agree with the sum of items owing to rounding.
[d] Definitions of 'abroad' used in this table are not identical.

Sources: British Home Tourism Survey and *British National Travel Survey.*

Economic and Social Determinants

The examination of holiday propensities of the resident populations of a number of countries and of sources of origin of international tourist traffic suggest that, in broad terms, the highest participation in tourism is to be found in countries with a relatively high standard of living, in which a large proportion of the population is urbanized. These characteristics are dominant in North America and in Western Europe, the two regions of the world which also dominate domestic as well as international tourism as the principal generators of tourists.

A high *standard of living* manifests itself in high disposable incomes, which tend to be accompanied by reductions in hours of work and by lengthening of holidays with pay. Thus the standard of living embodies two requisites of tourism — money to be spent on holidays and free time in which holidays may be taken. Moreover, a high standard of living finds expression in a high level of car ownership, which is itself conducive to travel away from home.

Whilst the standard of living may be considered as the most significant single determinant of tourism, available evidence suggests that participation in tourism is affected by a number of *demographic and socio-economic factors*, such as age distribution, the pattern of stages in the life cycle of families, terminal levels of education, occupation structure and population concentration.

All of these characteristics change only very gradually in any society and may be taken as static over a number of years. Some, in particular education and occupation, are closely correlated with income and may be, therefore, submerged in income in a general assessment of determinants; others, such as age and life-cycle patterns, are also linked with income, and whilst of undoubted significance in explaining individual behaviour and, therefore, in marketing, there are practical difficulties in their use as determinants of tourism growth generally, and in comparisons of tourism propensity between countries. However, in the long term certain consequences may be expected to follow not only from changes in the size of the population, but also from changes in particular age groups and in different life-cycle stages.

In Chapter 4 tourism was divided into holiday, business, and common interest tourism. Different determinants apply to each. The level of business tourism is to a great extent dependent on the level of economic activity, and various forms of common interest tourism on various influences. The discussion in this section is largely concerned with determinants of holiday tourism, which involves discretionary use of money and time.

Other Influences on Growth

When buying an article, the ability and willingness to pay the price make the demand effective. When buying a holiday, the buyer must have not only the money but also the time. Availability of income and leisure time make the purchase possible. When on holiday, the tourist uses public or private transport, stays in hotels or other accommodation, eats in restaurants and engages in a multitude of activities. The providers of these services exercise a significant influence on the level of participation in tourism through the availability, quality, and price of their services and through their promotion activities.

Rarely has this been demonstrated more clearly than in the case of transport in tourism. Transport developments in the nineteenth century made tourism possible, the transport revolution of the twentieth century created tourism as a mass phenomenon. Each reduction in fares and each increase in speed of transport adds to the volume of tourism: on the one hand those who can afford the lower fare, and on the other hand those who can spare the time to travel at all or who can travel further afield or who can stay longer at the destination.

The *price, frequency, and speed of transport* can thus restrict the volume of tourism but they can also positively stimulate tourism growth. These effects are of limited significance over short distances but of primary importance on long distances, where air transportation has experienced rapid technological and commercial development since the Second World War. In that time the replacement of the passenger shipping industry by the airline industry has been one of the most dramatic changes in tourism. At the same time the price of air travel reduced and the speed increased significantly. The major expansion on the transatlantic route, the busiest long-haul route in the world, began with the introduction of tourist class and economy class in the 1950s, to be followed by group and excursion fares in the early 1960s, an upsurge of charter flights in the late 1960s, and the growth of various forms of incentive fares in the 1970s, all of which led to a massive increase in tourism to many destinations.

At times similar even though less dramatic increases in tourist traffic have been brought about by railway excursions, bus and coach operators, hotels, and holiday camps, through differential pricing and other incentives to travel and stay away from home. However, a more far-reaching impact on the growth of tourism in the 1960s was made through the package tours, basically a combination of accommodation and transport at a price in which the two elements are indistinguishable, particularly by the package tours by air to foreign countries, which now account, for example, for well over a half of UK holiday traffic to Western Europe.

To the extent that developments in transport and in the organization and servicing of travel actually generate new tourist traffic, that is participation in tourism which would not take place otherwise, to that extent they represent creative forces in tourism. By influencing not only the pattern and the distribution of tourist flows, but also their magnitude and the overall volume of tourism, these developments also constitute determinants of tourism.

Last but not least, however difficult it is to quantify its effects, the role of *promotion in tourism* must be raised in a discussion of determinants. In all countries in which the participation in tourism is significant, the communications and information environment is dominated by the mass media. Newspapers, magazines, films, radio, and television, play a major role in the marketing of most consumer products. In the 1960s they began to play an important role in influencing the use of leisure through the dissemination of information about leisure activities, including travel and holidays. Tourism promotion may be instrumental in creating and fostering a tradition of travel generally, as well as to particular destinations, and in placing tourism in the range of purchases in which it did not figure before. It is, therefore, less than realistic to overlook the effects which promotional activities of individual operators and of official tourist organizations may have on the growth of tourism. The actions of the tourist industry, including promotion, may be viewed as a separate set of determinants, which enhance the natural growth of tourism, brought about by economic and social determinants.

Motivations

In the search for the determinants of tourism the discussion in this chapter has been concerned with the economic and social factors and with the influence of the providers of tourist services, which stimulate the growth of tourism. When the reasons why people wish to become tourists are considered, we are dealing with motivations. In examining motivations it is useful to distinguish between two broad groups of travellers.

The first group comprises those who have to visit a particular place and includes businessmen and some elements of those who may be described as common interest travellers, such as those visiting friends and relatives. The decision to travel, where to go and when to go, is to a greater or lesser extent outside their control. They are less influenced by price or distance and particularly demand for business travel is relatively price-inelastic, that is, not susceptible to price inducements.

The second group — holiday tourists — have a freedom of choice. They decide for themselves whether they should apply a part of their income and a part of their leisure time to participate in tourism, where to go and, to a greater or lesser extent, when to go. Their demand for travel is highly price-elastic, that is susceptible to price inducements.

The reasons for travel away from home by businessmen and by others in the first group are self-evident. Each may, indeed, be marginally influenced by those considerations which affect the second group, the pleasure travellers. This may be reflected in the frequency of visits or in the consideration of alternatives where they do exist as, for example, in the choice of venues for conferences. But no particular problem is faced in identifying the motivations.

In tourism conceived as pleasure or holiday travel the reasons are varied and not always clearly evident or easily identifiable. It may be said that the prime motivation to engage in tourism is to be elsewhere and to escape, however temporarily, the routine, constraints, and stresses of everyday life. From this basic motivation two main and distinct motivations may be postulated as dominant, which have been described by Professor Gray[9] as *wanderlust and sunlust*.

Wanderlust describes the desire to exchange the known for the unknown, to leave things familiar and to go and see different places, people, and cultures or relics of the past in places famous for their historical monuments and associations, or for their current fashions and contributions to society.

Sunlust generates a type of travel which depends on the existence elsewhere of better amenities for a specific purpose than are available in the domicile; it is prominent with particular activities such as sports and literally with the search for the sun.

The significance of the two types of travel relates to the degree to which they are likely to be international rather than domestic and to the type of facilities required at the destination. In a large country both types of desire may be satisfied but, on the whole, wanderlust is more likely to be international, even in a large country such as the United States. Sunlust is more likely to be satisfied in the country of residence, except where that country is small. Wanderlust calls for facilities geared to transient visitors and for means of movement at the destinations; sunlust requires facilities for a longer stay and for recreation.

A journey to a resort in a foreign country motivated by sunlust contains an element of satisfaction of wanderlust; conversely a tourist seeking to satisfy his wanderlust also expects some of the amenities of a resort holiday. But the distinction, even though one of degree, expresses realistically the flows of modern tourism. The dominant search for satisfaction is usually clear. The dominant flows of tourism in Europe are from the North to the Mediterranean, within Britain to the south coast and in the United States to Florida, for winter sports to the Alps and other mountainous regions, for shopping and entertainment to the cities and resorts. Wanderlust flows follow less marked routes, as climate is less important, and as more than one country or more than one place are commonly visited.

Within the two main types of pleasure travel variations exist — from a desire for quiet and seclusion to centres of activity, from complete relaxation to constant activity, from freedom and independence to organized activity. As a result the travel market at any time is highly fragmented. Moreover, people do not necessarily display constant motivations and the same people may buy different tourist products at different times.

In conclusion, it seems that whilst the long-term determinants of tourism can be identified with some certainty and whilst they show a high degree of stability over a long period of time, motivations to tourism are less precise and tend to change more frequently. We can describe the 'who, when, where, and how' of tourism, the economic and social characteristics of tourist and their behaviour; we are far less confident in assessing and predicting their gratification.

6 *The Significance of Tourism*

The importance of tourism was formally acknowledged when the XXI United Nations General Assembly designated 1967 as the International Tourist Year with a unanimous resolution recognizing that 'tourism is a basic and most desirable human activity deserving the praise and encouragement of all peoples and all Governments'.

In creating a better appreciation of other people's ways of life and institutions, tourism may create goodwill for a country. Each year many tourists travel to participate in particular events ranging from congresses to coronations; their visits also afford opportunities to improve co-operation as well as to project an image of a country to the outside world.

When travelling away from home, tourists come in contact with the places they visit and with their inhabitants, and social exchange takes place. Their presence and their social background affect the social structure and mode of life at the destination; tourists are in turn affected by the experience and often carry back home with them new habits and a new outlook on life.

Much tourism has an educational significance. In the widest sense it has the altogether beneficial effect which contact between people of different races and nationalities can bring about. In a narrower sense much tourist activity takes the form of study trips and attendance at courses and conferences with specified educational aims in view.

Tourism is often accompanied by cultural exchanges and by cultural enrichment of those who travel as well as those at the receiving end. Cultural factors attract tourists to destinations — architecture, historical monuments, and birthplaces of the famous are some of the places most visited by tourists; festivals and exhibitions rely heavily on visitor traffic for their audience and attendance.

In bringing together people of different backgrounds from different countries tourism, therefore, has a political and social significance; in this and in the activities in which tourists engage, there is often also educational and cultural significance. But the manifold significance of tourism does not arise only when people visit other countries. Internal, domestic tourism promotes similar interaction between people and places and contributes to that knowledge and awareness, which may enhance understanding.

Politics, society, education, and culture thus often provide motivations for tourists to travel away from home; they influence tourism and tourism in turn has an influence on them. These factors also help explain participation in tourism generally as we have seen in the last chapter when considering determinants of tourism. An evaluation of the significance of tourism may be extended to such aspects as organized sport and religion, and to its interaction with technology. Some of the most important aspects arise in the relationship between tourism, the economy and the environment.

The main economic significance of tourism — that money earned in places of normal residence is spent in places visited — is common to all tourism, whether international or domestic. Each year vast sums are transferred from the economies in which they are earned, to economies in receiving areas where they provide a source of income, a means of livelihood, and amenities for the resident population. The outstanding economic effect of tourism lies in the purchasing power generated in receiving areas through the expenditure of visitors who tend to spend at a much bigger rate than when they are at home. The flow of money generated by tourist expenditure finds its way into the overall economy of the tourist destination, as the money is turned over and re-spent.

But international tourist expenditure introduces an additional aspect of economic significance, as countries which are separate political and economic entities have to balance their transactions with the rest of the world. International tourism, therefore, enters into the balance of payments accounts of individual countries and is of major significance in international trade. For countries which generate tourist traffic, it represents an import, in much the same way as do imports of merchandise; for countries receiving tourist traffic it represents an export, in much the same way as do exports of merchandise. Globally tourism constitutes a major item in world trade, which has shown as much faster rate of growth in recent years than world trade in goods.

In this chapter tourism is evaluated mainly in terms of its economic significance, but reference is made also to its role as a source of other, less quantifiable, benefits and to some of the problems which tourism presents to individual destinations.

Tourism in the National Economy

The part played by tourism in the national economy may be seen in broad terms when tourist expenditure is related to estimates of National Income and Expenditure. Official estimates of National Income are made annually by most countries, which arrive at the value of all goods and service produced in the course of a year. The approach, which produces this aggregate, known as the output method, is matched by the income method, which adds up all personal and corporate incomes, and by the expenditure method, which totals up the value of all that people buy and what they save. Each of the three approaches classifies the composition of the National Income in a particular way — by output or income or expenditure — and acts as a check on the other methods. The outcome of all three methods of estimating is the same — the value of the Gross National Product (GNP), from which an allowance is made for depreciation or maintaining capital intact, before arriving at the National Income. That part of the Gross National Product which is spent by individuals is referred to as consumers' expenditure, and is classified by type of expenditure.

An indication of the economic significance of tourism may be derived by relating expenditure generated by tourists to the total Gross National Product, and to that part of it consisting of total consumers' expenditure. This approach is outlined for the United Kingdom below. The United Kingom income from tourism is made up of three main elements — expenditure on tourism in the country by UK residents, expenditure in the country by overseas visitors, and fare payments by overseas visitors to UK carriers.

The most comprehensive estimate of UK residents' expenditure on tourism is provided by the British Home Tourism Survey, which records British residents' tourism for all purposes of one or more nights away from home; expenditure is spending while away from home and on advance payments for such things as fares and accommodation. Overseas visitor expenditure may be derived from the International Passenger Survey, which records visits by overseas residents to the UK for less than a year; the expenditure includes only spending in the UK. Estimates of fare payments by overseas visitors travelling as passengers to and from the UK with the country's airlines and shipping lines are made by the Department of Industry. A broad estimate of the United Kingdom income from tourism for recent years may be, therefore, computed (using gross figures and ignoring imports required to produce the income) as follows:

Table 4

United Kingdom Income from Tourism 1975-79

	1975	*1976*	*1977*	*1978*	*1979*
	£ million [a]				
Expenditure in the country by British residents [b]	2,200	2,400	2,600	3,100	3,800
Expenditure in the country by overseas visitors [c]	1,200	1,800	2,300	2,500	2,800
Fare payments by overseas visitors to UK carriers [c]	300	500	600	700	700
Total	3,700	4,700	5,500	6,300	7,300

[a] All amounts are rounded to nearest £100 million.

[b] Expenditure on visits by British residents in Britain defined as England, Scotland and Wales; expenditure on visits by residents of Channel Islands and Northern Ireland to Britain and British residents' visits to Channel Islands and Northern Ireland is excluded.

[c] Includes expenditure on day visits.

Sources: See text above table.

Between 1975 and 1979 the United Kingdom Gross National Product and consumers' expenditure (which accounts for some 60 per cent of the GNP) increased by more than a half at market prices. Over the same period the UK income from tourism doubled, and by the end of the decade accounted for about

4 per cent of the GNP and more than 6 per cent of total consumer expenditure. UK residents received an income in the region of £130 per head of population from tourism, which accrued to providers of attractions, facilities, and services at the rate of more than £20 million a day.

It is often more difficult to evaluate tourism as a source of income for smaller tourist destinations but it is usually possible to provide at least a broad indication by means of special surveys of the destination. For example, in 1978 South East England, which covers Kent, Surrey, and Sussex, received some 11 million tourists, nearly 1½ million of them overseas visitors; tourists staying in the region spend £350 million, of which British visitors accounted for £210 million and overseas visitors for £140 million[10]. In the same year a study for Woodspring District Council by the English Tourist Board found that more than ¼ million tourists stayed in Weston-super-Mare in the summer of 1978, who spent £15.2 million; in the same period 1.4 million day visitors spent a further £5.25 million in the district[11].

Tourist expenditure increases the income of the destination by an amount greater than itself. The expenditure is amplified and this effect is known as the multiplier concept. The multiplier itself is the numerical coefficient indicating how much income will increase as a result of tourist expenditure. If, therefore, tourist expenditure is £10 million and the value of the multiplier is 1·9, the income will increase to £19 million. It arises as accommodation providers, restaurateurs, local transport operators, and others who receive income from visitors, pay wages, suppliers' bills, rents, and rates. In turn employees spend their wages, suppliers pay their employees' wages, landlords and other recipients spend their incomes. In this way the sum total of incomes is greater than the original sum spent directly by the tourists.

How large the multiplier is depends on how much of the original income is re-spent at each stage, i.e. not saved, and on leakages which occur through money leaving the economy through import purchases. For example, money spent by a tourist on imported goods increases income by very little.

Estimates of multiplier values in tourism have been made for Greece (1·2—1·4), Hawaii (0·9—1·3), Ireland (2·7), Lebanon 1·2—1·4), the Pacific and Far East (3.2) and Pakistan (3.3).[12] The considerable variations in the multipliers for the above countries and areas are probably as much due to methodological differences in computation as to differences in their actual values.

Suffice it to say for our present purposes that the initial tourist expenditure provides only a first broad indication of the impact of tourism on the economy of the tourist destination. In making an assessment of the value of tourism to the economy, as well as, for example, of the relative values of alternative investment projects, the multiplier technique provides an additional approach. In particular, it draws attention to the differences in the impact of tourism between destinations, which rely heavily on imports to supply the requirements of their tourism industries, and others, which can meet most of them from within the economy.

Tourism as an Employer

The provision of tourist services generates employment. However, the problems of defining the industry are particularly apparent when tourism is considered as an employer of labour. There are three main difficulties of analysis. First, those mainly employed in serving the tourist are rarely distinguished from others employed in the same or similar activities but not concerned with tourism. Thus hotels are usually combined with restaurants and often with other catering activities in official statistics; employment in various forms of transport is shown irrespective of its relationship with tourism; employment in smaller sectors such as travel agencies is usually not enumerated separately. Secondly, statistics of employment normally cover only employees and not others working as employers or self-employed; as tourist services are provided by many small units, the latter may often represent a significant proportion of the total manpower. Thirdly, much tourist activity is seasonal and numbers employed vary a great deal from one time of the year to another. Because of the problems of defining the industry and because of the limitations of the existing data, only broad indications are available about the significance of tourism as an employer in various countries.

A study of tourism-generated employment in the nine countries of the European Economic Community in 1972 estimated that between 8½ — 10 million people's jobs in the Community depended directly or indirectly on tourism, some 6—7 million of them on domestic and 2½—3 million on foreign tourists, including intra-EEC tourists.[13]

A study of employment generating effects of tourism in the United Kingdom in 1975 estimated that total tourism-related employment was in the region of 1½ million or about 6 per cent of total employment in the country.[14] In these and other studies it has been increasingly recognized that direct employment in tourism is only a part of total employment generated by tourism; employment arises also indirectly in other sectors of the economy which supply goods and services to those who serve tourists directly; further employment is induced throughout the economy as the incomes derived from direct and indirect employment are spent and re-spent.[15]

Tourism as a source of employment is particularly important for areas with limited alternative sources of employment, as if often the case in non-industrial areas deficient in natural resources other than climate and scenic attractions. Even in Britain there are many areas where more than 10 per cent of the working population is mainly engaged in catering for the visitor; the proportion is significantly higher in some districts and over 20 per cent in several coastal resorts.

The Beneficiaries

Who benefits from tourism? The simple answer is the tourist industry, that part of the economy which caters for the tourist, those firms and establishments which have a common function — supplying tourist needs. Some of them, such as holiday camps, many restaurants, and many souvenir shops are wholly or mainly dependent on tourism for their business. Others, such as many other retailers and some banks, may rely partly on tourism, but for the most part serve the needs of the resident population. However difficult it may be to define what exactly constitutes the industry in practice, those economic activities which serve the tourist comprise an entity with common interests, even though they do not correspond to the traditional concept of an industry. The industry is defined by reference to their particular market and includes the providers of tourist services, who derive their revenue from the tourist. But we have seen that it is not only the tourist industry, the direct recipients of the visitor expenditure who benefit; visitor spending becomes diffused throughout the economy. The beneficiaries may be, in fact, classified in two main ways — according to the relative importance of tourism to their business and according to the directness of receipts.

When we consider how important tourism is in the total activity of a beneficiary, we distinguish between primary and secondary tourist enterprises. Primary tourist enterprises are wholly or mainly dependent on tourists for their business; many hotels and restaurants, most travel agents and all tour operators fall in this category. Secondary tourist enterprises are only partially dependent on tourism, but for the most part serve the needs of the resident population; examples are banks, laundries, and retailers in important tourist destinations. Whether a particular tourist enterprise may be described as primary or secondary is commonly related to its location; a restaurant or a retail shop, for example, may be either, according to where it is located.

Another way of classifying the beneficiaries is according to whether they receive income from tourists directly or indirectly; the distinction is then between direct and indirect tourist enterprises. The direct ones receive the visitor spending from the tourist himself, as many hoteliers, transport operators, and retailers do, whether they are primary or secondary enterprises. The indirect tourist enterprises receive the benefit of tourist expenditure as a result of the consequent diffusion of receipts by the initial (direct) recipients. Thus many suppliers of goods and services who may never supply the tourists themselves, are beneficiaries from tourism, as are many farmers, builders, and other services, including public utilities, in tourist destinations.

In order to appreciate the full contribution and the total effects of tourism in the economy, probably the most effective instrument is the input-output analysis. This approach was developed and applied to tourism in the United Kingdom and Ireland by G. Richards of the University of Surrey.[16] By dividing the economy into a number of sectors and tracing the flows between them and the tourism sector, it becomes possible to identify the major focal points of the relationship between tourism and the rest of the economy, including individual industries and groups of industries.

Dr Richards found that the effects of tourism on the economy are spread over a large number of industries.

The contribution to incomes arises both from incomes generated in the tourism sector itself and from incomes generated in the rest of the economy. The import-content of outputs needed to meet tourism demand differs as between the two countries and between different industries within the two countries.

It is possible to analyse the requirements for labour and capital resources to meet a given level of tourism demand, both in tourism and in the input industries.

An income multiplier may be derived, which takes fully into account direct, indirect, and induced effects of tourism.

Tourism and Economic Development

In addition to being a source of income and employment, tourism is frequently a source of amenities for the resident population of the tourist destination. Because of visitor traffic, residents may enjoy a higher standard of public transport, shopping, and entertainment facilities than they would be able to support otherwise. The provision of incomes, jobs, and amenities for the resident population may therefore be regarded as the three main beneficial effects of tourism which apply to a greater or lesser extent to any tourist destination.

They are of particular significance to developing countries and to under-developed regions of a country. In comparison with other forms of economic development, an improvement in living standards may be generated through tourist traffic and its expenditure relatively quickly. No sophisticated technology is required to establish the basic facilities. As much of the industry is labour intensive, tourism can absorb unemployed labour resources, which is particularly valuable in areas with surplus unskilled labour. Many operational skills are relatively simple and can be rapidly developed by the inhabitants; such higher skills as are required can usually be imported. To say this is not to minimize the amount and quality of planning required to establish a tourist industry in a new area, but rather to indicate some of the advantages and attractions it may have as compared with other types of development.

In some locations tourism may provide an infrastructure, which in turn forms the base and the stimulus for the diversification of the economy and for the development of other industries. Tourism itself may be expected to create some demand for goods and services necessary for the creation and expansion of some local industries — to maintain the facilities, to meet its requirements for supplies, and to meet the requirements of the visitors directly. But over and above this, an established infrastructure often acts as an attraction to new and less directly related economic activity. Tourist expenditure may therefore be said to stimulate an economy beyond the sector concerned with tourism.

Last but not least, to a developing country tourism offers the prospect of early and substantial foreign currency earnings; moreover, where exports are largely dependent on only one or few primary commodities with widely fluctuating prices in world markets, tourism may provide a stabilizing influence on the country's export earnings.

Tourism and the Balance of Payments

Much of the evaluation of the significance of tourism applies to any geographical unit, whether a town, a region, or a country. But some of its impact occurs only for countries as a result of international travel, which finds expression in the balance of payments of individual countries. In order to appreciate how far-reaching these particular effects are, it is useful to list the principal types of transactions and monetary movements, both of current and capital nature, which arise between countries because of tourism:

(a) Current expenditure by tourists in countries visited (on accommodation, meals, shopping, local transport, and similar).

(b) Purchase of capital goods by tourists in countries visited (for example, antiques and motor cars).

(c) Imports and exports of goods for tourism purposes (equipment, furnishings, food, wine, and other supplies).

(d) Fare payments to other countries' international carriers (principally airlines and shipping lines).

(e) Various money transfers (for example, by nationals working in tourist enterprises abroad, to finance advertising and tourist offices in other countries).

(f) Foreign capital investment in facilities (particularly accommodation).

(g) Interest, profits, and dividends (transmission of return on investment to country of origin of capital).

Of the above transactions, items *(b)* and *(c)* are included with other imports and exports of goods in the balance of trade. Items *(d), (e), (g)* are included in the balance of payments with other invisibles, i.e. other imports and exports of services and monetary transfers. Item *(f)* is included in the capital account of the balance of payments. Therefore, six of the seven principal types of transactions generated between countries by tourism are not normally separately identified as such in the balance of payments. The only item which is so identified is the first, expenditure by tourists in the countries visited, in the travel account of the balance of payments. Sometimes official estimates are made of international fare payments, i.e. item *(d)* above; when this is the case, the amounts may be added to those in the travel account, to give estimates of identifiable foreign payments and earnings from tourism. These values may be illustrated from United Kingdom data, as shown in Tables 5—8.

Table 5

Travel in the UK Balance of Payments 1970-79

	1970	1971	1972	1973	1974	1975	1976	1977	1978	1979[P]
					£ million					
Earn's	432	500	576	726	898	1,218	1,768	2,352	2,507	2,764
Expen'e	382	442	535	695	703	917	1,068	1,186	1,549	2,091
Bal'ce	+50	+58	+41	+31	+195	+301	+700	+1,166	+958	+673

[P] Provisional

Source: Department of Industry International Passenger Survey

Figures of earnings and expenditure in the UK balance of payments for earlier years are shown in Appendixes J and K. UK residents' travel expenditure and changes in currency allowance are related in Appendix L, which covers the post-War period from stringent currency controls of the late 1940s and early 1950s, through the balance of payments crisis of the late 1960s, to the removal of all exchange controls by the UK Government in 1979.

Separate estimates of fare payments by overseas visitors to the UK to UK carriers have been made by the Department of Industry since 1966. Table 6 includes data for recent years in arriving at total UK earnings and indicates that in the region of 80 per cent of the total is made up of overseas visitor expenditure in the country and in the region of 20 per cent of their payments to UK carriers.

Tables 7 and 8 relate the contribution of tourism to the UK balance of payments in terms of tourism share of UK exports and in comparing tourism with other leading exports. In recent years tourism became a leading UK invisible export and also increased its share of total exports. It ranks among the top three invisible exports and among the top six exports overall.

Table 6

UK Total Earnings from Overseas Tourism 1975-79

	1975	1976	1977	1978	1979
	£ million				
Expenditure in the country[a]	1,218	1,768	2,352	2,507	2,764
Fare payments to UK carriers[b]	325	528	584	687	713
Total earnings	1,543	2,296	2,936	3,194	3,477

Sources: [a]Department of Industry International Passenger Survey
*   [b]Department of Industry estimate*

Table 7
UK Tourism and Exports 1975—79

	1975	1976	1977	1978	1979
Tourism earnings[a] as % of total invisible exports	14.4	15.7	17.9	16.9	16.5
Tourism earnings[a] as % of total exports	5.3	5.8	6.1	5.9	5.6

[a]including international fare payments by overseas visitors to UK carriers

Source: British Tourist Authority, Annual Reports

Table 8
UK Tourism and Leading Exports 1975—79

	1975	1976	1977	1978	1979
	£ million				
Visible exports					
Non-electrical machinery	4,255	5,058	6,079	7,082	7,615
Transport equipment	2,452	3,064	3,749	4,539	4,952
Chemicals	2,179	3,047	3,867	4,201	4,914
Invisible exports					
Interest, profits and dividends	2,836	3,711	3,873	4,055	5,219
Sea transport	2,634	3,089	3,378	3,241	3,442
Tourism[a]	1,543	2,296	2,936	3,194	3,477

[a]including international fare payments by overseas visitors to UK carriers

Source: British Tourist Authority, Annual Reports (adjusted for revision in 1979)

Some International Comparisons

The growth of international tourist arrivals and receipts between 1950 and 1979 is illustrated in Appendixes F & G. Over the thirty years international tourist arrivals increased from 25 million to 270 million and international tourist receipts from US $ 2 billion to US $ 75 billion.

Appendixes H and I provide a detailed breakdown of international tourist arrivals and receipts between six regions of the world for the years 1972—79. The highest rates of growth in what may be described as export tourism were achieved in Asia and the Pacific. But Europe continued to account for almost three-quarters of all arrivals and some two-thirds of total receipts, and the combined share of Europe and the Americas was over 90 per cent of all arrivals and close on 90 per cent of total receipts.

In most developed countries international tourism accounts for only a modest proportion of the Gross National Product. It is less than 1 per cent, for example, in Australia, Federal Republic of Germany, and the United States, but it is several per cent of the GNP in some developed countries with a developed tourist industry, for example, Austria, Switzerland, and Japan. Similar relatively high contributions of international tourism to the GNP are in several countries with a rapid rate of development in recent years, such as Greece, Ireland and Spain, and still higher ones in a number of developing countries.[17]

Generally tourism ranks high as an export in countries lacking in natural wealth and highly developed industry. For example, in the 1970s tourism accounted for a third or more of all export earnings for Jordan, Malta, Panama, Spain, and Tunisia: for a quarter or more for Greece and Morocco; for a fifth or more for Jamaica, Kenya, and Yugoslavia.[17]

The incidence of import tourism falls very largely on the twelve countries identified in Chapter 5, whose residents account for about 80 per cent of all international tourist arrivals and expenditure in other countries. But by contrast to the role of export tourism in the balance of payments of some countries, import tourism falls well below one-tenth of all imports of goods and services even in countries generating the highest numbers of international tourists, such as the Federal Republic of Germany and the United States. Moreover, the two countries which expressed most concern about the role of tourist expenditure in their balance of payments, the United Kingdom and the United States, actually experienced a decrease in the proportion of their residents' tourist spending abroad in relation to their total imports in the 1970s.[18]

International Tourism and International Trade

The part played by tourism in the international economy may be seen in broad terms when total international tourism receipts are related to total world exports. Table 9 indicates that international tourism receipts in recent years consistently exceeded the rate of growth in world exports and increased from less than 4½ per cent to 5½ per cent of world trade between 1975 and 1979.

Table 9
International Tourism and International Trade 1975—79

	1975	1976	1977	1978	1979P
International tourism receipts					
Total value (US $ 000 million)	38·6	43·7	52·4	65·0	75·0
Growth (% p.a.)	+13·2	+13·2	+19·9	+24·0	+15·4
World exports					
Total value (US $ 000 million)	873	991	1,124	1,300	1,365
Growth (% p.a.)	+4·4	+13·5	+13·5	+15·7	+5·0

P Provisional

Source: World Tourism Organization, Tourism Compendium, 1979 edition

Problems of Growth and Development

The growth and development of tourism are not without problems. The first is that of land use. When, for example, much of the area of a tourist destination is devoted to arable land and to other forms of agriculture, there may be a conflict in the demands which tourism makes on the countryside, both in its requirements for land for its facilities and in the need for public access. If tourism is to grow, more land has to be devoted to it and opened to tourists. This calls for provision of areas of land and increasing access, and raises the problem of the allocation of scarce resources in the most equitable and aesthetically satisfying way.

Secondly, there may be a conflict between the demands of visitors and the interests of residents of a town or region. Whilst both call for a high level of facilities for leisure and amenity, the larger the number of visitors, the greater the risk of inconvenience and loss of amenity and facilities to those living in the town or region. Tourism implies the injection into the destination of an alien element which may engender resentment on the part of the native population. It is an important task of the tourist organization to educate the resident population, as well as to attain the economic benefits of tourism at minimum social disturbance. This is also a planning and social problem.

Thirdly, tourism is to a considerable extent a seasonal activity. Relatively little of it continues throughout the year and most of its facilities are used intensively for less than half of the time. This leads to a wasteful use of resources and may, in particular, result in seasonal unemployment. This is an economic as well as a social problem. Apart from any attempts to lengthen the season, especially by taking advantage of the growing incidence of additional holidays, most of which are taken outside the main season, a careful examination has to be made of what facilities are least wastefully provided for a part-year use and of the extent to which they may be manned by seasonable labour, which may not be available for year-round employment anyway.

Last but not least, a healthy economy is a diversified economy which does not rely for its prosperity on one or two industries. It is necessary to decide what represents the optimum degree of diversification for a particular economy. At the same time, if tourism is to prosper, it must be realized that some industries are compatible with it and others are not. This is both an economic and a planning problem.

The challenge is clear. Each country, region, and town has to decide:

(a) whether it wishes to become an important tourist destination;
(b) how to maximize the economic and other advantages of tourism;
(c) how to meet the problems that the growth and development of tourism present.

The rewards can be high for those who understand the nature and the effect of tourism and who are able and willing to plan for tourism rather than let it happen. We return to the issues raised here again, in Part VIII of this book, in the context of planning and development in tourism.

Part III
Statistics of Tourism

Further Reading for Part III

British Tourist Authority: *Digest of Tourist Statistics,* latest edition
Burkart, A. J., and Medlik, S. (editors): *The Management of Tourism,* Part III
Organisation for Economic Co-operation and Development; *International Tourism and Tourism Policy in OECD Member Countries,* latest edition
World Tourism Organization: *Economic Review of World Tourism,* latest edition
World Tourism Organization: *Tourism Compendium,* latest edition

References to Part III

1 Ogilvie, F.W. *The Tourist Movement, An Economic Study*
2 Norval, A.J. *The Tourist Industry, A National and International Survey*
3 See, for example, Organisation for European Economic Co-operation, *Tourism and European Recovery;* Wimble, E.W.: *European Recovery 1948-1951 and the Tourist Industry*
4 Jeffries, D.: *The British Away from Home*
5 Lewes, F.M.M., Parker, S.R., and Lickorish, L.J.:*Leisure and Tourism*
6 Organisation for Economic Co-operation and Development: *International Tourism and Tourism Policy in OECD Member Countries*
7 International Monetary Fund: *Balance of Payments Manual*
8 United Nations: *Recommendations on International Travel and Tourism*
9 In July 1975 the OECD Tourism Committee accepted a list of common data to be collected within the framework of visitor sample surveys at frontiers and/or in tourist accommodation. This is based on the list of characteristics established at the meeting on tourism statistics organized by the Conference of European Statisticians of the Economic Commission for Europe of the United Nations in March 1972, and takes account of the proposals made by the European Travel Commission (ETC).
10 Business Statistics Office: *Business Monitor MQ6 Overseas Travel and Tourism*
11 Home Office: *Immigration Statistics*
12 Department of Industry and Trade: *British Business* (formerly *Trade and Industry*)
13 World Tourism Organization: *World Tourism Statistics*
14 World Tourism Organization: *Tourism Compendium*
15 World Tourism Organization: *Economic Review of World Tourism*

7 Statistical Measurement in Tourism

The beginnings of modern tourism date from the middle of the nineteenth century, but its systematic measurement began only in the twentieth century. The need arose as the volume of tourist traffic began to reach significant proportions in the early years of the century and, particularly, in the last sixty years following the First World War. Early in the century Austria, France, Italy, and Switzerland emerged clearly as tourist counties. Before the First World War began, Switzerland was known to have received half a million foreign visitors annually. In 1929 foreign visitors to Austria were estimated at about 2 million, to Italy 1¼ million and to Switzerland about 1½ million. Statistical measurement was largely concerned with foreign tourism.

Up to the Second World War such statistics of tourism as did exist were almost exclusively derived from government controls and enumeration for health, safety, taxation and, in particular, for police and migration purposes. They did not distinguish between tourists and other travellers, were secondary sources for tourism purposes, and provided at best only some indication of the volume and value of tourist traffic. This has been the case in many countries and many communities also since.

The other main sources of quantitative data about tourism were, and often still are, records of individual passenger transport and accommodation operators, the former giving numbers of travellers carried on particular routes, the latter giving numbers of travellers staying in hotels and similar accommodation establishments. Apart from their fragmentary nature, they rarely distinguish in any way between tourists and other travellers or between different groups of tourists. Although of value to individual operators in providing a measure of their own performance, only in some cases do they actually measure tourist traffic and are therefore also of limited value in the assessment of the volume and value of tourism.

In the last sixty years tourism received most recognition as an economic phenomenon and it is significant that it came into prominence and was studied most intensively in three periods in this country; most literature on tourism also dates to them.

In the 1920s and early 1930s tourism came to be examined against the background of economic problems of most European countries and this is reflected in English literature in *The Tourist Movement* by F. W. Ogilvie[1] and in *The Tourist Industry* by A. J. Norval.[2]

In the years after the Second World War European economies were dominated by reconstruction and recovery, by balance of payments problems, in particular by the dollar gap, to the solution of which tourism was seen as an important contributor. Numerous reports of national governments and of international agencies of the time, as well as subsequently, reflect this.[3]

In the 1960s much attention of individual governments and of international organizations was focused on the developing countries. This was United Nations Development Decade and a decade of consultants preparing development plans, in which tourism played a significant and often a dominant role. In this pre-occupation with the economic aspects of tourism statistics became an essential tool. The need arose for primary data on tourism to measure the flows of tourists to particular destinations and of their expenditure, to provide a basis for planning their future development.

The particular needs throughout the three phases identified above placed the main emphasis on international tourism and this partly explains the greater accuracy and comprehensiveness of statistics of foreign tourism as compared with domestic tourism in particular counties.

However, in the 1960s a particular concern also became apparent in many countries with regional economies and with the contributions of tourism, both domestic and international, to individual regions and districts within a country. Hence more recently the need has grown for tourist statistics of internal tourist movement and expenditure, its geographical distribution, and for statistics related to particular destinations within a country.

Last but not least, the application of the marketing concept and techniques to tourism on the part of individual destinations and on the part of individual operators, as well as the requirements of physical planning, have recently brought about the need for further quantified data, in addition to basic statistics of movement and expenditure, particularly for the profile characteristics of tourists and for details of their behaviour.

The reasons for statistical measurement in tourism may therefore be summarized as follows.

In the first place, statistics are required to evaluate the magnitude and significance of tourism to a tourist destination. Whether the destination is a country, region, or another geographical entity, statistics quantify the role and contribution of tourism to the economy and to society, and for a country also the part played by tourism in the balance of payments.

Secondly, statistics are essential in the planning and development of physical facilities. In order to assess the need for, and the capacities and the requirements of airports, roads, hotels, and other facilities, the volume and the characteristics of the tourist movement have to be determined quantitatively.

Thirdly, statistics are required in marketing and promotion, which can hope to be effective only if they are based on an assessment of the actual and potential markets and of their characteristics.

For all these purposes statistics of tourism provide a quantitative framework, in which various aspects of tourism are measured and can be seen as magnitudes, which can be subjected to further analysis. However, it will be made clear that the statistics required for all three purposes are not the same.

Users of Statistics

There is much difference in the interest and value of various statistics of tourism as between their main users: the government, tourist organizations, and the providers of tourist services.

Governments are mainly interested in immigration control, in travel as an item in the balance of payments, and in tourism as a source of employment and as a user of resources. Of these the former two have so far been their dominant concerns and official statistics have been collected primarily with the aim of controlling immigration and of measuring travel as an element in international trade. Hence most data collected are on a national basis and are concerned with the volume of inward and outward traffic, with the spending of visitors in the country and with the expenditure of the residents of the country in the countries visited; sometimes they extend to estimates of fare payments to international carriers and only very rarely to other information.

Tourist organizations exist in many countries at national, regional, and local levels and are, to a varying extent, concerned with the marketing of their destinations and with their physical planning and development. At national level their interest in statistics coincides with that of the government, in measuring the volume and value of inward traffic, which enables them to assess the magnitude and the significance of tourism. But their need for statistics is greater than that and so is that of other tourist organisations, according to the extent to which their functions include the marketing and the physical planning of their respective destinations. They need to know the geographical distribution of tourist traffic, the breakdown of total expenditure between accommodation, catering, shopping, entertainment, transport, and other disbursements, the market characteristics, and other information about the pattern of tourist activity.

The providers of tourist services are usually individual companies and other businesses, which are involved in marketing their own particular products and with investment in their own facilities. Relatively few of them operate at a national level and relatively few of them are large enough to identify their share of the market in the national picture. But irrespective of their size and level of involvement their business requirements call on the one hand for some of the data required by tourist organizations and, on the other hand, for data of particular relevance to their own operations according to type of business and location.

Some statistics are of particular interest to particular providers of tourist services. Specific detailed information on the use of different forms of transport is of main interest to transport operators, frequent data on hotel occupancy to hotel operators. Moreover, such information relating to individual industries engaged in tourism is also of importance in the assessment of their performance and of their plans, as well as in the evaluation of their roles in the economy. As compared with the functions of tourist organizations, which are concerned with the relationship of tourism as a whole to their destinations, industrial organisations have a more limited interest in aspects of tourism related to the type of business operated by their members. Tourism may be only a part of their market. However industry statistics can contribute substantially to the total statistics of tourism and particularly data on capacity, investment, and manpower can be most meaningfully provided by individual industries.

The distinction between different users of statistics of tourism and between their respective interests has a two-fold significance. It determines the nature and form of the required statistics and it suggests by whom they should be provided. If the respective roles are clearly seen, gaps in statistics can be remedied and duplication of effort avoided.

Statistics of Volume

The principal statistics of tourism may be divided into three main categories:

(a) Volume — counting events such as arrivals or visits and stays.
(b) Expenditure — measuring spending at the destination and on the journey.
(c) Characteristics — providing information on the profile and behaviour of tourists.

The basic statistic of volume is the number of tourists to a destination over a given period, for example, a year. In practice it is normally the number of arrivals or visits and not the number of tourists because it is impracticable to allow for those who visit the same destination more than once in the same period. Thus the 12·5 million overseas visitors to Britain in 1979 denote 12·5 million visits made by a somewhat smaller number of individual visitors.

The second main volume statistic is the length of stay, which is measured in terms of days or nights at the destination and is normally expressed as the average length of stay. Thus the average length of stay of overseas visitors to Britain in 1979 was 12·4 nights.

The product of the numbers and length of stay is the total tourist days or nights at the destination over a given period. Thus overseas visitors to Britain in 1979 spent more than 150 million nights in the country.

Statistics of numbers provide a general indication of the volume of tourist traffic to particular destinations. Statistics of length of stay provide a general indication of the nature of the traffic, in particular of the extent of transit and terminal visitors and of their demand for overnight accommodation. Total tourist days or nights, by combining arrivals and stay in one figure, provide the best single overall indication of the significance of tourism to a destination in physical terms.

The same three basic statistics of volume may be applied to the population of a country as distinct from applying them to the destination. The number of trips taken away from home, their average length, and the product of the two, measure the participation in tourism of the resident population.

Statistics of Expenditure

The value of tourism to an economy is reflected in tourist spending at the destination. For international tourism this commonly covers all tourist expenditure in a country including foreign tourists spending on transportation in the country and their purchases, but excluding payments to international carriers in respect of journeys to and from the country visited. Similarly, for other destinations expenditure covers that incurred at the destination, but not expenditure on the journey to and from the destination.

When the total visitor expenditure at the destination is divided by the number of arrivals or by the number of tourist days or nights, the result is the average expenditure per visit or per day or night. Whilst global estimates of tourist expenditure provide a general indication of the value of tourism to an economy, visit and daily averages provide respectively general indications of the type and quality of the traffic to a destination.

Payments made in respect of journeys to and from the destination do not necessarily accrue to the destination and they are therefore normally excluded from statistics of expenditure at the destination. However, for purposes of total estimates of tourist expenditure, they may be included or separately evaluated. For balance of payments purposes, fare payments by foreign visitors to a country's carriers represent income to the country visited. Although this item is usually included in the transport item of the balance of payments in conformity with international recommendations, it is part of tourist spending and part of the country's earnings from tourism.

A similar approach may be adopted to statistics of tourist expenditure by the resident population participating in tourism, i.e. to assess the generation of tourist expenditure. Tourist expenditure then often includes the cost of travel to destinations as well as expenditure at the destinations, i.e. the total amount spent by tourists while away from home and usually also advance payments on such items as fares and accommodation.

Tourist expenditure statistics thus comprise two main elements: expenditure at the destinations and expenditure on travel to/from the destinations. Both elements are often combined in estimates of tourism generation but rarely included with estimates of tourist destinations, and the two approaches are, therefore, not comparable.

Statistics of Tourist Characteristics

We have seen that in addition to statistics of volume and expenditure, those concerned with marketing and development require detailed statistics about their markets.

The total volume of trips or visits and nights have to be divided into market segments according, for example, to purpose of visit, place of origin, tourist profile characteristics, and behaviour patterns in order to provide meaningful information for marketing and development purposes.

In the case of international tourism, the places of origin are the countries or groups of countries of residence, which supply the major flows of tourists to a country. In domestic tourism the major sources of tourist traffic to a region are the other regions of the same country.

The principal profile characteristics of tourists are sex, age, occupation, and income. The behaviour characteristics include time of visit, whether travelling alone or in groups, whether on an independent or inclusive tour, the type of accommodation and the means of transport used, and the activities at the destination.

For promotion purposes the profile and behaviour characteristics are extended to include such information as the readership of newspapers and magazines, attitudes and impressions of tourists of their visits, and information on how and when holiday plans are made.

Equally important is the knowledge of the population which does engage in tourism but does not visit the particular destination under examination and of the people who do not engage in tourism at all. The knowledge of the numbers, of their profile, and of the reasons for visiting other destinations or for not going away from home, provide a basis for evolving a realistic marketing strategy and for the physical planning of the amenities of the tourist destination.

Like statistics of volume and expenditure, statistics of tourist characteristics may, therefore, also be compiled either for individual destinations or for the whole population of a country. The former describe that part of the total pattern which relates to that destination, the latter to the tourist characteristics of the whole population, from which tourists are drawn at present or may be drawn in the future.

General Problems of Measurement

Because of its nature tourism does not lend itself to easy measurement. In their movement and in their stay at destinations tourists can sometimes be readily distinguished from other travellers and from the resident and working populations of the areas through which they travel and in which they stay, but often they cannot. Therefore, the first general problem of statistical measurement in tourism arises from the difficulty of differentiating between tourists and other travellers (*see* Chapter 4) and between them and the resident and working populations.

In their movement to destinations tourists may use public transport but increasingly they use their own private transport. They normally enter various destinations without stopping and often without registering their arrival and they do so increasingly even when crossing many national frontiers. At the destination they use a variety of accommodation ranging from hotels to friends' and relatives' homes; they eat in the same catering establishments and buy goods and other services from the same outlets from which they are bought by those who are not tourists, using the same currency.

The collection of statistics of tourism relies partly on administrative controls such as those in use for immigration and for currency control purposes, and partly on the co-operation of the tourists themselves. Administrative controls suffer from the disadvantage that they are rarely designed and operated with tourism in view; moreover, they may be circumvented so that the information is neither complete nor accurate. When the collection of statistics is based on the co-operation of tourists, their comprehensiveness and accuracy depends on the willingness of tourists to be enumerated and to supply the required information.

In view of these problems and of the need of governments for information on migration and on international transactions, it is not surprising that in most countries more accurate and more comprehensive data are available on foreign tourism than on domestic tourism and that different methods are often applied to their respective measurement. The basic methods used and some of the related problems are described in this chapter; the specific approaches and methods of measurement of foreign and domestic tourism are described in greater detail in Chapters 8 and 9.

Main Methods of Measurement

Basic volume statistics — numbers, length of stay and days or nights — may be collected in three main ways:

(a) By enumeration at the point of arrival and departure.
(b) From accommodation records.
(c) By special surveys of tourists at the destination or in their homes.

The first method consists of counting tourists at the point of entry to or exit from the destination. Whilst of particular use in international tourism when entry into a country is stringently controlled, it is applicable to any destination to which there is a limited number of entry and exit points, as is often the case with islands. It is an accurate method of obtaining numbers and may also provide data on length of stay, as a statement of intent on entry or, preferably, as a statement of fact on departure, or by linking arrival and departure dates of individual visitors.

The second method consists of counting tourists at their place of stay, in which the registration forms of hotels and other accommodation units are the sources of information, and from which data are reported periodically to a central bureau. This method requires usually legal authority and enforcement. It provides information on numbers, length of stay and tourist nights, may provide some profile characteristics of tourists such as their places of origin, and may be classified by type of accommodation and area visited. Normally this method covers to a varying degree different forms of accommodation including private homes. Special care has to be taken to avoid double counting of arrivals when tourists change their accommodation at the same destination.

In contrast to the above two methods which measure the volume of tourism when and where it occurs, for example, at an airport or at an hotel, special surveys of a population by means of questionnaires and interviews, usually at home after the event, seek to establish the extent and details of participation in tourism during a past period. When the surveys are detailed enough and cover places visited, length of stay, and similar information, they may also provide basic statistics of volume of tourism to particular destinations, such as regions, in addition to profile and behaviour characteristics of the population in general. This third method is usually adopted as a means of measuring a country's domestic tourism.

The three direct methods may be supplemented by passenger transport records of carriers to particular destinations. These statistics are a by-product of their activities and do not normally distinguish between tourists and other travellers, but are sometimes useful to establish the density of traffic on particular routes as a basis for other surveys and they may provide a cross-check on other methods.

Tourist expenditure statistics may be obtained by a direct method or may be estimated by indirect methods. The direct method is based on obtaining information from the tourists themselves, who are asked about details of their expenditure immediately on leaving the destination or subsequently. The main indirect method consists of hotels and other providers of tourist services supplying estimates of tourist spending, from which an attempt is made to establish average spending per visit. In the case of foreign tourists, another indirect method is to derive foreign currency expenditure in the country from bank records of foreign currency exchanged in each country; this is considered further in Chapter 9. Despite certain problems associated with the direct method it is the one in growing use; in practice it is combined with obtaining also other information from the tourist at the same time.

When information is supplied directly by tourists, it may be through self-administered forms or questionnaires, such as landing cards or mailed questionnaires. Both may cover all tourists or, as is increasingly the case, involve sampling, i.e. only a proportion of the tourists are surveyed and the results from a representative proportion may then be extended to the total numbers. When a small number of tourists are selected to be representative of the rest, the major advantages are the saving of time and expense; in many situations it is the only practicable means available.

It will be apparent from the foregoing discussion that most statistics of tourism are estimates of varying degree of accuracy and reliability, which are compiled continuously or at intervals. For most purposes only broad indications of the order of magnitude are required rather than exact quantities and, as there is a degree of stability in some of the variables in tourism, periodical rather than continuous surveys are often adequate.

Summary and Conclusions

This chapter begins with the developing needs for statistics of tourism against the growing awareness of the economic significance of tourism in the last sixty years. Three main purposes of statistical measurement of tourism are identified and the different requirements of the main users of statistics according to type leads to a general discussion of the problems of measurement and of the main methods.

Statistics of domestic and foreign tourism are discussed separately in the next two chapters and illustrated from published sources. It will be seen that a high degree of comparability from year to year has been achieved in the main series in individual countries, especially in Britain. But statistics of individual countries do not always conform with standard definitions and are often compiled by different methods; consequently, they are not always directly comparable.

The need for uniformity and comparability in the statistics of tourism is generally recognised and has been receiving increasing attention by several international organizations. In three main respects some degree of success has been achieved in the last few years: there is now an internationally agreed definition of the term 'visitor', which has been recommended by the United Nations Statistical Commission; a uniform approach to the classification of international payments has been recommended by the International Monetary Fund; the Tourism Committee of the Organization for Economic Co-operation and Development has established a common framework for national holiday surveys. These and other moves to international comparability are also described in the next two chapters.

Notwithstanding these international moves, at the beginning of the 1980s even in Europe which receives and generates most of the international and domestic tourist movements, while available published statistics make, to a greater or lesser extent, possible an analysis of tourist flows for most individual countries, they allow only a broad assessment of intra-European flows, and of the flows within and between various regions of the world.

Relatively little attention has been paid so far by most tourist destinations to the measurement of travel and visits, which do not entail an overnight stay away from home. Yet, for example, between 700-800 million day trips are made by British people for recreational purposes each year, probably as many as ten times the number of holiday trips of one or more nights away from home.

A traditional view is that day trips are of uncertain importance and that only those who stay overnight are genuine tourists. Tourist boards tend to classify them separately, if at all, as recommended by various international agencies concerned with tourism, and day trips play little or no part in tourist board marketing. Yet day trips are important to consumers, particularly to those who cannot afford a staying holiday away from home, but also to many others with a preference for day trips. They are also important to many transport operators and to many tourist attractions.[4]

Available evidence suggests that the incidence of day trips is growing. Their measurement is an important task ahead for many destinations and a need for many parts of the tourist industry.

8 Statistics of Domestic Tourism

The tourist activity of residents of a country within their own country, which does not cross national boundaries, is described as domestic or internal tourism. Two main needs are present for its measurement: to obtain the volume, value, and characteristics of tourism of the population of the country, and the same information related to individual destinations within the country.

Historically the most common source has been accommodation records. Where they are highly developed, much of the required information may be obtained from them as the main source — for individual destinations by aggregating the data of individual establishments—for the whole country by aggregating the data of individual destinations. However, complete reliance on accommodation records does not usually suffice. We have seen that they normally cover only certain types of accommodation and, therefore, only part of the traffic. Moreover, they rarely provide adequate information on tourist flows and on profile and behaviour of tourists. For these reasons it is generally accepted that accommodation records can at best provide only some of the required information, that according to their scope they lend themselves to combining with other sources and methods, and that direct methods, which obtain information from the tourists themselves, provide the best means of adequate statistical measurement.

Two main approaches, both of relatively recent origin, are increasingly adopted in practice:

(a) National holiday and tourism surveys.
(b) Surveys of individual destinations.

In this chapter the two types of survey, in which sampling is used in obtaining information from tourists, are discussed as the two principal types of statistics of domestic tourism.

National Holiday Surveys

The most comprehensive means of measuring holiday travel is a household survey carried out in the country as a whole, which covers originating traffic and its characteristics. This consists of a sample survey of the whole population of the country, the sample being representative of the population, and is carried out at the places of residence in respect of the residents' travel during a specified period.

This approach has been used successfully in Britain since 1951, to measure the volume, value, and characteristics of holidays of the British population, first by the British Travel Association and, more recently, by its successor, the British Tourist Authority in co-operation with the three national boards in their annual British National Travel Survey. In recent years similar surveys have been undertaken also, for example, in France, Germany, Italy, the Netherlands, and in other countries.

In 1967 the OECD Tourism Committee recommended common data to be obtained and a common method to be used in national surveys to facilitate their comparability.

The recommendations specify that the surveys should cover only holidays, i.e. a stay outside the place of residence for health and recreational purposes and extending over at least four consecutive nights, that data should be collected by verbal inquiries, and that each survey should be based on a random sample of 5,000 to 10,000 people or of a sufficient number of families or households to ensure an adequate degree of statistical reliability.

The common data to be collected are: numbers and breakdown by sex, age, socio-occupational and income groups of persons who have taken a holiday and those who have not taken a holiday away from home; number of holiday trips, average length of main holiday, and the main holiday period in the country of residence and abroad; numbers of holidaymakers and nights' stay in the country of residence and abroad (including main countries for which the sample is representative); their breakdown by specified main forms of accommodation and specified principal forms of transport; total holiday expenditure divided into expenditure in the country of residence and abroad.

Holidays abroad are included in the surveys to provide an indication of the total holiday propensity of the population, irrespective of the destination, and to enable comparisons to be made between holidays taken in the country of residence and abroad.

Non-holidaymakers are included in the surveys to enable information to be collected and related to the whole population and comparisons to be drawn between the profile characteristics of holidaymakers and non-holidaymakers.

These extensions of the surveys from those who take holidays in their country of residence to those who take a holiday abroad on the one hand, and to those who do not take a holiday at all on the other hand, mean that in practice the surveys are not confined to domestic tourism. However, they enable information on domestic tourism to be seen separately and, as they relate to the resident population of the country, it is convenient to deal with them in this chapter in the context of domestic tourism.

As regards domestic tourism, a national holiday survey provides in the first place basic data on the volume of holidays, holiday expenditure, and characteristics of the holiday market. According to the extent of geographical breakdown adopted, it may also provide substantial information on the volume and value of holiday traffic to particular destinations, its sources of origin and many of its characteristics.

The British National Travel Survey is described below as an illustration of this type of survey.

British National Travel Survey (BNTS)

The British National Travel Survey is an annual sample survey carried out to establish details of holidays taken by the British population in the previous twelve months. Its scope may be summarized as follows:

(a) The Survey is concerned only with holiday travel and not with travel for other purposes.

(b) It is restricted to holidays of four nights or more away from home.

(c) It covers both holidays taken within Great Britain and those taken abroad.

(d) Holidays are divided into main holidays and additional holidays. When only one holiday is taken, the main holiday is the longest or, if there are two or more holidays of equal length, the one in or nearest to the peak summer period.

(e) The Survey establishes the proportion of population aged sixteen and over who have taken a holiday, the number of holidays taken, and the destination of those holidays.

(f) Basic profile information about holidaymakers collected includes age, socio-economic group, and region of residence.

(g) The information collected about holidays taken includes the length of holiday, the month in which it took place, the method of transport used to reach the holiday destination, the accommodation used, the size and composition of the party travelling on holiday together, the average cost of holiday per person (including travel). This information is collected in the same form each year so that comparable data are available over a period of years.

(h) In any one year further information may be added, because it is of topical interest or because it is of particular interest to a group of Survey users, such as particular providers of tourist services. For example, when restrictions were imposed in the United Kingdom on the amount of foreign currency available for foreign travel, information was collected to establish their effect on people's holiday plans. From time to time the Survey also sought to establish to what extent holidaymakers staying in hotels had private bathrooms, showers, radios, or telephones in their rooms — information of particular interest to hoteliers. In recent years information has been also collected on regions stayed in Britain and on all holidays abroad of one or more nights.

The British National Travel Survey uses a stratified random sample of the population aged sixteen and over. For example in 1970 nearly 20,000 people were contacted in order to achieve the following numbers of interviews:

    3,000 with people who had a holiday in Great Britain;

    2,000 with people who had a holiday abroad;

    1,600 with people who had no holiday.

These interviews were achieved in stages. In the first stage a random sample of 6,000 people was contacted. Among these, interviews were carried out with all those who had taken a holiday in Great Britain in the course of the year (3,000 interviews), with all those who had taken holidays abroad (500 interviews), and with a selection of those who had taken no holiday in the period (1,600 interviews).

The second stage consisted of contacting a further random sample of some 13,000 and all the people in this sample who had taken a holiday abroad were interviewed, which brought the number of interviews with holidaymakers who went abroad in 1970 to 2,000. This second stage was necessary because the number of people who had been on holiday abroad contacted in the initial sample, was too small to enable a reliable analysis of these holidays to be made. Less than 20 per cent of the population of sixteen and over in Great Britain have a holiday abroad in any one year.)

When survey results are analysed, sample proportions relating to holidays of the population of sixteen and over may be extended to the total population by making an allowance for the number of accompanied children.

The Survey results are subject to normal sampling errors, which may represent several hundred thousand people when percentages are applied to millions of people. However, they do provide broad indications of the order of magnitude, and when studied over a period of time they provide a reliable and useful indication of trends.

The main type of information provided by the British National Travel survey for a single year is illustrated below by reference to the 1979 Survey, which reveals the position in a particular year (Table 10). The value of a series of Surveys as indicators of holiday trends is illustrated below by reference to the main changes in the holiday market between 1955-1979, as disclosed by the Surveys for particular years during that period (Table 11). These changes can be seen against a background of the increasing holiday propensity of the population and greatly increased holiday expenditure.

In the late 1970s in the region of 60 per cent or more of the British population took a holiday of four nights or more away from home each year, some 20 per cent more than one holiday, some 20 per cent of all holidays were taken abroad, and total holiday expenditure, including the cost of travel to and from the holiday destination, approached £5,000 million. South West England continued to be the most popular holiday region in Britain and Spain the most popular country for holidays abroad by British residents.

Although only one in five holidays are taken abroad each year, since 1978 holiday expenditure abroad exceeded holiday expenditure in Britain and the British National Travel Survey demonstrates a continued loss of market share of a growing British holiday market to destinations abroad.

Since the 1950s there has been relatively little change in the main destinations of British holidays in Britain, their duration and timing, as reflected in the BNTS; the most fundamental changes occurred in the type of transport and accommodation used. The most important changes in holidays abroad have been in the popularity of the countries visited, and in the transport and accommodation used on holiday.

Table 10
British Holidays in 1979

Holidays [a]		of four nights or more	
		in Britain	abroad
Number		38.5 million	10.25 million
Expenditure [b]		£2,380 million	£2,570 million

Holidays [a]		in Britain of four nights or more		abroad of one night or more
		main [c]	additional [c]	
Main destination regions and countries	%	22 South West 12 South 12 Wales 10 Scotland 9 East Anglia 7 South East 6 North West 6 Yorkshire and Humberside	18 South West 11 Scotland 10 South 10 Wales 9 South East 7 North West 6 Yorkshire and Humberside 5 East Anglia	25 Spain 13 France 7 France 7 Italy 5 West Germany
Holidays began in June July August September Other months	(%)	16 29 30 11 14	9 8 17 17 49	12 16 16 14 42
Transport used [d]	(%)	71 car 13 bus/coach 13 train 4 other	72 car 11 bus/coach 12 train 5 other	71 air 24 ship 3 hovercraft
Accommodation used [e] Service (hotel etc) Self-catering Friends'/relatives' Other	(%)	30 47 20 5	28 35 37 3	60 17 13 8

[a]   Holidays taken by adults and by children.

[b]   Expenditure includes the cost of travel to and from the holiday destination. It has been calculated by multiplying the number of holidays by the average per capita expenditure.

[c]   Where only one holiday is taken, this is the main holiday; where two or more are taken, the main holiday is the longest or, if two or more were of equal length, the one in or nearest the peak summer period.

[d]   Some details may not equal the sum of their parts because of rounding.

ᵉ Columns add to more than 100% because some people used more than one type of accommodation. Holiday camp holidays, on which meals were provided, are included in service accommodation, those without meals are included in self-catering.

Source: British National Travel Survey

Table 11

British Holidays 1955-79

		1955	1965	1975	1976	1977	1978	1979
All holidays of four nights or more								
Population taking a holiday (%)				60	61	59	61	63
more than one (%)				19	18	17	20	19
Number of hols in Britain	(m)	25	30	40	37	36	39	39
Number of hols abroad	(m)	2	5	8	7	8	9	10
Total number of holidays	(m)	27	35	48	45	44	48	49
Holiday exp're in Britain	(£m)	365	460	1,270	1,460	1,570	1,700	2,380
Holiday exp're abroad	(£m)	100	265	1,080	1,210	1,360	1,860	2,570
Total holiday expenditure	(£m)	465	725	2,350	2,670	2,930	3,560	4,950
Main holidays in Britain of four nights or more								
Transport used	(%)							
Car		34	60	71	68	71	70	71
Bus/coach		33	21	13	14	12	12	13
Train		37	21	12	10	13	12	13
Other				4	5	5	6	4
Accommodation used	(%)							
Service (hotel etc.)		45	47	38	34	35	34	30
Self-catering		18	25	37	42	42	41	47
Friends'/relatives'		31	25	22	20	20	22	20
Other		11	8	8	6	9	6	5
All holidays abroad of one night or more								
Main destinations	(%)							
Austria		10	9	3	3	3	2	3
Benelux		18	17	4	5	4	3	3
France		33	26	14	11	11	13	13
Greece				4	6	4	6	7
Ireland, Republic of		15	9	4	4	5	5	4
Italy		17	21	7	8	9	8	7
Spain incl. Majorca		10	22	33	27	29	30	25
Switzerland		14	14	3	2	2	2	2
West Germany		11	13	5	5	5	4	5
All in Europe				84	82	83	82	81

Transport used	(%)						
Air		48	66	70	69	69	71
Sea		52	34	29	30	30	30
Accommodation used	(%)						
Hotel		63	60	60	59	58	58
Pension		13	4	3	3	3	2
Other		37	44	46	45	46	48

[a] See notes to previous table.
[b] Some later results are not strictly comparable with earlier years.

Source: British National Travel Survey

Table 12
British Residents' Tourism in Britain 1972—79

		1972	1973	1974	1975	1976	1977	1978	1979
Trips, nights and spending									
Number of trips	(m)	132	132	114	117	121	121	119	118
Number of nights	(m)	605	590	535	550	545	545	530	525
Estimated spending	(m)	1,375	1,450	1,800	2,150	2,400	2,625	3,100	3,800
Destination of trips									
England	(m)	107	107	92	96	101	98	95	97
Scotland	(m)	12	12	11	10	11	12	12	11
Wales	(m)	13	13	12	11	11	12	12	11
Duration of trips									
Average	(nights)	4·3	4·4	4·7	4·8	4·5	4·5	4·5	4·4
Short 1-3 nights	(m)	81	78	61	63	69	69	69	67
Long 4 nights or more	(m)	51	54	53	53	51	52	50	51
Purpose of trips		%	%	%	%	%	%	%	%
On holiday, solely		40	39	41	41	40	39	40	41
On hol. with friends/rel's		24	25	20	21	22	22	20	19
To visit frnds/rel's solely		19	20	21	21	20	20	22	22
On business or for conf's.		13	13	15	14	14	16	14	15
Other reasons		4	3	3	3	4	4	4	3
Month trip started		%	%	%	%	%	%	%	%
June		8	10	10	9	10	10	9	10
July		12	14	14	14	13	13	13	13
August		14	16	16	15	15	15	15	16
September		10	9	10	9	8	9	9	10
Other months		58	52	51	55	52	54	52	51
Transport to destination (trips)		%	%	%	%	%	%	%	%
Car		69	73	70	69	74	72	72	71
Bus/coach		11	10	11	11	10	11	9	7
Train		13	12	13	13	10	11	13	13
Other		7	5	6	6	7	6	6	8
Accommodation used (nights)		%	%	%	%	%	%	%	%
Service (hotel etc.)		26	25	25	24	23	24	22	25
Self-catering		28	28	31	29	31	28	32	29
Friends or relatives		40	41	39	39	40	42	39	48
Other		6	7	5	6	6	7	7	8

[a] All tourism by British resident adults and children under 16 accompanying them to destinations in Britain of one or more nights away from home, for holidays, business and conferences, visits to friends and relatives, or any other purpose except such reasons as boarding education or semi-permanent employment.

[b] Spending is expenditure while away from home and on advance payments for such items as fares and accommodation.

[c] Trips are rounded to the nearest million, nights 5 million, spending £25 million.

[d] Britain is defined as England, Scotland, Wales. Other destinations are defined as abroad, including the Channel Islands and Northern Ireland.

[e] Some totals may not equal the sum of their parts because of rounding.

[f] Columns may add to more than 100% because some people take more than one trip or use more than one type of accommodation on some trips. All use of holiday camp is included with service accommodation.

Source: British Home Tourism Survey

All Tourism Surveys

After the creation of national tourist boards for England, Scotland, and Wales, with responsibilities for all forms of domestic tourism, the need was felt for a regular and more comprehensive measurement of domestic tourism to include not only holidays of four nights or more, but also holidays of less than four nights, and also tourism for other purposes than holidays, including business and conferences, visits to friends and relatives, and other trips away from home.

In 1971 the British Home Tourism Survey (BHTS) was launched to meet this need. The BHTS is a continuous inquiry commissioned by the English Tourist Board on behalf of the national tourist boards for England, Scotland, and Wales, and the British Tourist Authority, and is carried out by NOP Market Research Ltd. Each month questions are included in an Adult Omnibus Survey and personal interviews are carried out with about 4,000 randomly selected British resident adults about all trips of one night or more made by them and children accompanying them during the previous two months. Thus results are accumulated on all trips started in a particular month from two monthly surveys in the following two months. Results for a particular month are available separately. Results for the whole year are analysed in detail at the end of the year. A series of data over a period of years provides a valuable indication of trends in British tourism, as shown in Table 12, which illustrates trends in selected aspects of British residents' tourism in Britain between 1972-1979.

Although trips abroad are recorded in the BHTS, the number of such trips covered by the survey is relatively small. Information about holidays abroad continues, therefore, to be in the main derived from the BNTS and about British residents' travel abroad for all purposes from the International Passenger Survey, which is described in the next chapter.

The regular use of the Omnibus Survey is particularly useful when information is required at frequent intervals, as is the case when close monitoring of the market is desired, and the research method has to rely on a short recall period on the part of the respondents. The Omnibus Survey covers in its questionnaire more than one topic for more than one client, which reduces the cost to each of them.

Destination Surveys

In destination surveys the object is to establish the volume, value, and characteristics of visitor traffic to individual destinations with a country. When the destination is an island, traffic flows to the island may sometimes be treated in a similar way as foreign visitor traffic to a country; the methods described in the next chapter in relation to the measurement of tourism are then often applicable to the measurement of tourism to an island.

However, a different approach is required for destinations within a country, which are not physically separated from the rest, a situation which applies to many regions and many small entities, such as individual towns and districts.

When national holiday and tourism surveys attempt to holidays by region, some basic information about flows to an individual region is available. When accommodation records at the destination are highly developed, some basic data about staying traffic may be derived from this source. But in most cases the only way of making a comprehensive assessment of the volume, value, and characteristics of visitor traffic to a destination is by means of a special destination survey.

A destination survey may consist of two related parts — an accommodation survey and a visitor survey. The object of the accommodation survey is to establish the number of staying visitors at the destination during the survey period. The object of the visitor survey is to obtain information about visitors and about their stay at the destination.

When a system of accommodation records in operation at the destination can provide comprehensive data on arrivals, length of stay and total nights of staying visitors during the survey period, this information may be used in conjunction with the direct visitor survey, However, if all this information is not readily available, a special accommodation survey is necessary to supplement the direct visitor survey.

The approach, which may be adopted when no accommodation data are available, is described below; parts of this approach may be omitted if parts of the information are available.

A Possible Method for Destination Surveys

As a basis for calculating the total numbers of staying visitors, one particular category of accommodation, for example hotels and guest houses, is chosen. The most comprehensive accommodation list available is taken and questionnaires are mailed to all or to a sample of establishments in the list, to obtain the available bed capacity and the number of sleeper nights spent at the establishment. The mailed questionnaire may be supplemented by personal calls at establishments. From the returns an estimate is made of the overall percentage sleeper occupancy.

This occupancy percentage is applied to the maximum possible number of sleeper nights in the chosen accommodation category, i.e. the number of beds multiplied by the number of nights over which each bed was available in the survey period, in order to obtain a figure of total sleeper nights spent in the chosen category in the survey period. This figure is divided by the average length of stay in the chosen accommodation category as observed in the visitor interview survey, in order to estimate the number of visitors staying in that form of accommodation.

The percentage of all tourists using the chosen accommodation category is derived from the visitor interview survey, in which visitors contacted are asked in what type of accommodation they have stayed. By relating the number of visitors in the chosen accommodation category to the percentage share figure, an estimate is made of the total number of staying visitors in all categories of accommodation.

Having arrived at the total number of staying visitors, the total staying visitor expenditure is arrived at by multiplying the number by their average expenditure as obtained from the visitor interview survey. Similarly other information, such as visitor profile characteristics and their behaviour pattern at the destination, may be arrived at by applying such information from the visitor interview survey to the total number of staying visitors.

In order to obtain an estimate of the number of day visitors to the destination, interviewers keep a record of the number of day and staying visitors contacted during the visitor interview survey, whether or not an interview was carried out with them. As the number of staying visitors is known, the ratio reveals the total number of day visitors as it would be, if the likelihood of both groups of visitor being contacted were the same; in order to allow for the much greater likelihood of each staying visitor being contacted, the ratio figure is multiplied by the average length of stay of all staying visitors, to arrive at an estimate of the total number of day visitors. If interviews are carried out with day visitors, the expenditure and other information obtained in the interviews may be extended to the total number of day visitors.

Information from the accommodation and visitor surveys may be cross-checked and supplemented by other indicators, such as statistics of bus and rail transport, records of car parking, visits to particular places of interest, and estimates of receipts from various trading activities at the destination.

The method outlined above and its application to a survey of Worthing carried out by the British Tourist Authority with the Worthing Borough Council in 1969 is described by L. J. Lickorish in *Leisure and Tourism* (Heinemann).[5]

In the accommodation survey questionnaires were sent to 134 hotels and guest-houses in Worthing. From the replies the percentage sleeper occupancy was estimated to be 57·6 per cent. By applying this percentage to the estimated bed capacity of all hotels and boarding-houses it was estimated that some 246,000 sleeper nights were spent in this category of accommodation during the five survey months. The interview survey revealed that the average length of stay of visitors using this type of accommodation was 9·1 nights. Therefore, the number of staying visitors in hotels and guest-houses was in the region of 27,000. The visitor interview survey revealed that 49 per cent of all staying visitors used this type of accommodation. The total number of staying visitors was therefore, 55,000 (100 per cent).

The total number was allocated between independent and inclusive holiday-makers in the ratio observed in the visitor interview survey and the two figures were multiplied by their respective average expenditure figures. The expenditure of independent holidaymakers was estimated at £870,000, the expenditure of inclusive holidaymakers at £80,000, giving a total of £950,000.

The number of visitors contacted during the survey was 2,540, 1,267 day and 1,273 staying visitors. The average length of stay of all staying visitors was 9·65 nights. The number of day visitors during the survey period was thus estimated as

$$\frac{1,267 \times 55,000 \times 9·65}{1,273} = 520,000$$

Average day visitor expenditure was £1; total day visitor expenditure during the survey period was, therefore, £520,000.

In the five months Worthing, therefore, had some 55,000 staying and some 520,000, nearly ten times as many, day visitors. Their combined expenditure in the town approached £1½ million. In addition to providing this assessment of the volume and value of visitor traffic, the study produced other information useful for planning the development of the destination. It indicated the accommodation and amenities to be provided, as well as the type of traffic to which the facilities and amenities would appeal — information useful for marketing to attract the traffic.

Summary and Conclusions

In domestic tourism statistical measurement seeks to provide information on the volume, value and characteristics of tourism of the residents of the country and of individual destinations in the country. The two main methods of statistical meansurement in domestic tourism are national holiday and tourism surveys, and destination surveys, through which the required information may be obtained by sampling. Holiday surveys, such as the BNTS, are first and foremost, surveys of the volume, value and characteristics of participation in tourism, which make it possible to determine, *inter alia* the holiday propensities of the population. All tourism surveys, such as the BHTS, using Omnibus Survey methods, focus primarily on the volume, value, and characteristics of trips, and do not provide a basis for the calculation of tourism propensities.

The scope of national holiday surveys and destination surveys is shown dia-grammatically in Figures 1 and 2 (proportions not to scale).

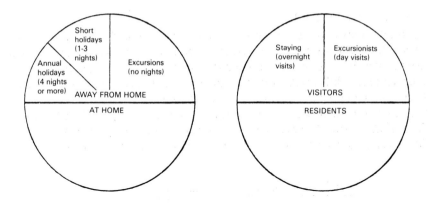

Figure 1. The Holiday Population   Figure 2. The Destination Population

9 *Statistics of International Tourism*

The main development in statistics of tourism in which residents of one country visit other countries can be traced to the three main periods identified in Chapter 7: 1930s, late 1940s and 1950s, and 1960s.

In the 1930s the growing appreciation of the economic importance of tourism was reflected in growing efforts to measure international travel movements and payments. In 1937 the Committee of Statistical Experts of the League of Nations recommended the first definition of the term 'foreign tourist', which gained some international acceptance and which remains in essence to this day: 'Any person visiting a country, other than that in which he usually resides, for a period of at least twenty-four hours.'

The following were to be considered tourists within this definition:

(a) Persons travelling for pleasure, for domestic reasons, for health, etc.
(b) Persons travelling to meetings, or in a representative capacity of any kind (scientific, administrative, diplomatic, religious, athletic, etc.).
(c) Persons travelling for business reasons.
(d) Persons arriving in the course of a sea cruise, even when they stay less than twenty-four hours. (The latter should be reckoned as a separate group, disregarding if necessary their usual place of residence.)

The following were not to be regarded as tourists:

(a) Persons arriving, with or without a contract of work, to take up an occupation or engage in any business activity in the country.
(b) Other persons coming to establish a residence in the country.
(c) Students and young persons in boarding establishments or schools.
(d) Residents in a frontier zone and persons domiciled in one country and working in an adjoining country.
(e) Travellers passing through a country without stopping, even if the journey takes more than twenty-four hours.

This definition was also considered appropriate for national purposes. A 'tourist' was then 'any person visiting a place for a period of at least twenty-four hours'.

Persons travelling on holiday for a period of less than twenty-four hours were to be treated as 'excursionists'.[6]

The 1937 definition was adopted after the war when the rapid development of international travel and its increasing economic importance led to action in reporting international travel movement and payments on a regular basis.

The efforts made after the war in Western Europe and in the USA to establish international tourism as an important element in the recovery programme led to an initial concentration on intra-European and transatlantic travel, to be followed by a global approach.

The first regular reporting was developed through the ETC (European Travel Commission), the OEEC (Organization for European Economic Co-operation), and through the IUOTO (International Union of Official Travel Organizations). The ETC was a non-governmental body mainly concerned with the promotion of American travel to Europe, whose members were national tourist organizations, including several Ministries of Tourism, of Western European countries. The OEEC established a Tourism Committee in 1950, composed of senior officials and those responsible for tourism in member countries and began annual reports on tourism in member countries in 1952. The IUOTO, representing national tourist organizations on a world basis, established a Study Commission on International Travel Statistics and in 1947 began the publication of its *Digest of Tourist Statistics,* a collection of national statistics of tourist arrivals and travel payments of some forty countries. A permanent IUOTO Research Commission to study and recommend improvements in statistical methods was established in 1950.

In the 1950s a major international confrontation on definitions between researchers and statisticians seeking precise data of a particular type, legal enforcement authorities not specifically concerned with tourism, and various interests providing tourist services who were concerned not to inconvenience the tourist, took place through the United Nations Statistical Commission, which reported on definitions in 1957. What was largely a statement of the existing situation and problems, resulted in no immediate progress on statistics of tourism, which came to be pursued more succcessfully in the following decade.

In 1960 the OEEC became the OECD (Organization for Economic Co-operation and Development) with an enlarged membership and took over the work in tourism of its predecessor. Both the OECD and the IUOTO publications were gradually enlarged and improved. In the same year the IMF (International Monetary Fund) made recommendations on methods of reporting travel receipts and payments as a basis for travel estimates in the balance of payments; the main recommendations are summarized below:[7]

(a) Travel covers expenditure in the compiling country of nearly all foreign visitors (credits) and expenditures abroad by nearly all residents visiting foreign countries (debits).

(b) Five categories of people whose expenditure constitutes foreign travel receipts or expenditures are suggested as tourists, business travellers, students, government officials, and others.

(c) The main exceptions, to be excluded, are the crews of international carriers whose temporary presence is caused by their professional duties, diplomats, and other personnel of foreign governments including military personnel stationed in the country, and migrant workers.

(d) Travel should cover all expenditure in the compiling country incidental to travel, including local transport within the compiling country and all

purchases of goods other than for business purposes. Payments to foreign carriers should be recorded separately and not with travel, except when made in respect of local transportation within foreign countries.
(e) The five categories of people are intended to suggest a possible classific-ation of travel receipts and expenditures by purpose of travel, but it is recognized that other purposes; e.g. pilgrimage or medical care, may be more significant for the compiling country; also that in addition to a classification by purpose of travel, travel receipts and payments may be divided according to other criteria significant for the compiling country, e.g. between border and other traffic, or between motor vehicle, railway and other traffic.

In 1963 the United Nations Conference on Travel and Tourism held in Rome recommended the following definitions of 'visitor' and 'tourist' in international statistics:

'For statistical purposes, the term "visitor" describes any person visiting a country other than that in which he has his usual place of residence, for any reason other than following an occupation remunerated from within the country visited.
This definition covers:
Tourists, i.e. temporary visitors staying at least twenty-four hours in the country visited and the purpose of whose journey can be classified under one of the following headings:
(a) leisure (recreation, holiday, health, study, religion, and sport);
(b) business, family, mission, meeting.
Excursionists, i.e. temporary visitors staying less than twenty-four hours in the country visited (including travellers on cruises).
The statistics should not include travellers who, in the legal sense, do not enter the country (air travellers who do not leave an airport's transit area, and similar cases).'[8]

An Expert Statistical Group on international travel statistics convened by the United Nations Statistical Commission recommended in 1967 that countries use the definition of 'visitor' proposed by the Rome Conference in 1963. The Group considered that it would be desirable to distinguish within the definition of visitor a separate class of visitors who might be described as 'day visitors' or 'excursionists' defined as consisting of visitors on day excursions and other border-crossers for purposes other than employment, cruise passengers, and visitors in transit who do not stay overnight in accommodation provided within the country. The special characteristic of this category of visitor, distinguishing it from the main class of visitor, is that there is no overnight stay.
In 1968 the Commission approved the Rome definition. The definition has two important features — it clearly distinguishes visitors from travellers arriving to take up permanent residence or employment; it also establishes that visitors be

classified by country of residence and not by nationality.

In the same year the IUOTO approved the Rome definition and also recommended that the term visitor be sub-divided into two categories by all its members, i.e.:

(a) tourists to include the visitors making at least one overnight stay;
(b) excursionists to include visitors not making an overnight stay in the country visited.

Thus the basic definitions for use in compiling national statistics of foreign tourism have been agreed and accepted internationally. In these tourism is generally synonymous with international travel for purposes of enumerating tourists and for estimating their expenditure. The outstanding problem is the implementation of these definitions in practice.

Volume Statistics

Basic statistics of volume call for an assessment of the number of visitors, their length of stay, and the total number of days or nights in the country.

In practice the number of visitors is measured in terms of arrivals or visits. These are usually recorded either at the frontier or in all or some types of accommodation. At present some sixty countries record foreign arrivals or visits at the frontier and some forty countries in various types of accommodation.

Frontier statistics are normally derived from immigration and/or customs controls and are therefore particularly accurate when stringent controls operate, as is the case, for example, in the United States and in the United Kingdom, where basic data are collected by means of entry cards or landing cards and by means of similar forms completed by visitors on departure. However, normal frontier recording presents problems as the volume of traffic and the freedom of movement increase.

Accommodation records are of value when recording at frontiers is not practicable, when legal enforcement operates effectively, and when it covers all types of accommodation. The latter is rarely possible and volume statistics based on accommodation records therefore rarely cover all traffic.

An assessment of the volume of outward holiday traffic by residents of a country to destinations abroad may be obtained through *household surveys* in the country of origin. This method was described in the preceding chapter in connection with national travel surveys of the population of a country.

In view of the problems and limitations of the two basic methods, increasing use is made of *sampling*, based on known densities of traffic on particular routes which, in addition to supplementing basic volume data, also provides information on expenditure and on profile and behaviour characteristics of tourists.

Expenditure Statistics

Foreign travel expenditure is divided into expenditure in the country or countries visited and fare payments to international carriers.

The traditional method of estimating foreign visitor expenditure has been to rely on *foreign currency exchange control* and *bank records*. Its effectiveness depends on the habits of tourists and the pattern of tourist traffic, as well as on the effectiveness of control. With the growth and changing forms of tourism and reduction of control this method has become increasingly unreliable. At any time considerable amounts of foreign currency are exchanged in most countries by residents, particularly foreign residents; increasingly large amounts of bank-notes are exchanged by tourists. With the growth of inclusive tours a large proportion of travel payments are made by tourists in their country of residence in respect of travel abroad; transactions of international organizations including carriers tend to result in net payments. Moreover, when exchange control or currency restrictions are in force, bank records tend to underestimate foreign visitor spending by the amount of smuggled currencies and overestimate it by the extent to which currencies allocated for travel are used for capital expenditure in the countries visited.

The second indirect method consists of estimating foreign visitor expenditure from surveys of hotels, travel agents and other *recipients of tourist expenditure* who sell services to visitors, from whom are sought estimates of foreign visitor spending. These are sometimes used in global terms or in arriving at expenditure per visit, which is then applied to volume statistics to arrive at global estimates. However, this approach is also unreliable; providers of tourist services find it difficult to separate tourist from other receipts and it is particularly difficult to ensure that all expenditure including shopping is included.

In view of these problems and limitations, the most reliable expenditure estimates are derived from *sample surveys of departing visitors,* in which information is sought about their spending during the trip. In order to ensure the reliability of the results, information provided by respondents is cross-checked with other sources, such as hotel tariffs, fare lists of carriers and, in the case of inclusive tours with the tour operators themselves; sample surveys are related to traffic flows, so as to be representative of the visits to the country. This method also enables estimates to be made of international fare payments generated by tourist traffic.

Types of Sample Surveys

Sample surveys of foreign tourism may be divided into several types according to purpose and scope and according to where and when interviews take place.

The most comprehensive survey endeavours to include all or most visitors to the country and to obtain volume and expenditure data, as well as qualitative data about the tourists themselves and about their trip; it is carried out at points of arrival and departure or *en route*. In order to be representative of the total traffic, interviews must be carried out at all major points of arrival and departure of foreign tourists and on all or most routes continuously throughout the year.

When it is desired to obtain more detailed information about one part of the traffic, separate sample surveys may be used to cover that part only, for example, businessmen or motorists, in which case interviews are carried out only with the visitors on business or those arriving and departing and by car, which may be restricted to certain times of the year.

Similarly, sample surveys may cover separately visitors of particular nationalities or countries of origin. In this case interviews may be conducted *en route* or at points of arrival and departure, but there are sometimes advantages in the survey being undertaken in the country of origin rather than in the country visited, in the visitors' own language. Since only a small proportion of the population in a particular country has visited the country studied as a destination, it is first necessary to locate them. This can be done, for example, by including questions in an omnibus survey in the country of origin, from which names and addresses of past visitors provide the contacts for interviews.

Simple information about foreign visitors to particular destinations within a country may be derived from the above types of survey, if interviews include questions about places visited and if the sample is large enough. However, detailed information can only be obtained by destination surveys of the type described in the last chapter in connection with domestic tourism.[9]

Statistics of Individual Countries

Tables 13 and 14 illustrate basic statistics of volume and value of international tourism for selected OECD countries for 1975, extracted from the annual report of the OECD Tourism Committee. However, the statistics produced by different systems and often using different definitions in individual countries are not directly comparable.

Table 13

Volume of Foreign Tourism in Selected OECD Countries 1975

	Arrivals (m)	*Average stay (nights)*	*Total nights (m)*
Recorded at frontiers			
Canada	13·7	5·6	77·0
France	13·1	7·6	100·0
Ireland	1·3	13·5	17·4
Portugal	0·9	12·0	10·2
United Kingdom	8·8	13·6	119·9
United States	15·7	7·0	110·0

Recorded at registered accommodation			
Austria	11·5	6·9	79·9
Germany	7·4	2·2	16·2
Italy	13·2	5·6	74·0
Netherlands	2·8	2·3	6·6
Spain	12·8	5·5	70·5
Switzerland	8·0	4·0	32·3

Table 14

Value of Foreign Tourism in Selected OECD Countries 1975

	Expenditure in the country (US $ m)	International fare payments US $ m)
Austria	3,034	130
Canada	1,534	251
France	3,470	n.a.
Germany	2,848	888
Ireland	201	70
Italy	2,578	521
Netherlands	1,107	365
Portugal	241	n.a.
Spain	3,404	n.a.
Switzerland	1,608	469
United Kingdom	2,462	891
United States	4,839	767

Figures for Canada, Ireland, UK, and US are based on sample surveys; figures for other countries are based on bank returns.

Home Office Immigration Statistics

The main basic source of foreign visitor arrivals (as distinct from all overseas visitors) in Britain is the Home Office Immigration Statistics, which are based on a comprehensive census of all foreign arrivals, excluding nationals of the Commonwealth and the Irish Republic.

The data are derived from landing cards completed by arriving foreign visitors and supplemented by Immigration Officers. The cards include surnames and first names, date and place of birth, sex, nationality, passport number, and address in the United Kingdom.

Published monthly statistics differentiate between arrivals of nationals of EEC countries (excluding the Irish Republic) and arrivals from non-EEC countries, which are sub-divided into several categories, and include a seasonal adjustment to eliminate the effects of the varying date of Easter. The information is also published quarterly as an appendix to *Business Monitor MQ6 Overseas Travel and Tourism*,[10] and in the annual White Paper *Immigration Statistics*[11] which contains a more detailed analysis by nationality and by purpose of visit.

Tourist statistics based on Home Office records are a by-product of immigration control. It is a series of long standing, which enumerates comprehensively foreign visitors by month of arrival and by nationality, and provides separate visitor numbers for a large number of countries; no information other than visitor numbers is provided. The main limitations of the Home Office statistics are that they exclude between one-third and one-quarter of the total traffic to the UK and that the analysis included is by nationality and not by country of residence. Some of the information obtained through the landing cards, such as age and sex distribution, is not analysed at all.

Until 1963 United Kingdom tourist statistics were based largely on the Home Office Immigration Statistics, to which were added estimates of visitors from the Commonwealth. Sample surveys of the British Travel Association were used to supplement the Home Office data, particularly to provide expenditure and other estimates.

International Passenger Survey

By the beginning of the 1960s the volume and expenditure of overseas visitors to Britain and to British residents abroad reached significant proportions. The substantial expenditure of Commonwealth visitors to Britain was difficult to measure when the large number of such visitors reaching the country by air and short sea routes from the Continent of Europe was unknown. At the same time the relaxation of exchange control made the estimates of travel expenditure by British residents abroad increasingly unreliable. These and other reasons called for a new system of measuring foreign tourism to and from Britain.

The Government was encouraged to adopt a new system based on interviews with a small proportion of the traffic, which would enable travel expenditure to be measured without interfering with the free flow of passengers at sea and airports, by the Tourism Committee of the OECD, which in 1961 recommended the sample survey method to obtain tourist statistics, after making a study of the sampling techniques used by certain member countries. The first surveys were carried out by the Government Social Survey on behalf of the Board of Trade during 1961 and 1962 and since 1964 United Kingdom statistics of international travel and tourism have been based on the new system, known as the International Passenger Survey. Its main aspects may be summarized as follows:

(a) The Survey is carried out for the Department of Trade by the Office of Population Censuses and Surveys and the results are based on their interviews with a large sample of passengers. This information is supplemented with estimates in respect of the Irish Republic provided by the Central Statistics Office of the Irish Republic and in respect of the Channel Islands (in the case of earnings and expenditure only and from 1975 onwards) by the Economic Adviser's Office of the States of Jersey.

(b) Similar main information is collected regularly for overseas visitors to the United Kingdom and for visits abroad by residents of the United Kingdom: number and purpose of visit, area of residence/area visited, mode of travel, inclusive/independent travel, length of stay, expenditure. Other information on such matters as places visited and the type of accommodation used has been collected from time to time.

(c) An overseas visitor is a person who, being permanently resident in a country outside the United Kingdom, visits the United Kingdom for a period of less than twelve months; included in this are United Kingdom citizens resident overseas for twelve months or more coming home on leave. Visits abroad are visits for a period of less than twelve months by people permanently resident in the United Kingdom (who may be of foreign nationality).

(d) The numbers are visits, not visitors, and relate to those ending during each period, i.e. to overseas visitors leaving the country and British residents returning to it. Average length of stay for overseas visitors covers stay within the United Kingdom, for United Kingdom residents travelling abroad time spent, including journey spent outside the country.

(e) Visits are classified by main purpose into holiday, business, visits to friends and relatives sporting events, health, religious, and other purposes, together with visits for more than one purpose where none predominates (e.g. visits both on business and on holiday). Migrants and persons travelling to take up employment together with military personnel, merchant seamen, and airline personnel travelling on duty are excluded.

(f) Published expenditure figures cover expenditure in the country or countries visited, including estimates of expenditure of visitors in transit and on day trips; consequently some expenditure figures do not exactly correspond to the figures for numbers of visits, which exclude visitors in transit, but include day visits.

(g) Published expenditure figures exclude payments for air and sea travel to and from the United Kingdom, though they include small amounts in respect of international rail fares. Expenditure in this country does not include the personal export of cars purchased by visitors to the United Kingdom (estimated at about £36 million a year), which is included in the Overseas Trade Statistics. Also excluded are overseas visitors' purchases on British carriers and at duty free shops.

(h) The Survey is carried out by personal interviews with a stratified random sample of passengers entering and leaving the United Kingdom on the principal air and sea routes, other than those to the Irish Republic, about whom information is obtained annually from the Central Statistics Office of the Irish Republic. The composition of the sample is determined according to known density of flows, i.e. previous year's traffic adjusted in the light of current density. Some 300,000 successful interviews are made each year.

(i) Some routes are not surveyed continuously, and others carrying relatively few passengers are not surveyed at all. Estimates are included in respect of the routes not under survey in any period, the total numbers travelling on which are known. About 70 per cent of the passengers entering and leaving the United Kingdom, other than those on routes to and from the Irish Republic, travel on routes which are covered by the Survey and at times when passengers were interviewed.

(j) The numbers of visits in the International Passenger Survey are estimated within fairly close limits of accuracy; expenditure estimates are subject to standard sampling errors within 1 per cent for the annual estimates of expenditure and within 2 per cent for earnings.

The results of the International Passenger Survey are published quarterly and annually in the *Business Monitor MQ6, Overseas Travel and Tourism,* [10] and also in *British Business.* [12]

The United Kingdom in International Tourism

Three appendixes include post-war statistics of the United Kingdom in international tourism. Appendix J records visits to the UK by overseas residents and their expenditure for 1946-79, and includes estimates of visitor nights since 1971; Appendix K shows similar information in respect of visits abroad by UK residents; Appendix L relates UK residents' foreign travel expenditure and changes in foreign travel currency allowance for 1945-79. Overseas travel and tourism to and from the UK for recent years, as measured by the International Passenger Survey, is summarized in Tables 15 and 16.

Until 1977 the United Kingdom experienced a relatively fast growth in visits by overseas residents, a continuing decline in the average length of stay until 1978, and the combination of the two produced a growth in nights, which stopped in 1978. The growth between 1975 and 1977 showed even more impressively in overseas visitor expenditure.

The trend started changing in 1978 and the changes continued into 1979. The growth in visits slowed down in 1978 and there was actually a small decrease in 1979 — the first since the Second World War. Expenditure continued to grow at current prices but since 1978 not in real terms. The bright light of 1979 was a reversal in the long-term decline in the length of stay; as a result total nights increased in spite of the decline in the number of visitors. The strengthening of the pound sterling, the high inflation in the UK, and the world economic recession, especially in North America, are the main explanations of the trends in 1978 and 1979.

Travel abroad by UK residents has been always more volatile than traffic in the opposite direction, but what happened in 1978 and 1979 was in sharp contrast to the trend in incoming traffic: big increases in numbers going abroad, nights spent abroad, and money spent abroad by UK residents. Three main factors explain the recent British exodus abroad: the strengthening of the pound; the reduction in air fares on many routes; the aggressive competition of many foreign destinations combined with the skills of the British tour operating industry.

The UK travel account continued to make a major contribution to the UK balance of payments in the late 1970s but this contribution declined after a peak in 1977 and in 1979 was the lowest for four years.

Table 15

Overseas Travel and Tourism to and from the United Kingdom 1975-79 by Volume and Expenditure

		1975	1976	1977	1978R	1979P
Overseas Visitors to the U.K.						
Visits	(m)	9·5	10·8	12·3	12·6	12·5
	(+/− %)	+11	+14	+14	+3	−1
Stay	(nights)	13·6	12·4	12·1	11·8	12·4
	(+/− %)	−3	−9	−2	−2	+5
Nights	(m)	128	134	149	149	156
	(+/− %%)	+8	+4	+11	—	+4
Expenditure (£ m current prices)		1,218	1,768	2,352	2,507	2,764
(+/− %)		+36	+45	+33	+7	+10
(£ m 1975 prices)		1,218	1,531	1,751	1,630	
(+/− %)		+24	+26	+14	−7	
U.K. Residents Abroad						
Visits	(m)	12·0	11·6	11·5	13·4	15·5
	(+/− %)	+11	−4	—	+17	+15
Nights	(m)	165	160	157	176	205
	(+/− %)	+14	−3	−2	+13	+16
Expenditure (£ m current prices		917	1,068	1,186	1,549	2,091
(+/− %)		+30	+17	+11	+31	+35
(£ m 1975 prices)		917	856	859	1,068	
(+/− %)		+6	−7	—	+24	

R Revised
P Provisional
Figures include day visits

Source: International Passenger Survey

Table 16

Overseas Travel and Tourism to and from the United Kingdom 1975—79
by Area, Purpose of Visit and Mode of Travel

Overseas Visitors to the UK	1975		1976		1977		1978		1979P	
	000	%	000	%	000	%	000	%	000	%
Area of residence										
North America	1,907	20·1	2,093	19·4	2,377	19·4	2,475	19·6	2,196	17·6
Western Europe — EEC	4,651	49·0	5,352	49·5	6,069	49·4	6,202	49·0	6,159	49·3
Western Europe — non-EEC	1,196	12·6	1,464	13·5	1,701	13·9	1,663	13·2	1,721	13·8
Other areas	1,736	18·3	1,899	17·6	2,134	17·4	2,306	18·2	2,417	19·3
Total	9,490	100·0	10,808	100·0	12,281	100·0	12,646	100·0	12,493	100·0
Purpose of visit										
Holiday	4,433	46·7	5,253	48·6	5,944	48·4	5,876	46·5	5,538	44·3
Business	1,778	18·7	1,934	17·9	2,142	17·4	2,295	18·1	2,391	19·1
Visits to friends & rels·	1,761	18·6	1,849	17·1	2,032	16·5	2,193	17·3	2,261	18·1
Other purposes	1,518	16·0	1,772	16·4	2,163	17·6	2,283	18·1	2,304	18·4
Total	9,490	100·0	10,808	100·0	12,281	100·0	12,646	100·0	12,493	100·0
Mode of travel										
Air	5,705	60·1	6,370	58·9	7,229	58·9	7,580	59·9	7,603	60·9
Sea	3,785	39·9	4,438	41·1	5,052	41·1	5,067	40·1	4,890	39·1
Total	9,490	100·0	10,808	100·0	12,281	100·0	12,646	100·0	12,493	100·0

UK Residents Abroad	1975		1976		1977		1978		1979P	
	000	%	000	%	000	%	000	%	000	%
Area visited										
North America	514	4·3	579	5·0	619	5·4	782	5·8	1,087	7·0
Western Europe — EEC	6,135	51·2	5,996	51·9	6,037	52·4	6,946	51·7	7,983	51·6
Western Europe — non-EEC	4,333	36·1	3,958	34·2	3,829	33·2	4,571	34·0	5,033	32·5
Other areas	1,010	8·4	1,027	8·9	1,040	9·0	1,144	8·5	1,361	8·8
Total	11,992	100·0	11,560	100·0	11,525	100·0	13,443	100·0	15,464	100·0
Purpose of visit										
Holiday	7,743	64·6	7,024	60·8	6,834	59·3	8,439	62·8	9,860	63·8
Business	1,807	15·1	2,054	17·8	2,154	18·7	2,261	16·8	2,510	16·2
Visits to friends & rels	1,792	14·9	1,911	16·5	1,913	16·6	1,970	14·7	2,178	14·1
Other purposes	650	5·4	571	4·9	624	5·4	774	5·8	917	5·9
Total	11,992	100·0	11,560	100·0	11,525	100·0	13,443	100·0	15,464	100·0
Mode of travel										
Air	7,296	60·8	7,235	62·6	7,300	63·3	8,416	62·6	9,785	63·3
Sea	4,696	39·2	4,325	37·4	4,225	36·7	5,028	37·4	5,679	36·7
Total	11,992	100·0	11,560	100·0	11,525	100·0	13,443	100·0	15,464	100·0

Source: International Passenger Survey

Global Statistics of International Tourism

Two main international organizations draw on estimates of individual countries of their incoming and outgoing foreign tourism and produce estimates of international tourism on a world-wide basis.

The Organization for Economic Co-operation and Development (OECD), which replaced in 1960 the Organization for European Economic Co-operation (OEEC), reports cover about three-quarters of the international tourist movement in the world and include all the main generating and destination countries. Illustrations of statistics from the OECD reports are included throughout this book.

The World Tourism Organization (WTO) was created as an inter-governmental body dealing with all aspects of tourism in 1975 and succeeded the International Union of Official Travel Organizations (IUOTO), a non-governmental body first set up in 1925. The development of tourism is reported by the WTO annually in *World Tourism Statistics,*[13] and in alternate years in *Tourism Compendium*[14] and *Economic Review of World Tourism,*[15] the principal statistical publications of the Organization, which covers more than one hundred countries and provides global estimates of the world tourist movement.

Appendixes F and G, based on WTO statistics, record the growth of international tourist arrivals and receipts between 1950 and 1979. The WTO estimated that by the end of the decade total international tourist arrivals reached 270 million and generated 75 billion US dollars in international tourisim receipts (excluding international fare payments).

Although the growth of international tourism slowed down in 1979 and registered only a 4 per cent increase over 1978, compared with 6·5 per cent increase a year earlier, and tourism receipts registered an increase of 15 per cent, compared with 24 per cent a year earlier, in 1979 international trade, compared with 5 per cent in 1978, demonstrating a more rapid growth in international tourism than in world exports.

Appendixes H and I provide a breakdown of arrivals and receipts between six regions of the world for the years between 1972 and 1979, and show differences in growth between the regions, as well as the shares of individual regions in total international tourist arrivals and receipts.

By the end of the 1970s statistics of international tourism have been developed to the point where they provide a broad indication of its main dimensions and of its global distribution.

Summary and Conclusions

The main elements of travel to a country may be summarized diagrammatically as in Figure 3 (proportions not to scale).

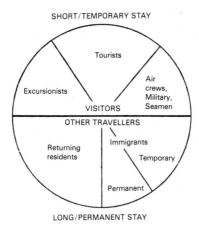

Figure 3. Main Elements of Travel to a Country

Statistics of international tourism have been developed by individual countries to meet their need for the measurement of the volume and value of tourism, using methods which have been in the main derived from immigration and exchange control systems. However, increasing efforts have been made to produce on the one hand more specific statistics and on the other hand to achieve a greater measure of comparability between statistics produced by individual countries.

With the growth in the volume of international travel and with increasing freedom of movement between most countries, statistics based on indirect methods derived from administrative systems make it no longer possible to obtain adequate information and direct methods based on sample surveys of tourists are increasingly used in addition to and instead of indirect methods. At the same time standard definitions have been agreed internationally; however, individual countries, whilst recognizing the value of these definitions, often find it difficult to apply them in practice.

In Britain sampling has been used extensively in the measurement of tourism for a long time and in the early 1960s a major improvement in statistics of international travel and tourism was achieved with the launching of the International Passenger Survey, which replaced the country's reliance on immigration statistics and *ad hoc* surveys. Britain also played a leading role in international organizations concerned with statistics of tourism.

Part IV

Passenger Transportation

Further Reading for Part IV

(Beeching Report): *The Reshaping of British Railways*
British Road Federation: *Roads and Tourism*
Burkart, A. J. and Medlik, S.: *The Management of Tourism: A Selection of Readings,* Part IV
Car Ferries between Western Europe and the UK, International Tourism Quarterly No.1 1977
Department of Trade: *Future Civil Aviation Policy* (Cmnd 6400)
Department of Trade and Industry: *Civil Aviation Policy Guidance* (Cmnd 4899)
(Edwards Committee): *British Air Transport in the Seventies* (Cmnd 4018)
European Air Fares, CAP 409
Milne, A. M. and Laight, J.C.: *The Economics of Inland Transport*
Monopolies Commission, *Cross-Channel Car Ferry Services*
Rosenberg, A.: *Air Travel within Europe*
Select Committee on the Nationalised Industries: *The Ownership, Management and Use of Shipping by Nationalised Industries,* HC 346
Straszheim, M. R.: *The International Airline Industry*
Wheatcroft, S.F.: *Air Transport Policy*

References

1 Hotels and Catering EDC: *Report to NEDO* January 1977
2 *British Air Transport in the Seventies,* (Cmnd 4018)
3 *Civil Aviation Act 1971*
4 Department of Trade and Industry:
   Civil Aviation Policy Guidance (Cmnd 4899)
   Future Civil Aviation Policy (Cmnd 6400)
5 Civil Aviation Authority: *Domestic Air Services* (CAP 420)
6 Burke R.: 'Civil Aviation Policy in the European Community', *Aerospace* Vol.7 No.1, January 1980

10   *The Pattern of Tourist Transport*

If one wanted to identify industries which clearly mark out the modern post-Renaissance world as distinguishable from earlier periods of history, one would choose printing and passenger transport above all as characteristic of the modern world. Both these industries represent forms of communication, and it is the rapidity of communication, the speed of the spread of ideas, which has been a crucial factor in the growth of the modern world.

Tourism is about being elsewhere, and a major component of any tourist activity must necessarily be an element of transportation. But the transport industries which serve the needs of tourists also operate their systems for other kinds of market, for freight for example, or for commuters. In many cases it may be possible to provide services exclusively designed for the tourist, but often the kind of services used by tourists is in part at least determined by the needs of the various transport undertakings to draw on other markets. Indeed the tourist passenger may benefit from the existence of other markets available to the transport operator. An example of this is the carriage of mail. The early days of developing a new transport facility may be made easier for the transport undertaking by the granting to it of a contract to carry mail: in the USA the award of mail contracts has been used as an explicit subsidy to foster the development of local air services.

Like the printing press, a transport system is extremely productive and large economies of scale appear at an early point in production. This has led the managements of transport systems to be concerned with a high degree of utilization of their capital equipment in ways which will be shown below. This characteristic of transportation has tended to induce kinds of reduced fares aimed specifically at the leisure or holiday tourist.

The Track, the Vehicle, and the Terminal

A transport system can be analysed in three parts: the track, the vehicle, and the terminal. There must be, to put the matter another way, a control of direction, a moving element, and a place at which to rest to pick up and set down passengers. Historically, the original form of mechanical transport, the railways, was conceived in this way, with the ownership and operation of the three components in different hands. Throughout the history of transport concern has been felt that if these three functions were in the same hands losses arising from the use of the track might be made up by higher prices for using the terminal. The problem was solved for the railways at an early date, and the majority of the vehicles used soon came into the ownership of the railway company. But in freight carriage by rail, at least until very recently, collieries used their own wagons to run over the railway companies' tracks, and the Pullman and the Wagon-Lits concepts in passenger carriage have perpetuated the original notion of track, vehicle, and terminal in distinct ownership.

The debate is far from a historical one, and problems still arise today. How should terminal facilities for the private car be provided and paid for? A private car needs a terminal, i.e. a place to park in, as much as a train needs a station or an aircraft an airport. How shall air traffic control facilities be provided and paid for? By the airline operators? Or by the government of the country over which the air routes pass? And how, if at all, shall the costs of these navigational facilities be reflected in the price of the ticket?

The Analysis of Transport

Transport services may be viewed in different ways. An obvious classification for the purposes of the study of tourism is to look at transport services as providing carriage inland, that is within the national boundaries of a sovereign territory, which is referred to as cabotage carriage, and complementarily we can also speak of international transportation. There are already, and with the increasing liberalization of movement between sovereign territories there will be, some disadvantages in analysing transport in this way.

Alternatively, transport may be analysed by mode, that is to say, by a classification based on the technologies employed. In this approach, the analysis would classify transport services as rail service, air services, the private car, and so on. This has the advantage of being readily identifiable physically.

In fact, there is no one ideal way of approaching the analysis of transport. But one or two caveats must be entered. For an island like Britain, international transport using the private car implies a sea crossing, and the statistics of cross-Channel ferries are to be found in shipping statistics. Hovercraft are regarded as aircraft for the purposes of safety specifications, but their commercial significance is as rivals to conventional sea ferries in the transport of vehicles and passengers.

For the most part, the modal analysis suits present purposes best and the overview of the principal methods of transport available to tourists which follows will be from that standpoint. Inevitably, a good deal of space will be taken up by discussion of the private car and of air transport. These two modes of transport dominate tourist movement in the second half of the twentieth century.

The Private Car

The increase in car ownership in Britain has proceeded rapidly in the last thirty years. The ownership rate has doubled about every ten years. For example, in 1949 there were 140 cars owned per thousand households, by 1959 this figure had increased to 310, and by 1970 rather more than 600 cars were owned per thousand households. More families owned one or more cars than owned no car. The ratio of car-owning families to non-owning families would be somewhat greater, if one excluded from the reckoning those non-owning families which consisted of low income single person households. Thus in recent years Britain has become a country where more families have access to a private car than families who have not.

Private car ownership in the United Kingdom in terms of cars per thousand population over a period of forty years is shown in Appendix Q and in selected countries in late 1970s in Appendix R.

A household acquires a car in the first place for non-tourist uses, for taking the children to school, to go to work and so on. The propensity to own a private car is thus related to a family's life-cycle stage and therefore to the family income. Car ownership is evidently related to income, and is most attractive to a family when their young children are relatively difficult to move around. The combination of these two factors enables one to see the influence of the car on patterns of tourist demand for transport. For few people buy a car primarily for leisure or holiday purposes. They will have bought a car for general household purposes, and the fact of their car ownership will be a significant influencing factor in their choice of holiday and of holiday transport. Moreover, only a small minority of tourists account for their car-owning costs in a rigorous way: for most owners the cost of motoring is perceived as the out-of-pocket expenses of fuel and oil, and depreciation and replacement are not estimated. The car owner thus calculates that it is not only more convenient but cheaper to travel by car.

The tourist taking his holiday in Britain has increasingly used his car for the purpose. As the proportion of families owning at least one car has increased, so has the use of the car for holidays. The British National Travel Surveys report that whereas in the mid 1950s car, bus/coach, and rail travel accounted for about one-third each of main holidays of four nights or more in Britain, by the mid 1960s the respective shares were three-fifths, one-fifth, and one fifth, and by the mid 1970s the use of car reached 70 per cent of the total, as shown in Table 11.

If attention is now directed to the use of the car by the British holidaying abroad, the picture is complicated by the island character of Britain and the influence of the inclusive tour by air. In the mid 1960s about the same number of holidays abroad used air and sea transport. By the mid 1970s two-thirds went by air and one-third by sea. In the late 1970s air travel accounted for some 70 per cent and sea travel for about 30 per cent of the total. This major growth in holiday travel abroad by air occurred in spite of growing numbers of British holidaymakers going abroad taking a car with them. The major contributing factor to the increased use of air transport for holidays abroad was the growth and development of the inclusive tour to Spain and to a lesser extent to other holiday destinations.

The expansion of the inclusive tour holiday has probably been partly responsible for a shift in the choice of destination. The nearer destination countries are likely to be associated with travel by car. In 1955, for one or more nights spent there, the rank order of British holidays abroad was France 33 per cent of holidays, Benelux countries 18 per cent, Italy 17 per cent, Republic of Ireland 15 per cent, Switzerland 14 per cent, with Austria, Germany and Spain in the region of 10 per cent each. By 1975 Spain headed the list with 33 per cent, France had dropped away to 14 per cent and Italy to 7 per cent, and the share of none of the other countries exceeded 5 per cent.

Other factors have to be taken into account, but if a family are using their car on holiday abroad because of its convenience and low cost, because they are at a life-cycle stage where cost and convenience matter, they will not be able to do more than visit nearer destinations. The decline in the relative popularity of France is at least as much as a preference for visiting Spain by air as it is evidence for a distaste for France. The British National Travel Survey 1970 demonstrates this point: only 16 per cent of all holidays of four nights or more abroad were taken in France, but of all taken abroad (excluding Ireland) with a car, 40 per cent were taken in France. Grossing these percentages up for 1970, approximately 550,000 holidays were taken by the British in France; of these, 320,000 (58 per cent) used a car as the means of transport, even though this figure includes those whose final destination was beyond France.

The British experience as an island is not entirely typical. However, Germany is a country with which it is useful to make a comparison. It has a common frontier with Austria and with Switzerland and France, and thanks to the major road networks Italy can be easily reached. The bulk of German tourists to these countries use the car, especially to Austria; as the distance increases, so the car passenger yields to the airline passenger.

The private car has facilitated camping and caravanning. The proportion of holidays involving camping in the UK has remained fairly constant at around 5 per cent, although the absolute numbers have tended to increase. By the end of the 1970s the proportion of holidays in Britain involving caravanning was one-fifth of the total. A distinction must be made between the static caravanner and the mobile one, but even if the static caravanner is to be regarded as the user of a particular type of accommodation, he will certainly depend on a car to reach it. For campers and mobile caravanners, 90 per cent or more naturally depend on their car. The total numbers of both campers and mobile caravanners who go abroad for their holidays are relatively small, presumably because of Britain's island situation. Finally, campers and mobile caravanners are rather better off than the population as a whole, but form rather larger households with more children; this is again a life-cycle effect closely related to income.

Going by Air

The principal internal air services in the UK are the shuttle services operated by British Airways, the state-owned airline. These services do not require advance booking and virtually offer a guarantee of carriage, and operate between London and the cities of Edinburgh, Glasgow, Belfast, and Manchester. Conventional services are provided by British Caledonian from London Gatwick. There are a number of secondary routes operated by smaller airlines and the development by Air Anglia, now part of Air UK, of an east coast oil-related route connecting to Amsterdam is welcome evidence that new entry is still possible in British aviation. These routes are principally meeting business demand, while the principal holiday routes are those to the Channel Islands and the Isle of Man, the traffic in both cases being markedly seasonal. In the north and west of Scotland there is a network of services supported by a grant in aid which satisfy the social need to maintain communication with the remoter parts of the Highlands and Islands.

For travel abroad, the air predominates both for holiday and for business purposes. Again, British Airways is by far the largest British operator. Under the provisions of the Civil Aviation Act 1971, British Caledonian was envisaged as a 'second force' carrier with routes to South America, West Africa, and the USA. More recent legislation, however, has impaired the position of British Caledonian as one of special privilege and Laker, for example, has secured substantial services to the USA. The operations of all these private airlines remain small compared with BA.

Since 1965, when the regulatory process made it possible, there has been some shift of interest from scheduled services to charters. The inherently lower operating costs of charter operation have enabled the airlines to offer very low fares or prices (in the case of inclusive tours) to a very price-conscious market. One popular device was the affinity group charter for groups of passengers with a common interest other than the pursuit of cheap air travel. However, abuse of the regulations relating to affinity led to the devising of advance booking charters, primarily on the North Atlantic; as the name implies, a crucial condition was the need to book in advance, originally 90 days but soon shortened to as little as seven days. The advance booking charter has had only a limited success chiefly to Canada: in Europe the inclusive tour (charter) or ITC seems to hold an unchallenged position, and on the North Atlantic the scheduled carriers have offered brisk competition with a range of discounted promotional fares.

Charter traffic entails the attainment of very high load factors, that is to say, a high proportion of the available seats to be occupied. Thus charters predominate on routes of high traffic density such as those from the UK to Spain. These large volumes of traffic present problems for airports and airport policy.

Measured by traffic passing through it, London Heathrow is the largest international airport in the world. At the end of the 1970s there were three major airports serving London and its environs, London Heathrow and London Gatwick, both operated by the state-owned British Airports Authority, and Luton owned by the local authority and handling chiefly charter traffic in the shape of ITCs. The development of Stansted, also a BAA airport, is envisaged in the 1980s. London Heathrow is the main base for British Airways and handles mostly scheduled traffic, while London Gatwick handles a mix of both charter and scheduled operations, and expects to increase the number of flights and of passengers during the 1980s. Foreign carriers use both London Heathrow and London Gatwick, and helicopter services as well as conventional ground services link the two airports in order to facilitate the interlining process.

In 1979, the International Passenger Survey recorded 12·5 million overseas visitors to the U.K. Of these, 7·6 million came by air. Some 15·5 million visits abroad were made by UK residents in the same year, 9·8 million by air. The importance of air transport to the UK is clear. This importance derives in part from this country's island situation, whereas, for example, German visitors to Austria or French visitors to Spain use the car as their principal mode of holiday transport. But the use by the large American carriers of London as the principal gateway to Europe is also a significant factor.

Crossing the Sea

The major part of sea travel today consists of short crossings from point to point, on a ferry which typically will carry both cars and passengers on foot. Liner service, the sea-going equivalent of scheduled services, has virtually disappeared under the pressure of rising costs for crew and latterly for oil. Some residual activity remains in cruising but it is not immune from the pressure of rising costs either.

Europe (once the main generator of transatlantic sea traffic) has proved to be a fertile place for the development of ferry traffic, due to its heavily indented coastline (e.g. the Baltic and the Adriatic), its large offshore islands (e.g. Crete, Sicily, and the UK itself), and its high car ownership. In the summer of 1979 there were between two and three hundred ferry services operating in Europe, mostly using conventional roll-on roll-off vessels, but with hovercraft (air cushion, ground effect) and hydrofoils also in service.

Ferry traffic between the UK and continental Europe accounts for about one-third of the total, the nearer EEC countries accounting for the larger part, and the densest routes being the short sea English Channel crossings. The principal operators are British Rail in collaboration with French, Belgian, and Dutch interests trading under the brand name SEALINK, and European Ferries Ltd trading as Townsend Thoresen. Recently a number of new entrants have appeared, notably P & O Ferries, Brittany Ferries, and the services operated by Mr Lauritzen under several names. The revived interest in a Channel Tunnel does not seem likely to affect the ferry operators during the 1980s. But the hovercraft services seem to have failed to make satisfactory profits and their long-term future must remain in doubt.

Although car passengers account for only about a quarter of the total traffic, the existence of adequate road systems behind the ferry ports is important, not least to facilitate the haulage traffic, on which the ferry services depend especially during the winter off-peak periods. Ferry traffic is highly seasonal and the re-introduction of something like free competition on the cross-Channel routes has created marked rivalry between the principal operators, with many fare reductions particularly during the shoulder months. The ferries to Scandinavia and to Ireland seem to have escaped the fierce competition of the English Channel.

As long ago as 1957, passenger traffic by air across the North Atlantic exceeded for the first time the seaborne traffic. By the end of the 1970s, passenger liner scheduled services by sea had virtually ceased between Europe and North America. Cunard, with the *Queen Elizabeth 2*, provided a dozen or so round trips from Southampton to New York, and the Russian shipping company provided services to Canada. Both these are summer services.

Cruising on the other hand seems to attract continuing interest. The Caribbean and the Mediterranean cater to the sunlust of the industrialized populations that lie to their north. In the Pacific, also, there remains a demand from Australia, Japan, and California for cruising. The main challenge to the cruising companies is to bring their prices down to a level more comparable with that of the air inclusive tour. Granted that cruising will always attract a limited market, the cruise operator is faced with the marketing problem of engaging the attention of a very small number of people in each country. Allied to this is the problem of getting the passengers to the ship, which cannot (as used to be the case) make a long itinerary around North European ports to pick up passengers. The use of air services to feed passengers to the ship is vital, and today there could be no cruising without adequate air services.

By Train or Coach

The use of the train as a mode of transport for tourism purposes depends on a rail service still being supplied, and all countries with developed rail systems subsidize their rail services heavily. In Britain, the provision of rail services has concentrated on commuter services and fast inter-City services. Because of their demand characteristics, commuter services require a massive subsidy if they are to attract traffic; the fast inter-city services probably are just profitable. What is lacking is adequate rail transport to the resort areas. The point was well made in a report by the Hotels and Catering EDC in 1977; after stressing the need for co-ordination in tourism development, the report continued:

'This should also be reflected in the policies of the nationalised industries such as the airlines, railways and other carriers. Yet frequently there seems to be a conflict between the needs of tourism and policies in other areas. This is reflected, in for example, the field of transport in the consideration by British Rail of cuts and line closures in the very type of area that the statutory [tourist] Boards are being urged to promote'.[1]

Appendix S shows the use of passenger transport in Great Britain for all purposes, i.e. reflects the supply of transport, and rail is doing well to hold its own against the continuing increase in the use of private transport, which is making inroads into the public service vehicle (bus/coach) sector in particular. The British Home Tourism Surveys confirm that the rail as a means of tourism transport has held its share at about 12 per cent in the 1970s; this represents a decline from a figure of around 35 per cent in the 1950s.

Recently, at the end of the 1970s, British Rail has offered dramatic fare reductions to families, old age pensioners and similar segments of their market for off-peak travel extending over the whole network. Aimed at 'Visits to Friends and Relatives' traffic in particular, these initiatives appear to have had at least some initial success and are to be welcomed, even if only to bring nearer the day when the railways will measure their performance by maximizing passenger/

kilometres rather than profits.

Throughout the first half of the 1970s, the bus/coach sector held its share of the British tourism market at around 11 per cent, but by the end of that decade there were signs of a further contraction at a time when, against all logic apparently, the use of the car was expanding. When the cost of running a private car was increasing rapidly, the cheapest form of public transport apparently failed to attract the tourist traffic.

It is instructive to compare the fuel efficiency of the various transport modes and Table 17 reproduces some estimates made in the aftermath of the energy/oil crisis of 1973-74.

Table 17
Fuel Used per Passenger-Mile

Mode of transport	No. of Passengers	Typical load factor %	lbs fuel per passenger mile
Coach	53	60	0·023
Train	450	30	0·073
Advanced passenger train	700	60	0·083
Medium car	4	40	0·180
Jumbo jet	347	40	0·347
Large car	4	40	0·348
Concorde	128	60	0·550

Source: Goldsmith, H. A., *Development of Aircraft ..., Aeronautical Journal,* Vol. 78, No. 765, Sept. 1974

Clearly, a great deal depends on the assumptions made about load factors in such comparisons, but the fuel efficiency of the train and the coach are self-evident, although it should be noted that the Jumbo jet and the large car are both of equal efficiency but much lower than train or coach.

If the coach in particular is fuel-efficient, and enjoys more flexibility in routeing than the train, what is its future in tourism? With all the evidence showing that the car is always the preferred means of transport and that the air is preferred to surface transport where the use of the car is inappropriate, the future of the coach would seem to lie in the provision of ancillary transport at the tourist destination. Currently in the UK, the typical coach passenger is elderly, i.e. over 50 years of age, predominantly female, and with a lower than average income. It is hard to see much change in the status of the coach except at the lower end of the market.

11 *Economics of Passenger Transportation*

All transportation systems are extremely productive, in the sense that once capital costs have been recovered, the incremental cost of the additional unit of output tends to be very low. Typically too transportation systems tend to be capital intensive. In the particular case of passenger transportation, demand for transport tends to occur with both seasonal and daily peaks. This gives rise to periods of under-utilization, in the sense that no revenue is accruing in the off-season troughs in demand, while at least the fixed costs are continuing.

The accepted measurement of transport performance compares the relationship over a given period between the capacity generated by the system or by the vehicle and the load actually carried. This relationship is expressed as the percentage of capacity which is under load. For example:

Available tonne kilometres (ATK): the product of the capacity available for payload and the distance performed.

Revenue tonne kilometres (RTK): the product of the load actually carried and the distance performed.

Load factor (LF): the relationship of RTK with ATK expressed as a percentage.

The Route

Between any two points, there will be one optimal route, the least-cost route, which will normally be the shortest route either in terms of time or of distance. It follows that if the route can carry just one transport operator, subsequent operators will suffer an additional economic burden if forced to employ some route which is not the least-cost route. From this consideration arises the element of 'natural monopoly' alleged to be present in transport operations; if an element of competition is to be introduced, all operators on the least-cost route must share the route in an equitable way so that all bear the penalty of using sub-optimal variations from time to time. The importance of this consideration will appear in Chapter 12 which discusses the regulation of transport.

The total demand for a particular route will tend to be somewhat price-inelastic, and inelastic to promotion and marketing effort as well. To put it in a non-technical way, it will be relatively difficult to persuade the papermaker with business in Stockholm to go to Milan instead, whatever inducements of price or otherwise may be offered him. But if each transport operator on one route is free to determine his own fares without restriction, it may be expected that all the traffic will travel on the cheapest carrier. In other words, demand *between carriers* on a route will be relatively elastic; demand *between routes* will be relatively inelastic. Again, it can be seen that if the situation is left to market forces, another kind of 'natural monopoly' will arise. Accordingly, it has been found desirable to secure common fares and prices which are charged by all operators on a route, as a step to prevent undue monopolistic practices. Such price fixing may be reached by mutual agreement between carriers on a route or it may be imposed on them by governments.

In developing a new route, the pioneer carrier on the route will incur costs at the beginning of operations which will not be faced by later operators. Such costs may arise from his sole use of, say, port or airport installations, Additionally, the pioneer operator may face lower-than-normal revenue in the first period of operation, at least until demand for the new service has built up. The pioneer operator thus hopes to have the new route to himself, so that he can recover in subsequent periods the losses he has made in the pioneer period. But in an unregulated situation, his very success will attract competitors to the route, and these later arrivals will enjoy the advantages of an already developed traffic, the development of which the pioneer carrier has already paid for. This effect is sometimes known as creaming, but it is often recognized that the pioneer should in equity be allowed to gather the rewards of his pioneering. This situation again calls for a degree of regulation, either by governments or by mutual agreement, or perhaps by subsidizing the pioneer.

Empirically, there seems often to be a threshold point on any one route in the minimum capacity and frequency to be offered. A certain intensity of operation seems to be necessary to draw out demand for the route. This will entail sub-optimal operations by the pioneer for a period, when he is offering more capacity and a greater frequency of service than the demand warrants. All transport systems, roads and bridges as well as airline routes, have a property of generating new demand for the facility, additional to the initial demand.

Identifying Transport Costs

Transport costs can be identified as fixed costs, which do not vary with hours flown or driven, or with distance travelled, and as variable costs which do vary in proportion to distance travelled or with load carried. In most transport under-takings fixed costs are relatively high, and this leads transport managements to look for a high degree of utilization of the fleet and its servicing installations. The exact relationship between fixed and variable costs will be different according to the technology employed, the density of traffic and the nature of the network. (The case of the private car presents some difficulty: the owner of a car is probably not influenced in the use he makes of it by the same considerations which an airline or shipping company, for instance, would entertain. Moreover, the true cost of using the track — the road — is difficult to calculate with certainty.)

   (i) Airline costs: *fixed* — depreciation, obsolescence, interest, insurance, engineering overheads (e.g. the engineering base), flying crew administration, and all ground costs;

variable — fuel and oil, direct engineering costs (e.g. overhauls), air crew expenses, landing fees, passenger meals, and attendance.

A distinction may be made also between costs associated with cruising performance and those associated with landing and take-off. This becomes important in distinguishing between the short-haul operation and the long-haul. In the case of short-haul operation, the ratio of time on the ground (i.e. non-revenue-earning time) to flying time is higher than in the long-haul case. Further, landing fees will be incurred more often and the aircraft will consume relatively more fuel (because of increased periods of full power at take-off) than a long-haul aircraft.

(ii) Shipping costs: *fixed* — depreciation, interest, protection and indemnity and insurance, annual survey and overhaul, all shore costs;

variable — deck and engine costs (water, salaries of non-hotel crew, voyage maintenance and fire-watching), hotel and catering costs (victualling, salaries of hotel crew, entertainment and furnishing, cleaning and maintenance), master's costs (fuel and oil, master's salaries, marine insurance), port costs and fees, loading and discharging.

Cruising employment reduces costs as compared with liner (scheduled) service. The hotel staff ratio to passengers can be lower, a less demanding schedule reduces fuel consumption, and port costs are generally lower, cruise ships being charged usually on a yacht basis.

(iii) Public service vehicle: *fixed* — depreciation, interest, overheads of workshops, all head office costs;

variable — fuel, oil and tyres, salaries and uniform clothing of crew, vehicle licences, insurances, ticketing, and vehicle cleaning.

A large part of the total costs of public service vehicle costs are variable or can be made so. Licences and insurance are obtainable for example for quite short periods.

Ground and Shore Costs

Administrative ground and shore costs will vary in pattern from organization to organization depending on the managerial practice of each one. It is, however, of the essence of international transportation that it links countries with different requirements, and these differences are most acutely incurred in the marketing area. For example, a British airline flying to the USA will be faced in that country with a level of marketing costs which would not 'normally' be considered appropriate to the share of the traffic obtained. The British airline establishing an office in New York is competing with the head offices of its American competitors. To win a footing in the American market, it may feel the need to open a public sales office on Fifth Avenue, to engage in widespread and continuous advertising and to incur other marketing costs such as reservations systems on a scale not readily to be seen as warranted by the traffic carried. *Per contra*, in Eastern Europe where facilities for winning traffic by the application of modern marketing methods are limited, unnaturally low ground costs may be incurred. These anomalies arise not from the nature of the network operated, but from the nature of the markets traded in.

Analysing Costs

If the fixed costs are taken to be relatively inescapable in the short run, including the administrative costs as well, the variable or direct operating costs per unit of output (i.e. revenue load) are good criteria by which to judge the economic performance of transport.

It must be noted that for aircraft at least a balance has to be attained between payload carried and fuel carried; if extra passengers are to be carried, fuel has to be sacrificed and, therefore, the range reduced. In the case of ships and land vehicles, comparable considerations apply theoretically, but are not of practical importance. But in airline operation the fuel/payload relationship is critical, because the weight of fuel is a significant fraction of the all-up weight.

The factors influencing the costs of operation are here discussed in airline terms, but, *mutatis mutandis*, the analysis applies to other forms of transport as well.

Costs are to a large extent under the control of management, in a way which is not true of revenue. Efficient operators will thus spend a good deal of time and trouble in minimizing the unit cost of payload, that is, the cost per available tonne kilometre. An example will make this analysis clear:

$$\text{Cost per ATK} = \frac{\text{operating cost per hour}}{\text{ATK per hour}}$$

Using British Airways Annual Report and Accounts for 1978/79, we find for that very large operator

Operating expenditure for year	£1,327·7 million
Revenue hours flown for year	469,000
ATK per hour for year	16,112
Cost per ATK	17·6p

Costs will be influenced by the degree of utilization of the fleet, by the nature of the routes flown, and, of course, by the ground costs incurred. For the year 1978/79 the costs of British Airways can be analysed as follows:

	£ million	% of total
Aircraft standing charges	75·2	6
Aircraft maintenance	181·6	14
Flying operations (1)	455·6	34
Passenger services	176·9	13
Station costs	184·5	14
Sales and publicity (2)	215·7	16
Administration	37·8	3
	1,327·3	100

(1) Fuel and oil accounted for £240 million.
(2) Commission to travel agents and others on traffic revenue is included at £102 million.

During the 1970s, the airlines and, indeed, other transport undertakings were faced with very large increases in the cost of fuel. Where total operating costs for airlines had increased by three and a half times, the costs of fuel had risen seven-fold.

Table 18
Index of Operating Costs of UK Airlines
1970 = 100

	1970	*1971*	*1972*	*1973*	*1974*	*1975*	*1976*	*1977*
Aircraft fuel	100	125	149	229	446	536	664	749
Total operating costs	100	116	134	163	208	248	307	367
Fuel costs as a percentage of total operating costs	11	11	12	15	23	23	23	21

Source: CAA Annual Statistics (CAP 424) 1978

Ground costs can contribute significantly to total costs. In addition to marketing costs referred to above, terminal costs (airport, port, station costs) will likewise be minimized by intensive utilization of the terminal facilities, and terminal costs will also depend on the quality of service the operator feels it necessary to provide. From these considerations the cost advantages that accrue to the charter (non-scheduled) operator can be seen. The charter operator's passengers may be content with less elaborate ground services, and the nature of charter operations may dispense with, for example, the kind of reservations systems which are essential to scheduled operation.

Similar figures of operating costs can be derived for other forms of transport. High utilization will keep daily or hourly costs down for coach operation, for railways, for ships and, indeed, for the private car, if the car owner would be interested in the economics of car ownership. The second observation one should make at this point is that, generally, large vehicles have lower operating costs than small ones because their payload is greater. But the use of large vehicles is justified only if there is sufficient density of traffic so that there need be no reduction in the frequency of operation which might inhibit demand. Typically, a transport undertaking is obliged to put a new large vehicle into operation when there is insufficient traffic at first; but it dare not reduce the frequency of operation lest such demand as there is be frightened off. Increases of supply in transport capacity tend to come in lumps, and the demand for the new supply tends to arise gradually. The introduction of the Boeing 747 aircraft illustrates the problems the undertaking faces with the introduction of additional capacity.

Apart from its attraction to the traveller, speed is generally desirable for its effect on utilization. The faster vehicle can perform more journeys in a given period than a slow one. Generally, particularly in the airline case, a smaller, faster vehicle is to be preferred to the larger, slower vehicle, and the productivity of the faster vehicle is greater than that of the slower.

Revenue and the Demand for Transport

High utilization (of vehicle, fleet, and crew) is desired in order that the unit costs of operation can be kept low. This will enable the transport undertaking to keep the price of the fare down and low fares will tend to attract more traffic. The improved level of traffic will result in lower operating costs because higher load factors are achieved, and further reductions in fares are possible. Thus a benevolent spiral is set up. In fact, this spiral does occur in practice, most notably in the increases in travel by air which followed the introduction successively of tourist fares and economy class fares.

The actual load factor achieved will be determined by the frequency of operation and by the traffic density on the route in question. A high traffic density will enable larger vehicles to be operated (i.e. vehicles with low operating costs) and will enable a high service frequency, thus improving the utilization of the fleet, and incidentally attracting yet more traffic.

Demand for transport is not homogeneous. From the tourism point of view, three major categories of demand may be identified as holiday travel, business travel, and common interest travel. It is very important for the holiday traveller, especially if the party travelling numbers several people, to seek out the cheapest method of transport. He will tend to travel by the cheapest route, subject only to markedly different journey times. He can be deterred from travelling to certain destinations by fares which are kept high, and encouraged to visit others if the fares are sufficiently low. Thus the transport operator can influence both the choice of destination of the holidaymaker and the time of day and season of the year in which he travels. The holiday traveller is thus very sensitive to the level of fares, and demand for holiday transport is highly elastic to price. A small reduction in price will generate a more than proportionate amount of traffic.

The business traveller requires transport in response to the nature and state of his business. This will decide the destination and the occasion of his travel to such an imperative extent that considerations of cost (the fare charged) will not enter into his decision within very wide limits. No formally feasible reductions in fare will tempt him to travel, unless his business interests demand it. Business travel is thus rather price-inelastic.

The group or market segment identified as common interest travel embraces the large category of other travellers, but is often largely composed of people visiting friends and relatives, or engaging in some educational activity. The nature of the demand created by the common interest traveller is between that of the business traveller and that of the holidaymaker. For example, his destination is fixed by the place of residence of his friends or relatives or by the location of the educational institution he proposes to attend. He may be able to give himself some latitude in the timing of his journey. He will generally be as sensitive to the level of fares as the holiday traveller.

These varying degrees of responsiveness to price and to price changes influence a transport operator in deciding his fares policy. Ideally, there might be three fare levels to attract these three segments of the market. However, in practice the three individual passengers are going to ride the same vehicle, and a means must be devised to make it difficult for the business traveller (capable of paying a rather high fare) from taking advantage of fares designed for holiday-makers. The method by which most transport undertakings achieve the goal of charging fares appropriate to each segment is by attaching various degrees of validity to the fare. Thus a cheaper fare may only be valid for travel on certain routes, or at certain times of the day or week or year, or for minimum stay periods between the start of the outward journey and the start of the return journey. Such a practice is intended to prevent a business traveller using holiday fares, and it might be that the holiday fare has its validity restricted to travel at certain specified times, e.g. only between 0001 hours and 0600 hours in the morning, which are judged unattractive to the business traveller. All transport operators with a differential fare structure try by means of varying validities of this kind to avoid 'dilution of the revenue'.

Railway systems embody such thinking in a series of cheap day return fares, etc., valid only for off-peak periods; between say 1000 hours and 1600 hours, a low fare may attract suburban and provincial housewives to shop in the city centre, but evidently the business traveller commuting outside these hours can be charged a higher fare. In Europe, the scheduled airlines have built up an intricate structure of differential fares, such as fares for travel at week-end day times, week-end night, mid-week day and mid-week night, off-season and high-season fares, fares with validity only between a specified pair of points and so on.

Some encouragement has been given to scheduled airlines to reduce their fares in this way to match identified segments of the market by the entry of charter operators on a large scale both on transatlantic routes and within Europe. Because they need not support the fixed costs of the scheduled operator (i.e. elaborate station costs, large reservations sytems, etc.), the charter operator's costs tend to be less than those of a scheduled operator, even if both are flying the same type of aircraft. A charter operator will have his passengers presented to him in a systematic fashion by the charterer (an affinity group or a tour operator) and the marketing burden is borne by the charterer. He will fly with very high revenue load factors. As a result, something like one-fifth of the total transatlantic traffic in 1970 flew in chartered aircraft, at fares half as expensive or even less than the cheapest scheduled fare.

In 1980, British Airways began to close down its first class services in Europe, and to substitute a club class instead. The effect of this is that by abolishing the first class section of seats with a generous leg-room between the seats (technically, the seat pitch), the airline can significantly increase its economy class capacity. First class traffic amounted to less than 5 per cent of the total, and its removal in European operations meant an additional 5 per cent in economy class capacity. The economy class aircraft will thus carry the new club class, which will be entitled to free drinks and other privileges, mostly in the same cabins as those paying the discounted economy class fares. It is hoped to attract the businessman on the short European routes by club class fares and the leisure or holiday traveller by a range of excursion and standby fares, to which a variety of special validities are attached and which are limited to a certain number of seats per day.

Economies of Scale

It is natural to ask whether for each mode of transport there is an optimum size and whether there are economies of scale to be attained. The anwer to such questions is not entirely clear. There is evidently a threshold level, below which costs are unduly high in relation to the capacity operated. An engineering workshop designed to service just three vehicles can probably handle six or twelve as well. But in general the larger does not mean the better. One of the temptations facing an expanding transport operator is to operate routes not themselves profitable in order to deny them to a competitor. Economies come primarily as a result of improved utilization, whether it be a coach operator or an airline, and it is the intensity of operation rather than the sheer size that produces economies.

The question in the airline case was examined by the Edwards Committee.[2] It suggests that big airlines incur higher unit costs than the airlines in the next size below them. Reasons suggested for this include that by definition the biggest airlines operate between big cities and thus face high rental and labour costs, that they face more competition, not least from airlines smaller than they are, that they offer system-wide standards of service, and that they have public service obligations.

Excess Capacity

It will be argued below that the setting of minimum prices for fares, which is a widespread practice in transport, encourages excess capacity to be operated. But prior to that discussion it must be noted that in the airline case excess capacity is encouraged by the need of a country to operate its own airline. Most international routes have the national carrier of each country operating on it. The room for more than one carrier from each country hardly exists on any routes. The reasons for most countries operating an airline stem from considerations of defence, of the need to earn foreign currency, and often of the prestige that would be lost if there were no national airline. In the following chapter the bilateral nature of international air transport is examined.

12 *Economic Regulation of Transport*

Historically most forms of transport have been regulated by governments, and today it is hardly possible to drive, sail, or fly without encountering the need for permissions or licences to do so. Some of this regulatory apparatus derives from safety considerations, which in turn may carry economic penalties, but in the context of the study of tourism, it will be primarily economic regulation which will be discussed, that is to say, regulation whose principal aim is to secure the economic well-being of transport systems in response to national economic policies. Thus the economic regulation of transport seeks to ensure, for example, that the public get adequate transport services at an acceptable cost to society.

Why Regulate Transport?

Tourism implies transport, but the reasons for which governments have regulated transport do not necessarily spring from concern with tourism. Indeed, since the concern of governments for tourism is fairly recent, it cannot be expected that many of the arguments for regulation are tourist arguments. But the existing regulatory practices, even if they were devised originally to deal with the problems of moving freight for example, still condition the framework within which tourist movement must take place. A number of reasons can be offered for regulation of transport:

1. The fares charged to the passenger do not cover the full cost to society of providing the transport in question. In the construction of roads or railways, land may have to be expropriated; users of roads pay a flat tax which is unrelated to their use of it; generally in such cases society grants an economic privilege (compulsory purchase of land, for example, at less than market price) and the *quid pro quo* exacted is a measure of control over the transport operator.
2. A special case of the foregoing is concern with noise, pollution, and congestion, where regulation is placed on the transport operator, to compensate society for being disturbed.
3. Control of monopoly characteristics in transport, and conversely control to avoid excessive competition, have been two arguments for regulation about which policy has oscillated like a pendulum. The early railways were accused of monopoly, the early bus and coach services of excessive competition, and both were felt to be operating too little in the public interest.
4. Transport has been seen as a public utility, which should offer its services to all on a non-discriminatory basis, e.g. all journeys should be priced at a uniform price per mile to all passengers.

5. The economic characteristics of transport operation (the need for year-round operation, the problem of peaking in demand, and so on) make regulation necessary for the benefit of the public, who would otherwise not be provided with a full service by profit-maximizing firms.
6. Transport conveys unearned economic benefits, e.g. enhances the price of land near to it, and its operations must be directed to ensure that society benefits from this enhancement. Conversely, it may convey economic penalties.
7. A variation of this theme is the promotion of transport technology. For example, it has often been urged that a country needs an air transport industry to provide a market for the aircraft manufacturing industry; if this is not done, the country will be in danger of losing the benefits and spin-off from this advanced technology.
8. In the more advanced countries, regulation is proposed to bring about inter-modal co-ordination, for example, between the private car and the urban bus, between inter-city rail services and the short-haul air services.
9. In international transportation, regulation may be justified to ensure flag discrimination, so that a given proportion of visitors to a country shall travel in that country's ships or aircraft. A new turn has more recently been given to this argument by the expansion of tourist movement.
10. In the late 1970s the need for fuel conservation has led to attempts to rationalize transport services in a fuel-efficient way.

The Requirements of Economic Regulation
Although it should not be necessary perhaps to say so, the first requirement for the successful operation of a system of economic regulation is a clear statement of policy — to answer the question 'with what objective are we regulating?'. Britain has not been too skilful in this, perhaps because the country has a pre-dilection for unwritten constitutions and a pragmatic approach to policy-making. Refuge has been taken in both such phrases as 'to further the interest of . . .' and also in enunciations of a non-binding character by the Minister of the day. US practice has been clearer though often contradictory. The Edwards Committee[2] in the UK has discussed this point, and the Civil Aviation Act 1971 does set out explicit policy objectives for civil aviation. Since 1971 civil aviation policy has been amplified by the publication of two guidance documents issued by the Government of the day.[3, 4]

The second requirement is that the regulatory body must have power to pre-scribe conditions of operation to meet the policy objectives, and to conform with international obligations. Prescribed conditions may apply to safety, schedules, periodic inspection, and so on.

The third requirement is the control of entry and exit to the transport industry in question. This characteristically takes the form of licensing to operate. The regulatory body will issue licences for domestic or internal operation and licences to operate internationally in discharge of treaty obligations with other states.

Fourthly, there must be some control of fares. This may take the form of requiring prior approval to changes in fares mutually agreed among the operators, or of imposing actual fares on the operators or limits between which operators may charge their fares.

Subsidies and taxes are also occasionally used to influence the development of transport. Fuel taxes, licence fees, and remissions of tax, have all contributed to the regulation and economic management of transport. Direct subsidies may be paid to keep a transport undertaking in being, and special payments for the carriage of mail, often referred to simply as mail pay, have often been used in Europe no less than in the USA to secure a socially desirable but economically unsound service in operation.

In the international field, the policy of the USA in regulating its own operators, airlines, and shipping lines, has had a far-reaching *de facto* effect on world-wide operations. Strictly, of course, the regulatory system of the United States cannot apply outside its national jurisdiction. But the North American market is so large and so remunerative to the operators who ply there, that they are obliged to conform to the specifications of the US systems. This is particularly true of air transport, it has been true of shipping, and the need of the European car manufacturer to conform to US standards of exhaust emission, if they wish to export to the USA, are merely recent examples of the importance of the USA.

As will be seen shortly in detail, the operation of a regulatory system usually entails first the control of entry to the transport industries in two ways, by restricting the number of enterprises by the issue of licences to operate, and by restricting the amount of capacity that may be offered by the operators; and secondly by prescribing the conditions of operation in respect of such matters as frequency of service, pick-up and set-down facilities, and above all by regulating the fares to be charged for the transport service. This is usually achieved by a quasi-judicial licensing authority, as in the USA and in the UK; or by a Ministry of Transport or similar body.

The Effects of Regulation

The fact of regulation produces some distorting effects in the natural market forces, no matter what particular method of regulation is applied. Where the motive behind the introduction of regulation has been to prevent excessive competition, the mechanism of regulation tends to favour the existing operator. If a new entrant is seeking a licence to operate, the existing operators possess several advantages; they may well have acquired over the years a specially skilled staff in matters of licensing, who have many years' experience of applying for licences (and opposing new entrants) before the licensing body. Moreover, if as is often the case the licensing body wishes, or is obliged by law, to establish 'a public need' for a new proposed service, the established operator has the advantage of his record going back maybe several years to prove that there is no such need. The applicant trying to enter the industry has to rely only on hypothetical argument or at best on local market research. This disadvantage need not of course be over-whelming, but it does favour the existing operator.

Where the determination of prices or price ranges is made by the licensing authority, changes in price and fare levels can only be made at infrequent intervals. When these changes are made in relatively large steps, they not only infuriate the public, they also imply that for the first part of a fare period the operator has got a price rather higher than he wants, so that his financial position may be better than in the second part, when his prices are rather lower than he wants. There is generally not much latitude extended by the licensing body to an undertaking to enable it to adjust the fare more sensitively to shifts in demand.

The prevention of excessive competition as a goal of a regulatory system stems from the fear that 'cut-throat competition' among operators will lead to the eventual disappearance of any transport service at all, due to strains of cutting prices. Thus the public will be ill-served. From the proposition that cut-throat competition will lead to no service, it is a short step for the licensing body to see that one of its roles should be to save the operators from their own predilection for competition. Unless at the same time capacity is restricted, and minimum fares determined, it appears that control of price, but not of capacity, leads to the encouragement of new entrants and the operation of excessive capacity. For if the licensing body sees minimum fares as a way of keeping operators financially sound in the public interest, then all operators will be inclined to offer as much capacity as they can, in the expectation that their total revenue will be helped by the high minimum fare, rather than by well-filled capacity.

The protection given by a licensing system to the existing operator tends to inhibit innovation. In the period between the two World Wars, when road service licensing was introduced in the UK, the railways and their bus companies opposed applications for licences on the grounds that new coach or bus services were supplying a public need the railways could fill. In the 1950s, in the case of air transport licensing, the argument against the private airline and its associated tour operator, and against the private airlines' bid for scheduled route licences, turned on questions as to whether the new applicant's service would materially divert traffic from the existing operators' services — at that time the State-owned air corporations. No doubt it would be very difficult to prove that innovation was often stifled by the regulatory system, but there can be little doubt that by maintaining existing services rather uncritically, regulation has tended to delay intermodal substitution. Why encourage a new road to be built, when the existing railway, albeit with difficulty, can supply the demand on the route, is an expression of the discouragement that could be meted out to those prepared to assault the existing operators.

By the same token, these rigidities generated by the regulatory system encourage the use of the private car, and substitution between different forms of public transport is further discouraged.

Finally, a regulatory system may be peculiarly susceptible to political pressure. The extent to which political pressure can be exerted on the licensing authority will depend on the status of that body. If it is quasi-judicial or responsible to an elected parliament (as the US Civil Aeronautics Board is responsible to Congress and not to the Executive), the licensing body will feel one kind of pressure; if the licensing body is merely advisory to a Minister in the Government, the pressure may be stronger and less easy to resist. In either case, the very existence of a regulatory system concentrates attention on the licence-granting procedures and, unless the statute creating the system has been very explicit, or unless the Minister has clearly enunciated his Government's policy, or unless the history of the system has been long enough to give rise to a corpus of decided precedents, the licensing body will remain vulnerable to political pressure.

The Regulation of the Railways

The early railways were created by Act of Parliament, and in return for privileges in such matters as land purchase the Railway Acts imposed, for example, dividend limitation or control of fares. The early disquiet of governments about the railways turned on protecting the public against the monopolistic tendencies alleged against the railway companies. However, by 1872 opinion had come to accept the good sense of co-operative agreements between companies and had recognized that competition between companies could not be enforced by legislation. Two World Wars in the twentieth century led to state control of the railways in Britain and to a lesser extent in the USA.

In Britain after the World War, the railways were taken into state control by nationalization. This did not in itself solve the problems of the railways. After several earlier attempts to put the railways' house in order, the Transport Act 1962 put the railways on a less-regulated stance by removing statutory control of fares (except for the London Transport Board) and relieving the railways of common carrier obligations. With the Transport Act 1968, the emphasis was placed on co-ordination of railway operation with other modes of transport, and the establishment of Passenger Transport Authorities and Executives made available to the railways methods whereby socially desirable services in and around the big cities could be subsidized by the local authorities.

In the twentieth century, the railways have been struggling to break free of the restriction imposed in the previous century in over 2,000 Railway Acts. New entry to the industry hardly arises, and the monopolistic power of the railways has quite disappeared. Apart from explicit obligations imposed by Act of Parliament, today the railways are not regulated in the sense the term is used in this chapter. The history of railway regulation is valuable for the light it throws on current practice in other modes of transport.

The Regulation of Passenger Transport by Road

In the UK the over-zealous competition among coach and bus operators in the inter-war years led to the introduction of a national system of licensing of their operations with the passing of the Road Traffic Act 1930. The principles of this Act remain virtually unchanged to this day, and they have been adopted with suitable modification into the regulation of civil air transport.

The Act provided for a number of Area Traffic Commissioners who in a quasi-judicial capacity heard applications for proposed services and, if satisfied of a public need for the proposed services, granted road service licences accordingly. Vehicle, drivers, and conductors require licences as well, but their grant was based on safely requirements and they were and are granted on a non-discriminatory basis to drivers and vehicles meeting the safety regulations. On the other hand, the issue of road service licences sought to control entry to the industry and to prescribe conditions of operation.

Public need for a proposed service has been the criterion used by the Traffic Commissioners in considering a licence application, and attention is paid to the adequacy of existing services; thus the proposed service has to satisfy also the policy of the Commissioners on the co-ordination of transport. In particular, the charging of lower fares on the proposed service than on existing services has explicitly been seen as not in itself amounting to sufficient reason for granting a road service licence. The basis for this policy lies in the fear of wasteful competition between operators.

The Transport Act 1968 brought about far-reaching changes in the organization of passenger transport by road, but these were largely concerned with commuter and other socially desirable services, rather than with services used by tourists.

As far as international coach traffic is concerned, a number of European countries restrict the use of foreign vehicles for tourist coach operation in their territories.

The use of the private car has hitherto been unregulated, even though resolutely taxed. The main problem in this area is to find means of charging the car owner with the true cost of his use of the road. Some progress has been reached by the adoption of a system of charging tolls for the use of expressways in the USA, and of bridges in the UK.

The Regulation of Shipping

There is only a small amount of passenger shipping still operating, with the notable exception of ferries. Further, some attempt has been made to rationalize the sailing schedules of ships operating in popular areas such as the Caribbean by mutual agreement between operators. But the notorious shipping conferences of the past scarcely exist today in passenger shipping.

One such conference however exists in the 'harmonization' conference of which the principal cross-channel ferries are members. The activities of this conference were referred to the Monopolies Commission in 1972 which reported that the conference did not operate in the public interest. At the same time the Commission recommended government supervision of fares, and this was entrusted to the Office of Fair Trading. The OFT succeeded in agreeing with operators an improved tariff designed to mitigate the high season peak. This unusual intervention by government seems to have been successful and the Minister concerned has suggested that even this degree of regulation could perhaps be discontinued in the near future.

The Regulation of Air Transport

After the First World War, in 1919, it was established that the air space above sovereign territory was within the jurisdiction of that sovereignty, and this doctrine was confirmed by the Chicago Convention of 1944. There exists no embracing freedom of the air comparable to that of the freedom of the seas. The Chicago Convention 1944 attempted to secure an agreed air policy among the Allied Nations, and the USA attempted to obtain a multilateral agreement to cover international air service operation. This was defeated by the other powers who feared American dominance of the air. Instead each country would conclude a series of bilateral agreements with other countries, which might include all or some of the freedoms of the air codified at Chicago. It is convenient to list these five freedoms as under, but it should be noted that they are privileges not rights:

1. The privilege of overflying a sovereign country without landing: as when a British non-stop flight to Rome overflies France.
2. The privilege of landing for technical reasons (to refuel for example).
3. The privilege of setting down passengers.
4. The privilege of picking up passengers: these two privileges are usually known as the commercial freedoms and cover most point to point traffic.
5. The privilege of setting down and picking up passengers in the territory of a third party: as when a British airline operating London-Beirut may be allowed to carry passengers boarding at Rome for disembarkation at Athens.

From this it will be seen that the philosophy of the Chicago Convention was that the scheduled traffic between two countries is to be reserved to their own airlines.

Within this framework, scheduled air services are the subject of bilateral treaties between countries. Two types of agreement may be distinguished. The first type may be called Bermuda-type, after the Anglo-American agreement concluded there following the Chicago Convention. This type of bilateral agreement is liberal in allowing the airlines concerned to put on unrestricted capacity, subject only to *ex post facto* review. Generally speaking the northern, prosperous countries concluded this type of agreement. The second type of bilateral agreement may be called predeterminist, because it will specify a fixed share of the capacity to be operated to each country. The southern and relatively under-developed countries prefer this type of agreement, because it reserves at least a half share of the traffic to the national airline. Bilateral agreements normally cover only scheduled operations. In 1977, the original Bermuda agreement was replaced by a new agreement, known as Bermuda 2, which moved the air services agreement between the USA and the UK nearer to the predeterminist model.

The determination of fares to be charged on international air services has, since World War II, been effected by the traffic conferences of the International Air Transport Association (IATA), subject to the approval of the governments concerned, and the air services agreements included a clause appropriately. IATA is the trade association of (principally) the world's scheduled airlines. It has derived its authority in the fare-making process by virtue of government approvals implicit in the air services agreements. By many commentators, it has been regarded as a producers' cartel which has kept fares unnecessarily high. While there is a need for some body to harmonize the world's air fares (to facilitate multi-carrier journeys for example), IATA has not been too successful in avoiding open rate situations, and it has experienced some pressure to amend its ways. In 1978, therefore, IATA changed its constitution so that an airline could voluntarily adhere to the fare-making process or could content itself with merely the other benefits of the trade association. Under pressure from the government, the American international carriers withdrew. It seems probable that at least an IATA-like mechanism will still be required in international air transport but that closer supervision by governments will be expected.

When agreement has been reached for air services between two countries the airlines who are to operate must be designated. In many countries, the appropriate minister will do this, but in the USA and the UK there is a quasi-judicial licensing procedure. Until 1978, in the USA, the Civil Aeronautics Board (CAB) licensed airlines to provide air services and conducted elaborate hearings in public. The US airline industry was closely regulated. But at the end of the 1970s, legislation was introduced to de-regulate air transport, and it was envisaged that the functions of the CAB would gradually disappear.

In the UK, a similar apparatus exists. The Civil Aviation Act 1971 created the Civil Aviation Authority to regulate and licence airlines and also to licence tour operators whose demand for capacity could deeply affect airlines. The negotiation of air services agreements is handled by the Department of Trade and the Foreign Office. The Civil Aviation Authority (CAA) in granting licences also approves or determines the fares to be charged or in the case of inclusive tours the price of the tour. Opinion in the UK moved in the direction of de-regulation and in the late 1970s, the CAA did not attempt a tight control on fares and prices within its jurisdiction. The CAA was far from inactive and undertook special investigations into such matters as the whole structure of European air fares.

The Significance of Regulation for Tourism

The well-being of tourism depends upon the adequacy of the available transport services, whether public or private. In the case of international tourism the air is of the greatest importance. Hence the way in which governments regulate air services is important to tourist authorities. Most tourist authorities will be seeking lower air fares from the airlines, but the regulations imposed upon the airlines may stem from considerations other than tourism policy.

The case for and against regulation is well set out in *Domestic Air Services,* a review of regulatory policy, published by the CAA.[5] In particular, the CAA points out that for reasons already mentioned, simple competition is not possible. 'The Authority believes that the air transport industry and the public are both likely to do better if regulatory intervention is kept to a necessary and unavoidable minimum . . . To an important extent regulatory intervention is needed in order to ensure those consumer benefits which competition might be expected to convey, if only it could be practised.'

The climate of deregulation and the modification of the IATA framework has made airlines readier to experiment. In 1980, British Airways announced its intention to cease first class services in Europe and announced new fares structures for the London-Paris route, offering some markedly cheaper fares than the ones replaced.

Air Transport and the EEC

Much of the work of the EEC in the transport field has been in freight rather than passenger markets, and has been concerned with the harmonization of procedures to facilitate the smooth passage of trainloads, of containers and so on across the road and rail systems of Europe. In air transport, which is of prime importance to tourism, much intra-European collaboration has been piloted by, for instance, the European Civil Aviation Conference (ECAC) or the Association of European Airlines (AEA).

In July 1979, however, the Commission published a Memorandum (*Contribution of the European Communities to the development of air transport service,* COM(79)311) suggesting a civil aviation policy for the EEC. The purpose of issuing this document was to encourage discussion. Among the subjects for discussion are the desirability of a wider range of low fares within the Community, the development of new scheduled services possibly operated by carriers new to the routes and cutting across the traditional five freedoms' regime, and a degree of liberalization in licensing and facilitation. The application of the competition rules of the Treaty of Rome to air transport is to be enforced, but, given the jealous nationalism of the European airlines, this seems to be the most difficult objective to attain.

The Commission has brought this Memorandum to public attention at a time when deregulation and its consequences, not merely in the USA, is engaging the notice of airlines and governments alike and when the energy situation will demand a rethinking of traditional attitudes to airline competition.[6]

Part V
Accommodation

Further Reading for Part V

Burkart, A. J. and Medlik, S. (editors): *The Management of Tourism*, Part V
Hotels and Catering Economic Development Committee: *Hotel Prospects to 1985*
Medlik, S.: *The Business of Hotels*
Medlik, S.: *Profile of the Hotel and Catering Industry*
Pickering, J. F., Greenwood, J.A., and Hunt, Diana: *The Small Firm in the Hotel and Catering Industry*

References to Part V

1 Organization for Economic Co-operation and Development: *Tourism Policy and International Tourism*
2 British National Travel Survey
3 Central Statistical Office: *National Income and Expenditure*, 1979 edition
4 Horwath & Horwath International and Laventhol & Horwath: *Worldwide Lodging Industry 1977*
5 Hotels and Catering Economic Development Committee: *Hotel Prospects to 1985*
6 Central Statistical Office: *Standard Industrial Classification*, Revised 1968
7 Central Statistical Office: *Standard Industrial Classification*, Revised 1980
8 *Development of Tourism Act, 1969*
9 Consultative Committee on Registration of Tourist Accommodation: *Report*, 1979

This Part of the book is based on

Medlik, S.: *The Business of Hotels*
and
Medlik, S.: *Profile of the Hotel and Catering Industry*

13   *The Market for Accommodation*

The demand for accommodation away from home is a function of travel and it is therefore not surprising that the main influence on the development of accommodation facilities has been developments in the mode of passenger transport. Until about the middle of the nineteenth century the bulk of journeys were undertaken for business and vocational reasons, by road, within the boundaries of individual countries. The volume of travel was relatively small, confined to a fraction of the population in any country. Inns and similar hostelries along the main highways and in the principal towns grew to become the hallmark of the accommodation market well into the nineteenth century, as most of those who did travel did so by coach.

Although the first hotels date to the eighteenth century, their growth on any scale occurred only in the following century when first the railway and later the steamship created sufficiently large markets to make the large hotel possible. For a hundred years or so, between about 1850—1950, the railway and the steamship dominated passenger transportation. A growing proportion of travellers went away from home for other than business reasons and holidays gradually came to represent an important reason for a journey, which particularly in the period before the First World War rarely took place by road. At the same time the new means of transport gave an impetus to travel between countries and between continents.

By the middle of the twentieth century, in most developed countries of the world (somewhat earlier in North America and a little later in a number of European countries), a whole cycle was completed and most traffic returned to the road, with the motor car increasingly providing the main means of passenger transportation. Almost concurrently the aircraft took over unmistakably, both from the railways and from shipping, as the principal means of long-distance passenger transport. On many routes, holiday traffic came to match and very often greatly exceed other traffic. A growing volume of travel away from home became international.

When, for example, less than a third of British holidaymakers stay in hotels when in Britain, it is not very meaningful to view tourist accommodation from the point of view of the hotel industry alone. In these circumstances, it is more appropriate to approach it from the point of view of the accommodation market as a starting point, and there are two groups of people engaged in this market. On the one hand there are the users, who range from the residents of the country to foreign visitors, and from holidaymakers to businessmen and common interest travellers: they represent the demand in the market. On the other hand there are the providers of accommodation facilities; they range from hoteliers to boarding-house landladies, from holiday camp operators to caravan site operators, from youth hostel organizations to farmers: these providers represent the supply in the market.

It will be readily apparent that some accommodation providers who serve the needs of tourists also operate their units for other types of user. Often the accommodation services used by tourists are to a greater or lesser extent determined by the needs of other users, who may represent the dominant market for the operator in a particular location. Thus a city hotel may cater primarily for businessmen, but also accommodate those on holiday. But from the early days of holidays away from home accommodation facilities, which are sufficiently distinct, have been also to a significant extent provided exclusively for the holiday tourist. The pension in Continental Europe and the boarding-house and guesthouse in Britain are prominent examples; the resort hotel designed for staying holidays is a common feature of the tourist accommodation market throughout the world. More recently, holiday camps in Britain, vacation motels in North America, and self-catering holiday units of some variety in a number of countries have become significant providers of tourist accommodation exclusively for that market.

Accommodation and passenger transport represent the two backbones of tourism. In this part of the book tourist accommodation is examined in three separate chapters devoted respectively to the market, the economics of operation, and to the industry.

Holiday Accommodation

Holiday accommodation may be conveniently classified into four main categories:

service accommodation, including hotels, pensions, guest and boarding houses;
self-catering accommodation, including camping, caravans, rented flats, and houses;
homes of friends and relatives, where no payment is made for the use of accommodation;
other accommodation, including, for example, boats, youth hostels, and similar.

In the 1970s in most developed countries, which included stays with friends and relatives in their holiday surveys, friends' and relatives' homes represented the largest single accommodation category used: for example, more than one-third used this type of accommodation in the United States and Canada, more than one-quarter in France and Great Britain. Various forms of self-catering accommodation were also prominent: for example, in the region of 20 per cent of holidays in Canada and 10 per cent in the United States were camping holidays, some 20 per cent used caravans and 15 per cent other rented accommodation on holidays in Great Britain. Service accommodation tended to account for less than one-third, and in many countries for considerably less than that.[1]

However, a somewhat different use of accommodation emerges from national travel surveys in respect of holidays abroad by residents of the countries, for which this information is separately identified. For example, in the late 1970s, some 60 per cent of British residents on holidays abroad stayed in hotels and other service accommodation, less than 20 per cent in self-catering and more than 20 per cent with friends and relatives.[2] In most European countries, where larger numbers go on holiday abroad by car, self-catering accommodation is more prominent on holidays abroad, but service accommodation is, nevertheless, more important than on domestic holidays.[1]

It appears that hotels and similar establishments are minority providers of holiday accommodation for people taking holidays within their own countries, when particularly rented accommodation and private homes account together for a significantly greater proportion of holidaymakers. However, for obvious reasons hotels figure prominently in holidays abroad and these reasons are reinforced by inclusive tours when they represent a large proportion of holidays abroad as they do for British residents.

British Holidays in Britain

The above pattern of holiday accommodation use emerges clearly from the examination of more detailed statistics of the *British National Travel Survey* in respect of British holidays over a period of time, which also reveal some significant long-term trends.

In the 1970s British residents took annually between 35—40 million holidays of four nights or more away from home in Britain, compared with some 30 million in the 1960s and some 25 million in the 1950s. The main long-term changes in accommodation used have been in the continued decline of unlicensed service accommodation, and in the proportion of holidays spent in friends's and relatives' homes, each of which accounted for a third of the total in the 1950s; the major growth occurred in self-catering accommodation, which doubled its share of the greatly increased market between the 1950s and 1970s. (*See* also Table 11 on page 87.)

Tables 19 and 20 show the pattern of use of holiday accommodation separately for main and additional holidays in the 1970s.

Table 19
Accommodation on Main Holidays in Britain 1970 and 1975—79

	1970 %	1975 %	1976 %	1977 %	1978 %	1979 %
Licensed hotel/motel	15	16	16	17	16	18
Unlicensed hotel, guest house, etc.	16	13	11	10	10	9
Holiday camp[a]	6	9	7	8	8	8
Caravan[b]	18	18	22	23	20	18
Rented accommodation	11	12	13	15	16	15
Camping	6	7	7	4	5	6
Friends'/relatives' home	24	22	20	20	22	20
Other	11	8	6	9	6	8
Total[c]	107	105	102	106	103	102

Table 20

Accommodation on Additional Holidays in Britain 1970 and 1975—79

	1970 %	1975 %	1976 %	1977 %	1978 %	1979 %
Licensed hotel/motel	15	14	15	17	15	17
Unlicensed hotel, guest house, etc.	11	9	10	6	6	9
Holiday camp*a*	2	4	3	2	4	3
Caravan*b*	14	17	17	22	19	15
Rented accommodation	6	6	8	8	10	11
Camping	5	6	5	4	4	4
Friends'/relatives' home	41	39	38	33	37	37
Other	10	8	7	8	9	7
Total*c*	104	103	103	100	104	103

a Includes both holiday camps with meals provided and self-catering holiday camps
b Includes both static and touring caravans
c Some used more than one type of accommodation
Source: British National Travel Survey

There are major differences in the type of accommodation used on main and additional holidays. Whilst friends' and relatives' home is the largest single category for both, it is particularly important for additional holidays. Holiday camps and self-catering accommodation account for a higher proportion of main and smaller proportion of additional holidays, which reflects the length and timing of additional holidays, as well as the availability of the accommodation.

British Holidays Abroad

In the 1960s British residents took some 5 million holidays abroad annually; by 1979 the number reached 10 million. Most of them have been main holidays. The use of different types of accommodation on these holidays in the late 1970s, recorded by the *British National Travel Survey*, is shown in Table 21, which includes all holidays abroad of one night or more.

Table 21
Accommodation of British Residents on Holidays Abroad 1975—79

	1975 %	1976 %	1977 %	1978 %	1979 %
Hotel/motel	60	60	59	58	58
Pension/boarding house	4	3	3	3	2
Holiday camp[a]	1	1	1	1	
Caravan[b]	3	2	1	2	17
Rented accommodation	5	5	7	8	
Camping	6	6	5	5	
Friends'/relatives' home	20	24	25	22	23
Other	9	8	6	8	8
Total[c]	108	109	107	107	108

[a] Includes both holiday camps with meals provided and self-catering holiday camps
[b] Includes both static and touring caravans
[c] Some used more than one type of accommodation

Source: British National Travel Survey

In contrast to British domestic holidays, the majority of British holiday-makers abroad stay in hotels. Their proportion grew from less than a half in the 1950s to some two-thirds in the early 1970s when self-catering begun to increase significantly also on holidays abroad. The use of pension accommodation, which accounted for a quarter of the total in the late 1950s, continued to decline throughout the 1960s and 1970s. These trends may be to a great extent explained by the growth and development of inclusive tours abroad and their extension to self-catering accommodation in the 1970s.

Overseas Visitors to Britain

The main source of data on overseas visitors to Britain, the *International Passenger Survey*, recorded 12.5 million visits and 155 million visitor nights spent in Britain in 1979. In spite of the importance of this traffic to the demand for accommodation generally, and even more so in particular locations and to particular types of establishment, the Survey has not included regularly the type of accommodation used by overseas visitors. A broad indication is available in respect of the year 1975, excluding visits by residents of the Irish Republic, and this is shown in Table 22, in which non-business demand is distinguished from business demand, in terms of bed-nights spent in the country.

Table 22
Accommodation of Overseas Visitors[a] to Britain 1975

	Non-business % bednights	Business % bednights	Total % bednights
'Hotel' sector[b]	26	59	29
Private homes (non-commercial)	54	20	50
Other	20	21	21
Total	100	100	100

a Excluding residents of the Irish Republic
b Including hotels, guest houses, bed and breakfast and all other kinds of commercial establishment where visitors pay (usually fixed rates) for their accommodation
c Including camping, caravans, boats, leased or rented houses, flats, villas, etc., as well as unknown accommodation used

Source: International Passenger Survey 1975 Accommodation Analyses

In interpreting the figures it has to be borne in mind that accommodation demand by non-business visitors accounts for some 90 per cent of the total nights and this is reflected in its influence on the distribution of total nights. The total demand is divided equally between 'commercial' and 'non-commercial' accommodation, but private homes are clearly the most important type of accommodation for non-business and the hotel sector for business visitors.

Expenditure on Accommodation

In recent years it has been consistently estimated that one-half of overseas expenditure in the United Kingdom was incurred on accommodation, eating and drinking out. The British Tourist Authority estimated the following breakdown for 1978, shown in Table 23.

Table 23
Overseas Visitor Expenditure in the UK by Sector 1978

	£ m	%
Accommodation	800	32
Eating and Drinking Out	460	18
Shopping	680	27
Internal Transport	250	10
Entertainment & Recreation	160	6
Miscellaneous	150	6
Total	2,500	100

Percentages do not add up to 100 because of rounding

Source: British Tourist Authority, Annual Report for the year ended 31 March 1979

It is more difficult to estimate domestic tourist expenditure on accommodation. The most comprehensive estimate of total domestic tourist expenditure in Britain is available from the *British Home Tourism Survey*, which records British residents' tourism for all purposes. For the year 1978, total British residents' tourist expenditure in Britain was estimated at £3,100 million. More than 20 per cent of this, some £700 million, was incurred by those staying with friends and relatives, leaving £2,400 million as expenditure by those using paid accommodation, albeit on all aspects of their trips. One-quarter of this, as representing accommodation expenditure, gives a figure of £600 million, one-third a figure of £800, equivalent to overseas visitors' expenditure on accommodation.

The combined total of overseas and domestic tourist expenditure on accommodation, in the region of £1,400—£1,600 million in 1978 was broadly equivalent to consumer expenditure on such items as books, newspapers, and magazines (£1,400 million), postal, telephone, and telegraph services (£1,500 million) or air and rail travel combined (£1,600 million); it was significantly greater than consumer expenditure on such items as betting and gaming (£1,000 million), fruit (£1,000 million) or footwear (£1,300 million).[3]

The Changing Demand and Its Implications

The main changes in the demand for tourist accommodation have come about from changes in tourist transportation and in the popularity of different forms of holiday, the two often being inextricably interconnected. The modern tourist is increasingly mobile and enjoys greater freedom and independence than his predecessor. The aircraft and the motor car enable him to be more adventurous, more flexible, and less formal; the type of holiday he chooses tends to be in growing contrast to his workaday life. As a result there are changes in the demand for accommodation in three main directions — in location, requirements, and in its volume and distribution in time.

The availability of the new forms of transport exercises a growing influence on the choice of holiday area. More remote countries and more remote regions of a country are increasingly accessible, often for the first time, and new holiday areas are growing up with a new demand for accommodation facilities. As popular tourist destinations become saturated or cease to attract, new hotels and holiday villages meet the accommodation demand in new locations, some entered by the tour operators, others by individual motorists. Thus the demand spreads from the Western to the Eastern, and from the Northern to the Southern Mediterranean and further East and South and to outlying villages in many countries.

As the touring holiday gains in popularity, the motor car greatly influences the length of stay in one location, creates a demand for one or two nights' accommodation, often without a previous reservation, and thereby disperses the demand geographically. It generates a demand for meals and refreshments along the route.

The type of hospitality required is changing, too, as the desire for informality is asserting itself — against having arrival and departure times regulated by set times for dinner in the evening and for breakfast in the morning, and in favour of eating at awkward times of day (and night), without changing before entering the dining-room.

The greater self-sufficiency of the tourist finds an expression in caravan and camping holidays and in self-catering accommodation ranging from chalets to flatlets, the former fostered further by the motor car, which is also conducive to week-ends and short holidays away from home, at all times of the year. Moreover, self-catering holidays are not a class phenomenon any more than are package tours; the changing pattern of holiday accommodation has been due as much to class and income changes as to other influences.

14 Economics of Operation

Hotels and other accommodation facilities display some characteristic features of economic significance, which distinguish them from most other establishments. These characteristics are largely derived from the nature of their activities and influence both the viability of individual operations and the structure of the accommodation industry. Some of them are examined in this chapter.

Nature of Investment

Investment in accommodation units is primarily an investment in land and buildings and the bulk of their capital is permanently sunk in fixed assets. Location in relation to transport and other amenities is often of crucial importance; therefore, hotels in particular frequently compete for sites in town centres and other situations where land values are high. Added to the high cost of the site is the cost of the building and of the interior facilities — equipment, furniture, and furnishings. In most investments in accommodation facilities, over 90 per cent of the capital is invested in fixed assets.

Fixed capital investment in accommodation units has a dual nature — on the one hand it is an investment in land and buildings, on the other an investment in interior assets. This distinction has been recognized in recent years in three particular ways. First, the land and buildings are sometimes owned by a developer, possibly as part of some larger project, and leased to an operator. Secondly, many companies have made use of sale and lease-back arrangements as a means of financing investment, thus reducing the capital requirements. Thirdly, interior assets may be leased by the operator of the accommodation unit rather than bought.

Variable assets form only a small part of the total and have a high rate of turnover. Stocks are usually low, and there is little or no work in progress. In spite of a recent increase in credit arrangements, cash trading still predominates; credit is normally extended to guests only for the length of their stay, and weekly settlement of accounts is customary where the length of stay is long.

The above characteristics of investment in accommodation imply that the ratio of capital to turnover is high and that most new projects have a long payback period; for hotels this is at least ten to twelve years. They generate demand for long-term finance for the land and the buildings, medium-term finance for three to seven years for interior assets, and short-term finance is required for operating and minor capital expenditure.

Much investment in hotels and other types of accommodation derives from personal savings (particularly in smaller businesses) and is often applied from the realization of other assets; some investment takes place from retained profits. Companies obtain investment finance by issues of shares. But increasingly investment in accommodation makes use of private and public external sources of funds.

Elements of Cost

Hotels, motels, and holiday camps generally offer three individual products and three main activites are therefore carried on in them: letting of bedroom accommodation, production and service of meals, service of drink; other amenities and services, ranging from entertainment to facilities for meetings and conferences, may be also available, and they may form a significant part of the total activity of a particular unit.

The provision of sleeping accommodation distinguishes an accommodation unit from other catering establishments. But it may or may not be the primary source of revenue, and the restaurant or bar activities may be the main sources; the relative proportions of each give the sales mix of a particular unit. The significance of the sales mix lies in the different gross profit margins derived from these activities, that is in the difference between the revenue and those costs directly incurred in earning that revenue. In broad terms, accommodation generates the highest gross profit margin, meals come next, and drink lowest. Thus a change in the sales mix for the same total turnover has an effect on the profit and ultimately on the rate of return on the capital invested. However, many costs are not easily identified with particular activities; this is the case with a significant proportion of costs of servicing the buildings, promotion and various operating costs, which are normally treated as costs of the whole hotel, motel or holiday camp.

The total costs may be divided into three main groups: materials, labour, and overheads. Materials include mainly food and drink; labour costs include not only wages and salaries, but also the costs of any additional emoluments received by employees from the employer, such as meals, and any other costs incurred by the employer for the benefit of his employees; overheads include the remaining operating costs, repairs and maintenance, depreciation of fixed assets, and interest on capital employed.

An indication of the relative importance of individual elements of revenue and costs in quality hotels is available from *Worldwide Lodging Industry*[4], which covers annually several hundred luxury and first class hotels of various sizes and locations. Data for thirteen regions and countries are shown in Tables 24 and 25.

Table 24 indicates that rooms represent the most important single hotel product in all regions and countries and account for from more than one-half to well over one-third of total revenue. Food represents between about one-third and one-quarter, and beverages less than one-quarter to less than one-tenth. Other sources range from about one-quarter to only a small fraction of the total.

The variations in operating conditions in different regions and countries are reflected in the cost structures of the hotels in Table 25. Materials (cost of sales) vary from less than 15 per cent to more than 20 per cent, labour (payroll) between less than 20 per cent to more than 40 per cent, other expenses from some 20 per cent to more than 40 per cent of sales. Profits range from less than 10 to more than 30 per cent of sales.

Table 24

Composition of Hotel Revenue
in Selected Regions and Countries 1976

	Rooms %	Food %	Beverages %	Other %	Total %
All hotels	48·4	28·0	12·8	10·8	100·0
Europe	46·5	26·4	14·8	12·3	100·0
Middle East	47·7	31·5	9·1	11·7	100·0
Asia	46·2	31·3	11·0	11·5	100·0
Far East	39·0	34·9	11·6	14·5	100·0
Australasia	37·4	32·0	22·7	7·9	100·0
Hawaii & Pacific Islands	53·7	29·5	9·4	7·4	100·0
Canada	44·8	30·4	19·5	5·3	100·0
USA	54·7	26·5	10·6	8·2	100·0
Mexico	49·9	24·1	19·1	6·9	100·0
Central America	47·5	27·9	12·7	11·9	100·0
South America	51·6	23·0	13·4	12·0	100·0
Caribbean	39·9	24·8	10·0	25·3	100·0
Africa	42·9	28·3	14·1	14·7	100·0

Source: Worldwide Lodging Industry 1977

Table 25

Composition of Hotel Costs as a Proportion of Sales
in Selected Regions and Countries 1976

	Total sales %	Cost of sales %	Payroll expenses %	Other %	Profit[a] %
All hotels	100·0	16·2	32·9	26·0	24·9
Europe	100·0	16·6	36·2	24·4	22·8
Middle East	100·0	16·8	25·6	21·1	36·5
Asia	100·0	17·9	23·3	24·9	33·9
Far East	100·0	21·4	23·9	21·8	32·9
Australasia	100·0	20·5	44·2	20·3	15·0
Hawaii & Pacific Islands	100·0	13·3	32·7	26·1	27·9
Canada	100·0	18·4	39·0	24·2	18·4
USA	100·0	14·1	36·3	24·6	25·0
Mexico	100·0	12·4	28·3	42·4	16·0
Central America	100·0	18·7	35·2	34·4	11·7
South America	100·0	16·0	31·9	27·1	25·0
Caribbean	100·0	14·5	37·3	39·1	9·1
Africa	100·0	18·2	19·4	28·8	33·6

[a] Including all income before rent, depreciation and other fixed charges

Source: Worldwide Lodging Industry 1977

Fixed and Variable Costs

A high proportion of the costs of accommodation operations are fixed or semi-fixed costs, which do not vary in proportion to the volume of business. In this category are management salaries and costs which can be attributed to the intensity of capital investment and to the high proportion of fixed capital employed: for example, rent, rates, insurance, depreciation, interest on capital; other costs, which must be appropriately described only as semi-fixed, depend only to some extent on the volume of business, but represent also a substantial charge against income: lighting, heating, communications, repairs and maintenance, and some labour costs. Materials vary directly with volume; the costs of food and drink sold are the main variable costs.

It is admittedly always difficult to classify sharply all costs into fixed and variable in practice; the time period has to be brought in and defined in any particular case. Only a broad generalization can be made about the industry as a whole. But it is clear that in broad terms it is appropriate to consider all costs of accommodation operation, except materials, as fixed, on a short-term basis of a few weeks or even months. Daily and weekly fluctuations in demand can, for example, only be partly met by the employment of casual labour. Even if an establishment closes down temporarily for the off-season months, certain costs continue; if this measure is not resorted to, most labour and overhead costs are incurred.

We have seen earlier that the main variable cost, the cost of sales, rarely represents more than 20 per cent of total sales, and that the payroll and other expenses make up most of the operating costs of hotels. Therefore, normally about one-half of total costs of normal working and sometimes considerably more must be incurred in order to make the facilities available at all, irrespective of the volume of business. The cost fixity of accommodation operations has important implications for their profitability.

Occupancy

The volume of business determines the degree of utilization of available facilities which is of major significance in firms with high fixed capital investment and high fixed operating costs. Hotels, motels, and holiday camps are therefore particularly conscious of the importance of a high degree of capacity utilization, which has a major bearing on profitability, and measures of utilization are prominent in any examination of operation.

Analogous to the transport operator's concept of load factor, there is the accommodation operator's concept of occupancy, in which the bed nights or room nights achieved are related to the bed or bedroom capacity of the establishment in percentage terms. The bed (or guest or sleeper) occupancy tends to be a more accurate measure of capacity utilization than room occupancy for any period; when, as often happens, double rooms are let as single, this has an effect on the revenue and is truly reflected in bed occupancy, but not in room occupancy. A more recent approach, which takes this aspect into account, as well as the relative utilization of higher — and lower — priced accommodation and sales at reduced rates, is the revenue occupancy rate — actual room sales are expressed as a percentage of the maximum attainable revenue from room sales.

Appendix T illustrates in summary form the results of the English hotels occupancy survey carried out annually by A. C. Nielsen Co Ltd on behalf of the

English Tourist Board, which highlights the importance of location as a determinant of hotel occupancy.

London hotels achieve highest occupancy levels and experience less seasonal fluctuation than hotels in other areas; they have higher than average length of stay and by far the highest proportion of arrivals from overseas. Hotels in urban areas achieve second highest occupancies after London, a relatively even monthly pattern of business, but a lower than average length of stay. Countryside hotels and particularly seaside hotels show the lowest occupancies and the highest degree of seasonality, relatively low proportion of arrivals from overseas, but seaside hotels have the highest average length of stay of all English hotels. Overall the available statistics demonstrate a substantial underutilization of English hotels outside London — no more than a half of the total available bed capacity is used each year.

Appendix U illustrates annual hotel occupancy rates in selected OECD countries, which reveal a similar pattern of low utilization. Few countries achieve an annual bed occupancy of more than a half of the capacity of their hotels and in some of them it is as low as a third. Only Japan approaches room occupancy of three-quarters of the available capacity.

Key operating statistics of quality hotels in selected regions and countries of the world are summarized in Appendix V, which draws on several hundred luxury and first class hotels included in the annual *Worldwide Lodging Industry*[4]. The combination of room occupancy and number of guests per room provides a two-fold approach to the measurement of capacity utilization.

The resort character of Hawaii & Pacific Islands and of the Caribbean is reflected in relatively high average number of guests per room, daily room rate, and length of stay in these areas. The data for Middle East reflect a shortage of capacity, which prevailed at the time. Overall the available evidence suggests a relatively high utilization and performance of the quality hotels, with a high proportion of international tourist business, which make up the sample covered by the survey.

Caution has to be exercised in interpreting the statistics included in the three Appendixes. None of them are based on a comprehensive census or on a representative sample of the hotels. However, they do provide a broad indication of the levels of utilization achieved in recent years by the hotels concerned.

Costs and Volume

The importance of high capacity utilization emerges very sharply from a close study of the relationship between costs of operation and volume of business in accommodation operation.

Total fixed costs are static irrespective of occupancy and total variable costs rise more or less proportionately with occupancy. When unit costs are considered, the variable unit cost remains static, but the fixed unit costs falls as occupancy increases. As each bed has to bear its share of operating costs, it follows that the income from each occupied bed must meet a higher proportion of fixed costs when occupancy decreases, because unoccupied beds are failing to cover theirs. In other words, the unit cost of operation — the bed/night (or room/night) cost — varies inversely with occupancy. Revenue from food, drink or other sales should not be allowed to obscure the profitability or otherwise of bed accommodation.

High fixed costs also provide an explanation of the substantial number of hotels with low occupancies remaining open in off-peak periods, and of their offering facilities at prices which suggest that they are below cost. There are several considerations involved but, other things being equal, on a short-term basis the entrepreneur will consider it worth his while to keep his establishment open as long as his revenue covers his variable costs and makes at least some contribution to his fixed costs; as long as the fixed costs incurred when the establishment is closed exceed the loss incurred by keeping open, it is financially advantageous to keep open. Whilst this simple rule would apply in any business when the question of temporary closure or price reduction arises, it is of vital importance in an industry in which so many units experience severe seasonal fluctuations in the demand for their services.

However, when demand is inelastic, differential pricing is a doubtful approach; price reductions do not result in a significant increase in demand and the suppliers simply share the same or similar volume of business at reduced prices. The loss of potential revenue is then equal in amount to the extent of price reductions and may represent that marginal proportion of revenue which would have accrued as profit.

The Influence of Size

The scale of hotels and other accommodation units has been traditionally expressed in terms of bed or bedroom capacity. The former is more satisfactory, as it takes account of the proportion of single and double bedrooms and, therefore, of the capacity to accommodate a given number of guests. Whichever of these methods is used, no regard is paid to the other activities of the hotel, which may account for a substantial proportion of revenue and of the numbers employed. An hotel with, say, fifty beds and substantial food and drink sales to non-residents, may, in fact, achieve a higher revenue and employ larger numbers than one with twice the bed capacity, which restricts its services to residents. Size measured in terms of turnover may, therefore, provide a better indication, although such information is rarely available.

An analysis of the size structure of British hotels in terms of bedrooms was made in the *Hotel Prospects* study[5] of the Hotels and Catering Economic Development Committee for 1974, which adopted a wide definition of the term 'hotel'. It included some 14,000 licensed and 20,000 unlicensed units with a total capacity approaching 500,000 bedrooms, over 300,000 of them in licensed and close on 200,000 in unlicensed hotels.

The analysis showed the small average size of the British hotel — over twenty bedrooms if licensed, and less than ten if unlicensed. Just over 1 per cent of all hotels had more than 100 bedrooms and less than 3 per cent between 50—100 bedrooms; the bulk of these were licensed hotels. By far the largest hotels were in London; London hotels accounted for less than 4 per cent of all British hotels, but for some 13·5 per cent of the total bedrooms. About one-half of all British hotels and of their bedroom capacity were in coastal areas; well over a third of all licensed hotels were in these areas and two-thirds of unlicensed hotels; coastal areas accounted for well over a third of licensed hotels' bedrooms and for two-thirds of the total unlicensed hotels' bedrooms in the country.

The present size structure of accommodation facilities in Britain, as in most developed countries, is a result of several sets of influences: the mode of entry into the industry over a long period of time, the nature of the operation, the size of the market, and the extent of competition; these have tended to favour the small unit. More recently, the growth of the market, the emergence of large firms, and the costs of building new units have been changing the position rapidly. Size is not a requirement of viable operation and technical economies of scale may not be substantial in accommodation operations, although such technical economies as do exist have not yet been fully exploited by hotels. However, the indications are that small hotels are not the most profitable ones.

After all that has been said about the factors, which tend to explain the present size structure of British hotels, the question arises as to the optimum scale of an hotel. In other words, is there an economically most efficient size, below and beyond which little advantage or even positive disadvantages exist? This is an extremely difficult question to answer simply in terms of a particular room or bed capacity, particularly as most hotels combine the letting of bedroom accommodation to a greater or lesser extent with the supply of food and drink, and sometime other sales. However, in broad terms, when the letting of bedrooms constitutes the main activity, there appears to be a critical size, which presents most problems in operation and which may be least viable. This is in the middle, probably between some 25 to 50 or 60 bedrooms or some 40 to 80 or 100 beds. Small units below this size can operate with family labour, have to rely only to a limited extent on outside staff, and can be supervised directly, without intervening levels. Larger units call for larger staffing and a supervisory structure, which is rarely financially viable until the unit reaches a larger size and reap certain other economies of scale. There would also appear to be significant economies for hotels with several hundred bedrooms, which tend to be the most profitable ones.

In this chapter the influence of size has been discussed in terms of an individual establishment. However, most increase in scale of accommodation operation has taken place through the increase in the size of the firm, which may control more than one establishment. This dimension is discussed in the next chapter in relation to the industry.

The Economic Problem

Hotels and other accommodation units differ from most other businesses in that they lack flexibility in supply. The output of their most important product — the bed/night — cannot be adjusted to variations in demand. A waste occurs when demand falls and there is an upper limit on the volume of business in a period of peak demand. As the capacity remains constant throughout the year while demand fluctuates, every night on which demand falls short of the maximum capable of being accommodated means idle capacity. Conversely, once all beds are occupied, the limit of earning capacity has been reached.

Moreover, the product is perishable — unoccupied beds on any night represent an irretrievable loss, as the product cannot be stored for future sale.

Thirdly, an accommodation unit has a fixed location and cannot follow the customer. The product has to be consumed at the place of production.

These characteristics are accentuated by the bulk of the capital in hotels, motels and holiday camps being invested in fixed assets, and by a high proportion of fixed costs in operation.

None of these characteristics are unique to the provision of accommodation, but are rarely, if ever, present in the same combination and in the same degree in other industries. In many other types of economic activity an adjustment of supply to demand is possible by a fuller utilization of plant, by overtime or shift working (especially in manufacturing) to meet an increase in demand. In others (for example, in retailing) surplus products may be stocked for future sale, and an increase in demand may be met by ordering additional supplies. In most commodity industries, products can be transported to different locations.

Some of the problems of providers of accommodation are significantly shared by the other main industry involved in tourism — by passenger transport. The total capacity of the carrier is also fixed at any one time, empty seats on a journey are also perishable and unused passenger seat miles cannot be recovered subsequently. Transportation also calls for a high intensity of investment and incurs high fixed costs. But even the transport operator has more elbow room — in the way he combines scheduled and non-scheduled services in his operations, in his ability to divert his fleet within limits to supply increased demand in a particular market, in abandoning old and in developing new routes.

Several key factors are, therefore, crucial in providing accommodation for the tourist and to the viability of an accommodation unit: the right location, correct capacity, and a high level of utilization.

15   *The Accommodation Industry*

The demand for accommodation away from home is met by a variety of facilities ranging from hotels, guest-houses, and boarding-houses to private homes, and from holiday camps and centres to caravan and camping sites. Many of them provide meals and refreshments and other services, but some confine themselves to the provision of accommodation alone. In many cases the facilities are available throughout the year, in some only for part of the year. Whatever the name given to the establishment, whatever the range of services, and irrespective of the time when they are available, when accommodation is provided for reward, this heterogeneous grouping of establishments forms a distinct economic activity which may be viewed as the accommodation industry.

The individual establishments have a common product and a common function and together they represent the supply in the accommodation market. However, their diversity presents particular problems of analysis, if a comprehensive view is adopted of the accommodation industry, as an individual type of unit may be meeting more than one type of demand under its roof; moreover the pattern of demand may be different and changing in time. On his way to his holiday destination the traveller may stay for a night at a motel which accommodates businessmen. The hotel on the coast, which accommodates families on holiday in the summer, may outside the holiday season attract residential conferences, which are also held in holiday camps and university residences. Charter flights, coach tours and other forms of group travel generate block bookings for one or more nights in hotels. Bed-and-breakfast lodging accommodation may be used by tourists, commercial travellers, and students. Static caravans provide permanent homes, second homes, and holiday accommodation for short periods and may share sites with mobile caravans and camping. This multiplicity of facilities and requirements is discussed in this chapter as the accommodation industry serving the accommodation market. Although not identical, two recent official definitions recognize the distinct nature of this activity in Britain.

The Scope of the Industry

The Standard Industrial Classification 1968[6], designed to provide a framework for the collection, presentation, and analysis of data about the performance of the economy, and to promote uniformity and comparability in official statistics of the United Kingdom, identified the supply of accommodation within the Miscellaneous Services group under the Minimum List Heading 884, Hotels and Other Residential Accommodation, as follows:

'Hotels, motels, holiday camps, guest houses, boarding houses, hostels and similar establishments providing furnished accommodation with food and

service for reward, but excluding licensed or residential clubs, which are included in Heading 887.'

The Standard Industrial Classification 1980[7], which is replacing the 1968 Classification, identifies the supply of accommodation within Division 6, Class 66, in two Groups:

Class Class Activity

66   665   6650   Hotel Trade

    1. Licensed Premises

       Hotels, motels, and guest houses providing overnight furnished accommodation with food and service which are licensed to serve alcoholic liquor.

    2. Unlicensed premises

       Hotels, motels, and guest houses providing overnight furnished accommodation with food and service but are not licensed to serve alcoholic liquor (including bed and breakfast places).

    667   6670   Other Tourist or Short-stay Accommodation

    1. Camping and caravan sites

       The provision of camping and caravan sites for rent. Rented caravan or chalet sites providing food supplies from a retail shop only are classified here but if the site includes a place providing prepared food it should be classified as a holiday camp.

    2. Holiday camps

       Provision of chalet or caravan accommodation having on the site a place providing prepared food.

    3. Other tourist or short-stay accommodation not elsewhere specified

       Holiday centres, conference centres, holiday houses, apartments, flats, and flatlets. Youth hostels, non-charitable holiday homes, private rest homes without medical care.

The Development of Tourism Act, 1969[8], defined *tourist* accommodation very broadly as 'hotels or other establishments at which sleeping accommodation is provided by way of trade or business.'

The United Kingdom Capacity

The facilities covered by the above definitions represent the stock of accommodation of a tourist destination, meeting various requirements of tourists at a particular time. When compared with the volume and pattern of demand, a shortfall or excess capacity of the industry emerges in total, in particular component sectors, and in particular locations.

Between 1970 and 1973 there was a massive increase in investment in the hotel industry in Britain. This followed the introduction of the temporary Hotel Development Incentives Scheme under the Development of Tourism Act 1969. The Scheme, which was administered by the national tourist boards for England, Scotland, and Wales, provided for grants and loans out of public funds for building and fixed equipment. It is estimated that prior to the introduction of the Scheme the number of rooms added to the hotel stock averaged some 2,000 annually. Between 1970—73 some 55,000 rooms were added.

The Government's main objective was to increase rapidly the capacity and quality of the hotel stock at a time when demand for accommodation was exceeding supply in a number of locations, in anticipation of a further major increase in overseas tourism to Britain. The objective was achieved beyond expectation. The Scheme stimulated a massive increase in capacity; more hotels were built in Britain in a few years than in the whole first seventy years of the century. Much obsolete stock was replaced and, in conjunction with the new bedroom capacity as well as separately, significant hotel modernization took place.

However, this was achieved with a much larger expenditure of public funds than was envisaged at the outset and it is arguable that much of the new investment would have occurred anyway, albeit at a slower rate. The non-discriminatory nature of the Scheme resulted in much indiscriminate expansion and no special stimulus was provided for particular types of development or particular locations. The overcapacity created as a result of the concentration of new investment in a small number of centres brought about major problems of viability for many operators, particularly as it was aggravated by the onset of recession.

A study by consultants of *Hotel Prospects to 1985*[5] for the Economic Development Committee for Hotels and Catering made an assessment of hotel capacity at the beginning of 1974.

For the purposes of the study an hotel was defined as 'an establishment of permanent nature, of four or more bedrooms, offering bed and breakfast on a short-term contract and providing certain minimum standards.' This definition covered a wide variety of establishments and included licensed and unlicensed hotels, motels, guest houses, and public houses offering overnight accommodation.

On the basis there was an estimated total of some 34,000 hotels with a total capacity approaching 500,000 rooms and 940,000 beds in the peak holiday season; some 14,000 of the hotels were licensed offering over 300,000 rooms and some 20,000 unlicensed offering close on 200,000 rooms.

At the time of the second edition of this book going to print, statutory registration of tourist accommodation had not been introduced in Britain and no statistics had been produced on the basis of the Standard Industrial Classification 1980. However, since 1974 only a limited new capacity was added to Britain's hotel stock, and much of this must have been offset by the loss of obsolete accommodation, particularly following the full implementation of legislation relating to fire precautions in hotels, as well as other influences. As cost pressures on hotels continued to increase, there was a further growth of self-catering accommodation, which increased its share of the market. In the absence of other evidence it is, therefore, unlikely that the capacity of the hotel industry in Britain changed significantly in total since 1974.

The total tourist accommodation is greatly enhanced by a substantial capacity available, for example, in holiday camps and centres, caravans, holiday houses and flats to rent, and temporary accommodation available in universities and other educational institutions during vacations. The peak capacity of tourist accommodation is likely to be two or three times as high as that identified by the EDC study and amount to between two and three million beds.

Location

Accommodation facilities provide an outstanding example of location in relation to the market. By their very nature, they are located where the demand is exercised, in person, by those requiring overnight accommodation. The resulting pattern is both a wide dispersal and areas of concentration of the accommodation industry.

We have seen innkeeping and hotel-keeping as the two parts of an evolutionary process, which followed the developments of the means of passenger transportation. Inns were situated along the roads and at destinations, serving transit and terminal traffic. The railways gave an impetus to terminal hotels at destinations. Motor transport created a new demand for transit accommodation. Although more limited, the influence of passenger shipping can also be discerned on the provision of accommodation in ports for incoming and outgoing traffic. Air transport has exercised a distinct influence on the location of accommodation facilities in the vicinity of air terminals and, more recently, near airports.

Although closely related to transport development, the influence of holidays may be regarded as a separate factor in the location of facilities. The movement to spas and resorts for treatment and recreation brought into existence distinct types of establishments and created concentrations of hotels, guest-houses, and similar facilities along the coasts and in inland resorts; it gave rise to holiday camps and centres and self-catering holiday facilities, including caravan and camping sites.

The third major influence on the location of accommodation facilities has been the location of industry and trade. Although again not separable from transport development, industrial and commercial activities have often created transit and terminal accommodation in and between population centres which could not have been supported by holiday visitors.

These complementary influences have produced the pattern of accommodation facilities in particular areas, including tourist destinations in various countries. However, the pattern has tended to be a historical one, and has rarely kept pace with the changing pattern of traffic.

A viable accommodation industry needs a close match between the demand for its facilities and their supply in individual locations. When examining the occupancy of British hotels in the previous chapter, we saw that no more than a half of their annual capacity is utilized. The extent of spare capacity emerges sharply when demand and supply are compared in particular types of location.

For example, in most years London hotels achieve annual room occupancies in the region of three-quarters and bed occupancies in the region of two-thirds of their capacity. By contrast room occupancies of seaside hotels are below a half and bed occupancies in the region of two-fifths of their capacity.

The relatively long time-lag between the conception of a large hotel and its operation accentuates the problem, as obsolete bed capacity in locations with static or declining demand is only gradually replaced by new capacity in areas of growth. Thus an established tourist industry in a developed destination is in a position to apply the marketing concept to its current operation only in part: the need to sell existing capacity represents the pressing task and usually dominates the marketing activity. The full realization of the marketing concept finds an expression only in the long-term. A new tourist destination offers full scope for a marketing concept to be applied to tourist accommodation as well as to the total tourist product: the discerned market needs can be translated into facilities developed to meet those needs.

Thus many old-established resorts devote most of their energies to promotion and so do their providers of accommodation. Some of them gradually cease to be resorts and become places of retirement and dormitory towns, when accessible to large centres of employment, as has been the case with Southend on the English coast; their hotels become flats, offices, hostels, and nursing homes or disappear entirely in re-development schemes. By contrast new recreation centres with new accommodation facilities emerge to cater for new traffic, as in Aviemore in Scotland; chains of motels and motor hotels come to spearhead the development programmes of leading hotels companies, as did Watney Lyon Motels and Trust Houses Forte Post Houses in many parts of Britain.

The Scale of Operation

Historically, the accommodation industry was made up of a large number of small independently-owned units. But as soon as the market became large enough, larger hotels appeared in cities and resorts. Between the wars the first large holiday camps with several thousand beds were a unique contribution to the provision of holiday accommodation, at the same time air travel began to demonstrate the potential for still larger hotels. The growth in size of individual units accelerated in recent years. The size structure of the industry is one of a growing number of larger establishments which account for a growing part of the bed capacity, with a much larger number of smaller establishments still providing the major part of the capacity of the industry at most destinations.

However, most of the increase in scale in individual countries and internationally has been taking place by the growth of the firm operating more than one establishment. Through the ownership of groups and chains of hotels, motels and holiday camps, the size of firms and concentration of ownership in the accommodation industry has come to resemble more closely that in other industries, with a small number of companies increasing their share of the market, the remainder being shared by a large number of smaller firms. Financial, marketing, and purchasing economies of scale continue to provide strong inducements for further concentration. There is a close parallel here with multiple retail trading, in which similar market considerations apply.

The main origins of the concentration have been essentially the same for a century or more. As the railways of the nineteenth century found it necessary to build hotels to safeguard their main business, the transportation of passengers, so do the airlines of the twentieth century. Some major hotel chains are subsidiaries of airlines and several followed in recent years the early example of Pan American Airways and Intercontinental Hotels, encouraged by the State Department. Others enter into agreements with hotel companies and form with them consortia to develop hotels, as has been the case with the European Hotels Corporation. The brewers who found the need to secure outlets for their beer and in the process created a massive tied-house system of public houses, have extended it to hotels, motels and motor hotels, which has at the same time allowed for a logical diversification into the accommodation market. Diversification and vertical and horizontal integration have also resulted in the entry into the accommodation market of property companies, oil companies, tour operators, and travel agents.

At the end of the 1970s there were some thirty hotel companies in Britain with more than 1,000 rooms, which operated a total of close on 1,000 hotels with more than 90,000 rooms. Their involvement in the industry is shown in Appendix W. More than a quarter of the total capacity of the thirty groups is operated by the largest, Trusthouse Forte, more than one-third by the two largest, Trusthouse Forte and Grand Metropolitan; the six largest, including Centre, Scottish & Newcastle, Ladbroke, and Crest, accounted for more than half of the room capacity of the thirty groups. Ten of the thirty groups were predominately or entirely hotel operators, seven were owned by brewery companies, four were hotel and catering companies, and nine were subsidiaries of diversified companies in various fields.

Holiday camps were dominated by the 'Big Four' — Butlin, Ladbroke, Pontin, and Warner — with a total of more than 60 camps and centres and some 150,000 beds in Britain, the bulk of the bed capacity in this sector, in addition to overseas interests.

Leading world hotel operators in the late 1970s are listed in Appendix X, which included thirty organizations with some 7,000 hotels and well over a million rooms; three of them are state-owned enterprises in Eastern Europe. The international scene is dominated by American corporations, representing eighteen of the thirty, of which several have a substantial involvement outside the United States. A number of the largest hotel organizations are controlled by others. Sheraton is a subsidiary of the International Telephone and Telegraph Company, Inter Continental Hotels is controlled by Pan American, Hilton International by Trans World Airlines, Western International by United

Airlines. Balkantourist, Cedok, and Intourist are tour operators and travel agents, as well as hotel operators. Trusthouse Forte and several others embrace substantial interests in catering outside hotels, leisure and entertainment, tour operation and travel agencies; hotels account for only a part of the business of Grand Metropolitan.

Franchises and Co-operatives

In the second half of the nineteenth century, breweries began to acquire retail outlets for their beer and thus began the tied-house system, which dominates alcoholic liquor distribution in England and Wales. The system preceded by almost a century a modern version of the tie, the franchise, under which the franchisor supplies the franchisee a developed advertised product with a brand image. In the United States franchising has been a major form of growth in several industries, including hotels: the largest hotel operator in the world, Holiday Inns, controls over 1,700 units. The arrangement limits the franchisor's capital investment, and enables entry into business with modest capital and reduced risk by a large number of prospective entrepreneurs. Although only in its beginnings in the provision of accommodation outside North America, the franchise in its various forms is a promising development for the small operator, who gains through it the advantage of size, whilst retaining a measure of independence.

In recent years major strides have been made with similar objectives by cooperative groups of hotels, which have been of two main types. Local groups of independent competing hotels have formed consortia, in which mutual trust and confidence have led to group marketing, purchasing, and other forms of cooperation at individul destinations, securing significant economies of scale for the participants. Torquay Leisure Hotels are an early example in Britain.

The other main form has been marketing consortia of independent non-competing hotels widely distributed geographically. Prestige Hotels, Interchange Hotels (now Best Western Hotels), and Inter Hotels have been outstanding examples in Britain, with varying degrees of integration and common strategy among members.

In considering the structure of tourist accommodation and in particular the growth of concentration, integration does not therefore stop at the level of the firm. As we can expect a further increase in size of establishments and firms in the supply of tourist accommodation, we may also see a growing impact of franchising and co-operative groups in the market.

Registration, Classification, and Grading

Tourist accommodation is an individual component of the total tourist product. As an individual product it is intangible, often bought in advance of its use, which the tourist cannot inspect and accept or reject at the time of purchase.

Accommodation, therefore, raises particular issues in its development and in its marketing, both as an individual product and as part of a package. It creates a need for reliable information for the tourist and the travel agent and it may require control and supervision.

From the point of view of a tourist board, which exercises a marketing and a development function, the need is for detailed knowledge of what accommodation exists and how it is changing, so that it can be related to market requirements. An individual operator needs to bring information about his accommodation to the tourist before he sets off on his journey and also when he reaches the destination. The tourist needs to know what accommodation is available in particular destinations, from which he can make an informed choice about where to stay.

In many countries there is a need to spread the tourist demand geographically, away from principal points of attraction and concentration to lesser-known destinations. There is invariably a need to spread the tourist demand more evenly throughout the year. Moreover, there is usually a need for intelligence networks so that the availability of accommodation is readily known to tourists and to travel agents.

These requirements are met by schemes of registration, classification, and grading of tourist accommodation and by central reservation systems. The aim of registration is to provide a complete list or register of tourist accommodation within a particular definition. Classification separates accommodation into different categories or classes on the basis of objective criteria, for example, by type of accommodation such as hotels, holiday camps, and caravan sites. Grading separates accommodation into different categories or grades on the basis of subjective judgments, or of a combination of these and objective judgments, such as standards of amenities and service.*

A registration scheme results in an inventory of accommodation which can be kept up to date. In order to be comprehensive, it normally has to have statutory legal authority and is administered by a government authority or a statutory body. Because of the wide range of accommodation used by tourists, it is desirable that a scheme of registration should cover all accommodation used by them.

A classification scheme seeks to present information about tourist accommodation in a form which would enable the user to find the information he requires easily and quickly and to be able to compare like with like. Therefore, apart from having the information classified by location, he needs to know the availability of accommodation which meets his requirements as to type, price, and other criteria.

A grading scheme provides qualitative judgments on the amenities and facil-

---

* Strictly speaking the separation of accommodation into categories is categorization; classification separates accommodation according to physical features, e.g. room with or without private bath. Grading can be by verifiable objective features of service, e.g. the availability of night porter and meals, as distinct from subjective features, such as cuisine and atmosphere, which call for a qualitative assessment.

ities of particular accommodation units in a form which enables the user to choose the quality of accommodation he requires. This may refer to the physical facilities, food and other services of the establishment, and grade them individually or collectively by numbers, letters, or symbols.

Schemes in operation in various countries differ. Some incorporate registration alone, some also classification, some also grading. Sometimes the registration and classification scheme is operated by an official body, which may also grade the establishments and subject them to inspection. However, often grading is undertaken by independent bodies, which also publish guides.

A statutory registration scheme for tourist accommodation was envisaged under Part III of the Development of Tourism Act 1969; Section 17 included enabling powers to bring a scheme into operation by an Order in Council without the need for further primary legislation, in the same way as Section 18, providing for statutory notification of prices, was brought into operation by an Order in the late 1970s.

In 1972 statutory registration was discussed by the statutory tourist boards with organizations representing the industry, consumer interests, and local authorities. As a result of these consultations, the tourist boards submitted to Government proposals for a compulsory registration scheme. The Government suggested that the tourist boards introduce a voluntary scheme, which would be reviewed after a few years. A scheme of voluntary registration was introduced in 1974 with the support of trade bodies and regional tourist organizations, and developed in subsequent years.

In 1978 the national tourist boards, having some doubt as to whether the original objectives could be fully achieved on a voluntary basis, decided to re-examine the matter and established a Consultative Committee on Registration of Tourist Accommodation with the following terms of reference:

1. To consider together the justification for a scheme of registration, either statutory or voluntary, in England, Scotland and Wales.
2. To consider together the objectives of a unified scheme of registering tourist accommodation in England, Scotland and Wales for the 1980s.
3. To consider the tourist boards' proposals for statutory registration of tourist accommodation and to suggest improvements, having evaluated the views of interested parties and examined the costs and benefits.
4. To consider the requirements of visitors to and within Britain in relation to tourist accommodation in the 1980s and beyond and, in particular, to establish the requirements for information about that accommodation and for assurance on its standards.

The Consultative Committee reported in August 1979, concluded that it was not timely to introduce a statutory system of registration of accommodation, recommended that the tourist boards develop further the voluntary registration system in operation on a consistent basis throughout Great Britain, and that the matter be reviewed again within three to five years time.[9]

Thus whilst a significant and increasing number of major tourist countries have some form of statutory registration of accommodation, and this is well-established and operating successfully within such areas of the United Kingdom as the Channel Islands, the Isle of Man, and Northern Ireland, Britain remains one of the few countries, where the stock of available tourist accommodation is known only within very broad limits and where marketing and consumer protection continues to rely on voluntary systems.

Part VI

Tours and Agencies

Further Reading for Part VI

Burkart, A. J. and Medlik, S. (editors): *The Management of Tourism: A Selection of Readings,*, Part VI
Economist Intelligence Unit: *The British Travel Industry*
(Edwards Committee): *British Air Transport in the Seventies* (Cmnd 4018)
Rosenberg, A.: *Air Travel within Europe*
Rosenberg, A.: *Air Travel across the North Atlantic*
World Tourism Organisation: *Distribution Channels*

References

1 *Travel Trade Directory 1979*
2 *British National Travel Survey*
3 Department of Trade and Industry: *Business Monitor M6 Overseas Travel and Tourism, Year 1971*
4 Economist Intelligence unit: *The British Travel Industry*
5 OECD: *Tourism in Member Countries 1970*
6 Wyatt, Sir Myles: *British Independent Aviation — Past and Future,* London, *Journal of Institute of Transport,* May 1963
7 A short summary history of air service licensing in the UK is to be found in *British Air Transport in the Seventies,* Appendix 2

16   *Retail Travel Agents*

By a coincidence, the two large world-wide travel agents, Thomas Cook & Son Ltd. and the American Express Company, may be said to have had their origins in the same year, 1841. Thomas Cook hired his first train in that year, and Henry Wells began his freight forwarding business in the USA at that same time. But neither was then a retail agent for, indeed, the modern complex distributive chain had not yet evolved in any trade. Thomas Cook began as what we should now call a tour operator, and Henry Wells as a shipper, specializing in bullion, and almost at once combining with similar interests to become the Wells of Wells Fargo, familiar to any folklorist of the West. The development pursued the line of financial facilitation at first, Thomas Cook inventing the hotel coupon in 1867, and extending into banking in 1879, the American Express inventing the traveller's cheque in 1891. Cook was in the retail business by the end of the century, and American Express by 1909 in London and in New York as late as 1915. The entry into retailing came about as a means to satisfy their tour clientele, with a large element of tour operation in their service. For example, American Express opened their Paris office as a service to the clients whose effects and baggage they had transported. Nearer home, Pickfords was in the haulage trade, Henry Lunn was an organizer of tours, Cox & Kings were primarily East India bankers. Not until after the First World War did the retail travel agent appear on the scene, to any significant extent.

There were other influences at work. So long as travel was a matter of rail and sea, the railway station and the shipping companies' offices sufficed as retail outlets for the travel product. When the coach operator and later the civil airline evolved, their tickets could not be sold by these existing outlets, because after all they were offering direct competition to the railway and the shipping line. This was particulary true of the embryonic airlines, as moreover airports were necessarily remote from town and city centres where the customers lived. The capital involved in airline operation precluded the emerging airlines investing adequately in the bricks and mortar of sales offices, and the use of independent travel agents was a natural solution to the problems of retail distribution. Since the Second World War, the world airlines' ticket sales have come to be the bread and butter of retail travel agents' business.

The retail travel agent must be carefully distinguished from the tour operator. These two functions are often performed by the same company; retailers undertake tour operation and tour operators have some retail outlets. But we may define a retail travel agent as one who acts on behalf of a principal, i.e. the original provider of tourist services, such as a hotel company, an airline, a tour operator, or a shipping company. The retail travel agent sells the principals' services and is rewarded by a commission on each sale. But he undertakes no liability for the principals' services. The tour operator, on the other hand, buys the individual elements in the travel product on his own account and combines them in such a way that he is selling a package of travel, the tour, to his clients. He is remunerated by a suitable mark-up on the prices he has paid the providers of the services, which make up the package. In practice many firms have both a retail and a tour operating function, but despite this common ownership, the functions are to be distinguished. The retail travel agent is just a retailer, while the tour operator is without doubt a manufacturer of a particular travel product. In this chapter, we are concerned with the retail travel agent; the discussion of the tour operator appears in Chapters 17 and 18.

The Role of the Retail Travel Agent

From the point of view of the tourist, the general public, the retail role is to provide a convenient location where the intending tourist may seek first of all information about his travel plans and, secondly, a location where he may purchase the various travel products he needs. The retail travel agent also normally provides ancillary travel services such as obtaining travellers' cheques, foreign currency, passports and visas, and holiday insurance. The tourist expects a reasonably expert retail travel agent's staff, and a reasonably convenient location.

From the manufacturer's, the principal's, point of view, the role of the travel agent is more complex. If we look for a moment at the function of a typical non-travel retailer, say a grocer, or a chemist, or a tobacconist, not only does the retailer provide a location where the product may be brought, but also, and crucially, the retailer buys from the manufacturer for his own retail stock. He normally has such a stock in his shop, for which he has contracted to pay the manufacturer. By so doing, he is sharing with the manufacturer the risk of production. Without this sharing of risk, much of modern mass production would be impossible. In the case of the retail travel agent, this sharing of risk does not exist, as it does not exist generally in service industries. The retail travel agent buys neither the seat nor the bed nor the tour from the principals until he himself has a customer standing at his counter. The retail travel agent carries no stock of the travel product, and the whole of the risk of production rests with the principal. From the point of view of the principal, therefore, the retail travel agent provides a location at which the public can obtain travel information, and at which access to the travel stock may be attained via the principals' reservations sytems; he relieves the principal of the need to open his own sales outlets over a wide area. The travel agent lacks a powerful incentive — nothing is more conducive to encouraging the retailer to promote sales than the overstocking of his shelves with the manufacturers' products. However, as we have seen, stocking the principals' travel products is not a function of the retail travel agent. In summary his functions can only be to provide information, to provide access to the principals' stocks via their reservations sytems, and to facilitate travel arrangements by providing various ancillary services.

Like most retailers, the travel agent enjoys typically an oligopolistic situation. His immediate competitors will be other retailers within his catchment area or hinterland. Each travel agent, like any other retailer, will draw on a limited hinterland. In the travel agents' case we may roughly pinpoint the size or area of the hinterland as being characteristic approximately that of the county town. A town like Reading or Guildford or Durham will provide generally the lowest stage in the hierarchy of travel agents' hinterlands. Towns that include, say, the offices of several building societies, may be expected to have five or six travel agents at most. Smaller towns for the most part will lack retail travel agents. We find, therefore, in the United Kingdom there were about 4,200 retail agents' offices in 1979. [1]

Travel agents are not the only retailers of travel products. Airlines and tour operators possess a number of retail outlets too. They will mostly be found in the next upper hinterland, at say the level of provincial capital, in cities such as Bristol, Leeds, and Manchester. Generally, in the United Kingdom the principals have not been anxious to put their capital into sales outlets (though they are more ready to do so, for example, in the USA); nevertheless, they have perceived a limited need to operate a small number of outlets. There are perhaps two reasons for this desire to own public booking offices in city centres. Airlines in particular have felt a need to secure a presence in large cities as a barrier to deter the entry of competition, and to be seen to be 'in the big league'. Bond Street, the Champs Elysée, and Fifth Avenue bear witness to this desire to bar the entry of competition. Secondly, in an industry where retail prices are maintained, the principals feel that malpractising by independent retailers can best be controlled by making their own product directly available to the public in limited quantities. This is felt to deter the unscrupulous retailer from overcharging or from attaching onerous conditions of sale. The principals' own offices serve additionally to give them a listening post to their market at the retail level. Shipping companies have done likewise, and increasingly the individual hotels of international hotel chains are acting as retailers for other establishments in the group. In the United Kingdom, there were in 1979 several hundred offices of airlines and shipping companies, [1] and to this must be added offices of hotel chains. All in all, there are approximately 6,000 retail outlets for travel in the United Kingdom, even though not all conduct the whole range of travel business. At the fringes of the market, in addition to principals' own outlets and travel agents described as such, there are other retailers who often perform that role — a newsagent selling tours for the local coach company is a familiar example.

The Appointment of Travel Agents

Throughout the travel industry a strong tendency is observable to retail price maintenance. Even in countries whose legislation specifically forbids price maintenance, as in the UK and the USA, exceptions are made in travel and in particular for transport. Part of the justification for this lies in the need to combine known and fixed fares into a multi-sector journey; an air ticket London-Beirut-Karachi, for instance, needs to have fixed fares for each sector before combination can be effected. As a result the transport carriers in particular have evolved a form of carrier licensing, which restricts the commission payable on ticket sales to travel agents who have been appointed to act on their behalf. We may identify the following reasons for this type of carrier licensing:

   (i) to enforce fixed prices and conditions of service;
  (ii) to prevent attempts at price-cutting (euphemistically called malpractising) by limiting the number of appointed agents within any one hinterland and thus restraining competition;
 (iii) to trade only with financially sound retail agents (there were some substantial failures in the 1950s and early 1960s);
 (iv) to restrict the number of locations with ticket stocks for security purposes (the airline ticket in particular is a cash-like document);
  (v) to restrict trade to active retail agents only, and thus reduce reservations and publicity costs;
 (vi) to restrict trade to professionally expert retail agents as a matter of consumer protection;
(vii) to protect a common fund or bonding scheme by restricting trade to members of the common fund or bonding scheme.

Thus only those agents who possess a principal's appointment or licence are eligible for commission on sales of the principal's ticket.

The mechanism by which this form of licensing works is to grant a licence for each approved location with appropriate conditions attached, and such licences are not transferable with the assets of the retailer's business. Licences are normally given in respect of a particular location and not to a firm. The most important of the carriers' licences is the IATA international airline appointment, which enables the retail agent to derive commission from ticket sales of the member airlines of IATA. In any one country, a committee of the IATA airlines scrutinizes applicants taking into account the factors listed above. Since something like 50 per cent of a travel agent's turnover often arises from airline ticket sales, the possession of an IATA licence is important.

In the case of British Rail, and in the case of internal air services, the transport operator grants his own licence. In the case of sea transport, the relevant conference of lines supervises the appointment of agents and may, for example, withdraw a licence from travel agents who sell the tickets of non-member lines. In the USA these arrangements have been strictly scrutinized by the Federal Maritime Commission and by the Justice Department, in the light of that country's anti-trust legislation.

Reference has been made above to the case where there exists a common fund to be protected, as in the case of the Association of British Travel Agents

(ABTA). The membership of this trade association includes both tour operators (who evolved in the main from retail travel agencies) and retail travel agents. During the 1960s, with the rapid expansion of inclusive tour holidays, there were a number of disturbing and widely publicized failures of certain tour operators, which left members of the public without the holidays for which they had paid, or worse strandard in a resort abroad and unable to return home. In apprehension of intervention by the government and the imposition of state licensing (as for example, in Belgium), ABTA introduced several measures to protect and safeguard the travelling public. First, in 1964 ABTA introduced a requirement for both tour operators and retail travel agents to submit their accounts annually to an independent qualified accountant; a copy of the accountant's report must be submitted within six months to the Council of ABTA. Secondly, in early 1965 ABTA established a common fund subscribed to by members, which was to be used to rescue the holiday arrangements of the public who were victims of the financial failure of a member. Thirdly, as a complement to the establishment of the common fund, in 1965 members of ABTA adopted arrangements whereby they would only sell the tours of fellow members, and tour operating members would only sell their tours through fellow retail members. In a short time, the majority of eligible non-members had joined the Association, and today membership of ABTA is essential to operate as a travel agent. By 1979 membership reached about 1950 firms, of whom some 1,600 were retail agents, 150 tour operators, and 200 both. (*See* Appendix Y.) This has placed some strain on ABTA, and a new constitution became necessary, whereby the specific interests of both retailers and tour operators are watched over by a Retail Agents' Council and a Tour Operators' Council. The new arrangements for safeguarding the public against the failure of a tour operator became known as 'Operation Stabilizer'. As an attempt by the travel trade to regulate itself, it has served the public well. When a very large tour operator, Clarksons, ceased to trade in the middle of August 1974, the implementation of the Stabilizer arrangements rescued a large number of British holidaymakers from the consequences of that failure. In 1972 ABTA had introduced a requirement for its tour operating members to be bonded and the CAA brought in a similar requirement as part of its supervision of tour operators. The events of the summer of 1974, however, prompted the government to establish an Air Travel Reserve Fund, financed by a levy on tour tickets, to supplement the bonding.

The Remuneration of the Retail Travel Agent

It is useful to consider how retailers generally are remunerated and at what level, and then to compare the general case with that of the retail travel agent. As a general rule, the higher the risk for the retailer in stocking the manufacturer's products, the higher is the retailer's mark-up, discount, or commission. Factors influencing the degree of risk include the rate of stock turnover, the capital employed (for machinery or large showrooms), and the perishability of the product. For example, newspapers, diaries, or fresh vegetables are all perishable goods, and retailers of them expect a relatively high mark-up. Car dealers may require elaborate showrooms and equipment, again expecting relatively high rewards. However, the retail travel agent neither holds stock nor, in general, does he need an elaborate showroom; he may indeed need a ground-floor shop in a prominent shopping centre, but in many cases even a first-floor office is not unsatisfactory. And he expects his principals to provide window displays, to provide or make available the reservations console in the case of computerized bookings, or to accept Freephone calls for making the reservations of his principals (in the USA similar facilities are provided). Thus only relatively modest capital is required in travel agency. The remuneration of travel agents is a small percentage of their turnover, usually about 10 per cent or more. (By turnover or throughput we mean the total amount of money received from customers; this amount less commission is remitted to the principals, becoming their revenue; the amount of commission earned thus becomes in the retail travel agent's hands his gross margin or revenue, from which he pays his outgoings.)

A travel agent is remunerated from the following sources:
  (i)   Commission on the sales he makes of his principals' services.
 (ii)   Commission earned from ancillary services, such as travel insurance, and charges made for such services as travellers' cheques.
(iii)   Income earned from the short-term investment of money received from his customers as deposits and pre-payments.
(iv)   Profit from the sale of his own tours if he operates as a tour operator.

The Retail Agent's Costs

60 per cent or even more of a retail agent's total costs are salaries and wages of staff. Not all, perhaps not even a majority, of a retail agent's staff will be highly trained. Much of the specialized work e.g. complex multi-sector ticketing can be taken over by the principals concerned. Further, the full impact of computerized reservations systems had not been seen by the end of the 1970s, and the implications of the microprocessor had not been fully evaluated. But there does not seem to be much scope for economies of scale in retail travel agency: if it takes twenty man-minutes to attend to one customer, it will take forty to attend to two. The other major cost facing the retail agent is the cost of the premises. Usually, the preferred location will be found on the periphery of main shopping centres.

There are two alternatives open to the ambitious travel agent. He can expand laterally and form a chain of agencies across, say, several counties. Economies of scale will be slight but the volume of turnover will be increased. The other alternative is to expand backwards into tour operation. Historically, tour operation has grown out of retailing and the number of applicants for air travel organizer's licences (ATOL: *see* p. 186) remains buoyant. But there also seems to be an increase in interest in forming chains of retail outlets, several existing chains expanding by acquiring new locations.

In a survey undertaken in 1966, the Economist Intelligence Unit[4] identified four chief types of retail travel agency, which are broadly still valid:

Business house agencies. Catering principally for the travel needs of commercial and industrial firms as clients. Such agencies will probably incur high staff and office costs since they will be located near their clients in city centres. They will, illogically, extend credit to their clients and their profits will accordingly be under some pressure.

City centre agents. Located in or very near to main shopping centres, they will need a high turnover to justify city centre costs. Branches of the big multiple agencies are typical of this type.

Country town agencies. The EIU found this type the most profitable with a mix of business and holiday traffic and comparatively low costs.

Suburban agencies: Selling principally tours with a markedly seasonal pattern of business.

The foregoing classification is still valid. The volume of traffic has of course increased enormously since 1966, and the increase in winter traffic as a result of the introduction of cheap winter tours has made the travel trade generally a profitable one. The suburban type of agency in particular has benefited considerably, becoming a year-round enterprise.

Principals (tour operators, airlines, etc) expect travel agents to promote actively within their hinterland by means of local advertising and so on. If they could deal exclusively, the argument goes, with creative or productive agents, they the principals would save a good deal of money. But the principal will always place a high value on the marginal sale and in any case it is doubtful whether a retail travel agent could for long incur the costs of effective local promotion.

In 1975, the Universal Federation of Travel Agent's Associations (UFTAA) and the International Air Transport Association (IATA) conducted a worldwide survey into the travel agency's costs. In detail of course these vary from country to country, but the global figures in the table below are fairly typical of the main generating countries' travel trade.

Table 26
Breakdown of Travel Agents' Costs

	% of total
Salaries	60
Rent, light, heating, etc.	7
Telephone, cables, stationery	7
Depreciation, financial expenses	3
Advertising and promotion	4
Travel and related expenses	3
Other expenses	16

Source: UFTAA

The Use of Travel Agents

Apart from business travel, the main market the travel agent currently attracts consists of holidaymakers. The use made by holidaymakers of a travel agent's services is determined by the type of holiday taken, as shown in Table 27.

Table 27

Use Made of Travel Agents by British Holidaymakers in 1970

Holidays in Great Britain

7% of all holidays were booked through a travel agent
25% of those using a bus or coach as means of transport used a travel agent
46% of those holidaying in the Channel Islands used a travel agent

Holidays abroad

68% of all holidays taken abroad were booked through a travel agent
84% of all holidays abroad by air were booked through a travel agent
90% of all package holidays (tours) abroad were booked through a travel agent

Source: British Tourist Authority, *British National Travel Survey 1970*[2]

Generally it may be inferred that the more unfamiliar the holiday or the greater its complexity, the greater the tendency to use a travel agent. But the influence of the package holiday (the inclusive tour) in directing traffic to retailers should be noted. The proportion of people going on holiday by coach in Britain and booking through an agent, though by no means necessarily a member of ABTA, is also to be noted. In the case of holidays taken abroad, the influence exerted by the inclusive tour by air is very clear.

Some Reflections on the Travel Agent

With the exception of British Rail, most carrier principals rely on retail travel agents to provide between two-thirds and three-quarters of the demand for their services; the proportion is even higher in the case of tour operators. There is thus a *prima facie* case for thinking that the distributive function in travel is well undertaken by the retail travel agent, at least in Britain. This is particularly true of journeys made abroad. Nevertheless, the principals are constantly seeking agents who may be termed creative or productive, and who are able to generate new business for the principals. This desire may be misplaced. As with all retailers, the volume of business generated by a travel agent depends on the size and wealth of his hinterland. Location, an important location, is the secret of success in retailing. Travel agents may be, therefore, most effective for the principals if they serve as efficient 'filling stations' or order takers of the travel product, rather than increasing their costs of retailing by local advertising and other promotional activity.

From the point of view of the consumer, the travel agent is seen in the same light. The buying decisions of consumers are founded increasingly on the advertising campaigns and on the elaborate brochures of tour operators and other principals. In this context the retail travel agent has an important informational role to perform in the distribution of those brochures. Where holiday packages are concerned, the expert guidance of the individual agent is largely irrelevant since the set of packages available cannot be modified to suit an individual tourist's taste.

Many large industrial and commercial companies own retail travel agencies within their group. Probably acquired in the first place to bring the volume of business travel within the firm's profit and loss account (10 per cent as commission on the travel expenditure of a large multi-national group is a significant saving), it seems quite probable that such companies will in time develop their dormant agencies, particularly where the parent company is engaged in the leisure/travel business. While entry to the trade is still relatively easy for the small would-be travel agent, it is to the big company that one must look for innovation.

The 1970s witnessed several noteworthy changes in the retailing of travel. One of these was the sale of Thos Cook & Son Ltd. In 1928, the ownership of this enterprise passed into the hands of the Compagnie Internationale des Wagon-Lits et du Tourisme. During the Second World War, control was assumed by the Custodian of Enemy Property, and after the war Cooks was one of a number of subsidiaries of the Transport Holding Company, a state-owned undertaking primarily designed to hold miscellaneous acquisitions resulting from the nationalization of the railways. In 1971, the government of the day offered Thos Cook & Son Ltd for sale and the enterprise was sold to a consortium of the Midland Bank, Trust Houses Forte and the Automobile Association. Expectations that this 'sleeping giant' might wake up under its new ownership were disappointed. The two minority shareholders disposed of their interest in 1979 to the Midland Bank which is now the sole owner. Thos Cook remains the largest multiple retailer of travel with worldwide interests.

The question may be asked whether there are enough retail agents. If one looks at the distributive trades for, say, consumer durables such as refrigerators, washing machines, and the like, whose price and frequency of purchase are not dissimilar to those of the travel product, one finds that they are sold through about three times the number of outlets as compared with the travel product. This suggests that the number of retail outlets for travel might be increased. The sale of travel through large hotel chains or through banks, as in Australia, seems a distinct possibility — both are involved in travel already. In Germany the mail order selling of tours has proved successful, probably in part because of the influence of the Deutsche Bundesbahn on retail agents whose selling of travel involving air carriage would not be welcome; however, the distribution of population between urban and rural areas is significantly different in Britain from that in Germany.

The selling of travel by mail order in Scandinavia and in Germany prompted imitators in the United Kingdom and opened up the whole question of tour operators selling directly to the public rather than through travel agents. In the late 1970s, Tjaereborg (Denmark) and Vingresor (Sweden) entered the direct selling race and soon established that mail order/direct selling was feasible in the UK. Vingresor is a subsidiary of SAS, the Scandinavian airline, and it must be noted that British Airways own a well-established direct selling tour operator (Martin Rook). There does not seem to be any magic formula for the success of direct selling, and all the normal criteria of price, etc. are as applicable in this form of tour operating as in any other.

Principals have always sold a proportion of their capacity directly to the public, but at the end of the 1970s there appeared to be a new interest in this method, signalled by the creation by Thomsons of a direct-selling subsidiary, Portland Holidays. The reason for this new interest by principals is a result of inflation and increased commissions paid to travel agencies. As the money price of a ticket has increased, and as a higher commission *rate* has become payable on the inflated price, the amount payable to agents by way of commissions has become large enough for it to be cheaper to sell directly to the public. This position may not prove to be permanent, as the costs incurred in direct selling rise in their turn. In 1980, Vingresor was taken over by Thomsons.

The arrangements for safeguarding the travelling public discussed above (pp. 170-1) have not entirely allayed disquiet about the operations of tour operators, and the extension of the provisions of the Restrictive Trade Practices Act 1956 to include services (hitherto it was only applied to goods) challenged ABTA's Operation Stabilizer and a number of consequential practices. ABTA reacted by quickly reaching agreement with the Office of Fair Trading by abandoning many of its rules and practices which were held to be objectionable, but decided to defend the core of Stabilizer, the exclusive dealing feature.

Finally, as often happens in rapidly growing industries, there is some public disquiet about the consumer's rights and expectations, which has been only partly mollified by the arrangement described above (pp. 170-1). As holidays abroad grow in number, so they will become a matter for increasing concern to governments — holidaymakers have votes. The licensing of retail travel agents together with compulsory bonding seems a not too remote prospect. It is to be hoped that any such scheme will not raise too many barriers to entry to the trade, and that there will be a place for the innovative new entrant. Innovation in travel retailing may be expected in the 1980s, as the tide of de-regulation advances and principals become free to vary commissions to travel agents.

17 *Tour Operation*

The idea of buying a package of travel, accommodation, and perhaps some ancillary services such as entertainment, became established in Western Europe in the 1960s. One of the familiar forms taken by the concept of packaging is the inclusive tour by air. For example, inclusive tour holidays from the UK to Western Europe by air, as reported by the International Passenger Survey,[3] grew from a figure of 630,000 in 1963 to 2,482,000 in 1971, nearly a four-fold increase. By 1970 tour operation had become a fully-fledged part of tourism. Its growth achieved something of a revolution in tourism. It succeeded in reducing the real price of travel abroad; in doing this, it brought holidays abroad to a segment of the market not reached by conventional methods of taking a holiday. By the construction of very cheap winter holidays, it succeeded in bringing about a significant extension of the season (a feat which has proved to be beyond the grasp of many other devices); in doing so, it has to a large extent turned the travel agency into a year-round business. Today, in most countries which are generators of tourism, tour operation is the dominating feature of the holiday market.

What is an Inclusive Tour?

Essentially an inclusive tour is a package of transport and accommodation and perhaps some other services, which is sold as a single holiday for a single all-inclusive price; that price is usually significantly lower than could be obtained by conventional methods of booking transport and accommodation separately from individual hotel and transport tariffs. There is commonly only one destination involved, and normally an inclusive tour does not embrace the idea of touring. Nor is an inclusive tour conducted by a courier, although it may be in some cases, as for example a motor coach tour. The popular term, package holiday, describes the nature of a tour more accurately than the technical term, inclusive tour.

The original demand for inclusive arrangements came from the convenience of buying a single travel product. The tour operator assembled a combination of accommodation and transport; he might have been able to secure reduced terms from hotels, not from the transportation companies, but by the time the costs of packaging and commission to retail agents had been allowed for, the price was not much less than could be attained by individual bookings. The development of these rudimentary tours played a part in turning Miami, for example, into a summer as well as a winter resort. A breakthrough came when airlines recognized that tour operation could fill the empty seats and introduced special fares for use exclusively by tour operators for combining into an inclusive tour.

Inclusive Tours by Charter (ITC)

Although at first the term charter implies a single purchaser, in the present case the air travel organizer, its use does not necessarily preclude the air travel organizer selling the chartered capacity on to the public. If he does so, he is offering to the public a genuine alternative to a scheduled service. If at the same time he offers accommodation and combines the transport and accommodation elements into a single package, he becomes an inclusive tour operator. (We shall see later that there are other ways of selling chartered capacity to the public.) The inclusive tour is sold to the public at a single price, so that the prices of the component elements cannot be identified by the public.

This form of package, chiefly for holiday purposes, has transformed tourism in Europe and the Mediterranean Basin. By chartering aircraft, and by making comparable long-term contracts for accommodation with the resort hotels, the tour operator is able to price a package holiday at a level lower than could be achieved by any form of scheduled service. Half Europe's air traffic now consists of charters, and the inclusive tour by charter offers the public such value that on many prime holiday routes between northern Europe and the Mediterranean conventional scheduled services have virtually been withdrawn.

The regulation of charter operations remains fairly informal. Initially, in the early 1970s, minimum prices were set for ITCs out of Britain, but this form of regulation was relaxed quite soon and at present the prices of ITCs are determined mostly by market forces.

Inclusive Tours on Scheduled Services (ITX)

The scheduled airlines, again especially in Europe, reacted to the growth of charter traffic by devising fares which were available only to travel agents for combination with accommodation into an inclusive tour, such tours using scheduled services being conveniently designated ITX. In operating scheduled services, load factors rarely exceeded 60% and the incremental cost of carrying passengers beyond existing loads would be small. ITX operations could thus usefully fill up seats which would otherwise be flown empty. This practice involves an element of discrimination, for the businessman paying the full fare may be sitting beside a holidaymaker (both enjoying identical service), but the latter has paid only a fraction of the full fare. European governments have been prepared to swallow this discrimination in the interests of high load factors, but the US Civil Aeronautics Board has been less willing. Today the pressure to lower fares in general may make devices like ITX unnecessary.

The Impact of Inclusive Tours

For holiday tourism by UK residents to western Europe, the impact of the inclusive tour can be seen from Table 28:

Table 28

Holiday Visits from the UK to Western Europe
by Mode of Transport 1963-78
(million)

Year	By sea	By air		Total
		Independent	*Inclusive tour*	
1963	1·51	0·61	0·63	2·75
1964	1·59	0·63	0·85	3·09
1965	1·64	0·57	1·09	3·30
1966	1·71	0·59	1·30	3·60
1967	1·64	0·56	1·36	3·56
1968	1·47	0·51	1·39	3·37
1969	1·66	0·57	1·58	3·81
1970	1·76	0·54	1·96	4·26
1971	1·88	0·49	2·85	5·22
1972	1·93	0·60	3·65	6·18
1973	1·84	0·77	3·98	6·58
1974	1·94	0·68	2·84	5·47
1975	2·43	0·64	3·13	6·21
1976	2·13	0·61	2·85	5·59
1977	1·98	0·67	2·73	5·38
1978	2·73	0·54	3·46	6·73

The years 1963—65 do not include travel to Scandinavia, and the Irish Republic is excluded throughout.

Source: International Passenger Survey

Almost all the growth in the fifteen years has been in the air inclusive tour sector.

Inclusive Tours to the United Kingdom

The International Passenger Survey also gives a picture of the situation of over-seas visitors to the UK who use inclusive tour arrangements.

Table 29
Visits by Overseas Visitors to the UK on Inclusive Tours 1968—78

Year		From		
	N. America	W. Europe	Rest of World	Total
1968	156	138	30	324
1969	234	152	34	420
1970	319	232	56	607
1971	370	317	81	768
1972	415	353	98	866
1973	402	422	107	931
1974	306	510	137	953
1975	273	677	147	1,097
1976	316	930	140	1,386
1977	316	1,201	160	1,677
1978	307	1,159	159	1,625

Excluding arrivals from the Irish Republic

Source: International Passenger Survey

During the ten years to 1977, inward inclusive tours have increased quite markedly although recessionary conditions affected the American market in 1974 and 1975. The very recent expansion in ITs from Western Europe should be noted. Even so, the proportion of inward traffic attributable to ITs is only 15% of the total. The relative unimportance of IT traffic inward compared with the UK originating traffic using ITs is due to several factors. The West European traffic is largely French, German and the nearer countries from which it is attractive to use a car or surface transport, whereas the principal destination for UK ITs is Spain. The UK hotel industry enjoys much year-round demand particularly in London and has little incentive to offer the very low contract prices, which have been obtainable in Spain and elsewhere in the Mediterranean. Thirdly, the relatively short flights from the European generating countries do not offer such dramatic reductions from charter operation as compared with the longer flights from the UK to Mediterranean destinations. Nevertheless, inward traffic including ITs was showing vigorous growth at the very end of the 1970s.

Other Types of Organized Travel

There are other types of organized travel which deserve attention. It is clear that the cheapness of chartered flying would make it attractive to anyone of an entrepreneurial cast of mind, if he were permitted simply to charter aircraft capacity and resell it to the public. It is equally clear that this would divert traffic from the

scheduled operators, and accordingly the airlines throug
and with the agreement, therefore, of governments dre
scheduled services from this diversion of traffic. The
that the chartering group must be of a certain size (to p
of neighbours), that it must have as a main object a s
securing cheap travel (e.g. the American Bar Association ha
lawyers as its main aim), and that the members of the group must
members for a significant length of time before boarding the aircraft. Su
charters are known as affinity group charters, and other forms of transport
besides airlines offer similar services for affinity groups.

However, in the early 1970s, abuse of the affinity group charter became widespread particularly across the North Atlantic; clubs were invented with spurious
common interests, membership documents were backdated, and in 1973 largely
at the initiative of the British authorities a new form of organized travel was
introduced, the advance booking charter (ABC). This enabled the travel
organiser to sell tickets for the chartered aircraft to the public without an affinity
requirement, provided that the seats were sold at a specified time in advance of
the departure date. Advance booking charters (and the travel group charters,
TGC, in the USA) have not perhaps fulfilled the hopes held for them by the Civil
Aviation Authority. Other European countries have steadfastly refused to admit
them, and even across the North Atlantic their use is diminishing before the wave
of other discounted fares and services such as Laker's Skytrain. In the USA, the
Civil Aeronautics Board has eliminated ABCs, TGCs, ITCs, and some other
forms in favour of a new concept the 'Public Charter'. No advance purchase is
required, no minimum stay, no restriction on discount pricing, no minimum
group size, and the charterer may not cancel later than ten days prior to
departure.

Cruising

Cruising is a form of organised travel which remains popular with a relatively
wealthy tourist, and it evidently includes both transport and accommodation.
With the decline of passenger liner services in the 1960s, the major shipping companies sought to use their surplus, and mostly unsuitable, tonnage in the cruising
mode, especially during the winter months. The Caribbean area became the principal cruising area, drawing upon the North American markets, and the number
of cruise ships operating at any one time occasionally threatened the very way of
life of the smaller islands as their population was temporarily swamped by the
passengers from four or five ships arriving simultaneously. A rather smaller
cruising area formed in the Mediterranean, and cruising in the Pacific from
Australia and off the western coast of the USA show that this form of holiday
tourism continues, although it can only provide for a minority market.

That there is still a future for this activity is shown by the fact that a small
number of new purpose-built vessels have been launched and successfully operated by companies such as Cunard with a long tradition of cruising. Much cruising is currently associated with air travel to and from the ship, and although there

ve been a number of world cruises, many of the berths have been sold on a
sector basis, with passengers joining and leaving the ship for only part of the
whole. Perhaps the most remarkable sign of the continuing appeal of deep-sea
cruising was the purchase by a Norwegian operator at the end of the 1970s of the
S.S. France. This elegant ship had been withdrawn from service after industrial
action by its crew and laid up. The new owners however refitted the ship to make
it capable of carrying nearly twice as many passengers as the original design
allowed for, and with reduced service on board, the *France* may provide a new
experience in cruising under its new name *S.S. Norway*.

Seasonality

The development of inclusive tours in the winter months has done much to even
out the marked seasonality of demand which originally faced the operator. For
him and for the retail travel agent, this has meant a considerable mitigation of the
problem of his winter cash flow. No other device has been so successful in tack-
ling the problem of seasonality as the reduction in price which accompanied the
early winter ITs in 1971. This was perhaps the first occasion when aggressive
pricing was applied to the holiday market in recent years.

Coach Tours

The coach tour probably represents for many people the quintessential idea of
touring, and it is pertinent to ask questions about its development. As has been
noted elsewhere, the market for holidays using the coach as means of transport
amounts to about 10 per cent of the total home holiday market and tends to be an
elderly female and lower income market. But this may not be inherent a characteristic and many operators perceive a future for the coach tour both at home and
for holidays abroad.

Three factors seem to be operating at the end of the 1970s in favour of the
coach tour. First, there is a climate of opinion in regard to deregulation of transport generally and it seems likely that a much more liberal licensing policy will be
adopted in Britain in favour of the touring coach at least if not extending to stage
operations. Secondly, there may be a general tendency to move towards fuel-
efficient forms of transport and the large modern coach is certainly the most
fuel-efficient form of public transport. Thirdly, the coach operators have felt for
some time that the shortage of suitable hotel accommodation has imposed a real
constraint on the development of coach touring: the additions to the hotel stock
in the 1970s may have the effect of easing the alleged shortage felt by the coach
operator.

While these factors also apply to overseas coach tours as well, the overseas
tour needs to compete with the inclusive tour by air on price as well. But it seems
likely that the motivation for the long continental tour is different from that for
the beach holiday, and a place must still be found for the coach, although like the
sea cruise it will attract a minority market.

The inclusive tour is not a new invention, but its post-war development by the British has come to be regarded as so dramatic as to constitute a kind of novelty. This development has been almost exclusively allied to air transport. It is now meaningful to write of an inclusive tour industry and, as in the discussion of tour operation in the previous chapter, a number of threads may be identified as making up the fabric of the industry and its market today.

One factor which has probably contributed to the growth of tour operation has been the rigid arrangements made by the airlines (and to some extent, by surface carriers) for the remuneration of the retail travel agents. Since the Second World War, the commission paid to travel agents who sell tickets on the IATA arlines' services has remained virtually unchanged. The effect of this has indeed been that the total remuneration of the retail agent has grown in line with the growth of air services. But another effect has been that the entrepreneurially minded travel agent has sought to improve his profitability and total revenue by becoming a tour operator, and nearly all today's tour operators have their origins in retail travel agencies. It may therefore be argued that if the scheduled carriers complain of competition from tour operators, they have themselves largely to blame.

The significance of the pioneering development of air inclusive tours by British operators is greater than merely national. The United Kingdom is one of the leading generators of tourism, especially to Southern European destinations. In 1970, tourist arrivals at frontiers in Spain from the United Kingdom amounted to more than 12 per cent of arrivals from all the OECD European countries, more than from any other country, except France and Portugal, which share a frontier with Spain. In the case of Italy, UK arrivals amounted to 7½ per cent of the arrivals from OECD European countries, again more than from any other country, if the four countries with common frontiers are excluded. For Greece, the comparable percentage is nearly 20 per cent and the UK led the field as the prime European market for Greek tourism. In all, in 1970 5·75 million holidays abroad were taken by residents of the UK[2] and the number increased to 10·25 million by 1979.

Historical Development

In the years immediately following the Second World War, the operation of scheduled services by air was reserved to three State-owned corporations: BOAC which was the successor, in 1940, to Imperial Airways, for long-haul services; BEA for European services; and the now defunct British South American Airways. Airlines in the private sector could only operate charter services, but the ready supply of war-surplus aircraft capable of performing civil tasks ensured that a large number of such operators came into existence. According to Sir

Myles Wyatt,[6] in 1946-7, there were no less than sixty-nine such private airlines. The Berlin airlift in 1948—9 obliged the British Government to press into service every available aircraft from the privately owned fleets. This unexpected situation placed the private airlines in a financial position of some strength earlier than could have been expected, and convinced the British Government of the value of the privately owned sector as a strategic reserve of aircraft. At about the same time, a committee under Lord Douglas of Kirtleside (later chairman of BEA) recommended that the private airlines should be allowed to operate services complementary to those of the State corporations, including the operation of trooping services and charters for inclusive tours. Accordingly under these arrangements the first air inclusive tour service was flown on behalf of Horizon Holidays to Calvi in Corsica in 1950.

With the change of government in 1951, a more liberal policy was devised for the private airlines, the Air Transport Advisory Committee was transformed from being a consumer protection body into a body to advise the government on which services could be operated without material diversion of traffic from the State corporations. Initially under new arrangements, trooping contracts made up the bulk of the private airlines' business, but inclusive tour charters nevertheless made up a fair proportion of their business too.

The use of the private airlines by tour operators in constructing charter inclusive tours enabled the tour itself to be priced at a figure significantly lower than could be attained by performing the same journey on one of the scheduled services. Not only were the tour operators able to make the economies inherent in the high load factors achievable from charter operations, but also the aircraft used for the purpose were generally obsolescent with a high proportion of their capital cost already repaid. This process was hastened by the re-equipment of the scheduled services with turboprop aircraft (Viscounts and Britannias), which resulted in the availability of technically satisfactory but somewhat outdated aircraft with piston engines. These substantially depreciated aircraft were used by the tour operators in offering tours at a significantly cheap price. A market was attracted by a product with a very low price, but with slower small aircraft than those of the scheduled operators.

The regulatory situation was radically altered in 1960 by the Civil Aviation (Licensing) Act.[7] This Act established the Air Transport Licensing Board, a quasi-judicial body, and to this Board all airlines (except for foreign ones) in the United Kingdom were to apply for an air services licence to operate. Thus the special status of the State-owned airlines, BOAC and BEA, was formally ended, and the private airlines were quite free to apply for licences on any route. The Board had powers to attach conditions to a licence and most frequently applied a condition known as Standard Provision 1, which obliged the tour operator to charge a minimum price for the inclusive tour. The scheduled airlines, particularly the European carriers led by BEA, replied to the steady growth of charter operations by the extensive use of ITX fares (*see* Chapter 17) and by the introduction of a range of reduced fares available to the public for travel at off-peak and off-season times.

From 1964 onwards, the ATLB began to adopt a more liberal attitude in granting licences for inclusive tour charters. In practice, though not without recourse to use of the appeal procedures, the Board was prepared to grant licences for almost any capacity applied for, still attaching the condition of minimum prices. At the same time, the new generation of turboject aircraft became available to tour operators, with technical characteristics as good as any operated in scheduled service, but requiring the same degree of utilization as could be obtained from that type of service. The gradual dismemberment of the colonial territories of the United Kingdom brought about marked reductions in the number of trooping contracts available for the private airlines and new types of business were sought.

It is convenient to identify the several strands which have contributed to the dramatic emergence of the tour operating industry since 1964:

1. Liberal licensing of capacity for inclusive tour charters; this amounted to identifying this type of employment as the 'natural' role of the private airlines.

2. The appearance of the smaller short-haul jet aircraft (such as BAC One-Eleven, Boeing 737); these aircraft placed the charter flight on equal footing with the scheduled airline, and required utilization of the same order. But the price of the new aircraft could only be met by the very largest operators.

3. Hence those tour operators who could obtain very substantial financial backing began to dominate the industry.

4. Devaluation in 1967 of the £ sterling had two effects: firstly the minimum price condition was breached — since international fares are quoted in dollars, the minimum applicable fare was automatically raised by some 14 per cent, higher than the operators required, and accordingly the supervising branch of the Government, the Board of Trade, permitted certain tours to destinations outside Europe to be priced lower than would normally be implied under Provision 1.[6] Secondly, the stringency in the economic affairs of the United Kingdom and the imposition of a limit of £50 per person in foreign currency for travel abroad for private purposes, both measures being associated with the devaluation, led tour operators to price down to the £50 at all costs (helped by the simultaneous devaluation of the peseta). This conscious attempt to reduce prices of holidays overseas brought an increase in holidaymakers going abroad and clearly demonstrated that the market for inclusive tour holidays in Europe was to be won by highly rivalrous pricing policies.

When all these factors operated together, they conspired to determine the nature and characteristics of the United Kingdom tour operating industry.

The Tour Operating Industry in the United Kingdom

The air inclusive tour is not the only holiday package that the intending holidaymaker can buy. The motor coach operators offer similar packages. But by 1970 only 3 per cent of holidays in Great Britain and 7 per cent of holidays abroad were packages involving the motor coach. Further, other kinds of travel organizers notably advance booking charter operators came to dominate the holiday scene.

The typical tour operator comes from a background in retail travel agency, although the largest operators have now little to show of their origins. As a consequence of Operation Stabilizer, the tour operator must be a member of ABTA in order to sell through ABTA retail travel agents, and the organization of ABTA includes a Tour Operators' Council and a Retail Agents' Council, from which bodies the National Council is formed. (At the end of the 1970s the exclusive dealing features of Stabilizer were under examination by the Office of Fair Trading.)

The holiday package consists of a combination of aircraft seats, hotel beds, ancillary ground transport, excursions, and other entertainment. Most of the sales will be made through conventional retail travel agents, although the tour operator will expect to sell 10 per cent or thereabouts directly to the public. Two Scandinavian tour operators, Tjaereborg and Vingresor, who specialize in direct selling, entered the UK market at the end of the 1970s, and the largest operator Thomsons set up its own direct selling subsidiary Portland Holidays. British Airways acquired Martin Rook a direct selling tour operator. In the summer of 1980 Vingresor sold out to Thomsons.

Tables 30-32 show the leading tour operators and their profitability towards the end of the 1970s. It is to be noted that Thomsons outdistance the second largest operator by a substantial margin and that a similar clear gap separates a small group of larger operators from the rest. These features reflect the struggles of the early years of the 1970s when there was a period of merger and failure, perhaps fuelled in part by the minimum price prescriptions of the Air Transport Licensing Board. In 1974, two large operators Horizon and Clarksons failed, the latter at the height of the summer season. This failure at least served to reduce the excessive capacity in the market and since 1975 the tour operating industry has enjoyed a period of comparative stability, which is reflected in improving profitability.

Table 30

Applications for Air Travel Organizer Licences (Return Passengers) in Excess of 100,000 Seats April 1979

Thomson Travel	734,000
Silver Wing SA Ltd	360,552
Cosmos Air Holidays	342,000
Horizon Midland	304,000
Laker Air Travel	174,000
Global of London	137,150

Intasun North	135,000
Owners Services Ltd	134,600
Intasun	130,950
Blue Sky Holidays	128,300
Thomas Cook	105,002
Martin Rooks	100,000
Total seats authorized	5,303,567

Source: Civil Aviation Authority

Table 31

Size of Air Travel Organizers at November 1979

Round trip passengers authorized	*% of all ATOL firms*
1,000 or less	53
more than 1,000 up to 10,000	31
more than 10,000 up to 50,000	11
more than 50,000 up to 100,000	1
more than 100,000	3

Source: Civil Aviation Authority

Table 32

Profits and Losses of the 30 Largest ATOL Firms
1972-78
(£ million)

Year	*Turnover*	*Profits*	*(Losses)*	*Net results*	*Net results as % turnover*
1972	206.0	1.9	(10.8)	(8.9)	(4.3)
1973	245.5	2.5	(2.9)	(0.4)	(0.2)
1974	226.7	1.8	(4.8)	(3.0)	(1.3)
1975	278.3	13.7	(0.8)	12.9	4.6
1976	326.1	12.8	(1.1)	11.7	3.6
1977	355.3	10.0	(2.1)	7.9	2.2
1978	530.7	35.1	(0.7)	34.4	6.5
1979	695.4	39.9	(2.6)	37.3	5.4

Where companies have failed, their losses in the year of failure are not included, e.g. Clarkson's losses are not included in 1974 figures

Source: Civil Aviation Authority

It has been a characteristic of tour operation to suffer from marked seasonality and in the earlier period the typical method of operation was to charter on a series basis for the summer season only. The effect of this was to give rise to problems of cash flow in the winter when neverthless expenditure would be incurred on such things as deposits on accommodation and the marketing costs of next season's programme. Latterly, however, the practice has grown at least among the larger operators of time-chartering aircraft and making similar long-term contracts for accommodation. In order to justify such arrangements, it was necessary to look for year-round use of both aircraft and accommodation, and thus the development of a substantial winter market came about. Notwithstanding the evolution of a firm winter market, tour operation still displays some seasonality, and it is to be noted that the larger operators are usually subsidiary companies of large organizations whose operations are rather less seasonal and may not be involved in any form of travel. Vertical integration is a common feature: thus Thomsons and Cosmos, for example, are affiliated to the airlines they principally use, and one of the newer large tour operators, Intasun, wasted no time in creating its own airline. The large operator may also own at least some of the hotels used and may include a number of retail outlets in his activities, either specialized outlets or a chain of full retail travel agencies or indeed a mixture of both.

The Civil Aviation Authority which succeeded the Air Transport Licensing Board as the regulatory agency for air transport was given powers in the Civil Aviation Act 1971 to license tour operators and other kinds of air travel organizers. Accordingly, four types of licence were introduced in 1972, at least one of which had to be held by an air travel organizer. The four air travel organizers' licenses (ATOL) are:

Type A — for advance booking charters
Type B — for inclusive tours
Type C — for other charters e.g. affinity group travel
Type D — for brokers of aircraft capacity

The airline of course is also required to hold the corresponding appropriate licence for its operations.

In order to give a greater degree of stability to the inclusive tour field, the CAA introduced compulsory bonding of air travel organizers. The purpose of this was similar to ABTA's bonding requirements and was designed to protect the passenger against being stranded abroad if his tour operator failed. After the Clarkson's debacle in 1974, an Air Travel Reserve Fund was created to supplement money which would be available from the calling in of bonds.

The Inclusive Tour as a Product

A typical inclusive tour is one which takes place in Spain, quite likely in Majorca (Palma is one of largest international airports in terms of passengers passing through), or elsewhere on the shores of the Mediterranean. The resort involved will probably be not more than two hours flying time from the point of embarkation and the length of the holiday involved will be about fourteen days. Such a programme is typical of the inclusive tour available to the residents of northwestern industrialized Europe. Typical costs of such a fourteen-day tour from the UK were in 1978 as follows:

Table 33

Costs of an Inclusive Tour by Air 1978

Price (mean but with seasonal variations)	£155	%
Air transport	50	32
Hotel accommodation	54	35
Commission to travel agents	14	9
Overheads, profit	37	24

Such a programme will be decided upon at least eighteen months before the date of departure. Increases in operating costs or fluctuations in currency rates of exchange may dangerously upset the calculations in which the costing rests. Most operators seek to compensate for this by levying surcharges at the time of final invoicing to the passenger. However, the demand for inclusive tours is highly price-elastic, and operators have tended to offer their customers guarantees that there will be no surchages.

The inclusive tour using chartered aircraft has powerfully transformed intra-European tourism. It represents the first real mass market in tourism. From the consumer's point of view, tour operation has made the holiday abroad as desirable and as normal as the consumer durables which are thought be part of the good life, refrigerators, cars, washing machines, and the like. Moreover, the product itself has been standardized and made repeatable, thereby making it possible to use modern marketing techniques to get it to the consumer. To judge from the tour operators' brochures, the product being demanded by the consumer is a fortnight's holiday in a modern white concrete hotel with a swimming pool and a bar, the whole bathed in sunlight under a cloudless sky. Little or no concern is shown about the country in which the resort is situated, and it may be inferred that the IT passenger is quite indifferent to the nature or status of that country.

It is also clear that the customer is extremely sensitive to price. The awareness of this sensitivity was the origin of the tour operators' objections to the fixing of minimum prices by the regulatory authority. The Civil Aviation Authority has generally not sought to fix minimum prices for inclusive tours, and the tour operating industry seems to have reached a level of stability by means of normal market forces.

The Future of Tour Operation

If the picture of tour operation is one of consolidation, it seems necessary to ask what of the future. The regulatory prospects should be examined first. The climate of opinion has favoured deregulation in aviation, and it seems likely that this will spill over into tour operation, and thus check the school of thought that would like to see more 'orderly' tour operation. The attitude of the deregulators has been confirmed by recent developments in the fight for low fares. With very low fares now available on other (not necessarily scheduled) services, the sale of ITCs with throwaway accommodation seems unnecessary. On the other hand, the ITC generation has never taken root outside Europe.

It is a dream that long-haul tour operation may grow on the pattern of the short-haul intra-European pattern. It seems likely to remain a dream if long-haul volume is expected to reach the scale of short-haul. It does seem that the volume market perceives two hours' flying time as about right, not merely in terms of costs.

Pricing and pricing policy still lie at the heart of successful tour operation and with that correct market segmentation. It is hard to see any innovation of a technical nature which will lead to lower prices. But more accurate market segmentation and greater flexibility in applying vigorous pricing policies would seem to offer the best prospect.

The impact of inflation at the end of the 1970s affected tour operators in a number of ways. The consumer found himself faced with surcharges to his original purchase to compensate the tour operator for increasing costs and in this connection it must be noted that tour operators have to quote prices determined as much as eighteen months in advance because of the long lead time required to prepare brochures and other elements in marketing. For the tour operator and the hotelier, inflation has made the long-term contract for hotel space much less attractive than formerly. Not only hotels but also carriers are unwilling to conclude contracts priced in figures that will be quite unrealistic in perhaps only a few months. These factors tend to work to the advantage of the bigger operator.

Part VII

Marketing in Tourism

Further Reading for Part VII

Baker, M.J. *Marketing: An Introductory Text*
Boyd, H.W. and Massy, W.F. *Marketing Management*
Broadbent, S.: *Spending Advertising Money*
Burkart, A.J., and Medlik, S.: *The Management of Tourism,* Part VII
Krippendorf, J.: *Marketing et Tourisme*
Medlik, S.: *The Business of Hotels,* Chapter 10
Schmoll, G.A.: *Tourism Promotion*
Wahab, S., Crampon, L.J., and Rothfield, L.: *Tourism Marketing*
Wood, M. (editor): *Tourism Marketing*
World Tourism Organization: *Distribution Channels*

References to Part VII

1 Krippendorf, J: *Marketing et Tourisme,* p.46
2 Burkart, A.J., Some Managerial Influences on a Firm's Pricing Policy, *Journal of Industrial Economics,* Vol. XVII, No.3, Oxford, Blackwell, 1969
3 *British Air Transport in the Seventies,* p.8
4 *Ibid,* p.9
5 *Civil Aviation Policy Guidance,* para 7 et seq.
6 Burkart, A.J. The Design Oration 1962: Design as an Instrument of Competition, *SIA Journal,* No.118, London, Society of Industrial Artists, 1962

19   *The Marketing Concept*

The principal generators of world tourism are the Western industrialized count-ries of Europe and North America, Japan, and a dozen of them account for 80 per cent of world tourist arrivals. Economic growth and a rising standard of living have been the declared political aims of their governments. Accordingly a conscious emphasis has been given to consumption; of consumable goods at first, at a later stage of consumer durables like cars or refrigerators, and in the most advanced societies, of consumer services. Prominent among the consumer service is tourism, particularly holiday tourism.

In placing this emphasis on consumption, the Western governments have been seeking to maintain full employment, even to the extent of tolerating a degree of inflation in order to maintain demand at an effective level. In turn the mainten-ance of full employment has led to increasing imports, and one of the imports, as it were, which has grown spectacularly fast has been the holiday abroad.

This was not always so. In the nineteenth century, most of an industrialized country's production was conducted in small manufacturing units. The market for a manufacturer was largely a local one surrounding his factory and few manufactured products achieved anything like what would now be called a national distribution. With considerable and chronic under-employment, the market for goods other than the necessities of life was small and limited to a frac-tion of the population. The change came about with the introduction of mass production. Mass production enabled lower unit costs to be attained and hence lower prices were possible, provided always that the increased production could be readily sold. A national market for groceries became possible, and indeed the consumer's choice began to be limited: where hitherto each grocer blended his own tea, for example, he could now stock Lipton's and other teas pre-packed. For the consumer, there was a choice not of an indefinitely large range of blends, but a limited choice among half a dozen pre-packed blends. However, if the con-sumer's choice was thus limited, he did enjoy the advantage of lower prices and an assurance of standards associated with a national brand.

The need to dispose of increasing production made possible by mass produc-tion was met by the growth in communication. Mechanized transport in the shape of the railway, and later the lorry, made the physical distribution of goods possible over areas much wider than the immediate hinterland of the factory. The telegraph and later the telephone served to widen the market for services. By the end of the nineteenth century the popular newspaper had been born, and its advertising columns were to be for years the chief medium through which the manufacturer could communicate with his market. Later the commercial radio and television challenged the supremacy of the newspaper as a medium of communication.

Three phases may be distinguished in the evolution of a consumer market. When industrial production starts, the manufacturer's pre-occupation will be with production. This was true in the last century for most consumer goods; demand for many manufactured goods potentially exceeded the capacity of manufacturing industry to supply it. A second phase occurs when the techniques of production have improved to the point that rather more goods are available for the market than there is potential demand for. This phase will be characterized by an insufficiency of demand for some manufacturer's goods, and will tend to lead to a concentration of manufacturing into a few large units, to take full advantage of economies of scale in both production and in marketing. Thirdly, there is the phase where production capability has progressed so far that continuous production of many goods is a condition of producing them at all. The need to secure a continuous off-take from the production line leads to a recognition of the necessity to produce to meet identifiable consumers' needs and tastes. Clearly, of course, not all industries will undergo these three phases consecutively and in step with each other. But the basic pattern has been from a seller's market and production orientation through a buyer's market and sales orientation to a buyer's market and marketing orientation. The three phases have been characterized by growth in output on the one hand and by growth of market on the other hand.

The Marketing Concept

For tourism the third phase referred to above was only just being reached in the early 1970s. The transition from production orientation to consumer orientation was beginning to be apparent. For example, the introduction of the Boeing 747 aircraft and the creation of very large hotels has made it clear that in these fields at least overproduction of both airline and hotel capacity is a real possibility, and again the very rapid growth of the inclusive tour in Europe has prompted some rethinking among tour operators. In the field of tourism, marketing is assuming a new significance.

There exist several formal definitions of marketing. The British Institute of Marketing has formulated the following:

'Marketing is the management function which organizes and directs all those business activities involved in assessing and converting customer purchasing power into effective demand for a specific product or service and in moving the product or service to the final customer or user so as to achieve the profit target or other objectives set by the company.'

Two points in this definition are significant: the marketing function is seen as co-ordinating *all* aspects of business, not merely a departmental one; the role of marketing is seen to include the assessment of consumer demand in the first place, and not merely satisfying demand as it appears. Krippendorf defines marketing in tourism in terms very nearly the same:[1]

'Marketing in tourism is to be understood as the systematic and co-ordinated execution of business policy by tourist undertakings whether private or state owned at local regional national or international level to achieve the optimal satisfaction of the needs of identifiable consumer groups, and in doing so to achieve an appropriate return.'

In the case of tourism, Krippendorf's definition stresses the co-ordination of the policies of several organizations, and this is a special feature of tourism which will be examined.

The Product in Tourism

The tourist product may be seen as a composite product, as an amalgam of attractions, transport, accommodation, and of entertainment. Each of these components is supplied by the individual hotel company, airline, or other supplier, and is offered directly to the tourist by them. From the individual consumer's point of view, there is an indefinitely large number of ways in which these individual tourist products can be combined: there may be one hundred possible destinations, each with a dozen hotels, each reached by at least two airlines. The potential choice facing the consumer is very large. The point about modern marketing is that it applies to situations where the choice can be limited to a relatively small number of brands, possibly in the field of consumables amounting to no more than ten or twenty, which gives the consumer a reasonable and 'handle-able' choice. This reduction in the choices open to the consumer is taking place in tourism by the increasing use of packaging (*see* Chapters 17 and 18 above). The real tourist product is a composite product, whether sold as a package or assembled by the tourist himself or his travel agent. The tourist product accordingly can be analysed in terms of its attractions, its facilities, and its accessibility.

Attractions may be defined as those elements in the tourist product which determine the choice of the tourist to visit one destination rather than another. They are the factors which generate a flow of tourists to their location. They may be local in character, as in the case of an individual resort, or they may be national, as for example French cooking. A further dimension can be distinguished by classifying attractions as site attractions or event attractions. Site attractions are those where the place itself is the major inducement to the tourist to visit it, for example the Swiss Alps or the Grand Canyon or Niagara Falls. Event attractions are those where the event staged is a larger factor in the tourist's choice than the site; for example, the Oberammergau Passion Play, the Olympic Games, or a trade congress or exhibition. Often the site and the event together form the major factor in the tourist's choice.

Tourist facilities are those elements in the tourist product which do not normally themselves generate tourist flows but whose absence might deter the tourist from seeking the attractions. The facilities complement the attractions, and comprise, for example, accommodation, restaurants, ski-lifts, picnic sites, and so on. They are thus basically utilitarian, even though they contribute significantly to the tourist's enjoyment — a well-appointed hotel may itself form a large part of the attractiveness of a resort; indeed, one man's facility may be another man's attraction.

Accessibility is the third component in the tourist product. It includes transportation to the attraction, and in a wider sense the proximity of the attraction to a sufficiently large population to constitute a market for the attraction. Nearness is best interpreted in terms of the time and the cost taken to reach the attraction rather than in terms of physical distance, i.e. as economic distance.

Tourist Markets

A tourist market may be identified corresponding to each tourist product. In this sense, the term market is used to describe the collective of buyers and potential buyers of each tourist product. The identification of this corresponding market, a segment of the total market, is of the greatest importance. If the marketing effort is to be cost-effective, it must be at a minimum level to avoid waste by reaching only that fraction of the total market which is likely to be attracted, and at the same time on a sufficiently large scale to reach some threshold level below which the marketing effort would be ineffective. Segmentation of the market is thus made in order to achieve the most efficient use of marketing resources.

By segmentation, therefore, is meant the identification of a section of the total market. The segment will be identified by purpose, by socio-economic or behavioural or similar characteristics. By way of illustration, the total tourist market may be divided into three major segments (even though within each further segmentation will be needed for practical marketing purposes):

1. *The holiday tourist.* The holiday tourist has proved to be very sensitive to price changes, and is readily influenceable by skilled marketing effort. He is resort-oriented (Paris, Rome, and New York are resorts as much as Venice, Miami, or Bournemouth). The holiday tourist market has hitherto been regarded as highly seasonal, but recent experience with winter package tour suggests that with aggressive pricing policies seasonal peaking of demand for holidays can be ameliorated.
2. *The business tourist.* The business tourist's choice of destination will be determined by the nature of his business, and to that extent his choice will not be readily susceptible to influencing by marketing efforts. Demand for business tourism will be relatively price-inelastic, will tend not to be extremely seasonal, and will tend to be big-city oriented. Business visits will be relatively frequent, but of short stay. On the other hand, this kind of tourism will be attracted by event attractions in the shape of exhibitions, trade fairs, and conferences.
3. *The common interest tourist.* This segment comprises visits to friends and relatives, visitors for educational purposes, for pilgrimages and the like. Demand for this type of tourism will be relatively price-elastic, and also sensitive to the absolute level of price. The tourist will not be very readily influenced by promotion, his stays will be relatively long, he will not be a significant user of hotel accommodation, and he will travel infrequently, spending relatively little on his stay.

Within these major segments, further segmentation is possible, using such criteria as, for example, income, family composition, taste, or past travel habits.

Special Features of Marketing in Tourism

Unlike the normal consumer product or service, the tourist product is marketed at two levels. The national, regional or local tourist organization will typically be engaged in a marketing campaign to persuade the potential tourist to visit the country, region or town which it covers. The official tourist organization will actually not sell a tourist product. Its marketing effort will have two major objectives. First, it will seek to create knowledge of its country in particular markets and to persuade visitors thereby to visit that country. Secondly, it will seek to create an identifiable image of its country's tourist attractions, subsuming to some extent the diversity of attractions within one country into a single coherent image.

Under this umbrella marketing campaign, the various individual providers of tourist services can market their own components of the total tourist product. Airlines and other transport operators, hotel groups, and tour operators can market their individual services to a market of potential buyers already aware of and predisposed to the destination represented by the official tourist organization.

The consumer as a tourist has special need of full and accurate information about the country he proposes to visit or within a country about the region of his choice. Unless he has previous acquaintance with his destination, he is purchasing an expectation, not a tangible product which can be inspected or sampled before purchase. A major function of the marketing campaigns conducted by the official tourist organization will be the provision of information about its country and the resorts within it. Within a country, a network of information bureaux may be set up to serve the needs of tourists once they have arrived.

The official tourist organization has special responsibility in formulating the tourist products, which are the subjects of its marketing campaigns. This may be carried out in various ways organizationally (*see* Chapter 25). But the formulation of the tourist products in terms of their attractions, accessibility and facilities of the product is in part at least among the roles of the official tourist organization.

The emergence of the tour operator has brought about a significant change in the marketing picture. The co-ordination of the policies of individual suppliers of components of the tourist product, which was referred to above as a prime part of marketing in tourism, is automatically achieved by the tour operator, who may thus be seen as conducting an entire marketing campaign, from formulation of the product to its ultimately being offered for sale and consumed.

Consideration of Pricing

The holiday tourist, it has been suggested above, is extremely sensitive to both the absolute level of price and to changes in prices. He is also susceptible to persuasion as to his choice of destination by the marketing campaigns of both official organizations and of the individual suppliers of components in the tourist product. This sensitivity of the holiday tourist to considerations of price and promotion is what makes the holiday tourist market so attractive to those organizations concerned with the promotion of tourism.

Pricing is a complex matter. Individual suppliers of tourism services, airlines, hotel groups, and others not only tend to determine their prices independently of each other, but also do so with an eye on the reactions of their immediate competitors. Thus the final price may or may not be strictly related to the costs of providing the services concerned, and an element of cross-subsidization may creep in. Moreover, while costs are reasonably predictable in the short run (because the fleet has been bought, the hotels have been built, the labour force engaged), revenue estimates are at best educated guesses. Demand can and does change overnight. It is, therefore, of the greatest importance that the tourist supplier, airline, hotel or whatever, should correctly gauge the sensitivity of its potential customers to changes in price, that is, should form a valid estimate of the price elasticities facing him.

In practice therefore a product may be priced at a less than optimal level, and because of the uncertainty of the revenue estimates, will as often as not be priced too highly. It is useful to define the short run as that period in which the price and product cannot be changed (because the brochure is already printed and so on), and the long run as a period after the point at which it becomes possible to vary the price and the product. In the short run, when prices cannot be altered, the importance of non-price marketing activity becomes very important.

The costs of manufacturing the tourist product will be reflected in the final price and also the costs of marketing. It becomes very important to divide the total market into segments according to various characteristics including price elasticity in order that the marketing effort be cost-effective.

The choice of appropriate marketing policies will itself influence costs and prices. For example, the decision has to be made whether to seek small volume and high-yield revenue and high profit margins, or alternatively to seek large volume, low-yield revenue, and small profit margins — a very familiar choice for enterprises concerned with tourism. Moreover the official tourist organization will normally incur only marketing costs. The way in which marketing strategy will influence costs, and therefore prices, may be seen also to arise from the skill with which market segments are identified; for example, a particular sort of market may be identified as suitable for some kind of affinity group travel. Hence, the sales force costs both of the official organization and of the firms supplying tourist services will be relatively low because only a few organizers of clubs and other affinity groups need to be approached. By contrast, a product whose appeal is very widely distributed and is thus sold through travel agents will incur relatively higher distribution costs.

Two questions must be asked about pricing policy. First, in what circumstances is it advantageous to reduce prices? The general answer to this question is that if a given proportionate reduction in price induces a more than proportionate increase in traffic, so that despite a lower price the new total revenue is higher than before the price reduction, then it is clearly advantageous to reduce the price. Secondly and conversely, it is advantageous to increase prices when by so doing the new total revenue is higher than it was before the price increase. Occasionally, it may be noted, it will be desirable to restrain demand for a particular tourist product; this may be achieved only if an increase in price in fact brings about a reduction in traffic, that is, fewer people but the same revenue. However, these changes in revenue affect also of course the physical volume of business and hence costs; only when both revenue and costs resulting from a change are assessed can the effect of price changes on profits be seen.

In practice, in tourism as in other fields there is a reluctance to vary prices frequently. This reluctance stems from several causes. First, there is the difficulty of ascertaining in advance the precise effect of price changes on the total revenue. Secondly, it is administratively complex to change prices frequently; new tariffs, for example, have to be printed and notified to travel agents. Thirdly, there is a fear that an increase in prices, in particular, may give rise to adverse reaction in the retail trade, which will become apprehensive about potential demand at the new higher price level, and the loss of trade confidence may aggravate the effects of the actual change itself. Because of this unwillingness to vary prices, promotion may be viewed as an alternative method of influencing demand. (One of us has discussed elsewhere[2] the administrative deterrents to price changes.)

For a large part of the tourism field, the freedom of the supplier of the tourist product to vary his prices at will is circumscribed by voluntary or statutory regulation. As part of their general supervisory function, official tourist organizations in many countries control or supervise the prices to be charged for accommodation, often linking this to a system of classification, and in Britain an Order made under the Development of Tourism Act, 1969 requires compulsory notification of accommodation prices. Taxi fares and other public transport fares are regulated in most countries, often with the needs of the tourist in mind; in all forms of international transport fares are fixed; the International Air Transport Association's fixing of international air fare is the most familiar example.

Consumer Protection

As in other fields, the 1960s witnessed an increasing concern in tourism for the rights of consumers. If marketing is about the satisfaction of consumer needs, then clearly the consumer should be entitled to say explicitly what those needs are. Obviously, the producer will engage in market research in order to establish actual or potential consumer needs. But the consumer protection argument is subtly different from the argument for market research. It postulates a right of the consumer to state his needs explicitly, and as of right to be regarded as a partner in tourism along with the voter and the shareholder in commercial enterprises. For example, the growth of the popularity of package holidays is *prima facie* evidence that the tour operation industry is indeed meeting a consumer's need. The proportion of complaints in relation to the several million package holidays taken by the British population was not very high in the 1970s, but the absolute number of complaints was high enough to attract the attention of the news media, and of the Consumers' Association. The latter organization has been particularly critical of the booking conditions which tour operators have in the past attempted to impose on their customers. The Association played a considerable part in changing the law in the United Kingdom with the Unfair Contract Clauses Act which has gone a long way to clearing up doubts about 'the small print' — not only in the case of tour operators' brochures, but also in insurance policies and other contracts outside tourism. The Consumers' Association after publishing in its magazine *Which?* several articles about holidays, formed a quarterly supplement *Holiday Which?*. In Sweden, The National Swedish Consumers' Council published a major study of European air fares in 1970 and a supplementary study extending to the North Atlantic in 1972. In the United States, an insurance-based organization, the Airline Passengers Association, was formed in the 1960s, which achieved fame in successfully intervening in the aftermath of a crash of a DC-10 airliner at Chicago in 1979, and has affiliated a similar association in the United Kingdom. In the UK also the Civil Aviation Authority has formed an Air Transport Users Committee to represent presumed consumers' interests. Further, an extension of the monopolies legislation and the creation of the Office of Fair Trading has provided further evidence in the UK at least that the consumer's interests are taken seriously.

Apart from the efforts of consumers' societies on behalf of their members, many of the regulatory bodies are statute-bound to take into account the consumers' interests. The Federal Aviation Act 1958 in the United States[3] lays down explicit objectives that the Civil Aeronautics Board must seek *vis-à-vis* the consumer, and in discussing American experience, the Edwards Committee Report in the United Kingdom[4] observes:

> 'One of the odd things about statements on civil air transport is that they very rarely talk about the customer in simple language. So let us say that in our view the primary long-term objective of a national policy towards commercial flying should be to see that each customer ... gets what he wants — not what somebody else thinks he ought to want — at the minimum economic price that can be contrived.'

The Secretary of State for Trade and Industry echoed these sentiments in his policy guidance to the Civil Aviation Authority[5] with the words:

> 'Civil air transport exists by serving the public; the Authority should inform itself of the public's needs and take full account of them.'

In the light of such evident concern for the interests of consumers, it may well be asked why anything further is needed. Unfortunately, the regulatory bodies have been given other objectives to meet as well, which may conflict with the consumer's interest, and a restatement of the rights of consumers is salutory. No doubt, as operators, transport undertakings and indeed hotel groups will seek to achieve their commercial objectives by paying full attention to what they believe the public wants; but the right of the consumer to say what he wants in a public forum has become recognized as legitimate in many of the countries which are the principal generators of tourism.

Marketing in Tourism — Some Guideposts

Unlike in most other industries, marketing in tourism takes place on two levels. At one level, the tourist organization is concerned with promoting the destination for which it is responsible. The advantages of a flow of tourists to an identifiable resort area are sufficiently important to justify what may be called destination marketing. Further, since the tourist product is an amalgam of several separate products supplied by individual enterprises, co-ordination of these separate interests is essential to effective marketing. Within this framework, under this umbrella, the marketing of the individual firms takes place. Destination marketing will seek to establish and identify the tourist products and their attractions for the relevant market segment. The individual firms supplying the tourists' needs may thus concentrate on developing the markets for their particular components of the composite tourist product.

The interests of governments in tourism are not likely to diminish; these interests include the control of immigration, the balance of payments, physical planning, regional policy, hygiene and public safety in order to name the more obvious interests. The tourist flows between many countries are sufficiently large for both receiving and generating countries to be keenly aware of the votes associated with tourism. These public issues are the business too of the official tourist organizations in devising a strategy for the development of tourism.

20 *Marketing Tools*

There are several activities and procedures which are commonly used in the conduct of a marketing campaign. Among these are, for example, advertising, the development of a sales force, and the use of public relations. The use made of these marketing tools will vary as between one firm and another and as between commercial undertakings and official tourist organizations. This chapter examines and assesses the marketing tools which are generally available in the field of tourism.

Market Research and Market Information

Market research can be defined as the systematic collection of information relating to the supply of and demand for a product or a proposed product, in such a way that the information may be used by the organization to formulate informed decisions about its policies and its objectives. The results of market research will often be presented in quantitative terms, and in any case may include the analysis of existing statistics, of non-quantified information, and the conduct and analysis of special investigations, often questionnaire surveys specially undertaken for the organization concerned. The conduct of market research is thus a matter of providing managements with information. There are, however, two different situations in which management needs this flow of information: the case of a new product, where its future place in the market has to be determined, and the case of the monitoring of the performance of an existing product. This distinction is an important one, for in tourism there has been a marked amount of innovation in holiday products in particular.

Before any market research programme is undertaken, it is important to identify the *managerial* questions to which answers are sought. If market research is not consciously directed to answer specific managerial questions, it becomes a matter of 'data dredging', of casting a net in the hope of catching an interesting fish. To take a simple example, it seems appropriate to many tourism enquiries to ask about car ownership. Further reflection leads to the view that it is not car ownership data which will be significant, but rather access to a car, or use of a car, and these will be influenced by location, family income and composition and so on, and car ownership *per se* will not be particularly relevant. In other words the questions to which management wants answers can be sought in envisaging the possible answers that might be disclosed by the research. Only in this way can market research prove fertile in the sense that management decisions can flow from it. Pure description, no matter how interesting, is not a role of market research: time and money will be wasted if the results of market research are not usable in the managerial decision-making process.

In tourism much of the basic information about markets is available from existing statistical series (*See* Part III above). But a good deal of the published material has been compiled with purposes in mind other than tourism. Despite this, a thorough examination of the existing statistics will be the starting point for market research. Where existing sources are inadquate, special investigations may have to be undertaken.

The most familiar tool for special investigations in consumer markets is the sample survey. A characteristic method of proceeding would be as follows. The population or 'universe' for which information is required is defined—for example, all households in a country might be the universe or population under investigation. Next, a statistically valid sample of the population is drawn and information is obtained from the sample. This procedure is advantageous, because firstly it will normally be markedly cheaper to gain information from a sample fraction of the population than by an exhaustive census of the whole population; secondly, it is statistically possible to determine the limits of probable error in the results of the survey. The actual obtaining of information from the sample units (i.e. households in our example) is often done in human populations by administering a questionnaire. In the industralized countries of the West, there are a number of specialized firms able to carry out sample survey enquiries, as well as government agencies similarly equipped. In Britain, the Office of Population Censuses and Surveys carries out the International Passenger Survey (*see* Part III) for the Department of Trade and Industry. The British Tourist Authority and the national Tourist Boards use specialized market research firms to carry out surveys on their behalf.

It is convenient to classify survey investigations by reference to the kind of information they seek to provide. First, there are surveys of market behaviour. A good example of this type is the British National Travel Survey (*see* pp.82-9 above), which records year by year the holiday habits of the British resident population, cross-analysed by socio-economic and other characteristics. Over several years, the trends in holidaymaking may be seen and inferences made about the motives of holidaymakers. It is important to distinguish between surveys which mainly record answers to questions of fact, from which the investigator may infer motivations, and another less frequently used type of sample survey, the motivation survey, which attempts to describe and forecast the motives of the population under investigation, by the use of techniques developed originally in psychology.

Secondly, the sample survey techniques can be used for retail audits. The population or universe here is, for example, the group of retailers selling or capable of selling the product. It measures not the behaviour of the final consumer, but rather the flow of products through the retail distributive chain. Common enough in the case of ordinary consumer goods marketing, it has only rarely been used in tourism, for the travel agent holds no stock. In those areas of tourism where there is a sophisticated reservations system, the system can provide the comparable information.

Thirdly, surveys may be undertaken to monitor the conduct of marketing campaigns. Although there exist in many of the principal tourist generating countries national readership surveys and television audience ratings, these general surveys may not be sufficient to monitor the progress of a marketing campaign in the specialized field of tourism.

There are, of course, other uses in which the standard market research techniques can be employed. In practice, a single survey properly designed may serve more than one use, but it is important to distinguish conceptually between the various ends which market research may serve.

Product Formulation and Development

With sufficient information available from market research and market information, it is possible to identify accurately the key market segments to be tackled. Characteristically, the criteria for distinguishing between segments of the total market will be demographic and socio-economic, but other criteria, such as purpose, motivation, and taste may also be used. The product must then be formulated and given a unique identity to match that segment of the market for which it is intended. In the case of tourism, the creation of a separate identity is particularly the task of the official tourist organization. Much of the physical character of the destination, its attractions and nature will be given and could only be changed slowly and perhaps expensively. To take a familiar example, the snowfields of the Swiss Alps are given; the special nature of their attraction has been based on the special identity given them by those responsible for stimulating tourism to Switzerland. A more complex case is that of Bermuda: originally a supplier of market garden produce to New York, Bermuda deliberately changed its identity to become a winter resort, when tariff barriers curtailed its market garden trade. The advent of the long-range aircraft, particularly the pure jet, dealt a heavy blow to Bermuda's trade as a winter resort by making the more certain sun of the Caribbean as easily and as cheaply reached as Bermuda. The island, therefore, refashioned the identity of its product to become a summer resort. Through all these successful changes in product identity, the basic physical plant of Bermuda tourism has remained unchanged. What has changed is the formulation and specification of what the tourist product is, and the skilful identification of markets to match each new formulation.

Development of the product will normally be possible. The construction of new accommodation, the construction of new amenities, the development of event attractions, and the conservation of natural attractions all form part of the development of the product. The most comprehensive example of product development has been the transformation of the east cost of Spain as the premier European resort area, but many later examples exist still in progress — the coast of Attica at Glyphada and Vouliagmeni or Mamaia on the Black Sea coast of Romania. The formulation or reformulation of the tourist product in these cases was a deliberate policy decision by the official tourist authorities concerned.

Selling the Tourist Product

In the marketing of consumer goods, the efforts of the sales force are directed towards ensuring that the retailers carry stocks of the product. This is a most important function in marketing; without an appropriate level of stockholding in a sufficient number of retail outlets, the final consumer may not be able to find the product, and thus at the point of sale the whole marketing effort is frustrated. Further, the purchase of a stock of the product constitutes a major incentive to the retailer to sell it and to promote it in his shop.

For the most part, the retailer of the tourist product does not buy for stock, but only orders from the supplier when he has the customer standing at his counter. He does not then draw down from his stock, but merely places an order via the supplier's reservation system. (For a discussion of the role of the retailer in tourism *see* chapter 16 above.) What then is the role of the sales function in tourism?

A distinction again must be made between the functions of the official tourist organization and the individual firm in tourism. The role of the former has developed conspicuously as the more progressive tourist organizations have come to appreciate the importance of the retail outlet in marketing. The term salesman may be inappropriate in the context of an official tourist organization, and some such term as trade relations officer may be preferred, but the function of educating and persuading the travel trade remains an important contribution. This eventuates in, for example, the concept of the tourist workshop, a kind of confrontation of the trade with suppliers and official bodies of the receiving country. At a typical workshop, the occasion and venue will be devised by the official tourist organization, and invitations extended to the retailer, tour operator, and other travel organizers to meet representatives of the suppliers of transport and accommodation. This kind of forum between the commercial firms of the generating country and the receiving country has proved highly successful and now forms an important part of the marketing campaign.

The sales function of a commercial firm as carried out by the sales representative covers three important areas of activity. There is an obvious 'trouble-shooting' role; for example, when a long and complicated itinerary cannot be readily constructed by the retail travel agent.

Secondly, the salesman's role as directed towards the retail travel agent is largely one of educating the travel agent's staff about the nature of the product and of training the agent's staff accordingly. He should be able to explain the merits of his firms's products, the locations and nature of the individual hotels in a group, the extent of the airline's network and its relations with other forms of transport. He should be able to train the travel agent's staff in his firm's reservations procedures, and to assist in the effective merchandising of the firm's product by installing and servicing window displays and in the display of brochures and other literature.

Thirdly, the sales force has typically an involvement with direct sales rather than simply with sales via a retailer. In both the accommodation field and in transport, a significant part of the sales effort will be directed to forms of bulk business, where the intermediary is not a retailer, but an organizer of travel and accommodation. Examples of this type of bulk business are affinity group charters, conferences, exhibitions, sales incentive holidays, and in the case of transport, the important interline sales. The change of emphasis from sales at any price to discovering what the needs of consumers are is nowhere more apparent than in the area of bulk sales. Only a few companies might unaided recognize their need for a sales incentive holiday scheme or for a conference, and it has been the specialized sales forces in several tourist industries which have seen and identified this particular need and have convinced their customers of its importance.

Reservations

The reservations procedure in some tourist industries, notably hotels, airlines, and some forms of entertainment, is analogous to the physical distribution network in the case of consumer goods industries. It is the means whereby the final consumer via the retailer draws upon the supplier's stock. Additionally, as is the case with consumer goods, it is a most important source of management information. Indeed the larger the company, the more important the reservations sytem becomes as a source of management information.

The significance of a reservations system lies in the opportunity it gives management to manage demand for individual units of production, e.g., at particular hotels or on particular flights. Reservations are not for the consumer's benefit primarily; his best interests would be served by being certain of being able to buy a bed or a seat of his choice at any time by simply presenting himself at the counter. The pioneer shuttle services (as this type of operation became known) were those between Boston, New York and Washington, a route of extremely high traffic density even in the 1960s. There are few routes which justify a no-reservations system with its implied guarantee of carriage. But in the United Kingdom, the domestic trunk routes were found to be suitable for this type of operation, the first shuttle service being started in 1975 by British Airways on the busy London-Glasgow route. London-Edinburgh was introduced three years later, followed by London-Belfast and London-Manchester, and by 1980 consideration was being given to overseas shuttles, London-Paris being the most favoured candidate.

The day-to-day management of demand is the proper function of a reservations procedure. If several units of production, aircraft, or hotels, are involved, the purpose of a reservations manager will be to distribute the demand for the seat or bed across the whole production in the most profitable way; it may be advantageous, for example, to have two aircraft flying with each carrying half the traffic than to operate the one with all the traffic and the other empty. Since typically a number of retail outlets will channel the demand for beds or seats, an essential feature of a reservations system will be an efficient communications network enabling the buyer (passenger or guest) to gain easy access to the stock of seats or beds. This easy access is via the retail outlet (travel agent, airline office, hotel), and it will be recalled that attention was drawn earlier to this role of the retailer.

The simplest form of reservations system is one person with a single list of available units, as will be the case in a small hotel or a small car hire company. Reservations procedures become complex as soon as there are two or more persons with two or more lists, as the harmonization of several booking lists becomes necessary. There arises the need for communications of a high order. Two systems, albeit with many variations in detail, can be distinguished. If the demand is not very big and the occasions of demand relatively infrequent, as for example in deep-sea passenger shipping today or in relatively small hotel groups, it is possible to make available to the retail outlets (including company offices) a statement of the status of the stock of berths or beds, listing at daily or weekly intervals what part of the stock may be sold and reported without prior challenge to the central reservations unit. However when the demand gets very large, as in the case of a large airline or a big hotel group, it will be necessary to institute a real-time system and to require every booking to be individually made. This will usually involve the use of a computer and a high speed communications system between the retail outlet or other booking point and the central reservations unit. Not only can such a computerized system handle very large volumes (a million bookings p.a. may imply 5 million transactions), but it is capable of performing the analysis of demand for management and also of initiating consequential procedures such as billing, load control, and so on.

The introduction of highly sophisticated reservations systems using computers gives rise to some speculation as to their implications for the future of management control in tourism. Three such speculations may be briefly considered. Firstly, in relation to sales through retail outlets, hitherto each company, airline, hotel and the rest, has relied on the telephone or the telex as means of communication between retail outlet and central reservations. The larger airlines have in the United Kingdom supported the Travicom system which enables a retail travel agency to contact the airline reservations via a single terminal. This obviates the difficulty of having several terminals in the retail outlet. The development of viewdata systems of information via an ordinary TV set also seems likely to have a part to play in travel reservations, with perhaps ultimately the traveller making a positive reservation and completing ticketing in his own home. But at the beginning of the 1980s, such a system looked still some way off, and conventional reservations for most travel through the intermediary of a travel agent looked good for some years yet.

Secondly, if an hotel group is to operate a centralized booking system by computer, it will be necessary to put all space on the system and not only that which the local manager regards as unsaleable. (The National Coal Board formed a subsidiary, International Reservations Ltd., which pioneered computerized reservations of hotel space in the UK and in Ireland. They experienced a larger feed of space from hotels in the winter than in the summer when unit managers preferred to keep the bulk of their space under their own hand. IRL did not succeed in getting the co-operation of the hotel industry on a sufficiently large scale, and operations ceased in the autumn of 1972.) It would thereby be desirable for each hotel to challenge the central reservations even for

...ᴄ upstairs known to be unoccupied. The implications of this world be to absolve in effect the local manager from responsibility for the profitability of his hotel (since he no longer controls the sale of beds) and make him a cost controller instead. Such a change is not so drastic as it sounds: the manager of a large group unit, say, in Paris, does not perforce contribute to the marketing of his rooms to any large extent.

Thirdly, in a large enough system, the demand for space will arise in a way which approximates to the operation of a perfectly competitive market. A computer system could in principle be programmed to adjust the price to be charged in the light of all other transactions completed, so that the price charged in any single transaction was a price which maximized profitability (or any other corporate objective). The consumer could be quoted a price for seat or bed which was unique to his transaction and reflected accurately the real state of demand and supply in the market. If the airline ticket is to be issued by a computer terminal, as is just around the corner, it does not seem so far-fetched to make pricing a matter for the computer too.

Advertising and Sales Promotion

The terms advertising and sales promotion as used here can be distinguished by reserving the term advertising to those methods which are available for communicating with the consumer when his identity is unknown and when the advertiser is not in direct touch with him. It thus embraces most forms of media advertising, TV advertising, Press advertising and so on. Sales promotion will be used to describe those methods of communication where the identity of the consumer is known, as when the advertiser is reaching his retailer by letter, or when he is in touch with conference organizers or club secretaries or other intermediaries. Clearly the terms do not lend themselves to absolutely precise definition without doing violence to the realities of actual usage, and some media advertising may still be directed to the retailer. Both advertising and sales promotion are methods of communicating with the consumer or with his intermediary.

The role of advertising can be summarized as that of impelling the consumer towards the point of sale, the retailer, where the product is stocked or where in the case of tourism and other services situations the product is accessible. The object of advertising is to persuade the consumer that he needs the product and in particular the advertiser's brand of it. It is essentially a method of communicating with the consumer in the belief that both manufacturer and consumer will derive benefit and satisfaction from the sale which will result.

Although the marketing concept is centred on consumers' needs, the foregoing paragraph may give rise to scruples about the morality of this view of advertising, particularly as media advertising is by definition obtrusive. But the advertiser must be assumed to face rational and responsible consumers who are capable of making wise purchases, or if they make unwise purchases, that they are fully responsible for their frivolities. It follows that advertising must not be fraudulent or misleading, but that an advertiser is not obliged to put the case for the prosecution. The advertiser is an advocate for his product, the rational consumer is the judge and jury. Further, it is sometimes said that advertisements should be factual and informative, as if this kind of advertisement were morally superior to advertisements which are emotive or persuasive. But if advocacy is the role of advertising, then facts and information will only find a place if these are the most persuasive ways of speaking to the consumer. Timetables and tariffs are very factual but hardly persuasive. (It may also be doubted whether it is possible to apprehend a fact without also forming an attitude to it; facts are always surrounded by a cloud of emotions and prejudices.)

In the great majority of cases, much of the conduct of advertising will entrusted to an advertising agency, who will undertake the planning of the campaign and its detailed realization. Advertising agencies are professional firms staffed by a variety of experts in the various facets not merely of advertising but of marketing in general. It is doubtful whether any but the very largest companies could afford to employ the whole range of expertise required in conducting an advertising campaign; in the same way a company will employ other professional advisers such as solicitors, or accountants, as well as having legally qualified members of its staff and qualified accountants on the payroll. Advertising agencies are remunerated by discount or commission from the advertising media owners, the newspapers, television networks, and so on. The practice is now widespread by which the advertising agency credits the client with the commission and recharges an equivalent fee, thus underlining the independent professional status of the advertising agency. A client company will undertake to brief its advertising agency, but when a campaign is agreed upon, the preparation of the advertisements for the Press, the booking of advertising space and time, the shooting of TV commercials, and the whole day-to-day conduct of the campaign will be managed by its advertising agency.

The effectiveness of an advertising campaign will depend chiefly upon the credibility of the message conveyed by the advertisement in the first place, and in the second upon the extent to which the message is seen by that segment of the market to which it is addressed, i.e. the coverage achieved by the campaign. Coverage will clearly depend not only upon the proportion of the market which sees the advertisements, but also on the frequency with which the advertisements are seen. A number of highly sophisticated methods of measuring the effectiveness of advertising have been developed, which are customarily used in planning and monitoring advertising performance.

Next, the broad characteristics of the most common advertising media must be outlined. The Press is a term used to cover newspapers of all kinds and magazines from the weekly woman's magazines to the official organs of professional bodies, the trade press, and a variety of specialized journals. Some countries, notably the United Kingdom, have a 'national' press, that is to say, one or more newspapers which are available throughout the country; other countries notably the USA and West Germany, have no national newspapers but several strong regional ones. The main feature of the Press as an advertising medium is its

.y; if the advertiser can identify the segments of the market he wishes to ᵼ, there will be a newspaper or magazine which is read by that segment. The wealthy business market can be reached via the *Financial Times* or the *Wall Street Journal,* a woman's market by *Woman* or *Fuer Sie,* most households by *Radio Times* or *Hör Zu,* and there is a wide range of specialist journals in most countries. Increasingly, colour reproduction is available in many newspapers and also of a high quality in many magazines.

By contrast, in most countries which have a developed network in operation, television advertising is very much a mass market medium and thus relativerly indiscriminate. Geographically, a degree of regionalization may be possible, but discrimination between markets of differing socio-economic profiles will be difficult, and the production costs of a TV commercial are such that it should be spread over a very wide audience. Colour is available in TV, and of course the medium can show movement and animation. For an appropriate product aimed at an appropriate audience, television is a very powerful medium inded; for many markets in tourism, however, the appeal of the product may not be large enough to justify the 'mass market' costs of television advertising.

Tourist Literature

Printed matter, such as brochures, prospectuses, tariffs, are not usually classed among advertising media, but it is justifiable to do so here because of the prominent part this type of literature plays in the marketing of tourism. Because the product in tourism is intangible, there is a need to describe very fully what the product is, and this can be done by producing an elaborate brochure. The advertising policy in this case will consider the prime objective to be to get the brochure into the hands of the final consumer, and then rely on the brochure to impel him to buy the product. This two-stage approach is used by tour operators and will be discussed in the next chapter. For the brochure itself, the very fullest use of colour is desired, and the cost of four-colour printing must be spread over very long runs if the cost per brochure is to be kept to a reasonable level. For long runs, heatset offset litho or gravure printing is desirable, and both these processes are fast and can produce good results from relatively poor quality paper. Even so, the presses must run well in advance of the booking period, and there is a considerable lead time from the finalization of the brochure contents to the time of its delivery at the retailer. A large tour operator's brochure may start printing in the spring, for delivery in the autumn for holidays that will be taken in the summer of the following year, thus giving a lead time of perhaps eighteen months. When completed, the brochure will be given the widest possible distribution, even wastefully so, for it forms the main marketing tool in many tourist campaigns.

Other Media

Other minor media which may find a place from time to time are commercial radio, outdoor poster advertising, direct mailing, and cinema film. For most of the principal tourism generating countries the main media will be press and television advertising integrated with brochure distribution, and the minor media will find a place in supplement to these.

A note should be made here of the importance of subsuming all advertising together with other manifestations of the product and the company under the umbrella of a corporate design policy. An airline must present the same visual impact in the countries it serves equally with that it manifests in its home territory. A world-wide hotel group needs to make it clear to its clientele that each hotel is part of a world-wide chain and can be seen to be so. The corporate design policy goes further than a mere trade mark; conventional advertising as well as the physical appearances should all be seen to come from the same stable.[6]

Public Relations in Tourism

Public relations may be defined as the continuous and consistent representation of an organisation's policies to the public at large and to sections of the public who have a special interest in the organization's activities, e.g. to shareholders, to Members of Parliament, as well as to its actual and potential customers. The public relations function should not merely be seen as the securing of 'free space' in newspapers and magazines, although this can be an important and valid aspect of public relations work. A positive attitude to public relations in an organization's activities is evidence that it recognizes a duty to keep the public aware of those activities, and of their impact upon society and its environment.

In tourism, the need for making full information available to potential and actual tourists places a special task on the public relations function in official tourist organizations — indeed, such tourist organizations may often be seen as public relations organizations primarily. Their main concern is the creation and maintenance of an attractive image of the destination. This is often promoted by giving facilities to journalists to visit the country or the region. Most large newspapers and magazines in the generating countries, and many broadcasting organizations carry regular features and programmes on travel and tourism. The distinction between new and existing tourist products is again to be noted: a new resort area will wish to invite journalists to experience for themselves the attractions of the area, so that the attractions may be fairly described in newspapers and other media. An existing resort area whose attractions are generally well understood will need to concentrate on retaining the image and flavour of those attractions against the competition from new resorts.

Tourism is singularly prone to natural disasters as well as man-made ones. Snowfields give rise to avalanches, many of the world's resort areas are in hurricane belts, or in earthquake zones. Hotels catch fire, aircraft do crash. Disastrous events which involve tourists attract the attention of the news media in a way not paralleled when only residents are involved. Tourist authorities who are caught up in a disaster have a special public relations need which can best be met by advance contingency planning for the possibility of disaster.

Tourist authorities experience a special need for public relations within their own country or region to explain to the resident population the benefits of tourism, in order that the tourists are sympathetically received, and also to explain to the appropriate legislature, national or local, how and why expenditure on tourist development and promotion is being incurred, and that the resources available are being efficiently deployed.

21 *Marketing Applications*

A single organization, whether an official tourist organization or a firm in the commercial sector, will not necessarily use all the available marketing tools. The particular mix of techniques will vary from time to time and from case to case. This chapter is concerned in exploring the use made of the available tools of marketing by providers of single products, for example transport and accommodation undertakings, by tour operators and by tourist authorities.

The order in which a marketing campaign is carried out logically will vary again according to whether the product is new or an existing one. The cycle of marketing operations bearing this in mind may be described as follows:

1. The tourist product is identified in broad terms, usually as a result of extensive market research. In the case of a new tourist product, market research findings will be a principal source; in the case of an existing product, there will be past experience available as well.
2. The exact product is formulated and priced, and the specific segment of the market to which it is to be directed is identified.
3. If applicable, the retail outlets are next acquainted with the details of the product, by means of, for example, workshops, special promotions to the retail trade, retailers' manuals, and staff training.
4. Advertising and sales promotion are directed towards the identified market segment, which will generate customers from the public in the appropriate market segment for the retail outlet, knowing about the product and prepared to buy it.
5. Once the public have started buying the product, the results of the marketing campaign can be evaluated, in the light of current experience, and possibly with the aid of further market research designed to monitor progress, and adjustments to the product be made.

As compared with ordinary consumer goods marketing, several further particular features of marketing in tourism must be noted in this context:

(i) The retailer, the travel agent, does not carry a stock of the intangible tourist product; he thus lacks the powerful incentive of a full stock to promote any particular product. There is thus a very low brand loyalty at the retail level.
(ii) The lack of a retail stock which in the case of consumer goods protects the manufacturer from the immediate and direct effects of minor fluctuations in demand. If retail stocks rise or fall temporarily, the consumer goods manufacturer does not feel the effect at once. In marketing tourism, the supplier feels at once a diminution of demand, and hence the volatility of demand is faced immediately by him.
(iii) The absence of brand loyalty at the retail level means that the tourist supplier's advertising has to work harder — the final consumer will rarely be faced by a retailer anxious to sell him a particular brand.

(iv) The composite nature of many of the toursit products offered makes the satisfying of the customer complex at the retail level; the tourist wants an airline seat and an hotel bed, and without the one, may have no demand for the other. The supply of one is dependent on the supply of the other.

This last point is of the greatest significance. The whole-hearted adoption of the marketing concept implies that airlines are not merely in the airline business, that hotels are not merely in the accommodation business, that the product is not the seat or the bed; both airline and hotel are truly in the business of tourism, and the true product is the holiday or the business trip.

The Marketing of Specific Tourist Services

Specific tourist services include notably the various forms of accommodation and transport which go to make up the composite tourist product, together with the attractions of the destination. This section deals with the tourist services and their marketing; later sections deal with the special case of tour operation and of the destination.

The accommodation industry has been discussed above (*see* Part V) in some detail. While an increasing part of the stock of accommodation is being marketed as part of an inclusive tour, the bulk of it is still marketed as a separate component in the composite tourist product. From a marketing point of view, the individual hotel has much in common with a retail outlet, particularly when the individual hotel is part of the hotel chain or is a member of a co-operative voluntary group. For the population of its immediate hinterland, an hotel is a special kind of bespoke retailer.

As in the case of a transport undertaking, much of the demand for accommodation is a derived demand, arising at random, and to an extent the success of an hotel will be closely bound up with its location. The two facets which engage attention here are firstly the possibility of gaining special kinds of business such as conferences, and secondly the effect of being a member of an hotel chain or group. The gaining of conference and similar business will be attractive at seasons of the year when other demand for accommodation is not buoyant. This kind of business rarely requires a full-scale marketing campaign, the approach being made as a matter of selling or negotiation with conference organizers.

However, the large hotel chains find it desirable to market their space in a more sophisticated way, particularly when the several units are situated in different countries. The Inter-Continental Hotels, owned by Pan American World Airways, were created deliberately to complement the airline's route network, and their marketing stance is to assure the traveller of reasonably consistent standards throughout the world. Their principal marketing pre-occupation has been towards the retail travel trade, and only to a limited extent towards the final consumer, the tourist. Within one country, however, an hotel group can usefully direct its marketing effort to the individual tourist, as Trust House Forte have done in the United Kingdom.

Membership of a chain or of a co-operative for marketing purposes has enabled hotels to promote bulk business of a package nature. By definition, bulk purchase implies the existence of an intermediary travel organizer, either a tour operator or the organizer of affinity groups. The Prestige Hotels co-operative in the United Kingdom is a good example of how a number of independently owned hotels can attract bulk purchases by combining their marketing efforts co-operatively.

A reservations system was seen above (Chapter 20) as a marketing tool in the management of demand. Several large hotel groups conduct their own centralized reservations systems. This is seen more as a direct convenience to the customer than as an instrument of demand management; in that respect a centralized reservations system is only performing part of its potential role.

Demand for transport in tourism is likewise a derived demand. Except in the limited case of sightseeing tours, it is not the transportation that is desired for its own sake, but rather the possibility of being elsewhere by its means. Of the two forms of transport chiefly involved in tourist movement, the aeroplane and the car, only the former can be said to be directly stimulated by the use of marketing techniques, but in the case of the United Kingdom, the car ferry shipping services (*see* Chapter 10) are important tourist services.

Transport undertakings may direct their marketing with two ends in view. They may co-operate deliberately with a given destination in cases where the particular undertaking faces little competition with rivals. Historically, there have rarely been in Europe more than two airlines operating on a single route and these two have usually operated pool agreements to limit day-to-day competition. It is logical in such circumstances for the three partners, two airlines plus the destination, to combine their marketing efforts to promote traffic to the destination, in the knowledge that the tourists are bound to use one or other of the airlines. Much of the development of the Spanish resorts was stimulated by joint marketing by BEA and Iberia and the Spanish National Tourist Office; similarly, for inwards tourists to the UK, British and foreign carriers joined with the then British Travel Association (now the British Tourist Authority — *see* Part IX below) in the co-operative marketing of Britain.

In cases where there are several transport operators in rivalry, as for example in cross-Channel ferries from the UK, or in transatlantic air routes, the marketing effort is extended less in increasing the size of the cake, and more on attracting traffic which will give the operator a larger slice of whatever cake is available. This effort to increase market share is encouraged when fares are fixed by agreement. Denied the possibility of competing on price, the transport undertaking competes with its rivals on the service it can offer, superior frequencies, more convenient departure times, better food, and more luxurious vehicles. Though perfectly familiar, it may be doubted whether this approach pays attention to what the tourist really needs. The close identification of the transport operator with the destination of the tourist recognizes what the tourist product is; and the identification, for example, of Eastern Airlines as the official airline for Disneyworld in Orlando, Florida, recognizes that Disneyworld is the true reason why the passenger is being carried to that particular destination.

The principal challenge to the scheduled airlines has been the emergence of non-scheduled carriers. This challenge is not merely an effect of cheapness possible in non-scheduled carriage. It is also a marketing challenge, just because the non-scheduled operator generally offers an entire tourist product, where the airline's identity is submerged in the concept of a total holiday package.

The Marketing of Inclusive Tours

The tour operator is the manufacturer of a true tourist product; he buys the components of the package, the inclusive tour (transport, accommodation, etc.) from the suppliers of the individual tourist services and packages and brands them into a single entity. The inclusive tour is the fastest-growing part of tourism in Western Europe, and it has been created with deliberate marketing policies. It is noteworthy that many of the successful tour operating companies are subsidiaries of large industrial or commercial organizations who are trading in other fields, and it is certain that they have been able to make a significant contribution to the marketing programme of their tour-operating subsidiaries from their experience of the marketing of ordinary consumer goods or other services.

The first step was to recognize that demand for a holiday, typically in the Mediterranean, was highly price-elastic. Given that low prices could be achieved, the next step was to create a package that would be amenable to the techniques of marketing. The product, it can be argued, that the tourist buys is a holiday in an attractive hotel, in a sunny climate on the shores of the Mediterranean. If this is true, then the name of the airline that flies there, the proprietor of the hotel, and the country in which it is situated are all of minor importance — they are not features of the tourist product which will substantially influence the tourist's buying decision. The holiday product could be standardized, irrespective of its site.

This standardization is highly significant for marketing. If a tour operator has several destinations which he serves, the level of marketing impact he could make, were each destination marketed separately, would not reach a threshold level. But by branding his packages and standardizing them, he can market his tours at a level of impact well above the threshold. The particular pack, as it were, in which he wraps his product is the brochure — his catalogue — in which all the tours offered are listed and which contains a booking form. The next task is to secure the distribution of the brochure (which is a substantial volume printed in full colour), and this is achieved by a very wide distribution to retail travel agents. Typically, as much as 90 per cent of his bookings will come from retail travel agents. The public is then urged to obtain the brochure by massive media advertising.

Thus the marketing of an inclusive tour is a two-stage operation. Firstly, the brochure itself is treated as a product in the same sense as any other consumer product (being tangible, this is possible) and it is stocked at the retail level and advertised to the public, exactly as discussed in the marketing cycle described above. Secondly, the brochure can be viewed as an advertising medium selling the intangible real tourist product, the holiday, and at this point the caveats mentioned above when considering the marketing cycle in tourism apply forcefully.

Only in the marketing of inclusive tours has the real power of marketing techniques been demonstrated in the market for holidays. Their success, not only in the United Kingdom but in West Germany and Scandinavia, also has transformed European tourism. The marketing function in this respect at least has passed from the individual provider of components to the tour operator, manufacturer, and marketeer of a genuine tourist product.

Marketing and the Tourist Organization

In most countries which are substantial receivers of tourists, a national tourist organization supervises and encourages the activities of the individual suppliers of tourist services (*see* Part IX below), and part of this function consists in influencing the quality of tourist attractions and facilities. The other main role of the national tourist organization is promotional and is concerned with marketing.

The contribution made by the national tourist organization in a tourism generating country to the marketing of its home country can be considered in two stages of development. The first stage is when the country is in the early years of its development as a tourist destination. The population of the generating countries may be only dimly aware of the attractions of Ruritania, they may be sceptical about the facilities for tourists in Ruritania, and doubtful about how to get there. The prime function in this case of the Ruritanian National Tourist Organization in the generating country is to create an awareness of Ruritania. This will be achieved as far as the public is concerned principally by advertising and by public relations. If the market is identified as large and undifferentiated, the advertising campaigns may need to be nationwide. This presents a problem for smaller, poorer countries who may not readily dispose of the money involved in advertising in the industrialized generating countries. Some geographical limitation in segmenting the market may be acceptable; for example, in the United Kingdom, the London and South East region shows the greatest propensity to travel abroad; on the other hand, the media available for regional coverage are limited basically to the London evening newspaper and the London television networks. In the USA there are no national newspapers, and the regional advertising media are rather more powerful; the principal generating regions are the Atlantic seaboard States, the area around Chicago and Detroit, and California. The content of the advertising may invite the interested reader to send for descriptive brochures.

Simultaneously with the attempt to create awareness of Ruritania goes the provision of information to the public. One or more ground-floor public information offices will be established in the principal generating areas where the public can obtain information about the country. In parallel with this will go a programme of education of the travel trade, by means of educational visits to Ruritania, film shows and other presentations, and travel writers will be invited to visit the country as guests of the national tourist organization. At this stage in the development of a country's tourist industry, the role of the national tourist organization is to support and pave the way for the marketing efforts of the commercial undertakings such as the airlines and the hotel companies. In the mind of the public, the role of the national tourist organization is akin to co-operative advertising conducted by trade associations (especially in the field of undifferentiated agricultural products).

The second stage of development in the marketing role of the national tourist organization comes when the volume of tourists visiting Ruritania is large enough for tour operators and other travel organizations to be able to specialize in that country. At this stage, the work of the national tourist office will be re-oriented towards the travel trade. Public advertising at this stage gives place to methods designed to aid the tour operator to construct inclusive tours. Public ground-floor information offices may be superseded by normal business premises whose prime purpose is liaison with the trade rather than with public. Film shows to the public yield to 'workshops' at which the travel organizers of the generating country can meet and do business with the Ruritanian suppliers of tourist services. The emphasis will shift from communicating with the public to securing facilities for the travel trade. This shift of emphasis occurred in the past, but with the emergence of the tour operator in the Western generating countries, even countries which do not at present receive very large numbers of tourists may begin the promotion with the tour operators rather than with the public. The offer of holidays in Ruritania may be particularly attractive to the public if packaged by a reputable and known tour operator, even if Ruritania is little known as a destination hitherto.

Further, the conduct or supervision of market research on behalf of all tourist interests may form part of the work of the national tourist organization. It is a curious fact that few national tourist organizations conduct large-scale market research in the countries that generate their tourist flows, whereas they do so in respect of their own country. Even in the United Kingdom, where the BTA has a proud record of market research in its principal markets, this effort is nothing like so comprehensive as the British National Travel Survey which records the holiday habits of the British population, and the International Passenger Survey (*see* Part III above).

Many established resorts and destinations have their own local organization to promote their attractions to tourists. These local tourist organizations may be more or less autonomous or may be grouped under the surveillance of a regional organization (*see* Part IX below). Within the limits of their available finance, the individual resort will mainly confine its promotion to the issue of a local guide-cum-accommodation list. The appeal of such guides is primarily to a known market that wishes to take holidays in Blackpool or Bournemouth or Margate and whose chief problem is to select accommodation.

The resort's brochure, often a substantial document, is distributed by advertising it in an appropriate series of newspapers and magazines or by means of commercial television. On receiving a copy, the intending visitor is expected to purchase his accommodation directly from the hotel or pension. In Britain, the main advertising for the brochures occurs in January and the bulk of the replies asking for a copy are received within a fortnight. The marketing of typical resorts is thus a primitive but effective operation. The larger resorts such as Torbay (Torquay), Bournemouth, and Scarborough supplement the brochure distribution by information bureaux which may keep a status diary of accommodation.

In the United Kingdom, the national tourist boards created by the Development of Tourism Act 1969 have recognized that the increasing affluence and motorization of the holidaymaking population make the region the most effective unit for marketing purposes: the modern holidaymaker is more interested in the whole of the South-West of Britain rather than in a particular resort. While the largest resorts like Bournemouth and Torbay may still handle a large part of their promotion, it makes sense for smaller resorts to merge their identity with the region in which they are situated.

Part VIII

Planning and Development

Further Reading for Part VIII

Association Internationale d'Experts Scientifiques du Tourisme, *Tourisme et Environment*
British Tourist Authority: *Tourism and the Environment*
British Tourist Boards: *Resorts and Spas in Britain*
Burkart, A.J., and Medlik, S. (editors): *The Management of Tourism*, Part VIII
English Tourist Board: Planning for Tourism in England
English Tourist Board (and others): *Tourism and Conservation*
Greater London Council: *Tourism — A Statement of Policies*
Kaiser, C., and Helber, L.E.: *Tourism Planning and Development*
Lawson, F.R., and Baud-Bovy, M.: *Tourism and Recreational Development*
Patmore, J.A.: *Land and Leisure*
Scottish Tourist Board: *Planning for Tourism in Scotland*
Wales Tourist Board: *Tourism in Wales — A Plan for the Future*

References to Part VIII

1 Outdoor Recreation Resources Review Commission: *Outdoor Recreation for America*
2 Burton, T.L., Outdoor Recreation in America, Sweden and Britain, *Town and Country Planning*, 34, 1966
3 British Travel Association and the University of Keele: *Pilot National Recreational Survey*
4 Government Social Survey: *Planning for Leisure*
5 Organization for Economic Co-operation and Development: *International Tourism and Tourism Policy in OECD Member Countries 1971*
6 Organization for Economic Co-operation and Development: *Tourism in OECD Member Countries 1970*
8 British Tourist Authority: *Digest of Tourist Statistics*
10 Law, S.: Planning for Outdoor Recreation in the Countryside, *Journal of the Town Planning Institute*, 53, 1967
13 Nicholson, M.: *The Environmental Revolution*
15 Middleton, M., in British Tourist Authority: *Tourism and the Environment*
16 Greater London Council: *Tourism and Hotels in London*
17 Greater London Council: *Tourism — A Paper for Discussion*
18 Greater London Council: *Tourism — A Statement of Policies*
21 Outdoor Recreation Resources Review Commission, *op. cit.*
23 Naylor, G.H.: *Contribution of Tourism to Quality of Life*

References 7, 9, 11, 12, 14, 19, 20, 22 are based on Patmore, J.A.: *Land of Leisure*

22   *Leisure and Resources*

The 1960s were known as the United Nations Development Decade, in which the attention of individual governments and of international agencies was focused on the developing countries of the world. In the same period the developed countries became increasingly preoccupied with leisure and with their own environment. Increased leisure time, higher disposable incomes and greatly enhanced personal mobility combined to create the challenge of leisure: how the leisure time is used; the demands it creates for facilities; the pressures it generates on land and amenity, as well as on the social structure of communities. In this the concerns of the developed and of the developing countries have soon become linked and shared. The former, whilst faced with their own environmental problems, have generated ever-increasing flows of traffic to the latter, thus creating concerns and problems similar to their own for the areas and communities visited.

Much of the increased leisure is spent in and about the home, much of it in the immediate environs of the towns and districts in whcih people live and work. Cinemas, theatres, dance halls, and concert halls provide many of the outlets for the increased leisure time of the community devoted to indoor pursuits outside the home, when leisure time is counted in hours, half-days, and evenings. Parks, sports fields, and other facilities fulfil the same roles as providers of local outdoor recreation. The daily and still to a great extent the weekly leisure time gives rise to the demand for essentially local leisure facilities.

But the annual leisure pattern in developed countries is of a different significance when it comes to determining how and where the disposable free time is spent. No less than four weeks' paid holidays have become universal for their working populations by the beginning of the 1980s and about a half of this time tends to be spent away from home. This proportion is growing, as is the incidence of more than one holiday away from home; a growing proportion tends to be spent abroad.

At the same time the sharp distinction between the annual and the weekly leisure pattern is becoming increasingly blurred. The two-and two-and-a-half-day week-end, with additional days on a number of occasions each year, gives rise to short holidays which are quite unconnected with the paid annual holiday entitlement. In 1979 over 60 per cent of the British population took an annual holiday and 19 per cent more than one holiday of four nights or more away from home, a total of almost 50 million holidays; but in the same year in the region of 50 million short holidays of one to three nights were also spent away from home.

Thus holidays represent a significant proportion of leisure time. We have seen earlier that they are highly concentrated in time: in Britain, France, and Sweden, for example, between 80-90 per cent of main holidays are taken between June and September and between one-half and two-thirds of them in July and August. No less important is the location of the impact: well over a half of main holidays in Britain, for example, include a stay by the seaside.

Added to the holiday pressures are those of other related activities. Often the holiday demand is superimposed on areas which are also visited intensively on day and half-day trips. Whilst the demand still continues to be highly localized, the mobility continues to increase. Already the coast may be reached in less than three hours' drive from any part of Britain and more than one-third of the population can reach the Lake District in the same time; most residents on the Continent of Europe can visit in the same time another country.

Some two-thirds of the population of Britain can reach almost any other part of the country on a week-end trip; similar proportions of residents of Continental Europe can do so within Europe. Most tourist destinations in the developing world are no more than a few hours' flight from large concentrations of population in the developed world.

The Need for Information

The challenge of leisure was recognized in the United States by Congress setting up the Outdoor Recreation Resources Review Commission in 1958. Effects of present and estimated future patterns of population, income, travel, and leisure time on outdoor recreation were studied and the Bureau of the Census conducted on behalf of the Commission a National Recreation Survey based on interviews with a sample of 16,000 Americans. The outcome of this massive effort is twenty-seven Study Reports and a final Report, *Outdoor Recreation for America,* published in 1962. In its analysis of demand and of its implications the work of the Commission provides a comprehensive appraisal and a firm basis for policy: on the need for facilities, on the requirements for land and resources, and on priorities for investment.[1]

Nothing comparable was accomplished anywhere else in the world by the time this book was written, but the awareness of the need was manifested, for example, in Sweden by a sample survey of the population aged 18-65 in urban areas in 1963[2] and in Britain by two major national surveys based on interviews with representative samples of the population, in addition to many regional and local surveys. In 1967 the British Travel Association and the University of Keele published their *Pilot National Recreation Survey* based on a sample of over 3,000 interviews carried out in 1965, and in 1969 Report No.2 gave a regional breakdown of the data.[3] The Government Social Survey, *Planning for Leisure,* was undertaken on behalf of the Department of Education between September 1965 and March 1966 and published in 1969. It was based on interviews with some 2,700 people in urban areas and separate samples for Inner London and the New Towns, taking into account special interests of the Inner London Education Authority and of the Ministry of Housing and Local Government.[4] Although direct comparisons between the three countries are difficult, because of differences in definitions of activities and in the different age groups and periods covered by the surveys, it is clear that the higher the income level, occupational class, and educational status, the greater the number of activities pursued, particularly those of an active nature, and it is people with these characteristics who comprise an increasing proportion of the population.* In other countries with higher income levels, participation in outdoor recreation greatly exceeds the levels reached in Britain in the 1960s; there was some evidence of an increase in the 1970s. Similarly, although the incidence of holidays at about 60 per cent of the British population is among the highest in the world, higher levels have been recorded in Scandinavia. And holidays are and are likely to remain the peak of leisure experience.

The Geographical Pattern of Demand in Tourism

Two main component sources of demand may be identified in tourism in individual countries: the residents and the visitors from abroad. The former represent the home market and constitute the most important source in most developed countries, the latter are the export market and tend to form by far the most important source of demand in tourism in developing countries. This broad generalization may conceal significant variations between regions, but provides a simple basis for the assessment of demand which is also reflected in major surveys of tourist traffic (*see* Part III). The pattern of demand of both groups tends to be well established in developed countries and changes only gradually; it tends to be highly volatile and to experience high and varying growth rates in developing countries. To that extent planning for tourism is a relatively easier exercise in most northern countries with a relatively stable pattern of demand and within the constraints of highly developed resources, facilities, and controls, which also tend to inhibit rapid change. By contrast demand predictions in most southern countries tend to be more hazardous, but resources and regulation of development allow for greater freedom of action and more rapid change.

Several broad patterns of demand emerge in relation to different types of location of tourist activity from various surveys of domestic tourism in individual countries, in particular the correlation between the topography of the country, especially the length of the coastline, and the popularity of different types of holiday location. In 1970, 45 per cent of summer holiday trips by the French population were to the seaside, 30 per cent to the countryside, 18 per cent to the mountains, 4 per cent on tours, and 3 per cent to towns.[5] The favourite geographical locations of Italians are the lakes and the seaside: 52 per cent of total domestic nights in 1968 were spent in these locations. [6] In Britain 75 per cent of all main holidays included a stay by the seaside, 16 per cent in other towns and cities, 11 per cent in mountains and moors, 7 per cent by lake and riverside, 9 per cent in other inland locations.[§7]

However, on short holidays, which have a different seasonal distribution, inland cities, towns, and other locations account for a higher proportion of holidays, particularly outside the main holiday months, and the seaside for a

* The three profile characteristics are, of course, related to and not independent of each other.

§ The proportions add up to more than 100 per cent because of double counting when a particular location is included under more than one designation and when a holiday is spent in more than one location.

much lower proportion of the total even in the summer.[8]

Whilst foreign visitors to Mediterranean countries tend to resemble the resident populations in their geographical distribution, this is distinctly less so the farther North one proceeds. For example, relatively few overseas visitors to Britain go to the coast; most of them concentrate on London and a limited number of inland towns and cities. A similar pattern emerges elsewhere in Europe, with the possible exception of mountainous regions of Austria, Germany, and Switzerland.

It is most difficult to generalize about the geographical pattern of tourist demand in developing countries. They offer a wide variety of attractions, ranging from sunny climates and beaches, as on the coasts of North Africa and the West Indies, mountains and scenery, as in Central Africa, history and folklore, as in Mexico, and sometimes a combination of these, as is the case with India.

The individual countries have reached different stages of economic and social development generally, and of tourism development in particular, and tourist flows are largely determined by the development of facilities, which is rather uneven.

It is already clear that the pattern of tourist demand in the Third World shares two prominent characteristics of the developed countries with their resultant problems: a geographical concentration in a limited number of locations and a seasonal concentration, both of which exercise extreme pressures on resources. Fortunately, both characteristics need not be permanent for them: commonly land is in abundance and demand may be spread in space as facilities are developed; it is also of crucial importance to the transport and tour operators in the generating countries to spread the demand in time, as they have begun to do successfully already.

Resource-basis and User-orientation

The geographer and the planner divide resources devoted to recreation and tourism into two broad categories — resource-based and user-oriented. The distinction is one of degree rather than one of kind and the two are not always mutually exclusive. The significance of resource-based lies in their quality which provides the attraction, irrespective of its location. It may be a unique landscape or an attractive coastline, an ancient monument or historic building, snow-covered mountains or a navigable river. Their character attracts those who wish to use them from considerable distances and their appeal is national or international rather than local or regional.

By contrast user-oriented resources are most important for their accessibility than for their quality. The quality must be adequate for the purpose for which the resource is to be used, but the resource must be above all accessible to the potential user. A prominent example is sites for sports, and also commons, parks and woodlands, which afford easy access in terms of both time and distance, although superior facilities of the same type may be available further away.

User-oriented resources cater, therefore, primarily for local or regional needs, rather than attracting nationally.[9]

Many studies suggest a strong correlation between the attractions of an area and the distance people are prepared to travel to reach them and it has been suggested that facilities may be classified into categories based on their relative powers of attraction as follows.[10] The first three are within the range of the half-day visitor, regional facilities within day-visitor range, national ones form the tourist destinations:

Zone of influence	Radius of attraction for bulk of visitors
local	5-10 miles
intermediate	
sub-regional	20-30 miles
regional	50 miles
national	unlimited

Thus the largest proportion of visitors to Southend come on half-day trips from the East End of London, to Whitley Bay on the Northumberland coast from nearby Newcastle upon Tyne, and to Southport from Liverpool. The largest numbers of visitors to South Coast resorts east of the Solent are day visitors from London, and to the Peak District from the industrial cities which surround it. By contrast the Irish Sea coast attracts in the main staying visitors from England, and such destinations as Edinburgh, Stratford-on-Avon, Cambridge, and Oxford not only from various parts of Britain, but also significantly from abroad.

It is the essence of tourism to be elsewhere for periods of time, and it is resource-based facilities which are of prime concern in the planning and development in tourism. The tourist may and indeed does enjoy user-oriented facilities in common with the resident of a particular area; the resident fortunate to live in a resource-based area has easy access to it, if he wishes to use it; to that extent planning and development has to take into account both types of user. But the main impact of tourism is in areas which attract tourists from some distance in large numbers because of the quality of their resources. If is therefore important to consider these resources as tourist resources, the kind of experience they provide, and the role they play.

Recreation surveys indicate that, apart from pleasure driving, swimming, fishing, and in some countries boating generate the highest levels of participation in outdoor activities. Holiday surveys suggest the dominant attraction of water as a holiday attraction. The sea coast and inland waters in the form of lakes, rivers, reservoirs, and canals represent therefore the most important resources in recreation and tourism. The countryside, including mountains, rank next. These natural resources are considered in broad terms in the remaining pages of this chapter.

The Coast

In most countries with access to the sea the coast is the most important resource for tourism. Nowhere is this more true than in the case of large islands, such as those which make up Britain, where one-fifth of half-day trips, one-third of day trips, and over a half of all holidays have the seaside as their destination, with no part of the country more than seventy-five miles away. As compared, for example, with a coastline of less than forty miles for Belgium, there are over 2,700 miles of coast round England and Wales alone.

Tourism competes for its use with other forms of development: ports and associated towns; oil refineries, power stations, and other industries; defence and other government uses. But the greater part of it is devoted wholly or mainly to recreation and tourism, through resorts and through the open coastline. The urban part is extensive and represents the focus: some 100 towns in Britain may be described as coastal resorts; the three largest, Blackpool, Bournemouth and Brighton are centres of urban areas, with over a quarter million population. The resorts absorb most of the pressure of demand and provide a particular outlet for the majority who prefer gregarious concentration, entertainment, and other facilities. Three further uses of resorts have developed significantly. The ownership of second homes, whether cottages, chalets, or caravans may in many cases legitimately be regarded as tourism; secondly, as places of retirement; thirdly, where suitably located, as dormitory towns for adjacent urban areas. A number of resorts already contain an element of each, in addition to holiday traffic; in several, such as Southend, Bexhill, and Whitley Bay in Britain, tourism has already ceased to be the dominant element in their economy.

Allowing for other uses and for the length of the urban resort coastline, the greater part of the coast in Britain is still one with open access, without any form of development. This applies not only to Scotland, but also to the coasts of Northumberland, Cumberland, and the West Wales in particular, and to long stretches in other parts.

Although the Victorian resort in England, with its intensively used foreshore, backed by a promenade and often extended into the sea by the pier, is in many ways unique, as we noted earlier, the sea coast as the focus of tourism is not. The parallels are, in fact, significant. The resorts absorb the seaside traffic even more exhaustively, as less of the open coastline is left in most European countries. Several cities in Northern Europe accommodate much of their working populations in near-by coastal resorts, which also attract increasing numbers of retired; the possession of a country cottage, often on the coast, is widespread in France and in Scandinavia. Many resorts also consciously seek and develop alternative complementary activities, to diversify the economy and to combat seasonality, e.g. the Canaries chrysanthemum cultivation, Bermuda offshore banking; at the same time Malta misses the dockyard, Gibraltar misses smuggling!

Inland Water

In countries with access to the sea, natural inland waters (rivers and lakes) and artificial ones (canals and reservoirs) are in many ways complementary to the coastal resources; for countries without such access, they are the only outlets for the lure of the water. Their supply is to a great extent finite and restricted in location; consumption for agricultural, domestic, and industrial use, as well as water-borne cargo transport, often compete for their use with recreation and tourism.

Much of the attraction of water is visual, as an adjunct to scenery, and for many uses, including fishing, the importance lies in the access to the banks rather than to the water itself. In comparison with such expanses as the Great Lakes in North America and even those of Northern Italy and Switzerland, which permit and can accommodate all or most water-borne recreation, there are no more than a few hundred square miles of inland water in Britain. There are few lakes of any size outside Scotland, the Lake District, and the Broads. Widespread river navigation is possible only with small boats, and sailing and cruising is confined to the relatively few broader and deeper stretches and to some canals, which have a cruising network of over 1,000 miles. Many of the 550 reservoirs are completely closed to public access and on others recreational use is severely restricted because of the risk of pollution.

Hence the pressure of recreational demand on inland water resources is great, particularly in the Lake District and the Norfolk Broads, the largest fully linked network in Britain, extending over some 120 miles. The number of holiday-makers in the region was estimated in 1938 at 100,000, in the mid-1960s it exceeded 250,000, with some 10,000 licensed craft, about a half of them for hire.[11]

Indeed, few resources for tourism in Britain experience such pressures and only the proximity of all parts of Britain to the coast provides relief. Moreover, all water-borne activities are not mutually compatible; sailing, power-boating, and water ski-ing are particularly difficult to accommodate in British inland waters. The initiatives of the Inland Waterways Association, the British Waterways Board, and other organizations in influencing the Government policy towards canals are noteworthy.[12]

Away from the Water

Away from the coast and inland waters, the countryside in its widest sense, including all areas outside the urban ones, presents most paradox and most problems in the context of tourism. On the one hand it represents the largest proportion of available land in most countries, yet in temperate climates most of it is in use as agricultural land or woodland, which is often not compatible with leisure use. Roads, which carry most tourists to their destinations in developed countries, may be seen as corridors of access, which make limited demand on land, as do railways and other transportation facilities. But most demands are made by various groups of visitors using the countryside in a variety of ways, particularly those using a car for their recreational experience. They represent a spectrum. At one extreme there are those who pass through without pausing, at the other extreme there are those who make for one particular destination where they remain as long as possible. The first group contribute to the volume of traffic using the road system, but make no specific demands on land; the second do; in between the two the intensity of the demand varies greatly.

However, the actual area demands, in the sense of land other than private land, being largely or exclusively devoted to recreation and tourism, are relatively small, even if day and half-day outings are taken into consideration. Their focus is networks of footpaths, roads and railway lines on the one hand, and nodes of intensive activity at parking and picnic sites on the other hand. Scattered in the countryside are historic houses and ancient monuments, zoo parks, and other 'honeypot attractions'. They are as important in the Loire Valley in France as in the Shires in Britain, and represent some of the most imaginative use of existing and new resources and tourism. Between them large expanses of land provide the scenery and the visual experience, but are devoted entirely to other uses.

Yet, these demands are at the core of the potential and actual conflict between tourism and the countryside, through lack of provision of access, as well as through the lack of care and consideration on the part of different types of user for each other's requirements. As on the coast, the problem is aggravated by the concentration of demand in space and in time. To this we shall return again in the next two chapters.

Tourism and the Environment

The resource-based land described above consisting of the coast, inland water, and the countryside represents in a nutshell the stock of natural resources for recreation and tourism, which assume varying relative significance in different countries and regions. These resources may be classified in greater detail to provide a comprehensive spectrum of the supply to match the demand made on them by increasing leisure, much of which is devoted to outdoor recreation and tourism. They also represent points of interaction between tourism and the environment. Whether as part of the overall concern with the quality of the environment and ecological balance in nature, so well explained, for example, by Max Nicholson in *The Environmental Revolution,*[13] or as part of the narrower concern with the demands and impact of outdoor recreation on land so ably demonstrated by Allan Patmore in *Land and Leisure,*[14] on which this part of the book has drawn heavily, tourism has to face the implications of its explosive share of man's leisure time.

The increased demand for leisure facilities is no transient phenomenon. The most pressing implications for tourism and other forms of recreation are still to come, as their growth continues. The purpose of this chapter has been to indicate the relationship between leisure, tourism, and mainly natural resources, as a general background to planning and development in tourism. The physical planning and development of facilities for tourism are discussed in the next chapter in the context of the requirements of tourism and of some of the problems which it faces. This is followed by a chapter devoted to conservation and management, which shows both the steps that have been taken in particular in Britain to conserve resources of importance in tourism, and the approach to the management of tourism which is necessary to ensure that tourism can not only develop in a way compatible with an enhanced quality of the environment, but also make a positive contribution to this enhancement.

23   *Infrastructure and Facilities*

Tourism takes many forms. A single trip may range from several miles to several thousand miles and include one or more forms of transport on the way. Stays of several days, weeks or months involve the use of one or more types of accommodation in one or more locations. Active and passive forms of recreation, conferences and meetings, sightseeing and summer schools, represent the spectrum of what the tourist does as part of his experience and in this he uses a variety of facilities and services, available more or less specifically for his use and enjoyment. The coast, inland waters, and the countryside, discussed in the last chapter, together with the climate, constitute the natural resources for his experience, which exist irrespective of the demands of tourism, although their availability and characteristics may be, to a greater or lesser extent, affected by tourism.

Superimposed on this variety of forms are resources of a different kind, which make tourism possible, and which are clearly identifiable, particularly in areas of intensive tourism development, where tourism shares them with few or no other types of activity. We refer to various forms of physical development, which make an area accessible to tourists, as well as to particular installations, which provide for the requirements of tourists in the area. They may be divided into two basic categories — the infrastructure and the superstructure.

The *infrastructure* includes all forms of construction on and below ground required by any inhabited area in intensive communication with the outside world and as a basis for intensive human activity within. It includes roads and parking areas, railway lines, harbours, and airport runways, as well as utility services of water supply, drainage and sewage disposal, electricity and power supply. The *superstructure* consists of passenger traffic terminals, hotels, restaurants, entertainment and shopping facilities, and the like. The dividing line between the two types of facilities is not sharp, but is nevertheless fundamental. The infrastructure has to precede the superstructure and has to be adequate to serve the needs of residents as well as of tourists. It is a condition of all the activities in tourism, and any repercussions of its inadequacy have been readily illustrated on access roads to tourist destinations generally, as well as by such problems experienced at the destinations themselves. Because of the scale of the development, the provision of the infrastructure normally extends over a wide area, with more than one ownership and more than one interest involved. For these reasons, and because of the heavy capital outlay, it is commonly provided by the government or other public authorities out of public funds. Because of the intensity of its requirements, and because it is often highly concentrated in particular places and at particular times, tourism creates special problems for the infrastructure. By contrast, individual facilities are often confined to limited areas of land, with more limited capital requirements, and as such may often be developed by commercial interests, if the infrastructure is adequate to begin with.

In the past much imaginative planning took place by private interests in towns and in the countryside, but until recently there was little physical planning and development in tourism in terms of a co-ordinated and regulated approach. Resorts have grown up spontaneously where natural resources provided an attractive setting and transportation links with other centres of population were created in recent times usually belatedly in response to the demands of heavy traffic; other cities and towns built to accommodate industrial and commercial activities and those engaged in them, often found themselves receiving increasing volumes of visitor traffic. Substantial tourist facilities were created piecemeal in individual locations, others came to be shared by the residents with the visitors. Existing infrastructure designed for the requirements of an earlier relatively static age came under the strain of a new mobile age in urban as well as rural areas in most developed countries. The need to re-plan existing uses of land and to plan for future ones became gradually more and more prominent, but it came to be acted upon in most countries only in the middle of the twentieth century; extensive war damage often provided the scope.

At the same time the transport revolution opened up new regions in individual countries and new parts of the world as potential tourist destinations. Abundant resources of land, untrammelled by existing uses, provided virgin conditions for systematic physical planning and development in tourism to meet the demands of the leisure explosion.

The Common Ground

We are therefore faced with two quite different tasks. One is physical planning and development in new areas with potential, but little or no existing tourist activity, and with most land and other resources uncommitted to existing uses. The other is the re-shaping of areas with significant tourist flows already, with existing patterns of land use and facilities. However, the two situations have several basic considerations in common.

The first is the need to assess demand; for new locations and facilities it is the potential demand, for existing ones the actual demand and how it may change if existing facilities are changed. What volume and what type of traffic may use a new holiday complex in the Southern Mediterranean or in the Highlands of Scotland, or a new conference centre in the Isle of Man, or a new hotel in the Outer Hebrides, are examples of the first order; how will the volume and type of traffic change if a marina is built, for example, in the Isle of Wight, a third airport is built for London, or existing hotels open casinos and night clubs in Brittany, are examples of the second order. Market research is the first essential step both in marketing and in development of both new and existing provisions of tourist facilities. Only when the market has been assessed can a meaningful and rational expression be given to the size and shape of the physical development.

The second common ground is the need for an assessment of the required resources of land, capital, and labour for any proposed development and of their alternative uses. The available land may be used for agriculture, industry, or residential development, as well as for tourism. The required investment capital may compete with its potential use in other forms of business activity if provided from private sources, and with the requirements for hospitals and schools if provided from public funds. If alternative sources of employment are available in the area, the quantity and quality of labour available for tourism has to be assessed in relation to the other sources of employment. However attractive tourism may be to its protagonists, it is often only one of several forms of development open to a community. When this is the case, normal commercial criteria of profit and return on capital are rarely adequate to evaluate the merits and draw-backs of alternative forms of development. In these circumstances there is much to be said for the use of cost-benefit analysis, which attempts to take into account all the consequences of alternative projects and where possible to measure them, and which applies yardsticks based on evidence about the worth the community attaches to benefits, or in the case of costs, benefits forgone. Some of the earliest and best known examples in Britain have been in the use of the technique as a method of investment appraisal in the transport field, with the assessments of the Victoria Underground line and the M1 motorway and, more recently in location studies, of the third London airport, and of port development.

The third matter of major common significance in tourism development to both new and existing areas is the respective needs of tourists and residents of the area and the compatibility of tourism with other activities. Physical planning and development control are normally in the hands of the local community through whatever planning machinery operates in a particular country. This is usually adequate to safeguard the interests of the resident population, when that machinery is adequate; however, often no one but the developers represent the interests of the tourists. Two problems, therefore, present themselves in varying degrees of acuteness, namely that the planning machinery may be inadequate or that it may be too restrictive against tourism. There is enough evidence to suggest that both problems do exist — the former in developing countries where mushroom growth of facilities has irretrievably mutilated some of the most attractive natural resources, as in Eastern Spain and the Balearic Islands, in the Canary Islands, and in large parts of the West Indies; the latter in some of the developed countries, including Britain. We have referred to this matter when examining problems of growth and development in the context of the significance of tourism in Chapter 6. We shall return to it again in Part IX when discussing the organization of tourism, for the interests of tourists can only be safeguarded by an effective tourist organization, which has to enter into the planning process.

The Changing Nature of Physical Planning and Development

It is well to remember that planning and development in the modern sense are largely post-war phenomena and less than a half a century old; we have seen that they are of an even more recent origin in tourism. The first national Town and Country Planning legislation in Britain dates to 1947; the first legislation of real relevance to tourism was the National Parks and Access to the Countryside Act in 1949 and it was not until the late 1960s that a positive stimulus to planning for recreation and tourism was provided almost simultaneously by the Countryside (Scotland) Act 1967, the Countryside Act 1968 in England and Wales, and the Development of Tourism Act 1969. In the 1970s the re-organization of local government gave local authorities considerable powers in relation to tourism including defining its place in the structure plans for their areas, and several other changes occurred in the nature of physical planning and development.

First and foremost, the growth of the tourist movement has changed the scale of development. The Jumbo jet and the massive hotel typify the scale in transportation and accommodation, the large tour operator in the organization of travel, the new tourist regions in Spain, Southern France, and Yugoslavia in the location of tourism. Where scale meant hundreds thirty years ago, it means thousands and hundreds of thousands today.

Individual projects, whether they be hotels or places of entertainment, have given way to holiday, conference, and entertainment complexes within tourist regions with a variety of attractions within a short drive from the tourist's base. Regional development in tourism has become a reality and increased personal mobility has widened the scope of planning and development geographically. The Aviemore Centre in Scotland is a major example in Britain, a country which as yet has not created a new tourist region.

Much development, earlier undertaken by local initiative and often financed locally, is now promoted and often financed internationally. Consortia of developers from several countries are the modern entrepreneurs and foreign funds, including those of international agencies, provide the investment capital for many projects conceived and designed by foreign consultants. Airlines, banks, mail order stores, oil companies, and developers are partners in tourism projects; in regions in developing countries and particularly in hotel development everywhere.

However, most physical development in tourism is also subject to growing control in the interests of the environment. All tourism activity is increasingly regulated in the interests of the consumer; physical planning and development are increasingly regulated in the interests of the tourist as well as the resident. The need for physical planning has come to be widely recognized, if not always readily accepted.

Planning the Infrastructure

There are two crucial aspects in the creation of the infrastructure: the capacity to serve a particular development and the range and type of facilities to be provided.

The assessment of capacity derives from the market assessment and the viability assessment of a project, the two comprising the outcome of a feasibility study. The number of users of a development determines not only the capacity of individual facilities within the development, but also the scale of the infrastructure required by these individual facilities and by the whole development. The infrastructure requirements may be divided into three main groups; those which provide lines of access and communication with the outside world, those which enable the movement of people at the destination, and those which supply essential services of lighting, heating, power, water, drainage, and sewage disposal for the development.

According to the location of the project, tourists may reach it by road, rail, on water, or by air, or by a combination of these means, and the provision of the infrastructure may accordingly call for the construction of roads, railway lines, harbours, and airport runways to carry the required volume of traffic to and from the area, with supporting facilities, telecommunications, and other means of communication.

The access network has to be extended within the area of development to provide means of communication and movement within the area and include adequate supporting facilities for those staying in the area.

A network of utility services extending over the whole area of development has to provide for the required volume of individual installations and for common services to the area as a whole, such as public conveniences and night lighting.

Because of the uncertainties involved in new developments, it is common for projects to be divided into stages to allow for gradual increase in size, as market assessments are confirmed in operation. This creates particular problems in the provision of the infrastructure, the overall design of which has to allow for such increase. Thus a dual carriageway may be envisaged when the development reaches its ultimate size, but a single carriageway is constructed in the initial stages; provision is made for a second airport runway; electricity and water supply are constructed, which may increase their capacity at a later date.

In existing areas of tourist activity the problem often arises that various parts of the infrastructure become inadequate in time to cope with the growth of traffic and the demands of individual facilities. An assessment of the current and future needs then has to be made to augment the existing provision.

These approaches are well illustrated in such major new developments as Disneyworld in Florida, the Languedoc-Roussillon region in France, and the projects sponsored by the World Bank in Tunisia, Yugoslavia, as well as on the Pacific coast of Mexico.

Planning the Superstructure

The individual facilities within a tourist area, ranging from passenger traffic terminals to accommodation, catering, entertainment, and shopping, comprise the superstructure in tourism. As they are commonly provided by individual developers and operators, they are also normally planned individually, particularly in existing tourist areas, but in comprehensive new developments they may be components of an overall plan.

Airport buildings and terminals, port facilities, railway, bus and coach terminals are usually planned in conjunction with the related infrastructure, as are car parks; their capacity assessments and spatial dispositions are derived from the related infrastructure facilities. Although individual forms of transport constitute some competition for each other, with the exception of car parks, one central facility of each type is normally adequate for most destinations. But their location and integration are of crucial importance to allow for proximity to key areas and for inter-change; in order to avoid congestion and the worst environmental effects of traffic, they also present some of the most difficult problems of planning in tourism.

The capacity of a destination for staying traffic is determined by the capacity of its hotels and other accommodation units. This is therefore a crucial dimension: to establish the optimum accommodation capacity which is economically viable for the operators and in turn for the economic prosperity of the community, whilst representing the optimum volume of staying visitors for the capacity of the whole destination and its individual attractions. We shall return to this aspect again shortly when we discuss planning for tourism in urban and rural areas, and again in the next chapter in the context of conservation and management in tourism.

The remaining facilities, in particular catering, entertainment, and shops, present few issues of principle and relatively few planning problems. They are some of the most volatile enterprises, which are readily provided by commercial entrepreneurs where the demand exists and, except to themselves, they rarely raise issues of capacity as an overall planning matter in tourism. But their nature and variety do, as an aspect of the overall physical harmony, which creates a visual impact, and which goes to the root of the nature of the tourist destination. It is for these reasons that they have come to be regulated, not only by the planning machinery, but also by the tourist authorities in a number of countries.

This discussion of the superstructure raises not only questions of capacity, but also of the right mix of different types of facilities, which constitute vital elements of the tourist products. As such they deserve attention in the context of physical planning and development, because they have also vital marketing implications.

Planning in a Rural Area

In the last chapter the coast, inland waters, and countryside were seen as the natural resources for which tourism is in competition with other uses. The focus of the pressure on theses resources is exercised in two main directions: in the networks of movement, represented by lines of communication, and in the nodes of activity, represented by concentrations of people. Therein lies the essence of the physical planning and development problem in tourism in a rural area in temperate climates.

Most available land in these areas has been committed to various uses for a long time. Tourism, as we know it today, is a relatively new phenomenon, which generates new demands on land for use and enjoyment on a scale not envisaged until recently. Although all its demands are relatively modest, tourism is a new-comer and is often seen as an intruder by the farmer and the forester in par-ticular, who have been sole users of the land before and unaccustomed to share their domains.

The concern is wider than that. Tourist traffic *en route* and where it concentrates in particular locations affects the rural environment. Cars and coaches create congestion on the roads and at sites, as well as noise and other forms of pollution. Aircraft noise disturbs the residents and causes damage to wild life. Tourists damage crops and flora and leave litter behind. Without tourism the rural environment would stand a better chance of being preserved, although its enjoyment would be confined to relatively few. Nevertheless the landscape may be spared some adverse effects without tourism.

Tourism also affects employment. Although the drift from the land to the towns has been going on in most developed countries for many years, tourism may take its toll in accentuating problems of rural employment in agriculture.

Planning legislation goes a long way to protect the physical character of the countryside and other means of protection have been devised in various count-ries which we examine in the next chapter. However, both rural and urban areas have become increasingly both workshops and playgrounds. It is therefore necessary to turn our attention also to the problems of tourism in places created by man, to cities and towns.

Planning in an Urban Area

With few exceptions towns and cities have been built as places for people to live and work. However, because of their attractions, many of them continue to receive large number of visitors. This has happened not only with those which are described as resorts, whether inland or coastal, but with many others which deserve the designation, because in the original sense of the term people do resort to them in large numbers. They have become tourist destinations and as such they constitute tourist resources.

We have seen that this is clearly the case with coastal resorts, which provide the focus for tourism as part of the coastline. In addition there are many cities and towns with historical associations, buildings and monuments as resources which cannot be replaced. They are commonly towns of character, which have retained their best old architecture and other special points of interest for visitors, and for which tourism has become a new use of old assets. Castles, cathedrals, museums, galleries, birthplaces of the famous, ancient universities, as well as whole streets and squares, make up these towns as tourist destinations.

The increased personal mobility provided by the motor car increases the appeal of the towns to visitors, as well as creating a major problem in an endeav-our to preserve their character. A tourist in a town is essentially an explorer on foot; a town that wishes to receive him has to make it possible for him to explore, as well as to park. New uses for old buildings of character, which have outlived their original purpose, enable them to be preserved. The design of new buildings in old settings must make for harmony. These points were made by Mr Michael Middleton, Director of The Civic Trust, when addressing the first conference in Britain on Tourism and the Environment in 1971.[15] He saw that many more towns of the right kind, besides Oxford, Stratford, Windsor, and Edinburgh, can now opt for tourism, as they once opted for, say, light industry.

London is one of the biggest single resorts in the world, visited annually by some 20 million people, 8 million of them from overseas and 12 million domestic visitors staying one or more nights in London; superimposed on this traffic there is a large unknown number of day visitors. Tourism in London, therefore, exemplifies on a large scale the main issues in physical planning and development in tourism in an urban area, which were highlighted by the Greater London Council in its Green Paper on *Tourism and Hotels in London*[16] in early 1971 and in subsequent discussions. The Paper identified three main planning problems, which have relevance in varying degrees for other urban areas.

The first is that of accommodation and its competition with housing: conversion of existing housing to hotels, use of building sites for hotel development, and the pressures on the building industry. Although the majority of visitors to London stay with friends and relatives, some use hostels, tents, and caravans in the vicinity, the bulk of the remainder stay in hotels. The growing holiday demand for accommodation is enhanced by growing conference and convention traffic. There is concern over the need to maintain the stock of housing in and around central London and over undue concentration of hotel accommodation in several central areas.

Secondly, tourism creates traffic. Cars, coaches, and taxis make for congestion on the roads and at sites of particular attractions. Air, rail, bus, and coach terminals cause congestion by their volumes of passenger movement and baggage handled. These phenomena in turn exercise pressures on police and public services.

The third problem postulated by the Council is that of employment and, in particular, the demands created by tourism for many lower-paid jobs and for housing employees.

To these problems are added others, for example the preservation of historic buildings and townscape generally and the demand for cheaper accommodation for the younger and less affluent visitors than can be economically available in central areas.

The 1971 Green Paper and subsequent pronouncements were superseded by the GLC publication in November 1978 of *Tourism — A Paper for Discussion*[17] and in February 1980 of *Tourism — A Statement of Policies.*[18] The policy statement recognizes tourism as of major importance for the future wealth and well-being of the city and outlines a co-ordinated approach to its development. In contrast to the statements of the early 1970s, the 1980 statement not only sets out a positive GLC policy and attitude to tourism, but also identifies the principal objectives within that policy and the possible means of achieving them. The five main directions are expressed as: the enhancement of London's gateway role, the encouragement of a wider seasonal and geographical spread of visitors, the promotion of higher standards of services and facilities, the promotion and marketing of London as an international centre, the improvement of the working conditions and image of the industry.

24 *Conservation and Management*

Demand for tourism is as diverse as the resources and for this reason alone the matching of supply and demand is no simple equation. A variety of sources from within and outside a country are generating a growing demand for a variety of facilities and both supply and demand are changing in time. The problem is not one of how many square miles have been conserved for tourism or how many miles are available, but in the effectiveness of both conservation and access, in the location of facilities, and in their uneven use at different times. Some requirements raise few problems, others impose acute pressures in particular locations and at particular times for which the facilities may be inadequate. This is the imblance which may lead to the lack of satisfaction from the tourist experience on the one hand and to the aesthetic and physical erosion of resources on the other hand. Pressures are increased by conflicts of use between the tourist visiting an area and the countryman who lives and works there, between the tourist and the town-dweller.

Only a clear appreciation of the issues involved, of mutual understanding of the legitimate demands of tourism and other users, and wise management can reduce conflict and ensure the full use and enjoyment of scarce resources in economic, social and aesthetic terms.[17] In considering the ways in which this may be achieved, we have the seemingly contrasting but in fact very analogous problems of the town and of the countryside — in both cases competing uses of resources, the movement of people and the congestion it creates, the social effects of changing patterns of activity and employment, the concern with townscape in one case and with landscape in the other. But we have also a whole spectrum of activity and resources from the intense and highly developed to the quiet, remote and not yet touched by development; between these extremes lies the tourism of the 1970s and 1980s, the playgrounds and the backwaters of the developed countries and regions and of the developing ones. The span of two centuries industrially and of more than one century in tourism development represent the spectrum of time, which is, of course, only partially accurate as a description. In these circumstances it is a meaningful illustration to trace the countryside and urban concerns for conservation, regulation and the environment in relation to recreation and tourism in a developed country such as Britain and to refer to others: the evolution provides significant pointers of a wide and general significance for those who have been through it, but even more so for those on the threshold of rapid change. It is also relevant to consider the means to progress.

Progress in Britain

In most countries the first pressures were in urban areas, and the urban resorts and urban parks were the major Victorian contributions to tourism and outdoor recreation in England, although the first Royal Parks were opened in London as early as the seventeenth century; but London was a special case; other urban dwellers had to wait until the nineteenth century for theirs and the concern for access to the countryside became apparent only towards the end of the century. The Yellowstone Park was established in the USA in 1872 with an area of 3,350 square miles, as one of the first manifestations of the American propensity to approach issues on a massive and imaginative scale in outdoor recreation, albeit brought about by horrified atonement for what the society had done to nature. Although it could form no prototype for European counterparts, the early attempts at amenity preservation in Britain were localized, defensive, and hardly spectacular in comparison. But to 1895 dates the founding of 'The National Trust for Places of Historic Interest and Natural Beauty' whose object was to acquire land and buildings by gift or purchase. In the period between the wars many local societies formed the Council for the Preservation of Rural England in 1926; a year earlier, in 1925, the expression of a dominantly urban concern was the formation of the National Playing Fields Association; in 1930 the Youth Hostels Association was formed as a reflection of the widespread use of the countryside for walking; in 1935 the Green Belt (London and Home Counties) Act secured an area around the London conurbation from the encroachment of urban and industrial expansion. It would seem that more pressing concerns in the 1930s than that with amenity were responsible for action being local and sectional, rather than national between the wars.

A separate Ministry of Town and Country Planning was created in 1943 and positive action on a wide front came since 1945 in two main phases. Until the 1960s the concern was primarily with active preservation, in recent years with more positive provision of facilities, partly in response to increased demand, partly to cope with pressure in areas of high amenity.

Following many private and public local initiatives, national physical planning began in earnest with the 1947 Town and Country Planning Act. Although initially the Act was mainly concerned with urban areas, it included powers for local authorities to define and submit for the Minister's approval areas of Great Landscape, Historic, or Scientific Value. In 1949 the National Parks and Access to the Countryside Act established a National Parks Commission with a two-fold duty: 'the preservation and enhancement of natural beauty' and the provision 'of opportunities for open air recreation and the study of nature by those resorting to National Parks'; ten National Parks covering some 9 per cent of England and Wales have been established. The Act also provided powers for the designation of Areas of Outstanding Natural Beauty and for the creation of long-distance footpaths. In the same year the Nature Conservancy was formed to provide additional protection to areas of particular natural history interest by establishing National Nature Reserves.

The growth of public pressure on the countryside and public concern with access and amenity led to the first of the Countryside in 1970 Conferences in 1963, followed by the second conference in 1965. In 1965 the National Environment Research Council was set up by legislation; the Sports Council was established 'to advise the Government on matters relating to the development of amateur sport and physical recreation services'. The National Trust launched the campaign Enterprise Neptune for preservation of the coastline. In 1966 the White Paper *Leisure in the Countryside, England and Wales* foreshadowed the Countryside Act of 1968 and the replacement of the National Parks Commission by a Countryside Commission with wider powers. Significantly the Act charged every Minister, government department, and public body to have regard to the desirability of conserving the natural beauty and amenity of the countryside. In 1967 the Civic Amenities Act provided new powers for the preservation of areas and buildings of architectural or historic interest; the Countryside (Scotland) Act established the Countryside Commission for Scotland. In 1968 a new Town and Country Planning Act established new concepts and procedures for development plans; the Transport Act gave the British Waterways Board recreation and amenity duties and powers. In 1969 the Committee for Environmental Conservation was formed at national level to enable voluntary bodies to speak to the Government on matters affecting the environment. In 1970 the Third UK Countryside in 1970 Conference was held in London. In 1971 the Department of Environment was set up.

The World Concern

The concern and activity were not confined to Britain. In 1963 the oil companies established an international study group for conservation of clean air and water. In 1964 the first natural area protected mainly by international effort, the Coto Donana Reserve of 25 square miles, was created in Spain with two-thirds of the cost covered by the World Wildlife Trust. In 1965 the White House Conference on Natural Beauty was held under the sponsorship of the President. In 1966 a major report on Physical Planning was published in the Netherlands, a country which is doing more than any other to its land surface and to reshape its natural environment by civil engineering. In 1967 appeared the United Nations list of National Parks and Reserves. In 1968 the Council of Europe launched European Air Pollution and Water Charters and the Water Conservation campaign; the African Convention for the Conservation of Nature took place. In 1969 *Problems of the Human Environment,* a report sponsored by the United Nations, was published. European Conservation Year was held in 1970; in the United States the Council of Environmental Quality was established and President Nixon promulgated a thirty-seven-point programme on environmental quality in a message to Congress; the World Bank announced that in future development projects considered for support would need to be 'ecologically validated'. In 1971 a meeting of governmental experts on problems relating to the environment was held in Prague. The centenary of National Parks took place in 1972; the Second World Conference on National Parks was held in the United States; the United Nations Conference on the Human Environment was held in Stockholm.

The selection of some fifteen events of environmental and planning significance in Britain and a similar number elsewhere in those ten years illustrated the intensifying activity in response to widespread concern. By the early 1970s influential opinion everywhere was alerted and the problems were recognized. Also a reasonably clear pattern of protected areas emerged in most developed countries, of importance to various tourist activities.

Schemes of Conservation

In Britain there is a pyramid of categories of designated land, in which the approach to conservation varies. At the apex are the National Parks, the prime example of conservation through planning designation, rather than ownership and management. As compared with the centenarian Yellowstone, they are a post-war development in Britain, in which it is sought to conserve landscapes of high visual appeal through special planning powers vested in local authorities, although the care of each park is vested in the hands of local park committees. Only limited parts are accessible to the public; they are not therefore parks in the true sense; neither are they truly national when their control is effectively in the hands of local interests.

The second tier of conservation are Areas of Outstanding Natural Beauty. Like National Parks they are selected and designated by the National Parks Commission and its successors, the Countryside Commissions. There are no special planning arrangements but grants are available to local authorities for improvements.

Areas of Great Landscape, Historic, or Scientific Value are designated by local planning authorities with the Minister's approval, but the designation does not attract grants for improvements and the main significance lies in the areas being specially considered when the planning authority consider applications for development in them.

The main function of Green Belts is to regulate urban growth and although they have an extensive recreational use, by their location they are largely of local rather than tourism significance.

As compared with the above areas, which rely on protection through planning designation, there are two types in which protection is based on ownership and management. Nature reserves are at one extreme — 130 tracts of land covering over quarter of a million acres, managed as a living musuem of natural history with controlled access, for which the Nature Conservancy, now a part of the Natural Environment Research Council, is responsible. There are in addition Forest Nature Reserves, Wildfowl Refuges, Local Nature Reserves, and Sites of Special Scientific Interest, managed under various arrangements between particular public bodies and owners. The other type are sites which the Department of the Environment has in its care: several hundred ancient monuments and historic buildings distributed throughout the country where the aim is to preserve, as well as to provide access.

Mention should be also made of the network of footpaths, of which the Long Distance Footpaths created by the 1949 Act are the best known. They have as their aim the development of a national system of public rights of way through some of the best mountain and coastal scenery and by 1970 over 1,400 miles had been approved.

Of the total area of England and Wales of some 58,000 square miles, about 5,000 square miles — about 9 per cent — is designated as National Parks and about 2,000 square miles are Areas of Outstanding Natural Beauty. The Nature Conservancy is interested in about 400 of the 2,700 miles of the coast.

Spreading the Demand in Time

The matching of supply and demand in recreation and tourism is a time and spatial problem. Activities are characterized by extremes of seasonality and periodicity on the one hand, and by extremes of geographical concentration on the other hand. In planning for recreation and tourism solutions have to be sought in these two directions, if adequate provision is to exist for all reasonable demand, to provide satisfaction for the tourist, and to safeguard the rural and urban environment.

Demand for most forms of tourism can be readily satisfied in most locations outside peak periods. Yet of all the problems the seasonal one, which also has such bearing on the economic viability of so many enterprises, appears to be the most intractable one. The principal causes — the timing of school holidays and public examinations, and of industrial holidays — have been well analysed and documented. However, any staggering of these has such implications for the pattern of living beyond recreation and tourism that institutional reforms have made little progress. As long as life is still not sufficiently leisure-oriented, it may well be that it is too much to expect for the demands of leisure to dictate its rhythms.

But there are hopeful signs. When a single fortnight in a year ceases to be the only focus of holiday experience and as second and third holidays become more common, the distribution of holidays becomes more evenly distributed throughout the year. As the sharp distinction in the weekly pattern of work and leisure becomes blunted by the introduction of a shorter working week, a real scope arises for a further growth of shorter holidays throughout the year. The scope for differential pricing is at last being realized and convincingly demonstrated by tour operators and some accommodation providers.

We may not see a radical reduction in the number of holiday departures in July and August, as the growth in demand from those entering the holiday market for the first time may counter the number of those who abstain from the peak period. We are likely to see a spread rather than a lessening of the growing demand. The main scope for relief of pressures must therefore be sought through more effective use of space.[18]

Segregation and Conservation

The Town and Country planning legislation focuses on development plans for individual areas in which land is designated for particular uses. It recognizes the principle of segregation in broad terms, of separation of agriculture, industrial, residential, and other uses. This is characteristic of many countries and of many existing uses and change has to be based on a careful evaluation of physical characteristics, visual quality, existing use and potential; recreation and tourism have to play a part, with classification of types of their own.

The classic approach of the Outdoor Recreation Resources Review Commission in the USA outlined six broad classes based on relationships between resources and public recreation needs ranging from the most remote to the most frequented; from those exclusively confined to those seeking extreme peace and quiet, through areas in combined use to those for most gregarious entertainment; it also laid down management principles for each.[19]

Zoning has more than one meaning in tourism, but the main principle is common: of designating areas, whether separate or adjacent ones, for different forms of activity, developing them accordingly, and regulating access and activity in them in accordance with clear guidelines.

It calls for identifying areas where conservation is of prime concern, both in terms of nature conservation and in terms of preservation of remoteness against all but the most determined walker as one end of the spectrum; in this sense the areas are more limited in extent than existing conservation areas. At the other end are areas of free access. Between them is a range of conservation and accessibility covering much of the existing National Parks and other protected areas.

The corollary is in highly developed, more limited geographical areas, such as resorts where active and passive, quiet and noisy, specialist and generalist interests are catered for in defined areas. This has been the principle adopted for the last century and more in the best designed urban parks; its application is more difficult but not less necessary in whole regions and countries. Different degrees of access in the same area can be used effectively to segregate demand in stages until only the most determined proceed any further.

Standards of Capacity

Where pressures of demand on particular attractions are great, it becomes necessary to lay down standards of capacity and to apply them. Capacity may be defined in various contexts; as physical capacity or the limits of a beach or historic building to absorb a given number of users engaged in particular activities; as social capacity or the degree of crowding users are prepared to accept before they seek alternative sites; as environmental capacity or the extent to which a site can be used before visual deterioration or conservation problems arise.

Capacity of sites has to be linked with capacity of access, as the latter often effectively determines the pressure of use, particularly with individual forms of transport. Not only the capacity of the roads, but the capacity of car parks, may determine the use of a beach or another attraction. The capacity of cable railways does the same for mountain tops.

The principle of capacity management is common in all sorts of facilities. The number of seats determines the capacity of a conference centre and of aircraft; even bus companies restrict the number of standing passengers. A finite capacity of these facilities helps; the concept becomes more difficult to accept and to apply in public spaces, which have conditioned people's minds to regard them as unrestricted and unlimited in capacity. Yet the experience of crowded attractions in the main tourist destinations, whether they be in urban or rural areas, calls for a similar approach.

Most standards of capacity have been devised in America, in particular, in intensively used managed areas of land and water. For example, in California, design standards range from 580 persons per acre of bathing beach to 40 persons per mile of hiking and riding trail. In Donegal empirical standards have been postulated for various resources and activities to suggest how many people could be served by each resource without congestion, crowding, and without physical or ecological damage, thus combining physical, social, and environmental criteria. For example the ideal standard for scenic driving on major roads was stated as one car every quarter of a mile, on minor roads every half a mile; for the beach 440 people per mile.[20]

Management of Space and Capacity

When entering a well-planned gallery or a museum we accept that we either go to see particular exhibits, or, more commonly, follow a route; occasionally an attendant may restrict access to a room or there may be a charge to see an exhibition. These aspects of an experience are part of the management of an attraction. Historical *laissez-faire* and egalitarian concepts have retarded the introduction of more rational and necessary approaches to cope with the demands of tourism in areas of high density.

A more adequate provision of some facilities is an obvious means to satisfy demand; it also helps to filter off some of the pressure on most intensively used resources. This may be difficult and expensive. New lines of movement may be created by the promotion of well-marked trails and scenic drives. Enhanced interest may be created by means other than scenery: such paths and highways can link places associated with people and events in history, as the Lincoln Trail in Illinois traces the journeys of young Lincoln in the State and others do in Boston and various parts of America. This approach may be combined with deliberate lack of emphasis in other areas. When new routes create costs, the toll system is a means for recouping them for those using the facility.

The pricing mechanism, as an instrument of strategy and as a means of ensuring a return for the cost of providing facilities, offers obvious scope for regulating demand in tourism as elsewhere. Price can be adjusted to stimulate or restrain demand to an acceptable level. Car parks with prices graded according to the attraction of the hinterland, as well as times of day, week, and year; routes with tolls charged according to intensity of traffic; admission charges to attractions on similar scales. There may be free times and free days and times and days with nominal charges, but these have to be provided according to demand and not in pursuance of social policies.

Some of the most imaginative approaches to management of space and capacity have been pioneered by accommodation, tour, and transport operators with beneficial effects on demand and profitability, as well as on the level of prices. The growth of tourism makes it necessary to adopt the same approach to the remaining facilities in tourism. One of the largest outdoor museums in America, Colonial Williamsburg in Virginia, the motor museum at Beaulieu in the South of England, as well as several instances of planned management of tourism in Continental Europe, provide the pointer for the environment problems of tourism in London and many other locations.

The Challenge and Responsibility

For decades physical development in tourism has been dominated by a micro-outlook: infinite care and thought concentrated on the optimum design of an hotel bedroom, aircraft, and conference hall, and these facilities have in some instances approached a high standard of visual impact and utility. Individual components have rarely been seen as part of total design of their towns and rural areas and still less so part of the total design for tourism. Unco-ordinated development of facilities, however well conceived individually, was highlighted by the growth of tourism and by the growing concern for the environment. The Second World War was a watershed in life in general, in tourism, and in physical planning and development in particular.

The need has emerged for a macro-outlook, in the attitude to leisure and in the use of resources for recreation and tourism. It has several implications in planning and development. First, as we have seen throughout, there are complementary and overlapping interests of recreation, travel and tourism, of urban and rural areas, of the infrastructure and superstructure, of the resident and of the tourist. Between them they need co-ordination and co-operation at various levels, and we shall return to this in our discussion of organization in tourism.

The second and no less important need is that for enhanced social responsibility, which any entrepreneur has to have in the development of tourism. His activities are of such magnitude that they can be accommodated only with a full awareness of the impact which they are creating and with a full acceptance of the consequences they have on others and on the environment. There is a case not only for an economic, but also social, and in the terms of the World Bank, ecological and environmental validation of tourism development.

There is a need for more and more meaningful research, to provide the answers as to the future pattern of needs and demand, the means of satisfying them, and the consequences of various forms of action.

Contribution of Tourism to Quality of Life

In May 1980 G.H. Naylor, Chief Executive of Wales Tourist Board, expressed the positive contribution of tourism in a paper to The Tourism Society, an organization established to promote and enhance professionalism in tourism, and the following extracts are taken from that paper.[23]

'The European Conservation Year 1970 began to direct attention to the benefits of tourism in catalyzing and justifying support for environmental conservation, particularly the unique architectural heritage of the great cities. Since then there has been a remarkable development in Britain. Many thousands of buildings all over the country, many of them country houses or farm buildings of indigenous style have been saved from demolition or dereliction by getting a new lease of life in accommodating, entertaining or catering for visitors. A great many hotels and guest houses were in buildings about 100 years old, and most of these were extensively refurbished in the last ten years, often leading to the saving and conserving of other buildings in the same area. In the countryside a great many of the characteristic stone buildings put up in that era of agricultural prosperity over 100 years ago have become obsolete and were saved in the 1970s by being turned into farm guest houses or holiday cottages.

'The arguments against tourism frequently demonstrate some new positive contribution to the quality of life of the 20th century Britain. London would not have as many theatres, quality shops, restaurants or taxis, without the massive spending of overseas visitors, and the London Underground transport system could not operate as many peak-hour commuter trains but for the £1 million a week contribution by tourists during the off-peak hours.

'Britain has been providing facilities on an enormous scale. The legislation which provided national parks has been followed by newer concepts such as country parks, long distance footpaths, areas of outstanding natural beauty, nature trails, heritage coast, and throughout Britain the provision of picnic sites, lay-bys and car parks by all local authorities and the creation of interpretation facilities by many. The National Trust has opened gardens, houses and beautiful countryside to the public on a courageous scale. The Forestry Commission has become an important innovator and provider of recreational facilities in opening more and more forest land, with over 600 forest walks and trails, 600 picnic places and 750 car parks, together with an increasing number of visitor centres, camp sites, forest cabins and forest holiday houses.

'English Tourist Board research shows that an average of 21 new sightseeing attractions had opened in England every year in the 1960s and 48 a year in the 1970s. Since 1970 England had acquired about 200 new museums and art galleries. Tourism was generating and sustaining industrial heritage in the regions in a dramatic fashion. Many of the newer attractions were built on the obsolete, redundant, derelict tumbledown or unwanted remains of earlier industries.'

Part IX

Organization and Finance

Further Reading for Part IX

Annual Reports of the British Tourist Authority, the English, Scottish and Wales Tourist Boards, and of regional tourist boards

Annual Reports of the Association of British Travel Agents, the British Hotels, Restaurants and Caterers Association, and other sectoral organizations

Burkart, A.J. and Medlik, S. (editors): *The Management of Tourism,* Part IX

Medlik, S.: *Profile of the Hotel and Catering Industry,* Part VI

Organisation for Economic Co-operation and Development: *Tourism Development and Economic Growth*

World Tourism Organization: *Tourism Compendium*

References to Part IX

1 Medlik, S.: *Profile of the Hotel and Catering Industry,* Chapter 19
2 See Chapter 5 for discussion of determinants and motivations
3 Quoted in the Debate on Tourism in the House of Commons on 27 February 1967, *see Hansard,* Vol. 778, No. 67, Col. 1948; World Tourism Organization, *Tourism Compendium,* Part III
4 Annual Reports of the British Tourist Authority, English Tourist Board, Scottish Tourist Board, Wales Tourist Board for the year to 31 March 1979
5 OECD: *Tourism Development and Economic Growth*
6 OECD: op.cit.
7 British Tourist Authority: *Annual Report for the Year to 31 March 1979*
8 OECD: op.cit.
9 OECD: op.cit.
10 British Travel Association: *Annual Report for the Year to 31 March 1969*
11 Department of Trade, Press Notice November 21 1974: New Guidelines for Tourism

25   *Organization in Tourism*

Men and women and the firms engaged in tourism have come together in a variety of organizations to further their common interests. It is possible to divide these organizations into two main categories in the present context: sectoral organizations, which are based on the main groups of providers of tourist services, and tourist organizations, which are based on tourist destinations. There are numerous other bodies with an interest in tourism, often governmental or statutory; however, as their main functions differ from the above two, they are referred to throughout this book, but are not considered specifically in this part, which is devoted, after a brief view of the sectoral type of organization, in the main to tourist organizations.

It is important to state at the outset that there are no 'rules' of tourist organization of universal applicability, but rather certain issues in and particular approaches to tourist organization. These issues and approaches are discussed in this chapter, in which the objects, scope, and forms are examined at various levels. Considerations of organization are closely related to finance and the requirements, sources, and problems of finance in tourism are dealt with in the next chapter. These two chapters look at organization and finance within a country and draw on a variety of practices and examples in different countries; they also consider what happens at international level. The third chapter in this part of the book concentrates in the main on Britain as a tourist destination, in which a new form of organization was created by an Act of Parliament, the Development of Tourism Act 1969. Britain thus provides a case study in three phases: of a situation before and leading up the 1969 Act, the framework created by the Act, and of some experience of the working of the new organization. In this review in Chapter 27 many of the issues and approaches involved in organization and finance in tourism are brought together and illustrated, which are of importance and relevance to tourism in Britain and elsewhere.

Organization in Sectors

Individual industries engaged in tourism have several types of organization. Voluntary organizations of individuals range from professional bodies to trade unions.

Professional bodies are organizations of individuals engaged in a particular occupation or group of occupations, normally of the nature of a vocation or calling, requiring a long period training or learning, which seek to provide standing and prestige for their members, and which control admission, usually by examination. Therefore, professional bodies adopt certain defined standards and members qualify for admission by formally meeting these standards, and by agreeing to observe them once they are admitted into membership. The standards are normally based on standards of competence shown in knowledge and experience, and often also on standards of conduct in the exercise of their occupation. The Chartered Institute of Transport (CIT) and the Hotel, Catering and Institutional Management Association (HCIMA) are the main examples in tourism in Britain. A multi-sectoral professional body, The Tourism Society, was established in Britain in 1977.

Trade unions on the other hand are associations of employees in a particular trade or industry, or of particular employees in more than one industry, whose principal function is the negotiation of wages and conditions of employment. Industrial unions such as the National Union of Railwaymen (NUR) in Britain cover one industry; they are common, for example, in the United States, but less so in Britain. Occupational unions, such as the British Airline Pilots Association (BALPA) and craft unions, such as the Electrical Trades Union (ETU), organize mainly skilled employees in a particular occupation in one or more industries. General unions, such as the Transport and General Workers Union (TGWU), General and Municipal Workers Union (GMWU), and the Union of Shop Distributive and Allied Workers (USDAW), include in their membership mostly semi-skilled and unskilled employees in more than one industry and in more than one occupation.

Trade associations are voluntary bodies formed by independent firms in a particular industry or a group of industries to protect and advance their common interests. Their principal functions are representation, in which they act as channels of communication with the Government and other organized groups, and services to members, in which they provide information, advice, and assistance to their members in the conduct of their businesses. To a varying extent trade associations are also concerned with the regulation of competition in their industries. In most countries there is more than one association in passenger transportation, covering particular modes of transport. One or more trade associations, such as the British Hotels, Restaurants and Caterers' Association (BHRCA), have in membership firms in accommodation and catering. The Association of British Travel Agents (ABTA) is a prominent example of a trade association of tour operating and retail travel agency firms.

In countries in which Government intervention in industry takes the form of setting up bodies for particular industries, statutory or 'official' bodies are also in existence for particular purposes. Three types of bodies are of particular interest in industries participating in tourism in Britain: Wages Councils, Economic Development Committees, and Industrial Training Boards.

There are close on fifty Wages Councils, which provide minimum wages and holidays for close on 3 million workers in a variety of British industries. Of these, three Wages Councils with an estimated coverage of well over half a million workers perform this role in hotels, restaurants, public houses, and clubs. Individual Councils consist of employers' and employees' representatives and of independents, and have statutory powers.

Some major British industries are covered by a network of Economic Development Committees set up by the National Economic Development Council, which assess the economic progress of their industries, encourage the means of improving their efficiency, and provide a channel of communication between the government and the National Council on the one hand and individual industries on the other hand. Among the fifteen EDCs covering some 11 million people in the 1970s, the Hotel and Catering EDC, and to a lesser extent the Distributive Trades EDC, were concerned with industries participating in tourism and covered about 1 million and 3 million people respectively. In its time the Hotel and Catering EDC made a major contribution to the development of its industry, and to an understanding of its role in the economy generally and in tourism in particular.

By 1970 Industrial Training Boards covering over 15 million employees had been set up in Britain under the Industrial Training Act, 1964, with responsibilities for training in their own industries. Three of them — the Air Transport and Travel, Hotel and Catering Industry, and Road Transport — and to a lesser extent the Distributive and Local Government Boards — are concerned with providers of tourist services. The former three cover together about 1 ¾ million and the latter some 4 million employees. The Boards consist of employers, employees, and educational representatives and have statutory powers.[1]

Table 34

Sectoral Organization

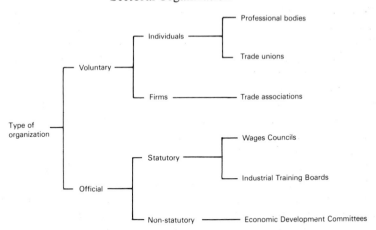

Tourist Organization Distinguished

As distinct from sectoral organizations concerned with particular industries participating in tourism, the tourist organization is defined by reference to the interests of a geographical area as a tourist destination, which may be a country, region, or an individual town. The tourist organization provides the framework in which tourism operates. Its purpose is to maximize the opportunities offered by tourism to the destination.

We have seen earlier that the determinants of success are, in the first place, the tourist qualities of a destination — the attractions, accessibility, and facilities. The extent to which these are present, the mix of the three, exercise the most important influence; the tourist organization cannot by itself create a tourist boom where the destination qualities are deficient. However, when the three qualities, and in particular the attractions, are present, tourist organization can develop and promote the tourist product, and enhance the success of the country, region, or town as a tourist destination.[2]

In any destination a variety of interests are involved in tourism. The government is concerned at all levels — in protecting its citizens, in providing essential services, and in creating the conditions in which their institutions, including industry and trade, can operate favourably. For example, as a protector of its citizens it is concerned with law and order, health and sanitation; as a provider of services it raises revenue through national and local taxation which is influenced by the prosperity of business and of the population; as the principal regulator of the physical environment it has direct interest in tourist facilities through its planning machinery. Although the government concern is usually dominated by the needs of the residents, it has to reconcile the needs of residents and visitors. Owners of tourist sites and attractions and a variety of providers of tourist services derive a greater or lesser part of their revenue from tourism; although each of them has an interest in the destination extending beyond his immediate contribution to it. There is therefore a need for co-ordination of all those concerned with tourism at particular destinations and this is provided by the tourist organization at national, regional, and local level.

Its scope is usually two-fold. In the first place the tourist organization can formulate and develop the tourist product or products of the destination; secondly, it can promote them in appropriate markets. It can base its approach to development and promotion on market research and thus achieve a close match between the products and the markets. In doing this the tourist organization is acting on behalf of all interests in tourism and on behalf of the whole destination and is complementary to the development and promotion activities of individual providers of tourist services; it also has to harmonize the activities meeting the needs of tourists with those of residents.

Background Considerations

The approach to and the type of tourist organization in a particular country are influenced by a number of background influences in that country.

The first is the political and economic system. Where there is a centralized government, this is likely to be reflected in the tourist organization, as is the case, for example, in Eastern Europe and most developing countries. By contrast, in countries such as Austria, West Germany, and Switzerland, with a federal State organization, the tourist organization consists of one or more co-operative bodies at national level and there is also a high degree of devolution to individual States or provinces in tourist matters.

Secondly, the tourist organization tends to reflect the importance of tourism to the national economy. Where tourism is very important in relation to other industries and activities in the country, it may have a Government Department wholly or substantially concerned with tourism, as is the case in a growing number of countries; in Italy it is a dual Ministry of Tourism and Entertainment, which is concerned in addition to tourism with historical monuments, theatres, and other forms of entertainment; in Spain the dual Ministry controls the press, radio and television, as well as tourism. In the minority of countries with voluntary co-operative bodies in tourism at national level, tourism does not often rank high in the economy, although Austria and Switzerland are prominent exceptions to this.

Thirdly, the tourist organization tends to reflect the stage of tourism development in the country. In countries with a highly developed tourist industry it is common to find a flexible, decentralized tourist organization, which has evolved over many decades, as is the case in Austria, Germany, and Switzerland. In countries where tourism on any scale is relatively new, where the prospects and the rates of growth are good, and where the Government takes a strong direct interest in its development, as is the case in Southern Europe and in many developing countries, a centralized form of tourist organization with statutory powers often provides the most effective means of rapid growth and development.

There are also other influences, which sometimes explain the existing tourist organization in a particular country. They may not always be logical and the type and form of organization in existence would probably not be designed now, if a new organization were to be created from the beginning. But there is rarely an opportunity to start from the beginning and the role of tradition and of other seemingly irrational influences often explain a particular pattern in existence. These influences taken together, therefore, often provide a stabilizing effect, which is conducive to a gradual evolution; but they may also mitigate against the achievement of the purpose for which the tourist organization exists, that is to maximize the opportunities offered by tourism to the destination.

The National Level

Three basic levels of tourist organization may be distinguished in most countries of any size — national, regional, and local — as part of what may be seen as a vertical structure.

At the national level, tourism is in the first instance a government responsibility, to formulate a tourism policy, which may be translated into a plan. Such policy clarifies how tourism is seen in the context of the national economy, what objectives are to be pursued, how tourism enters into national and regional planning; these objectives can be then translated into quantified targets and rates of growth. When the role of tourism is defined, the policy provides a statement of the means by which the objectives are to be attained; the means cover such matters as the administrative arrangements, the respective roles of the private and public sectors, and the fiscal arrangements.

Having defined its broad policy on tourism, the Government usually delegates its detailed formulation and its execution to a National Tourist Organization, which may be a governmental, semi-governmental, or non-governmental organization, with a given scope and sphere of influence. In 1969 there were 86 countries known to the International Union of Official Travel Organizations (IUOTO) to have an official tourist organization; of these the great majority were government departments, and the remainder was divided evenly between statutory bodies set up by governments and voluntary co-operative bodies recognized by their governments. In 1979 the World Tourism Organization listed 181 official travel organizations.[3] In the ten years a major growth appears to have taken place in government departments and statutory bodies; in relatively few countries the official tourist organisation now takes the form of a voluntary body.

According to which of the three basic approaches are adopted, the national level is, therefore, one (where the organization is retained as a Ministry) or may consist of more than one level (when the Government delegates the functions of the National Tourist Organization to a statutory body or to a voluntary body outside a Ministry). In the latter situation a Government Department exercises a general policy role, to a greater or less extent also a directing role in relation to the National Tourist Organization, and invariably is the channel through which the State provides finance. These roles usually fall to the Ministry of Economics, Trade or similar Government Department.

Whichever of the above approaches are adopted, there is a substantial variation in the scope and sphere of influence of the National Tourist Organization, which arises from the extent of delegation by the Government to the Organization, from the range of functions undertaken by the Organization, and from the extent of delegation by the Organization itself to other bodies. The two main functions of a tourist organization are the development and the promotion of the tourist product and they may be discharged by one or more separate bodies. The examples of various countries illustrate the many different approaches.

The Local Level

The two main functions of development and promotion exist in respect of every tourist destination. In a country of any size they are best performed at the level of each destination and this creates a need for a regional and local tourist organization as the second and third levels of tourist organization structure in a country. This enables tourism issues within specific areas to be dealt with by tourism interests in those areas, taking advantage of the knowledge and initiative in each destination.

Local tourist organization at the level of an individual town or district represents the oldest form of tourist organization, which came into being with the emergence and growth of resorts in most countries. Historically its main emphasis has been on promotion and this continues to be the case in many destinations to this day, as the main emphasis in physical development has been on the needs of the residents rather than of visitors. Soon information services for visitors at the destination were added to the promotional activities. With the growth of visitor traffic the need for planned development has assumed a greater proportion of importance in many areas in recent years.

Whilst the central Government does not always retain the National Tourist Organization within a Government Department, local tourist organization is often based on local government. This is on the one hand recognition of the significance of tourism to a locality and, on the other hand, of the complementary nature of the requirements of the resident population and of tourists; moreover, physical planning is normally the domain of local government. Whilst local tourist interests usually participate in the tourist organization, particularly in Britain the organization tends to be anchored to the local government organization.

Even where the local tourist organization developed separately, as had been the case for example in France, in recent years there has been a definite move from local organizations consisting mainly of private interests and generally not adequate to cope with complex modern problems of resort development, to greater participation in tourism by local government, even to the extent of undertaking commercial operations. In all the countries to which reference has been made earlier in this chapter, local organization provides a strong solid basis for the co-ordination of local tourist interests, for the provision of information services to visitors, and for the wider aspects of local promotion and development.

The Regional Level

Regional tourist organization is an intermediate level between the national and local levels and represents the latest development in tourist organization, which was brought about by three separate but complementary influences. First, by the gradual spread of tourist traffic away from a limited number of traditional tourist centres, which could no longer be developed, promoted, and co-ordinated centrally in larger countries; secondly, by the growing needs of regional economic development, to which tourism offers a promising contribution; thirdly, by the growth of touring holidays which extend the area visited by many in one holiday. These influences have important implications for physical development as well as promotion. A region often becomes a separate main destination within a country for a foreign tourist; it also tends to replace the individual resort as a destination for many domestic holidays. As such, regions provide a basis for the formulation of tourist products which can be promoted in appropriate markets and which call for information services based on a region. In this, regional tourist organizations may form a network of component bodies co-ordinated at national level and each regional organization may in turn co-ordinate local tourist organizations in its area.

Corresponding to tourist interests at national and local levels there are regional tourist interests, which comprise government authorities covering cantons in Switzerland, provinces in Austria, states in Germany and regions in France and other countries, transport and hotel companies and other providers of tourist services operating in those areas.

Table 35
Tourist Organisation

National tourist organization

Regional tourist organizations

Local tourist organizations

A particular problem arises in defining regions for purposes of tourist organization. There are obvious advantages if their boundaries correspond to government administrative boundaries so that administrative arrangements are facilitated. There are also advantages if tourist regions correspond to economic planning regions, where these exist, to stimulate regional economic development. But above all the areas should constitute natural tourist regions, which represent a community of common interest and which may be developed and promoted as such. Their size has to be such that they can support a viable tourist organization.

Having defined the boundaries, the scope of the regional tourist organization and its relationship with the National Tourist Organization on the one hand and with the local tourist organization within its boundaries on the other hand has to be defined. This may follow where it is part of a government or statutory structure, but a voluntary regional organization has to evolve its own relationships based on agreement with those concerned.

Cross-relationships

The tourist organization does not exist and function in isolation. In bringing the tourist product to the attention of the potential tourist through promotion, and in providing him with information when he is actually at the destination, its main relationship is with the tourist. But in development and in co-ordinating the efforts and interests of all involved in tourism, there are many links and cross-relationships between the tourist organization and other organizations at all levels.

Whichever Government Department has the ultimate responsibility for tourism, there are inevitably several Ministries with an interest in tourism and often a co-ordinating committee of interested Ministries is set up, which brings them together, as well as the National Tourist Organization, if not part of a

Government Department. In Parliament, Members connected with tourism, either in their business capacities or representing constituencies with a significant involvement in tourism, often form a co-ordinating committee, as is the case with the All Party Tourism Committee of the British House of Commons.

Two further main links have to be established at the national level. One is with the sectoral organizations, which represent various types of operators in tourism, described earlier in this chapter. The other is with a multitude of organizations, which exist in most countries, and which are concerned with such common and related matters as the environment, travel, and recreation. According to the nature and status of the National Tourist Organization, these cross-relationships find an expression in the membership of the boards, councils, and committees of the Tourist Organization, as well as in many reciprocal arrangements and informal links.

A similar pattern obtains and is recognized more or less formally at regional and local levels, where the need for consultation and co-ordination of all interests in tourism assumes even greater importance, as it is there that physical planning and development actually take place. The strength of the tourist organization and its effectiveness can be to a great extent determined by the way it works with others.

International Organization

The increasingly international character of modern tourism and the growing influence of international agencies in many fields are reflected in the growth of international organizations in tourism, which have been stimulated by the need for discussion and co-operation between individuals, firms, associations, and governments of individual countries.

International organizations have had a long history and it is interesting to note that many of the first came into being in the field of transport and communications. For example, the second half of the nineteenth century saw the beginnings of the Universal Postal Union and the International Tele-communications Union, the period after the First World War the setting up of the International Chamber of Shipping and of the International Union of Railways, and immediately after the Second World War the International Civil Aviation Organization was founded. International tourism organizations were founded between the two Wars and especially after the Second World War; for example the International Union of Official Travel Organizations in the 1920s, the OECD (then OEEC) Tourism Committee, the European Travel Commission, the Caribbean Tourism and Pacific Area Travel Associations in the 1950s.

There is a basic distinction between inter-governmental and non-governmental international organizations. *Inter-governmental organizations* are created by treaties between States and their members are States represented by delegates of member governments. The treaty which provides for their creation also defines their organs, functions, and competence. They are rarely able to take decisions binding on member States; draft conventions have to be ratified by member governments. The organizations normally possess a legal personality and enjoy certain privileges.

Non-governmental organizations are created by individuals, firms or associations and their membership consists of individuals and corporate bodies. They formulate their own statutes, cannot claim any privileged position in international law, and are subject to the law of the country where their headquarters are situated.

Inter-governmental organizations are of three main kinds — general, special agencies and regional organizations. The aims and activities of general organizations extend to all aspects of relations between States, including tourism; the United Nations Organization is the prime example. The aims and activities of special agencies are limited to specific aspects of international relations, are bound by special agreements with UNO, and work in close co-operation with UNO; the World Tourism Organization falls in this category. Regional organizations group together States with common interests in particular regions; for example, the European Economic Community and the Organization of American States do this with different degrees of intensity in Europe and the Americas.

Non-governmental organizations with tourism interest may consist of individuals, firms, associations, or their representative bodies, and be classified into four main categories — general, special, regional, and sectoral. General organizations are concerned with tourism as their main or sole field of interest in all its forms (e.g. International Association of Scientific Experts in Tourism), special organizations with particular forms of tourism (e.g. International Bureau of Social Tourism), regional organizations with tourism in general in their own regions (e.g. European Travel Commission), and sectoral organizations with component industries engaged in tourism (e.g. International Air Transport Association and International Hotel Association). There are altogether several dozen non-governmental organizations with an interest in tourism.

In the *inter-governmental* field tourism falls within the overall authority of the General Assembly, under the jurisdiction of the Economic and Social Council of the United Nations (ECOSOC). There have been several major resolutions on the development of tourism, including one leading to the United Nations Conference on International Tourism in Rome in 1963, and the year 1967 was designated by the United Nations the International Tourist Year. UNCTAD (United Nations Conference on Trade and Development) produced in 1971 guidelines for tourism statistics to assist member countries in the collection of information about tourism.

Many of the special agencies are not concerned or only indirectly concerned with tourism. Some include tourism and its particular aspects among their responsibilities, e.g. the International Labour Organization and the World Health Organization. Others are concerned with particular sectors, e.g. the International Civil Aviation Organization with the development of international civil aviation, and the Inter-Governmental Maritime Consultative Organization with co-operation in sea transport.

The two main inter-governmental organizations concerned with tourism are the World Tourism Organization and, through its Tourism Committee, the Organization for Economic Co-operation and Development.

The World Tourism Organization has more than one hundred countries in membership, in addition to many affiliate members. Article 3 of its Statutes states: The fundamental aim of the World Tourism Organization shall be the promotion and development of tourism with a view to contributing to economic development, international understanding, peace, prosperity, and universal respect for, and observance of, human rights and fundamental freedoms for all without distinction as to race, sex, language or religion.

The OECD Tourism Committee is composed of senior officials and others responsible for tourism in the 24 member countries of the organization and, as one of the committees concerned with reviews of various economic sectors, reports regularly on the development of tourism.

26   *Finance in Tourism*

Issues in and approaches to organization in tourism are closely related to questions of finance in tourism. The organization and its activities have to be paid for; in turn financing may influence the structure and working of the organization. This chapter, therefore, seeks to link the two. Although in the wide sense finance in tourism covers the investment in and the operation of individual enterprises participating in tourism, those aspects are dealt with in Parts IV, V, and VI of this book devoted to individual industries. Some financial aspects of marketing and of planning and development are referred to in Parts VII and VIII. In what follows we are concerned in the main with the vertical organization structure in tourism outlined in the last chapter and not with sectoral organizations.

In relating organization and finance in tourism in the present context we therefore refer the reader to other parts of the book, to complete the particular outline treatment of finance in this chapter. In this it is convenient to consider first separately the requirements of finance, the sources, and the methods by which funds may be channelled from the sources to meet the requirements.

In most countries there is a mixed pattern of financing in tourism, from public and private funds on the one hand, and from the same sources to more than one level of the vertical structure on the other hand. The former is considered appropriate, provided that the respective contributions of public and private funds are determined rationally as a matter of policy. However, it is more difficult to justify seeking contributions to more than one level from the same source, whether that source be a public one, or even less so, a firm, unless that firm also operates at more than one level geographically. The need for rationalization of financing in tourism may therefore be regarded as an important concern of this chapter.

Viewed in a different way, it is useful to consider separately two other issues: on the one hand the respective roles of public and private enterprise, and on the other hand of domestic and foreign capital in tourism. Analogous to a brief treatment of international organization in the last chapter, this chapter ends with a brief reference to tourism finance at international level.

Requirements of Finance

We have seen that the scope of the tourist organization is to a varying extent development and promotion of the tourist destination. Finance is therefore required for these two functions, according to the emphasis placed on each. The third requirement is other activities and administrations.

The formulation and physical development of tourist products calls for capital investment in the infrastructure and in individual facilities. Particularly in new tourist areas investment in infrastructure must precede investment in individual facilities and may represent a great proportion of the total investment.

For example, it has been stated that in the development of the Guadarrama area of Spain as much as 70 per cent of the total investment required was for roads, parks, snow clearance services, and the like, and only 30 per cent for cable railways, accommodation, and other individual facilities. The balance in this dual nature of investment in tourism does, of course, vary according to the stage of development of the area, but both call for long-term capital. Once created, physical development may continue through expansion, modernization, and extension schemes, which also generate the need for long-term and some medium-term finance. From the beginning the maintenance of the infrastructure and of individual facilties requires operating finance, which may be generated by the operation or call for short-term funds or both.

In the late 1970s the British statutory tourist boards spent each year between 15—20 per cent of their total expenditure on grants and loans for tourism development, and the greater part, normally over 80 per cent, to cover their operating costs.[4]

In contrast to the capital intensity of physical development, the operating expenditure of the tourist organization calls for current financing. In this tourism promotion tends to account for the greater part of the operating budgets of most national tourist organizations. For example, in 1978/79, the tenth year of its operation, the British Tourist Authority, which has very limited development functions, devoted some 80 per cent of its total operating expenditure to overseas publicity and expenses of its overseas offices. In the same year the English, Scottish, and Wales Tourist Boards spent in the region of one-half of their total operating expenditure on publicity. More than two-thirds of the total operating expenditure of the four organizations, which together comprise the British national tourist organization with complementary promotion and development functions, went on promotion in that year.[4]

The balance of operating expenditure of tourist organizations is incurred by other activities and administration. In the same year this accounted for some 20 per cent of the total operating expenses of the British Tourist Authority, for about a half in the case of the three national boards (including grants to regional organizations), or less than one-third of the total of the four organizations.[4]

Sources of Finance

Four main sources may be identified to meet the development, promotion and other financial requirements of the tourist organization: government, industry, tourists, and the tourist organization itself.

There are several arguments for the government at national, but also at regional and local level, to contribute to finance in tourism and, indeed, the government usually does do so. The economic benefits of tourism often extend directly and indirectly to a whle area and to the whole population; in those circumstances the government can enhance the material well-being of the community through its contribution. Secondly, even in a capitalist system it is considered legitimate for the government to intervene financially in circumstances in which private enterprise may not be able or willing to do so adequately; this may be the case in the initial stages in the development of tourism, and also subsequently. Thirdly, the goverent of a country has an interest in a healthy balance of payments, to which tourism may be able to contribute significantly. Last but not least, the government is itself a major recipient of revenue from tourism through direct and indirect taxation.

The main financial beneficiaries from tourism are the providers of tourist services who were described earlier in this book as the tourist industry. Whilst they make a return on the benefits they derive through taxation, which tends to be in proportion to their volume of business, it may be argued that their prosperity or otherwise is at least in part due to the tourist organization, which should be able to call on their financial support.

The main overall beneficiaries from tourism are the tourists themselves and this plain truth suggests that theirs should be the main contribution to the financing of tourism. Through the payment they make for the services they buy, including an element of tax in many of them, they are in fact the main contributors. But these channels rarely lead directly to the tourist organization and for this reason tourists are sometimes required to contribute directly in particular for purposes of improvement of amenity.

Finally, a tourist organization itself may generate income for its purposes through income from other sources, as it is often in a position to earn revenue for the provision of particular services.

Methods of Government Finance

The extent of government financial contribution to tourism and the means employed depend to a great extent on the background considerations discussed in the last chapter in relation to the tourist organization. When the tourist organization is a part of the machinery of government, the government itself normally plays a more active role in tourism and often uses the national tourist organization as its administrative organ for the purpose; when this is not the case, the government tends to be less involved in tourism financially and otherwise.

However, it is a common approach for government to assume prime responsibility for financing promotion, which enhances the impact of promotion undertaken by individual operators, although the cost of such destination promotion may be relatively small in relation to the total costs of individual promotion. It has been estimated, for example, in Spain that individual interests spend at least ten times as much as the Spanish Government does on promotion abroad.[5] According to the nature of the tourist organization, these funds may be applied by the Government itself or they may be channelled to the tourist organization by way of a grant, sometimes specifically earmarked for promotion, in addition to any other grant for other purposes, sometimes by way of a general contribution to the tourist organization. At local level the local government grant may be raised as a proportion of local taxes, as is the case in many countries where local authorities are empowered to apply the revenue from local taxes to tourism purposes. Sometimes a given contribution is required from other interests, which determines the size of the government contribution. For example, in Switzerland the Government levies 25 per cent of the cost of publicity from the beneficiary industries and localities and re-imburses them 25 per cent of the cost of their individual promotion.[5] Government contribution may also take the form of incentives, under which tourists are exempt from certain taxes, for example, by issue of tax-free petrol coupons.

The extent of Government financial involvement in physical development is related to the degree of development of the industry. However, even in advanced tourist destinations, governments are usually involved in a whole spectrum of activities ranging from investment in transport and accommodation, through various forms of assistance to fiscal arrangements. It is generally the case in free and mixed economies that government financing serves to stimulate and complement private enterprise rather than doing what private enterprise is able and willing to do. Thus the emphasis is on heavy capital requirements, particularly in initial stages of development, most often in the provision of infrastructure. But even here governments tend to involve increasingly the participation of private enterprise, banks and credit institutions. The outstanding case in recent years has been the massive Roussillon-Languedoc project in France, a country with a highly developed tourist industry and an active capital market, in which public and private funds have been associated from the outset in financing development in tourism, which covers some 5 per cent of the territory of France. Direct government investment in tourism superstructure is undertaken to stimulate private investment, as has been the case in Greece, Portugal, Spain, and in other countries, with Government sharing in ownership, or through subsidies to developers.

In all these schemes the Government can effectively influence the location, type, and quality of development, as it can using other methods, such as credit facilities, loans at preferential rates of interest, and fiscal arrangements both for investment and subsequent operation of facilities.

Finance for physical development in tourism is frequently administered by a separate government agency created for the purpose, rather than through the natonal tourist organization. This recognizes the specialist nature of tourism development, as well as the varying scope of the tourist organization. Thus the Caisse Centrale de Crédit Hôtelier in France, the Israeli Tourist Industry Development Corporation, the Portuguese Tourist Fund, and many other similar agencies provide means of channelling public funds into tourism development in their respective countries.

Finance from Industry

In many countries at all levels firms and industries participating in tourism contribute to the financing of the tourist organization. When the structure and composition of the organization provides for membership participation, individual interests pay subscriptions; they may also make donations and take part in specific co-operative research and promotion projects, sharing the costs of such schemes with others and with the tourist organization.

The level at which individual firms and industries contribute can be determined by the level at which they operate and a close analogy exists here with the level at which government contributes. In a district, resort, or town, local government is usually a prominent participant; hotels and other purely local operators can participate in the local tourist organization either directly or through their local association or both.

At regional level the participants in the tourist organization are the provincial or regional government or such public authorities as make up this level in a particular country, for example, county councils in Britain. Corresponding to them are firms with a regional coverage of their operations, in particular bus and coach companies and groups of hotels located in those regions.

At the country level the central government is sometimes the sole financer of the tourist organization, but other interests, such as airline, railways and chain of accommodation providers, travel agencies, and banks with a national coverage may be also legitimate contributors.

It may therefore be postulated as a general principle that the main participants at each level of the tourist organization are the government and private tourist interests whose geographical areas of operation correspond to that level of tourist organization, and that they also finance the appropriate level of tourist organization. When this approach is adopted, the general interest and the financial involvement of participants correspond at the level of a destination, which is the focus of attention. When individual tourism interests, whether they be public or private, are expected to finance more than one level of organization, they may face a conflict of interests, which is not in the best interests of the tourist organization.

Tourists as Sources of Finance

Some of the revenue required by the tourist organization may be raised directly from the tourists themselves by means of a special visitor tax, such as is applied in a number of countries, in particular Austria, Germany, and Switzerland. Apart from being a source of revenue to the tourist organization, such tax may be intended to offset in a more specific way the costs which tourists create, and to provide a more equitable basis for sharing the cost of providing and maintaining the amenities used by residents as well as visitors. Although foreign tourists can often export some articles free of purchase tax, they normally pay indirect taxes in the same way as residents; domestic visitors do not have the advantage of foreign visitors. However, it is usually impossible to differentiate between domestic and foreign visitors in the application of a tourist tax in practice, which is therefore a tax applied to visitors as distinct from residents. Visitors do not pay certain taxes paid by residents, usually those levied on property, although those subject to property taxes can, and usually do, recover some or all of them through the prices they charge for their service, if they are in business; only the private householder bears the whole cost himself. But visitors, particularly overnight visitors, normally spend at a much higher rate than the resident population; their contribution to public finance can therefore be even higher than that of the resident population. For example, in Ireland it has been calculated that an increase of £10 million in gross tourist receipts generated by multiplication of income, means an increase of £5 million in tax revenue.[6] A special tax on tourists can be tantamount to taxing them twice, and, in the case of foreign visitors, imposing a surcharge on exports.

Although it is conceivable to levy a tourist tax at points of entry or exit at the destination, particularly on foreign tourists, which then discriminates between them and other visitors, the main method open to taxing visitors is confined to those spending at least one night at the destination, and largely to establishments in which accommodation is provided by way of business. But it is important to distinguish in principle between a tourist or visitor tax and what has come to be called particularly in Britain a hotel tax, even though both may be collected through the accommodation establishment, which is the main practicable method. In the former case, the hotel acts as a collector of the tax on behalf of the community, in the latter case the tax is levied on the hotel, which recovers it from the visitor. The second important distinction is in the application of the proceeds. These may be applied for purposes of tourism — to finance the tourist organization, for the provision, improvement and maintenance of amenities and facilities for tourists, or even for promotion purposes; but they may be also retained by the authorities for general purposes.

The Tourist Organization as Source of Finance

The fourth main source of finance for tourism is the tourism organization itself and three main methods may be available in this context: a grant by a higher level to a lower level tier of the vertical structure; a levy or other contribution by a lower level to a higher level in the vertical structure; or thirdly, revenue earning activities.

When the national tourist organization wishes to stimulate the regional organization or the regional organization the local organization, a part of the requirements of finance of the lower level body may be provided by the higher level body by way of grant for specific or general purposes, or some other means of support. This approach has been used in two particular circumstances. In countries with strong central direction in tourism the course of direction is reinforced in its influence by its role as a source of finance. In other circumstances this form of financing may be appropriate particularly in the initial stages of an evolving organization structure and this may diminish as the lower level becomes established.

The reverse direction of financing — from the lower to the higher level — usually obtains when the need for a higher level organization is evident by those at the lower level and when it may be a necessary means of creating a viable higher level organization. In contrast to the former situation, this method of finance in tourism is more typical of a decentralized organization structure and of one which exists in countries in an advanced stage of tourism development.

The tourist organization at all levels may also earn revenue from its own activities. It may sell information material to tourists, advertising space in its publications to advertisers, research and other material to operators and other interested parties. It may provide advisory services to individual firms and industries participating in tourism for a fee. In 1978/79, the British Tourist Authority, for example, recovered over a quarter of its operating expenditure, £4·2 million, from such activities: £2·6 million from co-operative publicity, £1·1 million from sale of publications, £0·4 million from advertising.[7]

Table 36
Finance in Tourism

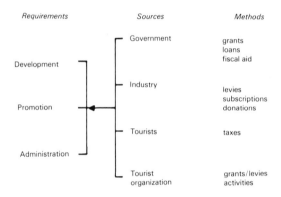

The Role of Public and Private Finance in Tourism

It has been suggested earlier that the respective roles of government and of private interests in tourism organization and in finance are not matters for empirical development but for a deliberate policy. Such policy provides a statement of the underlying philosophy and guide-lines for all concerned. In relation to finance the preceding pages have indicated the approaches adopted in general as well as in particular cases; these approaches may now be reviewed in three dimensions: in relation to the main requirements for finance, to the three basic levels of the tourist organization, and to individual countries — in all cases from the point of view of the respective roles of the public and private involvement.

Funds for each of the main requirements are not always clearly earmarked for development or promotion or other costs of the tourist organization. However, where they are so earmarked for the reasons indicated earlier, there is a clear tendency for public funds to be applied to promotion and administration, and for development to be financed largely by private enterprise. Departures from this and, in particular, for public finance used for physical development, can usually be discerned to exist with a view to particular objectives, to be concerned more with the infrastructure than with individual tourism projects, and to be administered by special arrangements, which may be within the scope of the tourist organization, but more often are not. On the other hand private funds, if used at all, tend to supplement the provision of public funds for promotion and other purposes.

There is a growing tendency for public finance to be the primary and often the exclusive source of finance at the national level of the tourist destination at which they operate, that is mainly locally and regionally. This identification of the individual interests with the corresponding levels of the vertical organization structure provides valid guide-lines for the direction of both government and private financial support to the tourist organization.

The third dimension for the definition of the respective toles arises in relation to individual countries. There the formulation of policy is likely to be influenced more by the background influences discussed in the last chapter than any guide-lines of general validity. The political and economic system of the country, the importance of tourism to the national economy, the stage of tourism development reached in the country, as well as histocial and other influences, taken together tend to determine also the respective roles of public and private finance in tourism. They also emphasize again that the tourism organization does not exist and work in isolation, but must be seen in the context of the economy and society of which it is part.

The Roles of Domestic and Foreign Finance

Whilst requirements for finance in tourism are related to particular countries and destinations, its sources range from those within to those external to the destination, and this distinction in turn extends the range of methods employed in financing particular requirements from particular sources.

We have seen that one level of the tourism organization may receive financial support from another level and thus a destination benefits from outside its own area of operation. The tourism organization may derive income for promotion purposes from collaborative schemes with transport undertakings, which handle traffice to the destination. But the main significance of this distinction arises in investment capital, the effects of which extend well beyond the year in which it enters the destination: the return on capital and, in the case of loans, the repayments, may or may not subsequently leave the destination. Whilst this is of importance to any destination, it assumes an added significance for a country, for which it has balance of payments implications. Of much relevance are, therefore, the respective roles of domestic and foreign investment, the latter of which may be subject to control in receiving and investing countries.

In developing countries local capital is generally scarce and foreign investment constitutes a necessary means of building up a tourism industry. For example, in the region of one-quarter of the total investment in hotels in Israel in the 1960s was from abroad, divided approximately equally between foreign loans and direct foreign investment. About one-quarter of tourism investment in Yugoslavia in late 1960s was foreign investment.[8]

The foreign sources are private developers and investors on the one hand and international agencies on the other hand. Both of them may undertake a whole project or, as is common, enter into partnership with local capital, both private and public. But international agencies, such as the International Bank for Reconstruction and Development (popularly known as the World Bank) and its affiliated Development Banks are the main sources of foreign investment in infrastructure. For example, the World Bank made possible the building of the Adriatic Coast Road and the Central Highway in Yugoslavia. Another means is employed, for example, by Israel, where the Tourist Industry Development Corporation, a government credit institution, sells debentures abroad, with interest guaranteed by the Government.

There is a much wider availability of foreign capital for individual facilities, particularly when an area has satisfactorily demonstrated its tourist potential. In addition to developers and investors, foreign tour operators represent a growing source of funds for hotel development.

But foreign capital in tourism is not moving only between developed and developing countries. As the freedom of capital movement between countries increases, it is clear that capital will move where best return is obtainable, and we may expect that the international character of tourism will increasingly find an expression also in the international ownership and operation of tourism industries in individual countries.

Table 37

Levels of Organization and Main Sources of Finance

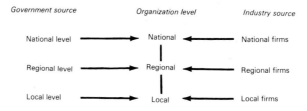

In 1966 an OECD Seminar on 'Tourism Development and Economic Growth' held in Portugal, classified countries into four broad categories as far as tourism prospects are concerned. First, there were seen to be countries where tourism is limited and is likely to remain so, i.e. countries with unpleasantly extreme climates, geographically remote from the high income areas of the world population, whose low level of overall development means that they lack the basic facilities that tourism requires; they cannot expect to build up a tourist industry of an appreciable size without considerable difficulty. Secondly, there are countries where there are some possibilities of advance, but of a limited nature; thirdly, those where tourism is already of some importance and with proper handling could become a very important factor in the economy; fourthly, countries which already have a highly advanced tourism industry, and for whom the question is how to maintain that advance.[9]

According to this classification, in the 1960s Britain could have been considered to belong to the third category, which embodies some of the most interesting issues and challenges of organization and finance in tourism for a democratic society and a mixed economy; Britain also had its share of traditions and other influences with a bearing on tourism organization, as well as on other aspects of its life and institutions. This combination of factors is a strong enough argument for a study of the issues and approaches in the organization and finance of tourism in Britain, quite apart from an obvious association of the authors of this book with that country. But a further reason for such study is that, in the late 1960s and early 1970s the organization of tourism in Britain was transformed from a voluntary framework to a largely statutory one with a strong Government interest and involvement. By the late 1970s Britain may be considered to have moved from the third to the fourth category of countries according to the OECD Seminar classification — one of the leading tourist destinations with a highly developed tourist industry. For all these reasons the British experience has a relevance beyond Britain, in bringing together much that is involved in the organization and finance in tourism. This chapter, therefore, looks at Britain as a country in transition from the time before the change took place, through the legislation of the late 1960s, to the first ten years of the new framework.

Tourism Organization in Britain to 1969

The British Government was interested in tourism for some forty years before 1969. During this period tourism was at Government level the general responsibility of the Board of Trade, a Ministry whose interests included an overview of industry and commerce in Britain, the export trade, as well as from time to time such matters as civil aviation and regional development. There was no stated policy on tourism. The functions of the national tourist organization were performed by the British Travel Association and its predecessors, under the direction of the Board of Trade.

The British Travel Association was a voluntary co-operative association of members, whose main concern was to promote travel to and within Britain and to stimulate the development of facilities. In its last full financial year 1968/69 the BTA had a total expenditure of £3·7 million. This amount was applied as follows: 75 per cent on overseas publicity including the expenditure on overseas offices, 18 per cent on head office administration, 7 per cent on travel promotion and information services within Britain. Eighty per cent of the income was in the form of a grant from the Board of Trade, 15 per cent from various activities including revenue from advertising and sales of literature, 5 per cent from members' subscriptions and contributions.[10] The Association had a staff of 450, of whom 150 (mostly local staff) were working abroad.

There were three separate semi-autonomous organizations for Scotland, Wales, and Northern Ireland — the Scottish Tourist Board, the Wales Tourist Board, and the statutory Northern Ireland Tourist Board, with promotion and development functions in respect of their own areas and some measure of co-ordination with the BTA, particularly in overseas promotion. Several statutory tourist organizations, more or less independent of the rest, operated in respect of the Channel Islands and the Isle of Man, which co-operated intensively with the British Travel Association.

At regional level the tourist organization was developed in the 1960s covering the whole of Wales through three regions, under the direction of the Wales Tourist Board; there were the beginnings of a regional framework in Scotland and six area/regional associations/boards were in existence in parts of England: the London Tourist Board, the Northumberland and Durham Travel Association, the English Lakes Counties Travel Association, the South West Travel Association, the Yorkshire Travel Association, and the Thames Valley Tourist Association.

There were many resort, town, and district bodies in existence under various designations, representing the local level in the vertical organization structure.

Problems and Weaknesses Before 1969

It was possible to identify five main problems and weaknesses in the organization of tourism in Britain in the 1960s.

Firstly, there was no clear comprehensive Government policy on tourism. In the absence of such guide-lines many actions of Government departments, tourism organizations, commercial and other interests were taken without reference to agreed objectives, rarely co-ordinated, and sometimes conflicting.

Secondly, the national tourist organization, the British Travel Association, and the Boards for Scotland and Wales had no statutory powers to secure action. The organizations had to seek to influence action by encouragement and persuasion, without adequate resources available to give enough attention to all of their functions.

Thirdly, and to a great extent due to the lack of statutory powers and resources, the development of facilities was lagging behind requirements and lacking in co-ordination with promotion on the one hand and as between various interests in development.

Fourthly, the regional organization was uneven and weak in most parts of Britain. The gap between the national and local levels resulted in a lack of co-ordination of tourism interests at the regional level and an uneven pattern of links between the local and national levels.

Last but not least, there was a diversity of financing. The confused roles of government and commercial interests at various levels resulted in individual public authorities and firms being called upon to play a role and to contribute financially at more than one level, some of them at all levels from the local association to the British Travel Association.

These five main problems and weaknesses resulted in demands and pressures for change in Britain in the late 1960s.

Background to Change

The problems and weaknesses identified above provided strong stimuli to change in tourist organization in Britain, but there were other influences at work at the time.

A dramatic growth of tourism took place in post-war Britain reflected in the holiday propensity of the British population and even more so in overseas visits to Britain. Some 15 million or one-third of the population took an annual holiday away from home immediately before the Second World War; this volume rose to 25 million or one-half of the population in 1950s, and to 30 million or about 60 per cent of the population in 1960s; at the same time an increasing proportion of the population took more than one holiday annually. Half a million overseas visitors came to Britain in 1937 and this number arrived again in 1947; it doubled to 1 million in 1955, to 2 million in 1963, to 4 million in 1967, with a prospect of doubling again to 8 million in early 1970s. A new organization framework was needed to cope effectively with growth.

The growth in the volume of tourism in Britain and the opportunities created by tourism brought about an increasing realization on the part of the British Government of the importance of tourism — to the balance of payments in particular, to the economy in general, and also to regional development.

In 1968, the Government announced three particular measures — an hotel development incentive scheme, intention to acquire powers to register and classify accommodation, and selective financial assistance for particular tourism projects. These measures were formulated piecemeal, but created a need for machinery to administer them.

At the same time there were other pressures and advocacies of various sectional interests which added momentum to a need for a new organization framework in British tourism. The search for a formula was under way.

The Available Options

We may discern five main alternatives available at the time to meet the requirements of the situation, in which a framework, which had become inadequate, was to give way to a new one:

(a) To give development and possibly other powers to the British Travel Association.

(b) To give development powers to the Board of Trade and for the British Travel Association to concentrate on promotion.

(c) To create a new development organization and for the British Travel Association to concentrate on promotion.

(d) To combine development and promotion in a government department, such as the Board of Trade, or in a new ministry, with adequate powers.

(e) To create a new statutory organization with adequate powers, to combine promotion and development.

It was not appropriate to give powers to a voluntary membership organization, such as the British Travel Association. There seemed to be a general reluctance for additional functions to be assumed by a government department and therefore to adopt the second alternative, similar to the pattern in existence in Italy at the time. This, together with the undesirability of separating promotion and development functions between two organizations, were also the main reasons for the lack of support for the third alternative, although some of the problems of separation could have been avoided by a common policy board, co-ordinating committees, sub-ordination of one organization to the other generally or in respect of particular matters, or by a combination of these and other approaches. Apart from the reluctance to assume additional functions within a government department, the commercial nature of promotion was not considered appropriate for a government department, and this effectively ruled out the fourth alternative. In the end, the fifth alternative, a new statutory organization outside a government department, and combining promotion and development, appeared to present the balance of advantages, and what was probably the most radical of the five available options was adopted. This pattern found an expression in the Development of Tourism Act 1969.

The New Statutory Organization

In 1969 the first Act of Parliament devoted to tourism was passed in Britain: the Development of Tourism Act 1969. The Act has three parts:

Part I set up four statutory boards with defined functions, structure and powers.

Part II provided for financial assistance for hotel development.

Part III provides certain enabling powers in respect of accommodation.

Part II of the Act was essentially temporary in its effect and operation and was referred to earlier in this book in connection with planning and development. Part III provides enabling powers for the registration of tourist accommodation by Tourist Boards. The Act does not set out any pre-determined scheme of registration, classification or grading, but provides for the introduction of a scheme by Order in Council. The same part of the Act enabled provision to be made by an Order in Council requiring hotels and other establishments in Great Britain which provide sleeping accommodation to display or otherwise notify their room charges. This Part of the Act is dealt with in Chapter 15 of this book. Our concern in this chapter is Part I of the Act, creating a new statutory organization for promotion and development of tourism in Britain, whose principal features may be summarized as follows.

The new statutory organization consists of four bodies — the British Tourist Authority and the English Tourist Board, both responsible to the Board of Trade (now the Department of Trade); the Scottish Tourist Board and the Wales Tourist Board responsible to the Secretaries of State for Scotland and Wales respectively.

Under Section 1 of the Act the British Tourist Authority is to have not more than nine members, the Boards for England, Scotland, and Wales not more than seven each. The four tourist boards are to be compact, functional bodies, and their members are not intended to be representatives or delegates for particular sectional or geographical interests. A link between the four bodies is provided through the chairmen of the Tourist Boards of England, Scotland, and Wales, who are members of the British Tourist Authority. Matters such as membership, staffing and proceedings of the four bodies are dealt with in Schedule 1 of the Act.

According to Section 2 the new organization has responsibilities for tourist publicity and promotion, as well as for encouraging the provision and improvement of tourist amenities and facilities. According to Section 2 and 5, the British Tourist Authority is responsible for the promotion overseas of tourism to Britain and for dealing with matters of common interest to the country as a whole, such as co-operation with other national organizations, general research, and advisory services. The development of tourism in England, Scotland, and Wales is the responsibility of their respective Tourist Boards, who also carry out publicity and promotion within the United Kingdom. All four bodies have powers under Section 4 to give financial assistance to particular tourism projects; there is also provision in Section 3 for general schemes of financial assistance to classes of projects, to be made by Order.

Under Section 5 the British Tourist Authority can carry out overseas promotion for the Channel Islands, the Isle of Man, and Northern Ireland at the request of their tourist organizations.

The Act draws particular attention to the desirability of co-operation between the three Boards (the ETB, STB, and WTB) and bodies such as area and regional organizations. Section 2 of the Act empowers the three Boards to give financial and other help to such bodies.

All four bodies are able to set up advisory and consultative machinery to maintain links with trade and consumer interests. All of them are encouraged to be outward-looking and, for example, to provide the Overseas Development Administration with technical experts to help in programmes of technical assistance to overseas countries.

Each body is responsible for recruiting its own staff, but it needs the consent of the relevant Minister and of the Civil Service Department as to the numbers and to the pay of their staff.

Although the British Tourist Authority and the three Boards are able to charge for their services and to earn commercial revenue, for example by the sales of advertising space and of their publications, they are in the main financed by money voted by Parliament, as provided for by Section 20 of the Act; there is no scope for industry financing through membership subscriptions and donations towards the administrative expenses of the four bodies and towards expenses incurred in the exercise of their functions. The general framework created by the Development of Tourism Act is shown in Table 38, its principal characteristics in Appendix Z1, and income and expenditure in Appendix Z2.

The New Non-Statutory Organization

The Development of Tourism Act provided a powerful stimulus to the development of the regional organization in Britain. We have seen that at the time of the passing of the Act regional organization was most highly developed in Wales, there were beginnings of a framework in Scotland, and there was a patchy framework in existence in England. The English Tourist Board and the Scottish Tourist Board gave a high priority to the creation and development of comprehensive regional frameworks in their countries and the developed framework has been consolidated in Wales since 1969.

The organization of tourism in Britain below national level was also affected by a major re-organization of local government in the 1970s. In arriving at the number and geographical distribution of the regions a number of considerations have been to the fore in the English, Scottish, and Wales Tourist Boards, in the local government, and in the other interests involved.

First, the desirability of the outer limits to be so drawn as to coincide with the government boundaries; at the same time, although Economic Planning Regions do not necessarily represent the right geographical areas for promoting tourism and developing facilities for tourists, they are closely related to natural tourist regions and have an interest in the development of the leisure potential of their areas.

Secondly, the need for each region to be of a size to support a viable and effective organization. Marketing considerations, the availability of finance, and the need to employ a team of professional staff impose a limit on the number and size of regions.

Table 38

Statutory Tourist Organization in Britain

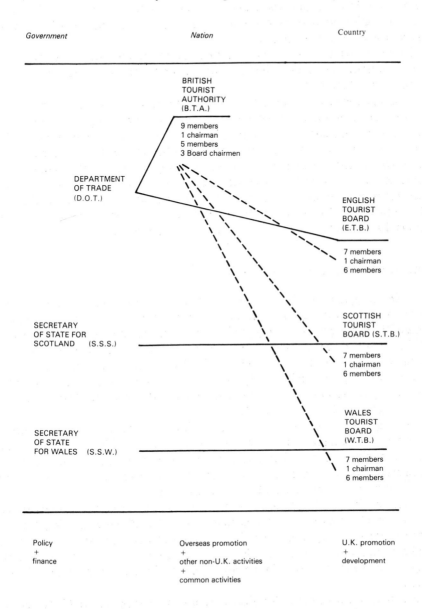

Government	Nation	Country

BRITISH
TOURIST
AUTHORITY
(B.T.A.)

9 members
1 chairman
5 members
3 Board chairmen

DEPARTMENT
OF TRADE
(D.O.T.)

ENGLISH
TOURIST
BOARD
(E.T.B.)

7 members
1 chairman
6 members

SECRETARY
OF STATE FOR
SCOTLAND   (S.S.S.)

SCOTTISH
TOURIST
BOARD (S.T.B.)

7 members
1 chairman
6 members

SECRETARY
OF STATE
FOR WALES   (S.S.W.)

WALES
TOURIST
BOARD
(W.T.B.)

7 members
1 chairman
6 members

Policy	Overseas promotion	U.K. promotion
+	+	+
finance	other non-U.K. activities	development
	+	
	common activities	

Following the creation of the Southern Tourist Board, England has 12 regional boards with local authority (i.e. county council and district council) and commercial participation, supported by the English Tourist Board.

In Scotland, in 7 of the 9 regions, supported by the Scottish Tourist Board, tourism is the responsibility of the regional government (i.e. regional councils), in one of them of a voluntary association, and in the Highlands and Islands, of a statutory Development Board, which covers tourism.

In Wales there are three regions operating under the direction of the Wales Tourist Board through regional tourism councils with local government (i.e. county and district council) and corporate membership.

The total framework of 24 regional tourist organizations in Britain is intended to fulfil basically the same roles in respect of each region, but differs principally in the degree of independence as between England, Scotland and Wales. In England marketing and development are integrated in the same organization, whilst in most regions of Scotland the two functions are the responsibility of separate departments within regional government. The activities of all regional organizations are to a greater or lesser extent co-ordinated by the 3 national tourist boards. Three main parties, therefore, normally participate in the tourism organization of each region: local government, the commercial and other interests, and the national tourist board.

The main focus for the organization of tourism at local level is normally local government, at county and district level in England and Wales, and at district level in Scotland. The local government level consists of 45 counties and 333 districts in England, 8 counties and 37 districts in Wales, and 53 districts in Scotland. The local authority usually acts as the destination organization in respect of development and promotion of tourism in respect of its own area, but often also acts as provider of tourist attractions, facilities and services. Within a local authority the two main functions are normally discharged by separate departments; one is variously concerned with leisure, recreation, tourism, and with attractions, amenities, entertainment, and promotion; another with physical planning. In a number of areas there are also voluntary associations, which seek to influence local government, and which may also conduct promotional activity

New Shape of Finance

In the reorganization of tourism in Britain some significant changes took place in financing, in addition to the hotel development incentives of Part II of the 1969 Act. Some progress has been made in defining the respective roles and financial contributions of the major sources of revenue in relation to the three basic levels of tourist organization and their respective voices in determining their direction of policy and activities.

The State has assumed responsibility for expenditure incurred by the BTA and the three Boards in discharge of the functions allocated to them by the Act, i.e. for promotion and administration; no commercial contributions are sought for these bodies which are, however, free to earn revenue through their own activities. Specific contributions from individual regions and resorts may be called for specific overseas promotions by the BTA, and from them and firms and other organizations or for co-operative promotion schemes, by all the four bodies. Specific development finance is available for particular tourism projects from public funds, through all four bodies.

Local tourism organization financing has not been affected by changes following the 1969 Act, but at regional level the identified sources of income came to be established as local government, the national tourist boards, commercial membership, and revenue-earning activities and services. These are shown for the 12 English Regional Tourist Boards for the period 1971—80 in Appendix Z3. Most of the Boards received major contributions from local government and the English Tourist Board, and achieved only limited success in commercial membership, but in recent years earned a significant part of their income themselves.

The First Ten Years

The end of the 1970s marked the first fifty years of active promotion of Britain abroad as a tourist destination, since the Travel Association of Great Britain and Ireland was formed in 1929, and the first ten years of the new tourism organization created by the Development of Tourism Act 1969. As the last pages of the first edition of this book came to be written in 1972, it was possible to discuss the first achievements and some of the weaknesses of the British framework three years after the first tourism legislation in Britain came into operation. The new edition affords an opportunity to take a ten-year view.

In that time the British Government became better informed and attuned to the prospects and problems of tourism growth and development within its shores. Two major reviews of tourism were made by the Government in the 1970s, from which a positive outlook and the first rudiments of tourism policy emerged.

The first inter-departmental review, which took place when a new Government took office, resulted in policy guidelines to the British Tourist Authority and the three national tourist boards in 1974 — to give more emphasis on publicizing attractions of Britain outside the main tourist centres and outside the peak season; to switch expenditure to develop untapped potential for tourism in areas that can readily absorb and benefit from more visitors; to cut heavy expenditure on generalized promotion both at home and overseas; to put more sponsored activities on a self-supporting basis.

The 1974 guidelines 'intended to bring the high importance of tourism for our balance of payments and for our regional economies into focus with the environmental and financial constraints of the foreseeable future',[11] represent a significant step forward in policy formulation and an alignment of tourism objectives with Government economic objectives; they were indicative guidelines and it was for the statutory tourist boards to formulate and implement the detail.

In 1978 the Government confirmed the continuing relevance of the 1974 guidelines, introduced capital building allowances for hotels, and also extended the development assistance for tourism projects from Development Areas to Intermediate Areas.

In 1979 the review conducted by a Steering Group chaired by the Department of Trade and including principal Government departments concerned with tourism as well as the four statutory tourist boards, concluded that Government expenditure on tourism should continue, and this was confirmed by a subsequent Government review of public expenditure.

By 1978/79 the Government grant-in-aid to the four statutory tourist boards reached £24 million and the White Paper on the Government's expenditure plans published in March 1980 indicated that the comparable amounts would be £27 million in 1979/80 and £26 million in 1980/81 at constant prices. Government financial support for tourism, therefore, continues on a significant scale. However, the experience of the 1970s suggests reluctance on the part of the British Government to formulate a more comprehensive policy on tourism and, unlike other governments, to create a permanent machinery for inter-ministerial co-ordination; broad policy guidelines, periodic review, and a more *ad hoc* liaison between the Government departments themselves and between them and the statutory tourist boards appear to be preferred.

In the 1970s the top tourism organization of statutory tourist boards became established, following a relatively smooth transfer of responsibilites from a voluntary to a new statutory framework, including the creation of the English Tourist Board, an interesting pioneering in constitutional practice in recognizing England as a separate entity, which had no precedent before 1969. Overseas promotion by the British Tourist Authority continued the work of the former British Travel Association, and to this the national tourist boards added a dynamic and innovative approach to domestic tourism promotion. The development function in tourism received increasing recognition in the work of the national boards, which also acted as the agencies of the Government in the Hotel Development Incentives Scheme and continue to do so in the administration of development assistance to tourism projects.

The relationships between the British Tourist Authority and the national boards were ill-defined in the 1969 Act and came to be largely clarified subsequently; broad strategic planning for British tourism has made some headway. However, whilst the co-equal status of the Authority and of the national boards has worked effectively in areas where their complementary roles were defined by the Act or were agreed between them by consensus subsequently, areas of overlap and lack of consensus remain, and the influence the national boards should have on the marketing of their countries overseas through the BTA continues to receive attention. The planned devolution to Scotland and Wales, which would have increased the size of the BTA Board and the representation on it of England, Scotland, and Wales, and which might have led to a clearer definition of roles, did not materialize; the arrangements and relationships of the 1970s, therefore, continue into the 1980s.

The priority given to regional organization by the national boards, which led to the creation and growth of regional tourist boards, has led to increased understanding of tourism, improved co-operation between local authorities and commercial interests, and help in the implementation of national policies. A comprehensive network of some 600 tourist information centres has helped to improve the dissemination of information and to disperse tourist traffic geographically and seasonally. At the local level, most local organizations have been adjusting themselves to their role as tourist destinations organizations in the context of their regions but this has been a slow process; the realization that only the largest and best-known resorts can still hope to promote themselves, has been very gradual in its acceptance among others.

Finance in tourism made some strides towards rationalization at national and to a lesser extent at regional level. But the same government and commercial interests often still continue to be asked to participate and to contribute financially at both regional and local levels.

There is a growing realization of the changing role of tourist organizations at all levels. Often the marketing concept still has to permeate the structure and to replace limited co-ordination in promotion and development. With time the emphasis is moving from promotion to development and to the basic task of reconciling the interests of residents and visitors. The tourist organization is gradually entering into the local planning process but it has made little progress in the educative process aimed at the resident population to increase the tourism consciousness of those whose towns and districts are tourist destinations.

There is also a growing recognition of tourism as an activity, which calls in its management for professional knowledge and skills of its own, rather than a mere layman's interest or an exercise of political judgement. The 1970s saw a major growth of education and training in tourism and the beginnings of recognized career structures in tourism. Over the decade the numbers employed by statutory and regional tourist boards in Britain more than doubled from less than 500 to well over 1,000 people; a significant growth took place in tourism employed in local government, and among the many and diverse providers of tourist attractions, facilities and services, travel organizers and intermediaries in the private sector.

At the beginnings of the 1980s tourism in Britain reached a stage where it calls for a growing number of professionals who can lead and take a positive part in the many boards and committees, who can influence local opinion as well as visitors, and who can plan for tourism rather than let it happen. Only planned education and training can safeguard the future success of British tourism.

Part X

The Future of Tourism

Further Reading for Part X

Burkart, A. J. and Medlik, S. (editors): *The Management of Tourism,* Part X
Medlik, S., *Profile of the Hotel and Catering Industry, 2nd ed., Chapter 20*
Edwards, A.: *International Tourism Development Forecasts to 1990*, Special
  Report No. 62
Archer, B.H., *Demand Forecasting in Tourism*

References

1 Archer, B. H., 'Forecasting Demand: quantitative and intuitive techniques', *International Journal of Tourism Management,* Vol. 1, No. 1,
  March, 1980

In this final part of the book, we discuss the prospects for tourism. First, in this chapter in terms of markets, flows and destinations, but in subsequent chapters we turn our attention to the facilities and resources, as well as to aspects of organization likely to influence the future pattern of tourism.

At the start of the 1980s, there are several constraints to be taken into account in attempting to paint a scenario of the future. First, we see no prospect of an abatement in the high rate of inflation which has afflicted the world since the mid-1970s. This has been caused to some extent by the oil/energy crisis that burst upon the world with the so-called Yom Kippur war in 1973 between Egypt and Israel. We think, or rather for present purposes, we assume secondly that the price of oil will continue to rise, that its rise will affect more than the price and cost of aviation fuel and of petrol, and that the level of economic activity and incomes in the main tourism generating countries will be static if not declining, so that tourism growth may be checked somewhat. Thirdly, some increased tension between the Western powers and the communist bloc may be expected in the early 1980s, as the military strength of the USSR approaches parity with that of the USA. Fourthly, we expect some expansion of militant Islam, which stretches from Algeria in the west to Indonesia in the east and spreads into Africa. The puritanical mien of Islam is fundamentally opposed to the western concepts of the good life, which includes holiday travel as a major ingredient.

The picture is however by no means gloomy and in discussing each factor which influences tourism, we shall try to show how the impact of these constraints may be modified.

Further, we make no claim to be forecasting. Nevertheless, it is appropriate to note here that the art and science of forecasting made great progress during the 1970s and management has at its disposal in the 1980s vastly improved techniques for forecasting tourism demand.[1] Reference should be made also to the several institutions, which have grown up to provide forecasts over a wide field of economic activity, and of which perhaps the best known is the Hudson Institute, whose director Herman Kahn may be said to have invented futurology.

Size and Structure of the Population

Demand for tourism is related to the size and structure of the population, particularly in the case of those countries with high propensity to tourism. In recent years that population has tended towards much slower growth and in Britain, for example, the population is likely to remain more or less unchanged during the 1980s; the population of the USA may grow from 220 million in 1979 to 240 million ten years hence. Within this limited growth the composition of the population is important.

Age alone is not the most meaningful predictor of participation in tourism. The other aspects of the population structure are more hazardous to predict. Such factors as age of marriage, the resultant rate of family and household formation, and the composition and age distribution within the family are often more important in influencing participation in tourism.

Traditionally, people in their twenties and thirties have been the prime consumers. Representing, for example, in Britain over one-quarter of the population, they are responsible for their children's expenditure and provide, therefore, well over one-half of the purchasing society. This group is likely to increase most in size by the early 1980s and account with their children for close on two-thirds of total consumers. The second age-group to increase most in size will be the over-sixties, to almost one-fifth of the population. The prime age groups continue to be better and better educated making them more receptive to new ideas and encouraging them to broaden their horizons. The age of marriage has been steadily reducing and although it is impossible to predict the changes in attitude to family size, it is clear that the control of the incidence of child births and of family size are within the grasp of each family. Although the number of working women may not change significantly, the number of working married women continues to increase, associated not only with earlier marriage, but also with their desire to get out of the house and to lead a more interesting life.

Incomes and Leisure

Disposable personal incomes have continued to grow in the tourism-generating countries, despite occasional setbacks in particular countries and at particular times. Subject to improvement in world trade generally, continued affluence is seen for the 1980s. If the experience of the UK is repeated elsewhere — and the UK has been a tourism pioneer quite often — expenditure on leisure, especially on foreign travel, will form an increasing share of total consumer expenditure.

Greatly increased leisure in the future is a popular assertion which has a little too readily passed into the contemporary mythology. Leisure needs closer scrutiny, and in particular it seems valuable to distinguish between leisure calculated on a daily or weekly basis and leisure calculated on an annual basis.

On a weekly basis, the week worked (as distinct from the standard working week on which normal time wages are calculated) has not shortened substantially in the last twenty years, and for manual workers in Britain seems to have stabilized around forty-six hours a week. This includes a fair amount of overtime, and is true of manual workers. It may be that in the case of clerical and administrative workers the week worked more closely approximates to the standard week. However, the general pattern seems to be that people are not prepared to work less long hours unless they receive an income which will enable them to spend on their newly acquired leisure. In a nutshell, leisure is not readily substituted for income. The effect of this seems to be that when the first employment offers a reduction in hours worked, the reduction is used by many to earn more income in a second employment, a practice sometimes called 'moonlighting'. The desire seems to be to secure a sufficient income so that a relatively short period of leisure can be more intensively enjoyed by increasing the money spent on each hour of leisure rather than by increasing the total amount of leisure.

For that part of the population susceptible to overtime, the need to earn more on a weekly basis to pay for costlier annual holidays may only lead to requests for more overtime. Many industrial disputes have turned on the question of overtime, and during the miners' strike in 1972 the popular press carried stories of miners on strike awaiting the settlement of their claims on holiday in Majorca by means of very cheap charter inclusive tours. If the stories were not well-founded, their philosophy was.

In the industrialised countries, the holiday entitlement of workers has steadily increased, until substantial sections of the population enjoy up to six weeks a year for holidays. The question that has to be answered is whether the increased income, which will make extended holidays possible, will be available. For no one envisages that a reduction in the time worked should be matched by a corresponding drop in income. Holidays and holidays abroad are seen by the western industrial worker as an essential part of his life style.

However, available evidence suggests that additional leisure time is not readily converted to holidays away from home as the holiday entitlement increases. When paid holidays constitute two weeks in a year, all or most of that time is devoted to a holiday by a large proportion of those entitled to it. When most have become entitled to annual holidays with pay of four weeks or more, two weeks' holiday away or its equivalent has remained for many the norm and only a small proportion have so far taken an additional leisure time as a third week's holiday away from home. According to the British Home Tourism Survey the bulk of holiday trips do not exceed two weeks and according to the British National Travel Survey only one in five of the population takes more than one holiday in any one year.

Car Ownership

The private car, all in all, is the most used method of transport in holiday tourism. Only about 2 per cent of all US holidaymakers travel abroad in any one year, but the use of the car for domestic holidays outpaces any other form of transport. The same pattern would be true in Europe, but for the multiplicity of nation states in that region, and much has still to be achieved in aiding unrestricted crossing of frontiers. Nevertheless, the big volume of German visitors to Austria and Italy, and of French visitors to Spain is a reflection of increasing car ownership and use in both Germany and France.

The private car occupies an increasingly prominent position in the developed generating countries. In the UK, for example, during the period 1968—78, car travel generally increased by 50 per cent and the number of cars rose from 11 million to 14 million. With such a commitment to the car, it is not surprising that by far the largest part of holiday transport in Britain is performed by car. The same phenomenon is found in the USA, in France, and in Germany. For travel abroad the car remains important, but less so in the case of the UK where the English Channel forms a natural barrier to its use and where the development of cheap inclusive tours to Spain and elsewhere has made the air the principal mode of travel abroad.

In the UK, the near-completion of the motorway network has facilitated the use of the car and in particular the south-west, already the country's prime holiday area, may expect even more holiday demand. The Lake District is another area where the pressure of demand may pose problems of control. The case for some kind of pricing system coupled with advance reservation in these areas looks strong.

In 1975 the British government abandoned the plans for a Channel Tunnel linking England and France and the cross-Channel traffic has to travel by sea. The privately owned operator in the early 1980s was introducing new and faster ships on the car ferry routes. This will make the crossing time by conventional ships comparable with the hovercraft services and one hovercraft operator is seeking to leave the route. In the late 1970s, there were several new entrants to the cross-Channel routes. The re-introduction of competition in the car ferry services seems likely to produce lower fares, and despite attempts to re-open the Tunnel issue, some growth in cross-Channel ferry traffic is seen, particularly for holiday purposes.

Propensity to Holidays

It is difficult to envisage that the level of holiday participation in any one year on the part of the population is likely to increase much in the countries where it is 60 per cent or more already, such as in Britain, although the frequency is. Permanent and temporary influences tend to exclude from holiday participation the old and the poor, those with preference to stay at home or to go only on day trips and other reasons for not going away on holiday in any one year include illness, very young children in the family, and a whole range of other reasons, each of which alone accounts for a small, but together for a significant number of people.

However, in many other countries with similar or even higher income levels, including France, Germany, and the United States, still less than 60 per cent of the population take holidays away from home. The potential for growth in propensity, as well as frequency, in these countries in the years to come is considerable.

We may therefore divide countries into two broad groups according to their current propensity to holidays. Those with high levels of population participation can expect in the main an increase in additional holidays, that is an increase in holiday frequency. Others can expect an increase in propensity as well as growing frequency reflected in more than one holiday on the part of a growing proportion of the population.

Travel Abroad

The extent of foreign travel depends in part on the same factors as domestic tourism, but also on the size of the country of origin and its geographical location. A European is much more likely to cross international frontiers than an American, but even in Europe most tourism is domestic.

Early in the 1970s the International Union of Official Travel Organizations (IUOTO), now the World Tourism Organization (WTO), estimated that international tourist arrivals throughout the world would reach 250-280 million by 1980, as compared with 169 million in 1970. The largest absolute increases in arrivals were foreseen in Europe and in America, the two regions which have always accounted for the great majority of them; Europe and the Americas were still expected to dominate international tourism with more than 90 per cent of all arrivals in these regions by 1980; Europe was to attract a little less than ten years earlier, the Americas were to retain or slightly increase their share. The largest proportionate increases were projected for the other regions, particularly for Africa, albeit from a small base.

The projections were prepared in 1971, before any signs of the energy crisis, which did not break out until late 1973. In the event there were only two years of low growth in the 1970s — 1973 and 1974, and in the mid 1970s international tourism resumed the growth rates of the early 1970s. By 1979 international tourist arrivals reached 270 million and by the end of 1980 the forecast could understate the reality (*see* Appendix F). Europe and Africa were close to the forecasts, the Far East gained more than was expected, largely at the expense of the Americas. But the overall outcome is likely to be close to the forecast (*see* Appendix H).

By the end of the 1970s the developed world was competing for most international tourists from developed countries; the whole of the developing world was competing for a small, mainly long haul market from the developed world. The developing world was generating few international tourists — for the developed world or for its own destinations. The dominant international tourist flows were, first, north to north, and, secondly, north to south, in that order.

New Generators of Tourism

It is important to ask whether there are in sight any new generators of tourism in addition to the existing twelve countries which generate some 80 per cent of current demand. We have seen earlier that countries with high discretionary incomes display a high propensity to tourism and this can be weighed against the other factors. In the first edition of this book, we placed Japan as our first choice as a major new generator. That we were right to do so is now a matter of history — Japan generated 3·6 million international tourist arrivals in 1975 ranking tenth among the leading generators. Our second choice for new generator status was the black Americans. So far as can be judged, the growth in their propensity to travel has been disappointing but difficulties of identifying their flows may lead to some understatement. We also hazarded the speculation that a relaxation of East-West tension might lead to an increased flow of Eastern European countries' tourists. There has been some increase but the hoped-for relaxation of tension has not materialized, and while we would still draw attention to the effects of any large surge of East European tourists on Europe's resorts, it seems unlikely that it will occur in the 1980s.

It is useful to divide the countries of the world into three categories, the developed countries, the countries in course of development, and the undeveloped ones. It is among the countries in the course of development that we must look for the new generators. Two countries stand out as likely to emerge as significant generators of tourism, Brazil and Mexico. The latter is already a substantial recipient of tourists chiefly from the USA, and generates no less than 11 per cent of arrivals for the USA. It should be noted that Taiwan and South Korea generate a similar proportion of arrivals for Japan, and should also be included in the list of new generators.

There remains a further source of new tourist traffic. For most of the developed world there is still a significant proportion of the population who do not holiday abroad at all. In the 1980s, further progress should be seen in extending and deepening the market by reaching these people. The introduction of very low fares across the North Atlantic at the end of the 1970s served to open up new market segments beyond the student-type traffic that was the original target of those fares. By the same token much has still to be done in increasing the intensity of tourism in the developed countries by encouraging, for example, second or even third holidays a year.

Immigration and the Future of Tourism

A feature of the last quarter century has been the flow of migrants from poorer southern countries to more prosperous northern countries. This flow is observable in North America in the immigration of Puerto Ricans to the northern parts of the USA (Puerto Rico having a special status *vis-à-vis* the USA), in the flow of immigrants from the Caribbean to the United Kingdom, and in the somewhat later flow of Asian immigrants from East Africa to the UK. All these flows have been possible because the immigrants had a recognized nationality status with the country receiving them. Rather different in kind has been the flow of migrants into Northern Europe from Southern Europe, from North Africa and from Asia Minor, in which cases the immigrants have been seen as a temporary addition to the receiving countries' workforce, rather than as an integral part of the population, in the northern industrial countries.

Inevitably, the major part of the immigrant flow has found employment initially at the bottom of the economic ladder, but on a ten-year plus view of the future it would be reasonable to expect to see the beginnings of a tourist flow generated by the fact of migration, closely analogous to the flows created by the earlier migrations from Europe to the USA. With little evidence to support the view, one might perhaps expect the second generation immigrant born in the receiving country, or at any rate very young upon arrival, to evince some curiosity about the land of his origin and to deploy the means to gratify it. Although there is not much evidence on the point, this seems to have been the pattern of the Europe-North America case: the first generation migrants appear to have little taste and perhaps not the means to revisit the country of origin, from which either economic or political pressure had expelled them. Their children and grandchildren seem to have generated the tourists.

Future Tourist Destinations

In the 1980s, it can be said with confidence that as the principal generators of tourism will be the developed countries of Europe and North America, so will those same countries be the principal destinations. Too much has been invested in the coast of Spain, for example, for it ever to be abandoned in the foreseeable future. Moreover, there will also be a limited demand for the exotic and therefore relatively expensive. Outer Mongolia was included in the largest British tour operator's brochures at the end of the 1970s, and Antarctica continued to attract cruise passengers and day excursionists who regularly flew over parts of that snowbound continent. Perhaps the best vehicle from which to visit the exotic was the cruise liner, but although cruising has survived, the world cruise has become something of a rarity.

Tourist flows to the exotic destinations do not herald their development as resorts. If the typical European tourist is looking for summer warmth and a good hotel, and one keenly priced as well, then the product he seeks can be manufactured on the coasts of the Mediterranean. As the resorts reach capacity, new ones can be created in North Africa, on the Black Sea and in Asia Minor. In so far as the American tourist wants the same, he can find it within his own country, in Hawaii or in the Caribbean.

The fragile disengagement between Egypt and Israel holds out some hope of the recreation of tourism to the Nile Valley and to the Holy Land. If some stability is attained there and is sufficient to encourage the much needed investment, one of the most important traditional destinations will again attract large numbers of tourists.

The attraction exercised by a new development will continue to be closely associated with the distance from the generating country. This no doubt reflects the costs of getting to the destination, and there appears to be something of a barrier to the development of longhaul tourism. The tourist destinations of the world seem to lie at about two hours' flying time from the point of origin, say, roughly 1,000 miles. For such destinations it proves possible to attract the tourists in sufficiently large numbers for the destination to 'take off'. But perhaps costs is not the only reason for the much slower development; it may simply be the result of the geography of the northern hemisphere. Go more than a thousand miles from the generating areas, and one is in the Sahara, the Panama Canal area or the mid-Pacific. The most likely developments at least in the early 1980s seem to be those expanded upon the existing structure. East Africa will continue to develop, south east Asia as well as the Far East, and the islands of the Pacific are possible candidates for further expansion.

Not least among the attractions of a tourist industry in a country are that tourism can make use of otherwise economically unproductive land and that little technology is required in the development of a resort other than building skills. The success of a new development is not dependent on the possession of a high technology. Any government can therefore embark on plans to develop tourism, in the knowledge that an attractive tourist destination can be developed without the need to have at its elbow sophisticated technical expertise.

However, in some regions the full potential may not be realized until a closer working arrangement is achieved between several countries. For instance, the natural game reserves may lie inconveniently across national frontiers; they may be served by an airport in one country, but the attractions and the accommodation lie in a neighbouring state. Some kind of co-operative organization may be needed by the states to rationalize such matters as airport siting, common rating of air fares, and the research and promotion for the regions as a whole.

A modest average growth of 4 per cent a year in international tourist arrivals would bring the total volume to more than 400 million by 1990. Europe and the Americas may drop their share from some 90 per cent in the late 1970s to some 85 per cent by 1990, and the rest of the world may be attracting as much as 15 per cent — some 60 million international tourist arrivals, which was the total volume of international tourism as recently as the late 1950s.

It is extremely hazardous to attempt to predict the particular shares of the individual destinations within the regions. They are competing destinations and the success of each in attracting tourist traffic will depend greatly on the type, quality, and price of the facilities provided, on the development of transport to reach them, and on the volume and quality of their promotion.

By the turn of the century or soon after, the world will move from being perhaps 25-30 per cent developed to being perhaps 50-60 per cent developed. As the populations of the developing countries are rising fast, by early next century there may be two-and-a-half to three times as many people as there are today living in countries, which will have reached for most of their populations a standard of living making international travel possible. How many hundred million will travel abroad and where will they go in the 1990s and in the 2000s?

Politics and the Future of Tourism

The foregoing discussions rests heavily on assumptions about the future prosperity of the world and also about its future peacefulness. It is appropriate to consider the effects on tourism of political upheavals less than war. If it is legitimate to say that there is little evidence that tourism contributes to a better understanding among the nations, the political complexion of a country seems equally to have little effect on its tourism arrivals and receipts. The growth of Spanish tourism was achieved while the government of that country did not command universal admiration in the generating countries, and more recently another less than popular regime in Greece did apparently nothing to deter tourists visiting that country when it was a matter of their free choice to do so.

Again one must conclude that the tourist himself does not see his purchase of tourist products as being affected by the political situation. Just as the consumer refused to see his purchases of South African oranges as a vote in favour of *apartheid,* so the tourist refused to see his holiday in Spain or Greece, or for that matter France or Britain as a vote for the country's particular political system. If it is correct that the tourist increasingly sees his holiday as if it were one with consumer durables, then it can only be concluded that he sees his annual holiday as too trivial, too ordinary a matter to have any political sentiment attached to it. Thus it is safe to assert that demand for tourism is neutral to politics — it neither encourages goodwill among nations nor deters governments from pursuing their chosen course.

Until quite recently Egypt used to be a major tourist destination as was Israel, as the Holy Land. Both still receive a considerable flow of tourists, but had they not been at war both might reasonably expect more. In 1971 and 1972, the disturbances in Northern Ireland seem to have brought about a marked reduction in British visitors to the Republic of Ireland. It is not necessarily the fear of becoming entangled in the conflict, but the fear of insult, discourtesy, or hostility which would spoil the holiday. To feel this is not to suggest that such hostility would ever be shown; it is simply the judgement that the game is not worth that particular candle — lending further support to the view that the consumer's view of his activity as a tourist is altogether modest and low-keyed. The tourist cares about politics only when he is personally quite likely to be the unwilling recipient of insult, contempt, or injury.

The Future of British Tourism

Until 1977 Britain experienced a relatively fast growth in overseas visitors, well over 10 per cent annually, a continuing decline in their average length of stay, well into 1978, and the combination of the two produced a growth in nights, which stopped in 1978. The growth between 1975 and 1977 showed even more impressively in expenditure, even if an allowance is made for inflation.

The picture started changing in 1978 and the changes continued into 1979. Visits slowed down in 1978 and there was actually a small fall in 1979, the first since the Second World War. Expenditure continued to grow at current prices but since 1978 not in real terms. In 1979 there was a reversal in the long-term decline in the length of stay, and as a result total nights increased in spite of the drop in the number of visits (*see* Appendix J).

Three main factors explain the trend in overseas visitor traffic to Britain at the end of the 1970s: the strengthening of the pound sterling, the high level of inflation in Britain, and world economic recession, especially in North America.

British residents' travel abroad has always been more volatile than traffic in the opposite direction, but what happened in 1978 and 1979 was in sharp contrast to incoming tourism: big increases in numbers going abroad, nights spent abroad, and money spent abroad (*see* Appendixes K and L).

Again three main factors explain most of this trend: the strengthening of the pound, the reduction in air fares on many routes, the effective competition of many foreign destinations combined with the skills of the British tour operating industry.

Early in 1980 a clear consensus emerged among leading economic forecasters that Britain was entering a severe recession, with a fall in output, high inflation, and high unemployment, although not much change was expected in consumer spending in real terms. These expectations, together with the continuing strength of the pound sterling, suggested a broadly static volume of British incoming, outgoing and domestic tourism in the early 1980s.

On a longer-term view an improvement in the economy has been projected on the assumption that the policies and measures introduced by the Government in its first year in office prove effective, from about 1982 onwards.

A forecast of key socio-economic factors of importance in tourism, prepared by consultants Pannell, Kerr, Forster for the English Tourist Board, which looked to 1990 from the 1978 base, suggested that by the end of the decade the national income would increase by a quarter in real terms; there might be more than two million unemployed; personal disposable income would be a quarter higher in real terms; the average person would enjoy an extra week's holiday; the pound would be less strong and air fares somewhat lower; motoring would cost almost twice as much, but staying away from home little more in real terms. Various estimates put forward suggest a growth in overseas visitors to Britain to reach over 20 million, a less dramatic growth in British holidays abroad, and a static domestic holiday market in the 1980s.

29   *Future Resources*

It is possible to consider much of the demand for tourist facilities as supply-led demand. New hotels, new airline routes, even new bridges, generate demand for their use by the very fact of their coming into being. The likely changes in the supply of tourist facilities and services therefore merit attention in considering future prospects for tourism. Throughout any discussion of the supply of tourist facilities, it is important to keep in mind the matter of relative costs and prices. Throughout our discussion of many aspects of tourism a constant refrain has been the sensitivity of much tourist demand to both the absolute and the relative prices charged to tourists. Looking at the global picture, many tourist movements may be represented as the populations of relatively wealthy countries enjoying holidays in countries where the general standard of living has been relatively low. However, in many successful tourist destinations the effect of tourism (as, of course, was expected) has been to close or at least narrow the gap. The northern European will go for his holiday to Florida when once he went to Spain, and Spain and its east coast resorts are no longer as inexpensive as they once were. Many tourist facilities are labour-intensive and the supply of labour becomes more costly and less flexible in its use. Tourism has benefited many once-underdeveloped areas and has improved the standards of living for the inhabitants, and in so doing has weakened its unique contribution to those areas.

The increasing cost of fuel has had and may be expected to have a considerable impact on tourism. The initial impact will probably be most apparent in both public and private transport, with periodic shortages at the filling station and diversions in airline operations in order to obtain necessary fuel.

Air Transport in the 1980s

The period since the Second World War saw an enormous development in the field of air transport, and the most significant feature of this development has been the introduction of various forms of gas turbine engines — first the turbo-prop where the engine power output was harnessed to a conventional propeller (the Vickers Viscount being the principal instance of this type), and secondly the pure jet where the reaction thrust of the engine provides the motive power (the Boeing 707 and its derivatives accounting for most of this type). Between the 1950s and 1970s a new aircraft type was introduced to the world's civil aviation approximately every five years, and this was accompanied after a two-year lag by surges in tourist flows. If a reason for this is sought, the best explanation lies in the fact that each new aircraft type was successively larger and cheaper than its predecessors in terms of operating costs, and the resultant reduction in unit costs per seat mile in real terms (and often in money terms too). The component factors of this reduction in costs are three; the gas turbine is a more efficient converter of fuel into power than the reciprocating engines it replaced (and more reliable too), the gas turbine engine enabled higher speeds thus permitting improved annual utilization of a pure jet fleet, and thirdly the earlier versions of these engines proved to be capable of significant uprating in power, thus permitting larger aircraft. The classic example of this development was the Boeing series, the original 707 having a capacity of about 160 seats, the 747 initially of about 350 seats but being capable of lifting almost 500 seats. However, demand for air travel rose fairly smoothly during the period, and the supply of new aircraft came forth lumpily in batches. Something like a two-year lag is apparent before demand catches up with supply, and hence the introduction of new aircraft tended to be followed by widespread price cutting in fares.

The increased speed of the pure jet aircraft has undoubtedly contributed to the growth of air traffic, particulary in the early days, but the lower fares rather than the passenger appeal of speed must be identified as the prime cause of the growth in traffic.

There do not appear to be any dramatic changes in the technology of air transport in the next decade, comparable with the introduction of the wide-bodied jet aircraft. The prospect rather is one of improving the performance of existing aircraft types by, for instance, improved control surfaces or by the use of composite materials to reduce weight. Of particular importance will be the modification of engine design to be more fuel-efficient. The succession of new aircraft that became available at five year intervals up to the 1970s will not be repeated in the 1980s.

The need to offer low fares on the principal routes will lead airlines to put as many seats as possible in the aircraft, and the future of first class services on board an aircraft also carrying economy class traffic seems to be in doubt. The trend is to offer full-fare (economy) service and discounted-fare service, with traditional first class service available only on supersonic aircraft from the handful of airlines operating the Concorde,.

⸱The Concorde will no doubt continue to fly its limited services, but because of its limited range, it has rarely flown with a full passenger payload. Long-range versions of the wide-bodied jets will mean that Concorde's superior speed will be counter-balanced by their greater range and consequent need for fewer stops.

⸱ Some interest may be shown in developing new supersonic aircraft but not for commercial operations in the 1980s. This decade seems to be the decade of the medium-sized aircraft like the A 300 airbus.

The provision of airport capacity is likely to command much attention, not least because there is lead time of perhaps ten to twelve years between identifying the need and completing the installations on the ground. The size of the task is not the only reason for the long lead time: increasingly, in the western world, a process of planning inquiry is becoming necessary as residents near an existing or planned airport demand reassurance about noise, pollution, and safety. The problems faced by airport authorities are not confined simply to those affecting the safe and compatible operation of aircraft; the numbers of passengers now being carried in a single aircraft impose great strains on many existing airport

buildings and the need for new terminals is becoming cle~ ~
the world.

The Future of Sea Transport
Air transport has captured almost all the market which ~
distances by sea. The last regular liner service may be though ~
the last voyage of the *Windsor Castle* to South Africa in 19 ~
time of writing the *Queen Elizabeth 2* contrives some sum__ ~ ~anlings from
Southampton to New York.

The major growth point in passenger shipping will continue to be the car ferry services. They are a prominent feature of European tourism in particular, because the coast of Europe is indented by large bights such as the Baltic and the Mediterranean itself, and because outside North America Europe is the most car-conscious part of the world, with more than half of all European holiday tourists using a car as transport on their holidays. In Europe there are over 200 car ferry operations ranging from the Baltic to the Greek Islands of the Aegean.

The monitoring by the Office of Fair Trading of the cross-Channel ferries between Britain and continental Europe has resulted in fierce price competition between the operators and new entry has been a feature of these routes. With the prospect of a Channel Tunnel still distant, the car ferries may be expected to become an even more significant form of tourist transport, and the largest private operator is introducing faster ships for the 1980s. It seems likely that the hovercraft services will be the main victims of competition on the cross-Channel routes.

At the time of writing the UK government was unfolding plans to transfer its interests in SEALINK to the private sector. Political concern apart, the SEA-LINK consortium has shown itself able to stand up to the brisk competition which has recently developed on its cross-Channel routes. European Ferries, the largest private sector operators, seem unlikely to be permitted to take over the SEALINK operation on anti-monopolist grounds.

At the end of the 1970s, after earlier abandonment of the original three-tunnel plans, the proposals for a Channel Tunnel seemed to take a new lease of life with a much less ambitious proposal for a single tunnel to carry rail only. In view of the past history of this project, it is hard to feel much confidence in any proposal.

Cruising at sea continues to attract a limited clientele and new tonnage is being constructed for cruising. The rising cost of fuel oil will however tend to restrict much further growth. The Mediterranean and the Carribean will continue to be the principal cruise areas. The cruise operator will find it difficult to keep his prices even broadly in line with comparable land-based inclusive tours, and cruising will remain a minority pastime.

The Private Car or Public Transport
It can be expected that the car will continue to share with the air the distinction of being a principal means of transport in the tourist product. Whatever its short-comings, the car is a most attractive holiday vehicle. It leaves from the home, it

.ves at the holiday accommodation, it can tow a caravan as holiday accommodation. It demands only immediate out-of-pocket disbursements. And it imparts great flexibility to the structure of a holiday, making changes of plan possible at very little notice. Western industralized societies are now geared to the car so firmly that it seems inconceivable that the level of car ownership will not continue to rise, in spite of increasing costs of motoring, albeit at a much slower rate than was the case in the 1960s and early 1970s.

Can public transport provide a viable alternative to the car as a means of holiday transport? Surface transport systems, the railway and road networks, were not chiefly constructed for tourist purposes, but for the haulage of goods, the railways for the haulage of chiefly bulk goods such as coal or grain, and roads for the distribution of those goods when bulk was broken. The carriage of passengers was largely incidental. Much of modern manufacturing today is based on frequent deliveries of supplies with a consequent reduction in manufacturing stocks. This has led to the cessation of bulk deliveries to the factory rail sidings in favour of the frequent delivery of small consignments. The bulk traffic of railways has largely disappeared, and the highly seasonal carriage of tourist traffic could not possibly justify the cost of operating whole parts of the railways system for it. It must be concluded that surface public transport can rarely provide an alternative to the car for tourist purposes, although for the highly specialized carriage of commuters there may be no alternatives to sophisticated rail services.

The problem of the private car will not be solved by wishing it had never been invented. The problem facing society is how to manage the car; in our discussion, how to manage it for tourist purposes. Like any other form of transport, the car needs a terminal, a place to park. For many recreational and tourist purposes, the car is preferred as a vehicle because the children are young and the grandparents old, and the car serves the need to have a mobile sitting-room from which no member of the party need stray more than a few yards. The small planned car park and picnic sites now being developed by the Forestry Commission and the Countryside Commissions in Britain seem to be going some way to provide for the car as a vehicle for family leisure.

The use of the private car for holiday purposes tends to increase in a direct relationship with the level of car ownership. The growth in car ownership slowed down in the 1970s: in the five years 1968-73 the number of cars on the road in the UK increased by nearly three million, between 1973 and 1978 by a little more than half-a-million (*See* Appendix Q). But there was no reduction in the use of the car in tourism, which remained in the region of 70 per cent of holidays to the end of the 1970s (*See* Tables 11 and 12). As the cost of private motoring may double in real terms (*See* p. 296) and car ownership grow only slowly in the 1980s, there is unlikely to be much growth in the total number of holidays using a car, unless there is a significant increase in holiday propensities.

Coach and Rail Travel

The use of the coach is very largely attractive to the less affluent segments of the

market. What has been said of the private car can also be said of the coach —
except that it is the cheapness of coach travel that is attractive. It may also be
noted that a large proportion of the current passengers are elderly, that is,
passengers who in earlier life did not possess a car.

It seems fair to hazard that the coach as a means of transport for tourism will
not increase in popularity, except as an intermediate vehicle for aircraft-hotel
transfers and for sightseeing. Nor can any substantial economies in operation be
seen, since the nature of the road network is not likely to permit coaches with 100
or more seats and fuel costs are likely to continue rising.

Like the coach, the railways account for relatively little of holiday tourist traffic, and only a small part of the total business movement. The fast Inter-City
traffic of British Rail and the earlier Trans-Europe expresses in continental
Europe have indeed attracted custom from the business community, but this
traffic is so small that it can never earn enough to enable the railways to adapt to
passenger requirements a track system designed for the carriage of bulk loads
like coal, oil, and grain. Unless subsidies are available, advanced trains will be
prisoners of the track and its associated signalling systems.

True, the optimists for a rail re-birth point to the Tokyo Tokaido line, but too
often fail to mention that no other traffic runs on the single track, that there are
no signals accordingly, and the train travels like a bullet in a tube. Interesting
though that is, it is not helpful in countries with a well-developed track, frequently crossed by points, equipped with sharp curves, and much of whose
traffic is slow-moving freight.

Engineering and operating problems apart, the claim is made for rail that it
goes city centre to city centre. But in fact this claim ignores the nature of the
travel market which for business and holiday traffic alone often wants suburb to
suburb transport. For anything but local or commuter travel, the rail terminus is
inconvenient, and the time taken between the terminal and a suburb is rarely
offset by the speed of the rail journey itself.

For holiday travel, similar problems arise, but to them must be added the
inherent attractiveness of the car for family travel. The railways traffic in all
developed countries is now a combination of commuter traffic, very costly
because of low utilization, and barely profitable passenger expresses, needing
substantial bulk freight traffic to earn the bread-and-butter traffic revenue.

It is too optimistic to anticipate a significant growth in rail travel for tourism
purposes in the 1980s. But the combination of increasing costs of motor
transport, both public and private, and the type of imaginative marketing of rail
travel demonstrated in recent years by British Rail, may bring about some
substitution of holiday transport mode from both the private car and coach to
rail. Any more than that could come about only more gradually, should energy
problems invoke greater government intervention than has been the case so far.
This is less likely in a country such as the UK, which is expected to be self-
sufficient in its oil requirements for the remainder of this century.

The Future Supply of Accommodation

The increase in tourist flows has seen a world-wide development of new hotels and motels. This has often been accompanied by governmental loans or subsidies to speed up investment in accommodation. Much of the new hotel construction has been along traditional full service lines and the sites concerned have been either major resort sites (such as London, Paris, and Frankfurt) or sites developed in the creation of new resorts (such as Glyphada and Vouliagmeni near Athens and the Algarve in Portugal). As has been seen, the user of many of these hotels has been the inclusive tour holidaymaker, travelling by air.

The other kind of accommodation development has been in the field of catering for the motorist, by means of motels, motor inns, and camping and caravan sites. This development has been brought about first by the needs of motorists using major road links, often for business purposes, and secondly by the self-catering preferences of the holiday motorist. Thus both consideration of time and money lie behind these developments.

In London and in Paris and in some other large cities, the re-allocation of property sites, which has been a feature of the first twenty years after the Second World War, concentrated on industrial and especially office accommodation. In part, the high content of service industries in the make-up of such cities was responsible for this preference. By the 1960s the property dealer was in the hotel business; in the United Kingdom by 1970 new hotels were being built under the stimulus of the Act of 1969, and the builders were really more property men than hotel men. If the future is to be looked at, will these sorts of circumstances still prevail? First, investment in a large city centre hotel with an international clientele is an attractive hedge against inflation and in particular against devaluation. So long, therefore, as the demand for this kind of accommodation is buoyant, this kind of property will be sought. If demand slackens, then the city centre hotel could be reasonably converted to office uses. A variant of this type of hotel is the airport hotel.

Much has been made of the need for medium-priced hotel accommodation in such city centres, particularly for inclusive tour purposes. It seems doubtful whether at present new building (as distinct from the conversion of older properties) can meet this presumed need, in the light of alternative uses for the site. Hotel building may be said to be in the pre-jet era by analogy: early inclusive tours sold at low prices because cheap obsolescent aircraft were used, but the pure jet aircraft were so much more efficient that the tour operator could use them and still undercut the scheduled airlines. In this sense then the hotel industry awaits its jet engine, some innovation which will dramatically enable the industry to offer lower tariffs in city centres.

The Second Home

Attention has already been drawn (in earlier chapters) to the trend towards self-catering holidays. The ultimate expression of this is the second home. In the major generating countries, but especially in France, Sweden, and the United

Kingdom, it is possible to detect a growing use of a second home. The idea of a country cottage, or log cabin, or chalet, has a powerful attraction for the city dweller, again particularly in northern countries. The growing ownership and use of the car can transform the idea to a practical reality. The impact of this trend on tourism may well be felt when a substantial part of the population is able to take more than one holiday each year; a pattern may then emerge whereby one holiday is taken in a normal resort, either at home or abroad, and the remaining holidays and week-ends are taken in the second home. Such a development would work against the interests of resort areas to develop a year-round traffic, and would be as detrimental to Palma as to Bournemouth. It seems likely therefore that the market for second homes will become institutionalized; the seeker of a second home need no longer hunt the countryside for the derelict agricultural cottage, but instead would seek his second home in purpose-built holiday parks in or near the traditional resorts, these holiday parks being developed and operated by companies or even co-operatives formed for the purpose. Such schemes would avoid the purchase in development areas of houses judged to be needed for local residents by outsiders from the city. Clearly, if depopulation in the development areas is to be checked, let alone reversed, occasional visitors from the city cannot be allowed to buy up the local stock of houses and to use them for only a few weeks a year. This problem is already beginning to be acute in western Scotland and Wales with the sale of crofts and cottages for second home purposes; the effect is to take housing off the local market, and at the same time to raise the market price against the resident.

Entertainment and Amenity in the Future

By the end of the 1960s, most governments had recognized the importance of tourism as an important element in world trade, and local and regional governments also began to consider afresh the desirability or otherwise of attracting tourists to their areas. The degree of attention paid to tourism varied with the state of development achieved so far, the older resorts being concerned with modernizing their attractions, and areas not yet recognizable as resorts asking how they might become one. Further, the existence of relatively affluent tourists, with leisure and the money to spend on it, attracted entrepreneurs to develop new attractions.

Pride of place among new attractions must go to Disneyland in California and Disneyworld in Florida. Based on the Disney cults, wildlife as well as fantasy stories for children, these two enterprises attract millions of visitors each year. They are likely to be repeated in other parts of the world, not necessarily by the Disney organization.

Interest in wildlife, felt to be threatened by the activities of man, has recently been canalized by the creation of extensive wildlife parks, notably in the United Kingdom. Originally expansions from the deer parks associated with the country houses of the British aristocracy, they have now developed into major attractions in their own right, and the aristocratic landowners have entered into partnership with circus and zoo families to provide a major tourist amenity. The early examples were Woburn Abbey (the Duke of Bedford) and Longleat (the Marquis of Bath), and more examples can be expected, not necessarily associated with a stately home. The Windsor Safari Park is an example of a simple wildlife park not associated with a ducal house.

The enterprises are attractive as honeypot attractions, which siphon off from the agricultural countryside the recreational town dwellers. But the pressure from conservationists to ameliorate the effects of economic activity on the environment is also causing the redevelopment for leisure purposes of worked-out gravel pits and other industrial sites. Gravel pits are being turned into yachting basins, and even simple coastal stretches of beach are being developed into complex marinas. These developments are generally to be welcomed, not least in that they tend to concentrate demand for recreation in one place where the demand can be met and managed effectively. For the future, more elaborate entertainment parks are likely to be created, with particular hotel and camping accommodation available to encourage more than day visits.

30 *Future Organization of Tourism*

It is appropriate to start this chapter with some observations about society's attitude to the environment, particularly as it concerns tourism. Since the Second World War, the environmental resources have come to be seen as finite, and perhaps for that reason as precious. This realization has been prompted by such matters as the prospect of substantial radioactive fall-out from the testing of nuclear armaments, by the identification of the large-scale penetration of insecticides into the human food chain, and sometimes also by the effect of very large tourist traffic itself on many traditional tourist attractions. These conspicuous manifestations of danger to the environment sometimes tend to obscure such real major causes as over-intensive cultivation, and industrialization, the effects of industrial technology and of the discharge of waste products, and the consumption of non-renewable mineral and other resources. Nevertheless, the effects of tourism on the environment, however insignificant by comparison, have not gone unnoticed.

Accordingly, the simple economic benefits of tourism have come to be weighed in the balance against the costs to society. It thus seems likely that the main focus of governments and of their national and regional tourist organizations will turn from the promotion of tourism towards the management of tourism, in the sense of regulating and mitigating the spontaneous patterns of tourist demand. Some early conservationist policies have produced bizarre results: restrictions on the hunting of elephants in parts of East Africa led to over-grazing by the elephants, so that herds which had been rescued from the hunter's gun were threatened by starvation. This example poses questions which conservationists find hard to answer — which species ought to be preserved, and what criteria are to be applied to which species?

Clearly policies of this kind can only be the province of national governments or international agencies. But the selection of an appropriate policy will affect the development of tourism. Because for many countries tourism is an important factor in the economy, it will become increasingly important that the voice of the tourist organization should be heard when national and international policies are being formulated, the tourist organization ought to be able to represent its views on the worthwhileness of preserving or demolishing this or that historic building and on the merits or drawbacks of particular developments.

International Organization

The need for influencing the policies of governments in relation to tourism led to the transformation in 1975 of the International Union of Official Travel Organizations (IUOTO) a non-governmental body, into the World Tourism Organization (WTO), an inter-governmental body concerned with all aspects of tourism. In addition to continuing the technical work of its predecessor, the

Organization is recognized by the United Nations, and as such speaks officially to governments on tourism.

In its first five years the WTO established and consolidated the working of its general assembly, executive council and six regional commissions, as well as secretariat and regional secretariats, organized a number of conferences, and extended the range of its studies and publications. Having achieved a membership of more than one hundred countries, it must be a matter of high priority for the Organization to extend further its influence by embracing several important countries into membership, which continue to remain outside the Organization: not only the United Kingdom, but also Canada, New Zealand, and all the Scandinavian countries. Other major tasks for the 1980s are to achieve an appropriate balance between its political and organizational concern on the one hand and the technical on the other, and to command a budget which would enable it to expand the latter and to become more fully involved in stimulating tourism development.

Progress in the achievement of the principal objectives of the European Economic Community has had much impact on tourism in such matters as the freedom of movement, employment, setting up business and investment, as well as to some extent in the harmonization of social policies. But only a limited amount of integration and co-ordination in tourism has come about as a result of more than twenty years since the creation of the Community, although co-operation developed between national tourist organizations of member countries. Some members consider that tourism can be dealt with adequately by the existing economic and transport committees; others would like to shape EEC policy in such fields as leisure and holidays including the staggering of school and industrial holidays, legislation and regulation of tourist services such as accommodation and travel agencies, and even joint promotion of the EEC as a tourist destination in third countries. Therefore, closer co-ordination of tourism interests may come in the 1980s.

Organization of Tourism in Britain

The current organization of tourism in Britain is discussed fully in Chapter 27. The four statutory tourist boards have succeeded in welding together the national, regional and to some extent also local levels within a national framework. But if a framework is there, it cannot be said that there is a clear and comprehensive policy on tourism. What policy does exist, is in the main expressed for Britain as a whole in the guidelines given by the Government to the statutory tourist boards in 1974 and confirmed in 1978 (*see* pp. 281-2); the Greater London Council statement of 1980 (*see* p. 239) represents a superior approach, albeit confined to the capital. However, the lack of a comprehensive policy for British tourism continues to cause problems of co-ordination and in achieving a most effective contribution of tourism to the economy.

We stated earlier (*see* p. 257) that we see tourism in the first instance as a Government responsibility and it is, therefore, for the Government to state the aims, for example, how tourism is seen in the context of the economy and what objectives are to be pursued with what ends in view. It is only then that the means — the administrative and fiscal arrangements and the funds — can be most effectively channelled to achieving the desired objectives, and conflicts can be resolved where they may exist. As the need continues to manifest itself, we would expect that in the 1980s tourism in Britain will call for a critical re-examination by a committee of inquiry, as for example, civil aviation and shipping did by the Edwards and Rochdale Committees which reported in 1969 and 1970.

Lack of a clear and comprehensive policy is not the only candidate for change during the 1980s. In the current arrangement the British Tourist Authority is responsible for the overseas promotion of Britain as a tourist destination, while the development of the tourist product is the responsibility of the national boards. Major dangers of conflict or imbalance inherent in this situation have not be realized, because the staffs engaged on their respective tasks have been closely associated with each other and have come to some consensus of common goals. This cannot be relied upon for ever; the threat of conflict and lack of co-ordination may be greater in the future. The courses most likely to be canvassed are that the BTA, itself perhaps reorganized, should be seen as the overall co-ordinating body with powers to direct the national boards, or that a new co-ordinating body should be created, stopping short of a Ministry of Tourism, which may also provide for continuing inter-ministerial co-ordination. What machinery should meet the need, may be also best dealt with by the committee of inquiry suggested above.

The statutory boards have very few powers. Since their temporary influence in the hotel industry through the administration of the Hotel Development Incentives Scheme, they are largely confined to stimulating tourism development through Section 4 of the 1969 Act, and in the longer-term may be extended to powers to register and classify tourist accommodation.

The 1979 report of the Consultative Committee on Registration of Tourist Accommodation (*see* p. 162) envisaged a further review of the question within three to five years. It is unlikely that the pressure for a comprehensive system will disappear in the 1980s. It is only to be hoped that in the meantime voluntary systems do not depart so widely from each other as to make a uniform system for the whole of Britain more difficult to formulate and implement.

The encouragement of foreign visitors to come to Britain is but one aspect of the tourism phenomenon, but it does represent the credit side of the balance of payments account for tourism. The statutory boards are charged with the duty to encourage the use of British holiday facilities by the British resident. Except at the Department of Trade, as the sponsoring Ministry, the credit and debit side of the tourism balance of payments account do not come together. Apart from temporary restrictions the debit side, expenditure abroad by British residents, in so far as it is subject to any regulation, is controlled incidentally by the licensing of air transport services and of tour operators. Yet the 1967 devaluation of the pound sterling proved to be a powerful stimulus to the tour operators to produce tours to Europe which came within the £50 travel allowance that accompanied devaluation. This was the trigger factor and the licensing of inclusive tour charters on a liberal scale gave a remarkable fillip to the demand for overseas holidays. Factors which were intended to improve the balance of payments position (successfully for a few years) in the long run have proved counter-productive. For the future, it is to be hoped that the co-ordinating body overseeing tourism in Britain will have the duty of looking at the whole picture and will be able to devise more subtle means of achieving policy objectives than resorting again to the unpopular travel restrictions.

The Organization of Air Transport

The traditional methods used to regulate air transport were being questioned as the 1970s drew to a close. The preponderance of charter traffic on some routes may be expected to prompt re-examination of the whole concept of regulation, and the apparent early success of thoroughgoing deregulation in the USA is likely to produce some sympathetic reaction elsewhere.

In assessing the traditional forms of regulation, it must be repeated that the authority of IATA to determine fares derived from the widespread practice of governments to state in their bilateral air services agreements that the IATA traffic conference would be the instrument of determining fares. Until recently this worked well, and indeed quite a powerful case can be made out that the unanimity rule within IATA was a means of securing the interests of the smaller airline against its larger competitors. In place of the IATA mechanism of traffic conferences, it seems likely that negotiations on fares in particular will be conducted in a semi-governmental way.

The future organization of air transport will be influenced by a number of external factors. The continued problem of fuel is one such. The price of fuel may be expected to continue to rise, and it may well be that sporadic and localized shortages of fuel will occur. Apart from increasing air transport costs, the fuel problem will lead to slowing down of economic growth in the world economy as a whole. This could lead to increasing pooling agreements between airlines.

Within one region, namely Europe, there has not been much criticism of the traditional system by the airlines or their governments. The peculiarity of the European scene is that it comprises so many sovereign states each concerned to protect what is believed to be their best interests. Nevertheless critics of the European airlines point to comparable experience elsewhere — notably in the USA — and to the lower levels of fares apparently obtainable in the USA. But in comparing unit fares in North America and Europe, account must be taken of the greater communality of interest between a city pair in the USA than may be expected in Europe. The citizens of, say, Detroit and Philadelphia have more in common and therefore generate more traffic, than, say, the citizens of London and Bucharest.

The Retail Travel Agent

As long as the retail travel agency provides an efficient channel for the distribution of the principals' products their future is assured. Three observations may be made. First, at the end of the 1970s, there was some interest shown by large tour operators in selling directly to the public; this clearly could weaken the position of the travel agent. Secondly, since the application of the restrictive trades practices legislation to include travel, the future of 'Stabilizer' is in doubt and therefore the protection it affords. Thirdly, in the consumer goods field, the abandonment of retail price maintenance has brought extra-ordinary power to retailers of consumer goods particularly to the large grocery chain. The question posed is whether the larger retailers in tourism and travel are likely to achieve comparable power.

The acquisition by the Midland Bank of Thos Cook and Son may be setting the scene for a more aggressive development of this multiple travel agent. But the initial interest of the Midland Bank is rather in the traveller's cheque aspect of the Thos Cook operations, and the earlier part of the 1980s is likely to witness a period of competitive rivalry in the traveller's cheque market.

The criterion on which the success or otherwise of the travel trade must be judged is by its ability to handle its principals' business. If the question is answered negatively, other outlets will be devised, and experiments with direct selling are in part a result of some dissatisfaction with the performance of the conventional travel agent. Moreover, the profitability of the individual travel agency will depend on the correct assessment of the alternatives in standard of service provided: whether to act simply as a filling station for travel or whether to endeavour to act as a travel counsellor. Clearly, the distinction is not absolute, and many agents will be capable of counselling, but it would be unrealistic to expect more than a minority of travel agents to be effective travel counsellors. For most retail travel agents, the correct policy will be to concentrate as far as possible on selling the packaged products of his principals and in so doing to minimize his staff numbers in the hunt for profitability.

The threat of increasing direct selling techniques by the tour operators hung over the retail trade at the beginning of the 1980s. While this practice may worry the travel agent who is heavily reliant on packaged holidays, it should not worry the agent with a good mix of business. The particular set of circumstances which make direct selling attractive may not persist for long, and the traditional importance of the travel agent to the marketing of travel may be re-asserted.

Tour Operation

The oil/energy situation appears to have affected the development of tour operation less directly than might have been expected. During the 1970s, two large tour operators, Clarksons and Horizon failed, the former at the height of the holiday season. Thomson Holidays has become the clear market leader in the United Kingdom tour operating industry. The reduction in capacity offered which resulted from the Clarkson's debacle make it possible for the industry to achieve profitability.

The Civil Aviation Authority has pursued a general policy of non-intervention in the affairs of the industry, seeing its task as one of creating conditions in which something approaching competition can flourish. There has been a further degree of concentration in tour operating and this trend is likely to continue. The leading tour operators have created new tour venues in Outer Mongolia, the west coast of Africa and elsewhere for a minority market, but Spain remains the prime destination offered by the tour operators. It seems certain that in the immediate future the substantial commitments made to Spain by tour operators in all the prime generating countries in Europe will ensure that that country remains the principal receiving destination.

The present state of tour operation owes much to the introduction of time-chartering of aircraft and similar arrangements with hotels. The onset of inflation, however, has made the long-term contract less attractive, and this seems likely to be true of the future too, unless and until the inflationary conditions throughout the world are brought under control. The effects of inflation on the general prosperity of the generating countries has been to reduce demand for packaged tours to some extent, and in an industry so sensitive to high load factors and occupancy rates, even comparatively small changes in demand are significant.

The regulation of the air charters on which so much of tour operation depends seems likely to remain on a fairly informal basis. The climate of opinion favours the philosophy of deregulation, and there seems to be little taste for creating further barriers to the operation of inclusive tour charters.

Education and Training for Tourism

Tourism covers a wide spectrum of activities, which include what are normally seen as separate industries or sectors of economy. Traditionally, courses of education and training for tourism have been in the main specific to a component sector, in particular to prepare people for careers in hotels and catering, transport, and travel agencies. These divisions have been reflected first in courses in further education and later for the first two industries also in higher education in Britain. Three main bodies have conducted professional examinations in these fields leading to corporate membership: the Hotel, Catering and Institutional Management Association (HCIMA), the Chartered Institute of Transport (CIT), and the Institute of Travel and Tourism (ITT), formerly the Institute of Travel Agents (ITA). Three industrial training boards have covered a similar spectrum: the Hotel and Catering Industry Training Board and the Road Transport Industry Training Board since 1966, and the Air Transport and Travel Industry Training Board since 1970 (as Civil Air Transport Industry Training Board since 1967).

A smiliar, basically sectoral, approach has been evident also in the rest of Europe, in North America, and elsewhere. Other educational programmes have treated tourism as a particular manifestation or application of a basic discipline, such as economics, geography or sociology, particularly in universities.

More recently some courses with a sectoral approach have included some study of tourism, to provide an understanding of the wider spectrum and market, in which, for example, many hotels and transport undertakings operate, as well as an appreciation of the interdependence of individual providers of tourist facilities and services. This is a welcome development in education and training in those sectors, which are essentially suppliers of tourist attractions, facilities and services, and in which individuals require first and foremost knowledge and skills specific to their particular business, but also an understanding or at least an appreciation of the wider field of tourism, to the extent to which tourism represents for them a significant part of their business and of their work.

However, the component sectors described so far do not account for the whole of tourism or all employment in tourism; this extends on the one hand to tourist boards and associations as tourist destination organizations, at national, regional and local level, and on the other hand to travel organizations and intermediaries other than travel agencies, such as tour operations. It is in these sectors that the need increasingly manifests itself for generalists in tourism; a similar need also exists in larger organizations in accommodation and transportation, in such specialist functions as marketing, research, planning and development.

Appropriate distinctions have to be drawn according to the background of the student (which may range from little or no previous knowledge or experience, to that of a practitioner for whom the learning about tourism represents a post-experience study), according to the level of provision (which may range from a more conceptual university study to more practical learning with an emphasis on particular skills, and in other ways. However, future education and training for tourism will have to recognize increasingly both the conspicuous interdependence of the various activities in tourism, and the need for people for whom the main requirement is a knowledge and experience of tourism *per se.*

The experience of the University of Surrey illustrates the needs and the ways in which they have been met in recent years, through three separate but complementary programmes. Since its beginning in 1967 the undergraduate degree course in hotel and catering administration has included in its final stage an option in tourism. Since 1972 the University has offered a postgraduate course in tourism, which may be seen as a conversion course both for practitioners and for new graduates in related disciplines. To provide for the continuing education and training of the practitioner, the University introduced in 1970 a Management Development programme of short courses in tourism.

The growing recognition of tourism as an activity which calls for knowledge and skills of its own in the management of its operations, and of the interdependence of the individual sectors in tourism, also found expression in the formation of The Tourism Society as a multi-sectoral professional body in tourism in 1977. In 1980 the Society completed a research study of tourism occupations, careers and body of knowledge, as a basis for the development of tourism education and training in Britain in the 1980s.

Tourism in the Next Few Years

In the early 1970s when much of the first edition of this book was written, the need to conserve the natural environment engaged the first attention of those whose business it was to study tourism. Whilst this need certainly remains, the text had a decidedly old-fashioned look in the years after the energy crisis first emerged. In the next few years the problem faced by tourist authorities will not be to prevent ever-increasing crowds of tourists trampling down what they have come to see. Their main concern will be to stimulate and manage tourist flows so that existing investment in airlines, hotels, and other facilities and services continues to show a proper return. Required for success in this task will be a knowledge and understanding of tourism and marketing skills in the widest sense; the matching of demand to meet a more adequate supply of tourist facilities and services in Britain and in many other tourist destinations will be a paramount requirement. Paradoxically, the same conditions which affect tourist demand also prevent tourist authorities from spending more on their task. Success then attends those who can make the available money more effective. Increased productivity in tourism will be only achieved by a cadre of professionals and it is for them that this book is written.

Appendixes

APPENDIX A

Select Chronology of British Tourism I: Before 1840

1539 Dissolution of monasteries provided a stimulus to the growth of inns
1552 Act of Parliament introduced a general system of liquor licensing in England and Wales
1663 First Turnpike Act passed for roads in Hertfordshire
1669 One-day coach service introduced (in summer) from Oxford to London
1753 Dr R. Russell published in English 'Dissertation concerning the Use of Sea Water . . .'
1773 General Turnpike Act consolidated governance of turnpike system
1774 First family hotel opened in Covent Garden by David Low
1783 Prince of Wales (later Prince Regent and George IV) first visited Brighton
1784 First mail coach initiated by John Palmer from Bristol to London
1791 Mail-coach services totalled 17,000 route miles
1796 Royal Sea-bathing Infirmary open at Margate
1825 Stockton-Darlington railway opened
1830 Liverpool-Manchester railway opened
1835 Brighton received 117,000 visitors by coach during the year
1836 John Murray's first Handbook published (*Holland, Belgium and the Rhine*)
1837 Peninsular Steam Navigation Company (later P. & O.) formed
1838 First railway terminal hotel opened at Euston
      22,000 miles of turnpike road in operation (a fifth of all public roads)
1839 Karl Baedeker's first guide-book appeared (*Belgien und Holland*)

APPENDIX B

Select Chronology of British Tourism II: 1840-1914

1840 Voyage of *Britannia* to Boston by Cunard
1841 Thomas Cook's first excursion train between Leicester and
      Loughborough
1842 2,000 miles of railway lines in use in Britain
      Railway Clearing House established
1844 Gladstone's Railway Act introduced parliamentary trains
1848 5,000 miles of railway lines in use in Britain
1851 More than 6 million people visited the Great Exhibition in London
1862 Brighton received 132,000 visitors by train in one day
1867 Thomas Cook issued first hotel coupons
      Cruise of *Quaker City* in the Mediterranean (recorded by Mark Twain
      in *Innocents Abroad*)
1869 Suez Canal opened
1871 Bank Holidays introduced in Britain
1872 Thomas Cook took the first group of tourists round the world
1878 First Baedeker guide to London published
1883 Dr Henry Lunn visited Switzerland for the first time
1889 Savoy Hotel opened in London
1902 Ruff's Hotel Guide listed some seventy railway companies' hotels in
      Britain
1903 Trust Houses formed in Hertfordshire
1909 American Express opened its London office
1911 Automobile Association's first hotel guide published
1914 22,000 miles of railway lines in use in Britain
      132,000 cars on British roads; 2 million on US roads

APPENDIX C

Select Chronology of British Tourism III: 1919-1979

1919 Daily air service introduced between London and Paris
1921 Amalgamation of British railways into the 'Big Four'
     Austin Seven popular car introduced
1929 Travel Assocation of Great Britain and Ireland established
1930 One million cars on British roads
     Road Traffic Act introduced licensing for bus and coach operation
     Scottish Travel Association formed
     First Youth Hostel opened in the United Kingdom and YHA formed
1935 RMS *Queen Mary* launched
     British Airways formed by non-subsidized airlines
1937 Butlin opened first large-scale holiday camp at Skegness
     488,000 overseas visitors came to Britain
1939 Pan Am introduced first commercial transatlantic air service
     Two million cars on British roads
1940 Imperial Airways nationalized and renamed BOAC
1947 British Tourist and Holiday Board formed
     First Town and Country Planning Act passed
1948 Half a million overseas visitors came to Britain
     Wales Tourist and Holidays Board established
1949 National Parks and Access to the Countryside Act passed
     Nature Conservancy was formed
1950 British Travel and Holidays Association established
     First charter inclusive tour arranged by Horizon to Corsica
1952 Tourist class air fares introduced on transatlantic routes
1953 First scheduled service by turboprop aircraft introduced by BEA from
     London to Cyprus
1955 One million overseas visitors spent £111 million in Britain
1957 Transatlantic air traffic exceeded sea traffic for the first time
1958 First commercial pure jet service from London to New York opened by
     BOAC
     Economy class air fares introduced
1959 M1 Britain's first motorway opened
1960 Skyway Hotel, first major hotel at London Airport opened.
     Caravans Sites and Control of Development Act passed
1961 Carlton Tower, first skyscraper hotel in London, opened
1963 London Hilton Hotel opened
     Two million overseas visitors spent £188 million in Britain
1964 British Travel and Holidays Association became British Travel
     Association
1965 Association of British Travel Agents introduced 'Operation Stabilizer'
     Civic Amenities Act passed
     Sports Council established

1966 £50 foreign currency travel allowance introduced for British residents
      Prestige Hotels, first major co-operative marketing group, formed
1967 Countryside (Scotland) Act established Countryside Commission for
      Scotland
      4 million overseas visitors spent £236 million in Britain
1968 Countryside Act established Countryside Commission
      Town and Country Planning Act introduced new planning concepts and
      procedures
      Transport Act gave British Waterways Board recreation and amenity
      duties and powers
      Interchange Hotels, second major co-operative marketing group, formed
1969 Development of Tourism Act created statutory tourist boards and intro-
      cuced an hotel development incentives scheme
      Inter Hotels, third major co-operative marketing group, formed
      Queen Elizabeth 2 made maiden voyage across the Atlantic
1970 Trust Houses merged with Forte
      British residents took more than 40 million holidays away from home
1971 Civil Aviation Act passed
      Seven million overseas visitors spent £500 million in Britain
1972 More than 10 million British residents travelled abroad for the first time
      British Hotels Restaurants and Caterers Association formed
      Thomas Cook & Son Ltd sold to a consortium headed by the Midland Bank
1973 United Kingdom joined the European Economic Community
      British Airways succeeded BEA and BOAC
      Oil/energy crisis became apparent with petrol coupons issued in UK
      8 million overseas visitors spent £726 million in Britain
1974 UK Government issued policy guidelines for British tourism
      Local government in England and Wales reorganized
      Tour operators Horizon and Clarksons collapsed
1975 High speed train made first public run
      British Airways started shuttle service to Glasgow
      Overseas visitors spent well over £1,000 million in Britain for the first time
1976 British Airways and Air France started transatlantic Concorde services
      Department of Environment encouraged local authorities actively to con-
      sider tourism
1977 Overseas visitors to Britain exceeded British residents travelling abroad
      USA and UK negotiated new air agreement Bermuda 2
      Tourism became top British net invisible export
      Laker Airways started Skytrain services to New York
1978 The Government confirmed the relevance of 1974 guidelines for tourism
      12½ million overseas visitors spent £2,500 million in Britain
      13½ million British residents spent £1,500 million travelling abroad
1979 Exchange controls wholly removed in UK.

APPENDIX D

Glossary of Basic Terms and Concepts in Tourism

Tourism

Conceptually
tourism denotes the temporary short-term movement of people to destinations outside the places where they normally live and work, and their activities during their stay at these destinations.

Technically
tourism represents various forms of short-term travel and visits and is variously defined for particular purposes, by reference to the purpose of travel or visit, duration, and other criterion.

Related Concepts

Leisure
is the time when a person is not engaged in employment or travelling to or from employment or for housewives or mothers when not engaged in domestic duties and caring for the needs of their families; the time may be put to various uses, including participation in tourism.

Recreation
means a use of time or an activity which has as its main purpose to refresh, entertain or provide a similar experience; recreation may be the main reason for participation in tourism and tourism may represent a particular form of recreation.

Travel
is journeys from one place to another, undertaken to and from work, as part of employment, as part of leisure, to take up residence, and for any other purpose; all tourism includes some travel, some travel constitutes tourism, but not all travel is tourism.

Migration
means travel with a view to taking up permanent or long-term residence in another country and constitutes emigration for the former country of residence and immigration for the new country of residence; migration is not tourism, nor are movements of seasonal and other temporary labour.

Basic Distinctions in Tourism

(*a*)   According to range   — domestic or internal (by residents within own country) and foreign or international (between countries)

(*b*)   According to distance   — long-haul and short-haul

(*c*)   According to purpose   — holiday, business, and common interest tourism (with a purpose common to visitor and visited, such as visits to friends and relatives)

(*d*) According to duration — day visits or excursions (no overnight stay)
staying visits or trips (overnight stay)

(*e*) According to number in
party — individual and group travel and visits

(*f*) According to arrangement— independent and inclusive travel and visits
Also quantitavely — mass tourism (refers to volume)
and qualitatively — popular tourism (refers to popularity)
— social tourism (refers to participation in tourism by disadvantaged groups of population)

Miscellaneous Terms and Concepts

Visitors — are non-residents of a locality and may be divided into day visitors (excursionists) and staying visitors; according to the definition adopted for a particular purpose, some or all visitors may be regarded as tourists.

Tourists — are people who travel to destinations outside the places where they are normally live and work with a view to returning within a few days, weeks or months; tourists may be variously defined and classified according to purpose, duration of travel or visit, and other criteria.

Tourist destinations — are countries, regions, districts, towns, villages or other geographical areas visited by tourists.

Tourist markets — may be viewed as networks of dealings between buyers and sellers of tourist products (i.e. between tourists and providers of tourist facilities and services) or as existing or potential tourists (existing markets and potential markets) and represent tourist demand.

Tourist products — in a narrow sense consist of what tourists buy; in a wider sense tourist products are amalgams of what tourists do at the destinations and of the facilities and services they use to make it possible (the destination products); the total tourist product includes also accessibility to the destination; elements of the tourist product may be classified as attractions (site or event), amenities (e.g. accommodation, catering, entertainment) and accessibility (distance and transport).

Tourist facilities and services — are facilities and services used by tourists; they include passenger transportation; accommodation, catering, entertainment; tour operations and travel agencies; other such as information services; tourist facilities and services represent tourist supply.

Tourist industry — is the sum total of providers of tourist facilities and services; that part of the economy which has a common function of supplying tourist needs; firms and establish-

	ments deriving income from tourists.
Sectors of tourism	are activities involved in the ownership, management, marketing, planning, development, education, training, consultancy and other services concerned with providing for the needs of tourists; sectors of tourism may be classified according to their main function or role in tourism or in other ways.

(The terms and concepts included in this glossary are discussed in Chapter 4 — Meaning and Nature of Tourism.)

APPENDIX E

Population, Incomes and Holidays
of Countries of the European Economic Community[a]

Country		Population[bl]		GNP per capita[bl]			Holiday propensities[c]			
		Number Mid-year	Growth 1970-77	Amount	Real growth 1970-77		Total net[d]	Total grs[e]	Abrd	Source f
		(million)	(% p.a.)	(US $)	(% p.a.)		(%)	(%)	(%)	
Belgium	1977	9.845	0.3	8.280	3.5	1976	47	63	35	(2)
Denmark	1977	5.076	0.4	9.160	2.3	1976	58	71	26	(3)
France	1978	53.182	0.7	8.270	3.1	1978	54	90	15	(4)
Germany FR	1978	61.212	0.2	9.600	2.2	1978	56	67	30	(5)
Ireland	1977	3.198	1.2	3.060	2.1	1977		75	14	(6)
Italy	1978	56.800	0.7	3.840	2.0	1978	38			(7)
Netherlands	1978	13.971	0.9	8.390	2.2	1978	58	77	47	(8)
Utd Kngdom	1978	55.918	0.1	5.030	1.6	1978	61	86	16	(9)

a   Excluding Luxembourg
b   Population and GNP per capita: all data are based on the same source and are
    generally comparable, but some refer to 1977 and others to 1978; 1977 figures are
    definite, 1978 figures preliminary.
c   Holiday propensities: data are based on various sources and refer to different years
    and are, therefore, not strictly comparable; the sources used for individual coun-
    tries are listed below. Generally they cover holidays of four nights (five days) or
    more away from home and exclude travel for other purposes. For some countries
    they include stays in second homes and visits to friends and relatives (e.g.
    Denmark, France and the United Kingdom). Other differences arise because of
    different definitions used for particular aspects of individual surveys.
d   Total net holiday propensity denotes the proportion of the total population who
    have taken at least one holiday away from home.
e   Total gross holiday propensity denotes the proportion of the total number of
    holidays taken to total population.
f   Gross propensity to holiday abroad denotes the proportion of all holidays taken
    abroad to total population.

Sources
(1) World Bank, *1979 World Bank Atlas,* Washington, 1979
(2) Westvlaams Ekonomisch Studiebureau, *Development of the Holiday Behaviour of
     the Belgian Population 1967-1976,* Brugge, 1978
(3) Danmarks Statistik, *Statistical News,* Special Publication, Copenhagen, November
     1979.
(4) Service d'Infomation et de Diffusion, *Le Tourisme en France en 1978,* Paris, 1979
(5) Studienkreis fuer Turismus, *Reiseanalyse 1978,* Starnberg, 1979
(6) Bord Failte, *Report and Accounts,* Dublin, 1977.
(7) Notiziario istat dell Instituto Centrale di Statistica, Luglio, 1979
(8) Centraal Bureau voor de Statistiek, *Mededelingen NR 1138,* Voorburg, January
     1980
(9) British Tourist Authority, *British National Travel Survey 1978,* London 1969

APPENDIX F

International Tourist Arrivals 1950-79

Year	Number[a] (million)	Index (1950 = 100)	Growth (% p.a.)
1950	25.3	100	
1960	71.2	281	
1961	75.3	298	+ 5.8
1962	81.4	322	+ 8.1
1963	93.0	368	+ 14.2
1964	108.0	427	+ 16.1
1965	115.5	456	+ 6.9
1966	130.8	517	+ 13.2
1967	139.5	551	+ 6.6
1968	139.7	552	+ 0.1
1969	154.1	609	+ 10.3
1970R	158.7	627	+ 3.0
1971R	169.4	670	+ 6.7
1972R	184.3	728	+ 8.8
1973R	191.3	756	+ 3.8
1974R	196.7	777	+ 2.8
1975R	206.9	818	+ 5.2
1976R	227.0	897	+ 4.1[b]
1977R	243.6	963	+ 7.3
1978R	259.4	1,025	+ 6.5
1979P	270.0	1,067	+ 4.0

R   Revised

P   Provisional

a   The totals of international tourist arrivals are not strictly comparable from year to year, as figures do not relate to the same number of countries owing to the increasing number of statistical series available. Nevertheless, these changes have only a marginal effect on the global totals and do not alter the general conclusions drawn from the trends shown by the figures available.

b   Percentage calculated on the basis of a total of 215.5 million. The figure of 227.0 million is the result of a change in series for France.

Source: World Tourism Organization, *Tourism Compendium,* 1979 edition

APPENDIX G

International Tourism Receipts 1950-79

Year	Amount (US $000 million)	Index (1950 = 100)	Growth (% p.a.)
1950	2.1	100	
1960	6.8	324	
1961	7.3	348	+ 7.4
1962	7.8	371	+ 6.8
1963	8.3	395	+ 6.4
1964	9.6	457	+ 12.0
1965	11.0	524	+ 14.6
1966	12.5	595	+ 13.6
1967	13.4	638	+ 7.2
1968	13.8	657	+ 3.0
1969	15.4	733	+ 11.6
1970	17.9	852	+ 16.2
1971	20.9	995	+ 16.8
1972	24.8	1,181	+ 18.7
1973	31.3	1,490	+ 26.2
1974	34.1	1,624	+ 8.9
1975	38.6	1,838	+ 13.2
1976	43.7	2,081	+ 13.2
1977	52.4	2,495	+ 19.9
1978	65.0	3,095	+ 24.0
1979P	75.0	3,571	+ 15.4

P   Provisional

Source: World Tourism Organization, *Tourism Compendium,* 1979 Edition

APPENDIX H

International Tourist Arrivals by Region 1972-79

Number (million)

Region	1972	1973	1974	1975	1976	1977	1978	1979P
Europe	131.8	136.7	139.7	148.0	165.0	178.3	189.0	196.0
Americas	38.1	39.5	40.0	41.6	43.5	45.1	47.5	49.5
Africa	3.4	3.5	3.9	4.3	4.1	4.5	4.9	5.3
Middle East	3.7	3.1	4.3	3.4	3.6	3.5	3.8	3.6
South Asia	1.1	1.25	1.3	1.5	1.7	2.0	2.1	2.0
East Asia & the Pacific	6.2	7.2	7.5	8.1	9.2	10.2	12.0	13.8
Total	184.3	191.3	196.7	206.9	227.0	243.6	259.4	270.0

Index (1972 = 100)

Region	1972	1973	1974	1975	1976	1977	1978	1979P
Europe	100	104	106	112	125	135	143	149
Americas	100	104	105	109	114	118	125	130
Africa	100	103	115	126	121	132	144	156
Middle East	100	84	116	92	97	95	103	97
South Asia	100	114	118	136	155	179	191	182
East Asia & the Pacific	100	116	121	131	148	165	194	223
Total	100	104	107	112	123	132	141	147

Growth (% p.a.)

Region	1972	1973	1974	1975	1976	1977	1978	1979P
Europe		+3.7	+2.2	+5.9	+3.7	+8.0	+6.0	+3.7
Americas		+3.7	+1.3	+4.0	+4.6	+3.7	+5.3	+4.2
Africa		+2.9	+11.4	+10.3	-4.7	+9.8	+8.9	+8.2
Middle East		-16.2	+38.7	-20.9	+5.9	-2.8	+8.6	-5.3
South Asia		+13.6	+4.0	+15.4	+13.3	+15.9	+6.6	-4.8
East Asia & the Pacific		+16.1	+4.2	+8.0	+13.6	+10.9	+17.6	+15.0
Total		+3.8	+2.8	+5.2	+4.1	+7.3	+6.5	+4.0

Share of Regions (% ot total)

Region	1972	1973	1974	1975	1976	1977	1978	1979P
Europe	71.5	71.5	71.0	71.5	72.7	73.2	72.9	72.6
Americas	20.7	20.7	20.3	20.1	19.2	18.6	18.3	18.3
Africa	1.8	1.8	2.0	2.1	1.8	1.8	1.9	2.0
Middle East	2.0	1.6	2.2	1.6	1.6	1.4	1.5	1.3
South Asia	0.6	0.6	0.7	0.7	0.7	0.8	0.8	0.7
East Asia & the Pacific	3.4	3.8	3.8	3.9	4.0	4.2	4.6	5.1
Total	100.0	100.0	100.0	100.0	100.0	100.0	100.0	100.0

Source: World Tourism Organization, *Tourism Compendium,* 1979 Edition

APPENDIX I

International Tourism Receipts by Region 1972-79

Amount (US $000 million)

Region	1972	1973	1974	1975	1976	1977	1978	1979P
Europe	16.2	20.6	21.5	24.8	27.7	34.7	44.0	50.0
Americas	6.1	7.4	8.7	9.7	11.0	11.5	13.5	16.0
Africa	0.6	0.8	0.9	1.1	1.0	1.2	1.5	1.8
Middle East	0.4	0.5	0.8	0.5	0.8	1.2	1.45	1.4
South Asia	0.15	0.2	0.2	0.3	0.5	0.7	0.8	0.7
East Asia & the Pacific	1.3	1.8	2.0	2.2	2.7	3.1	4.0	5.0
Total	24.8	31.3	34.1	38.6	43.7	52.4	65.0	75.0

Index (1972 = 100)

Region	1972	1973	1974	1975	1976	1977	1978	1979P
Europe	100	127	133	153	171	214	272	309
Americas	100	121	143	159	180	189	221	262
Africa	100	133	150	183	167	200	250	300
Middle East	100	125	200	125	200	300	363	350
South Asia	100	133	133	200	333	440	533	440
East Asia & the Pacific	100	138	154	169	208	238	308	385
Total	100	126	138	156	176	211	262	302

Growth (% p.a.)

Region	1972	1973	1974	1975	1976	1977	1978	1979
Europe		+ 27.2	+ 4.4	+ 15.3	+ 11.7	+ 25.3	+ 26.8	+ 13.6
Americas		+ 21.3	+ 17.6	+ 11.5	+ 13.4	+ 4.5	+ 17.4	+ 18.5
Africa		+ 33.3	+ 12.5	+ 22.2	− 9.0	+ 20.0	+ 25.0	+ 20.0
Middle East		+ 25.0	+ 60.0	− 37.5	+ 60.0	+ 50.0	+ 20.8	− 3.4
South Asia		+ 33.3	0.0	+ 50.0	+ 66.7	+ 32.0	+ 21.2	− 17.5
East Asia & the Pacific		+ 38.5	+ 11.1	+ 10.0	+ 22.7	+ 14.8	+ 29.0	+ 25.0
Total		+ 26.2	+ 8.9	+ 13.2	+ 13.2	+ 19.9	+ 24.0	+ 15.4

Share of Regions (% of total)

Region	1972	1973	1974	1975	1976	1977	1978	1979P
Europe	65.3	65.8	63.8	64.8	63.4	66.2	67.7	66.7
Americas	24.6	23.6	24.6	24.4	25.2	21.9	20.8	21.3
Africa	2.4	2.6	2.7	2.9	2.3	2.3	2.3	2.4
Middle East	1.6	1.6	2.4	1.3	1.8	2.3	2.2	1.9
South Asia	0.6	0.6	0.6	0.8	1.1	1.3	1.2	0.9
East Asia & the Pacific	5.2	5.8	5.9	5.8	6.2	5.9	6.1	6.7
Total	100.0	100.0	100.0	100.0	100.0	100.0	100.0	100.0

Source: World Tourism Organization, *Tourism Compendium,* 1979 Edition

APPENDIX J

Visits to the United Kingdom by Overseas Residents 1946-79

Year	Visits[a] 000	% increase	Visitor nights million	% increase	Expenditure[b] £ million	% increase
1946	203	—			12	—
1947	396	95			21	75
1948	504	27			33	57
1949	563	12			43	30
1950	618	10			61	42
1951	712	15			75	23
1952	733	3			80	7
1953	819	12			88	10
1954	902	10			95	8
1955	1,037	15			111	17
1956	1,107	7			121	9
1957	1,180	7			129	7
1958	1,259	7			134	4
1959	1,395	11			143	7
1960	1,669	16			169	18
1961	1,824	9			176	4
1962	1,955	7			183	4
1963	2,159	10			188	3
1964[c]	3,257	—			190	—
1965	3,597	10.4			193	1.2
1966	3,967	10.3			219	13.9
1967	4,289	8.1			236	7.4
1968	4,828	12.6			282	19.9
1969	5,821	20.6			359	27.2
1970	6,692	15.0			432	20.3
1971[c]	7,131	6.6	104.2	4.1	500	15.7
1972	7,459	4.6	108.8	4.4	576	15.2
1973	8,167	9.5	115.8	6.4	726	26.0
1974	8,543	4.6	119.2	2.9	898	23.7
1975	9,490	11.1	128.5	7.8	1,218	35.6
1976	10,808	13.9	134.2	4.4	1,768	45.2
1977	12,281	13.6	148.5	10.7	2,352	33.0
1978R	12,646	3.0	149.1	0.4	2,507	6.6
1979P	12,493	1.2	155.5	4.3	2,764	10.2

a   Visits by people who, being permanently resident in a country outside the United Kingdom, visit the United Kingdom for less than a year. Immigrants and persons coming to the United Kingdom to take up employment, military personnel, merchant seamen, and airline personnel on duty are excluded. Visits exclude visits from the Irish Republic before 1964.

b   Expenditure covers only spending in the United Kingdom, includes visitors in transit or on day trips, and from 1975 estimates for the Channel Islands.

c   Horizontal lines between years denote changes in the method of estimating.

P   Provisional,   R   Revised

Sources: 1946-63 Home Office for arrivals of foreign visitors, Board of Trade for estimates of Commonwealth visitors and of expenditure; from 1964 Department of (Trade and) Industry International Passenger Survey, except for numbers of visitors from the Irish Republic, which are provided by the Central Statistics Office, Dublin.

APPENDIX K

Visits Abroad by United Kingdom Residents 1946-79

Year	Visits[a] 000	% increase	Visitor nights million	% increase	Expenditure[b] £ million	% increase
1946					42	—
1947					76	81
1948					66	− 13
1949					75	14
1950					85	13
1951					104	22
1952					83	− 20
1953					89	7
1954					101	13
1955					125	24
1956					129	3
1957					146	13
1958					152	4
1959					164	8
1960					186	13
1961					200	8
1962					210	5
1963					241	15
1964[c]	5,897	—			261	—
1965	6,472	9.8			290	11.3
1966	6,918	6.9			297	2.4
1967	7,202	4.1			274	− 7.9
1968	7,269	0.9			271	− 1.2
1969	8,083	11.2			324	19.8
1970	8,482	4.9			382	17.8
1971[c]	9,497	12.0	134.2	6.3	442	15.7
1972	10,695	12.6	147.6	10.0	535	21.0
1973	11,740	9.8	162.5	10.1	695	29.9
1974	10,783	− 8.2	144.6	− 11.0	703	1.2
1975	11,992	11.2	164.6	13.8	917	30.4
1976	11,560	− 3.6	159.9	− 2.9	1,068	16.5
1977	11,515	− 0.3	156.7	− 2.0	1,186	11.0
1978R	13,443	16.6	176.4	12.6	1,549	30.6
1979P	15,464	15.0	205.1	16.2	2,091	35.0

a Visits for less than a year by people permanently resident in the United Kingdom (who may be of foreign nationality). Emigrants and persons travelling abroad to take up employment, military personnel, merchant seamen and airline personnel on duty are excluded.
b Expenditure excludes payments for air and sea travel to and from the United Kingdom but includes expenditure on day trips, and from 1975 estimates for the Channel Islands.
c Horizontal lines between years denotes changes in the method of estimating.
P Provisional,   R Revised

Sources: 1946-63 Board of Trade; from 1964 Department of (Trade and) Industry, International Passenger Survey.

APPENDIX L

United Kingdom Residents' Foreign Travel Expenditure
and Changes in Currency Allowance 1945-79

Year	Expenditure (£ million)	Annual Currency Allowance		
		Date	Amount	Notes
1945	—	Oct. 1945	Fixed at £100	To include dollar area
1946	42	Mar. 1946	Changed to £75	
1947	76	Aug. 1947	Changed to £35	
		Sept. 1947	Withdrawn	
1948	66	Apr. 1948	Fixed at £35	To exclude dollar area
1949	75	Apr. 1949	Changed to £50	
1950	85	Dec. 1950	Changed to £100	
1951	104	Nov. 1951	Changed to £50	
1952	83	Jan. 1952	Changed to £25	
1953	89	Mar. 1953	Changed to £40	
		Nov. 1953	Changed to £50	
1954	101	Nov. 1954	Changed to £100	
1955	125			
1956	129			
1957	146	July 1957		To include dollar area
1958	152			
1959	164	Nov. 1959	Changed to £250	Further amounts granted
1960	186			
1961	200			
1962	210			
1963	241			
1964	261			
1965	290			
1966	297	Nov. 1966	Changed to £50	Plus certain additions; no limit for sterling area
1967	274			
1968	271			
1969	324			
1970	382	Jan. 1970	Changed to £300	Per journey
1971	442			
1972	535			
1973	695			
1974	703			
1975	917			
1976	1,068			
1977	1,186	Nov. 1977	Changed to £500	Per journey
1978	1,549			
1979P	2,091	June 1979	Changed to £1,000	Per journey; £5,000 per journey for business
		Oct. 1979	No limit	All exchange controls removed

Source: Board of Trade for estimates of expenditure 1946-63; Department of (Trade and) Industry, *International Passenger Survey,* from 1964.

APPENDIX M

British Airlines 1978

All scheduled services		All IT charter services	
Airline	*Passengers carried* *000*	*Airline*	*Passengers carried* *000*
British Airways	15,916	British Airways	105
British Caledonian	1,380	British Airtours	762
Air Anglia	375	British Caledonian	406
Aurigny	222	Britannia	2,431
British Air Ferries	138	Dan Air Services	2,696
British Island	573	Laker	524
British Midland	606	Monarch	703
Dan Air Services	459	4 others	46
Intra	105		
Laker	264		
7 others	298		
Total	20,336	Total	7,673

Source: CAA, *Annual Statistics 1978*

APPENDIX N

Major UK Passenger Ports and Airports 1978

Airport	Port	Passengers *000*
London Heathrow		26,913
	Dover	8,422
London Gatwick		7,841
Manchester		3,480
Glasgow		2,187
Luton		2,061
	Harwich	1,707
	Folkestone	1,643
Birmingham		1,352
Aberdeen		1,211

Source: CAA, *Annual Statistics 1978*

APPENDIX O

Major International Airports 1977

Airport	Terminal Passengers on International Flights 000	International Air Transport Movements 000
London Heathrow	20,568	199.1
New York JFK	11,490	96.4
Frankfurt	9,634	128.1
Amsterdam	8,444	129.9
Paris C de G	7,550	86.8
Paris Orly	7,543	91.6
Copenhagen	6,795	115.2
Zurich	6,741	102.3
Rome (2) (1976)	5,825	91.7

Source: CAA, Annual Statistics 1978

APPENDIX P

Major UK Airports 1978

Airport	Terminal Passengers 000	Air Transport Movements 000
London Heathrow	26,488	269
London Gatwick	7,761	99
Manchester	3,442	52
Glasgow	2,154	45
Luton	2,072	21
Jersey	1,427	53
Birmingham	1,306	28
Belfast	1,173	26
Edinburgh	1,138	22

Source: BAA, Annual Report and Accounts 1978/79

APPENDIX Q

Private Car Ownership in UK 1939, 1946 and 1950-78

Year	Population (million)	No. of Cars (million)	Cars per 1,000 population
1939	48.0	2.0	42
1946	49.2	1.8	37
1950	50.6	2.3	45
1951	50.3	2.4	48
1952	50.4	2.5	50
1953	50.6	2.8	55
1954	50.8	3.1	61
1955	50.9	3.5	70
1956	51.2	3.9	76
1957	51.4	4.2	82
1958	51.7	4.5	87
1959	52.0	5.0	96
1960	52.4	5.5	105
1961	52.8	6.0	114
1962	53.3	6.6	124
1963	53.5	7.4	138
1964	53.8	8.2	152
1965	54.2	8.9	164
1966	54.5	9.5	174
1967	54.8	10.3	189
1968	55.0	10.8	196
1969	55.2	11.2	202
1970	55.4	11.5	206
1971	55.6	12.1	218
1972	55.8	12.7	227
1973	55.9	13.5	241
1974*	56.0	13.6	242
1975*	56.0	13.7	245
1976*	55.9	14.0	250
1977*	55.8	..	..
1978*	55.8	14.1	253

.. No census in this year
* From 1974 onwards various improvements were made and the figures are not strictly comparable from year to year
Population is the mid-year *de facto* home population

Sources: British Road Federation, *Basic Road Statistics 1979; Annual Abstract of Statistics*, HMSO, various years.

APPENDIX R

Private Car Ownership in Selected Countries 1977

Country	Population (million)	No. of Cars (million)	Cars per 1,000 population
Belgium	9.8	2.8	293
Denmark	5.1	1.4	269
France	53.2	16.9	319
Germany FR	61.3	20.3	332
Italy	56.0	16.6	277
Netherlands (1976)	13.9	3.8	271
United Kingdom (1978)	55.8	14.1	253
Japan (1976)	111.9	18.5	165
United States	215.9	110.4	511

Sources: British Road Federation, *Basic Road Statistics 1979:* populations from various national sources.

APPENDIX S

Use of Passenger Transport in Great Britain 1968-78
Estimated passenger/kilometres
(000 million)

	1968	1970	1972	1974	1976	1978
Air	1.9	1.9	2.2	2.3	2.3	2.4
Rail	33.4	35.6	34.5	36.1	35.0	35.2
Road Public Serv. Vhcle	59.0	56.0	55.0	54.0	53.0	52.0
Prvte Trnsprt	286.0	309.0	347.0	350.0	363.0	390.0

Source: CSO, *Annual Abstract of Statistics 1980*

APPENDIX T

English Hotels Occupancy Survey 1977-79

The English hotels occupancy survey is a sample survey of several hundred hotels drawn from hotels listed in major national, regional and local accommodation guides. The results are more representative of larger, higher priced and group-owned hotels than of less expensive, smaller and independent hotels, but are a useful guide to occupancy of all English hotels. Eight key sets of information are published monthly:

● Average bedspace occupancy in five different types of location by two price levels in each location.
● Average room occupancy with the same analysis.
● Average length of stay with the same analysis.
● Average proportion of arrivans from overseas with the same analysis.
● Average bedspace and room occupancy, length of stay and proportion of arrivals from overseas, for each of the twelve English tourist regions.

Annual results from the survey for three years are shown below. Full details are available from Planning & Research Services Branch, English Tourist Board, 4 Grosvenor Gardens, London SW1W 0DU.

	1977	1978	1979
Bedspace occupancy	%	%	%
Seaside	41	40	38
Countryside	44	42	40
Small town	48	50	48
Large town	48	50	48
London	65	65	54
England	48	47	44
Room occupancy	%	%	%
Seaside	47	45	44
Countryside	52	50	49
Small town	58	61	60
Large town	58	59	60
London	75	75	63
England	55	54	52
Length of stay	nights	nights	nights
Seaside	3.6	3.5	3.4
Countryside	2.3	2.2	2.1
Small town	2.1	2.0	2.1
Large town	2.1	2.0	2.0
London	3.1	3.0	3.0
England	2.8	2.8	2.8
Arrivals from overseas	%	%	%
Seaside	10	9	7
Countryside	15	13	11
Small town	15	14	14
Large town	14	13	11
London	61	58	54
England	19	17	14

APPENDIX U

Annual Rates of Hotel Occupancy
in Selected OECD Member Countries 1976-78

	1976 %	1977 %	1978 %
Bed occupancy			
Austria	28.9	28.9	29.2
Belgium (a)	42.7	43.2	40.9
Denmark	42	42	40
Germany	33.2	33.5	33.7
Ireland	..	42	45
Norway (b)	49.2	49.8	47.6
Portugal (c)	65.8	57.8	51.9
Spain	46.8	56	..
Sweden (d)	..	41	40
Switzerland (e)	37.1	39.4	38.8
Turkey (f)	57.6	53.3	46.3
United Kingdom (g)	48	48	47
Room occupancy			
Finland	56	56	57
Sweden (d)	52	..	..
Japan (h)	73.1	73.9	73.6
New Zealand	64.8	63.5	59.5
United States (i)	63	65	67

(a)	Belgium	Based on a sample of 16 pilot hotels in Brussels
(b)	Norway	Approved hotels only
(c)	Portugal	Excluding boarding houses and inns
(d)	Sweden	Room occupancy rates in 1976, bed occupancy rates from 1977
(e)	Switzerland	Rates of available hotels
(f)	Turkey	Hotels, motels, boarding houses, inns, spas and holiday villages
(g)	UK	England only
(h)	Japan	Hotel members of the Japan Hotel Association only
(i)	US	Sample survey results published in *Survey of Current Business* of total hotel/motel industry
..		Not available

Source: OECD, *Tourism Policy and International Tourism 1979*

APPENDIX V

Hotel Occupancy, Rates and Length of Stay
in Selected Regions and Countries 1976

	Room occupancy[a]	No of guests per room[b]	Daily room rate[c] US $	Rate per guest[d] US$	Length of stay[e] Days
All hotels	69.8	1.3	33.00	25.05	5.1
Europe	68.6	1.4	33.78	23.80	2.8
Middle East	72.2	1.4	43.31	30.70	5.7
Asia	71.7	1.4	30.71	22.50	3.7
Far East	81.2	1.4	29.88	21.66	3.3
Australisia	63.4	1.3	32.10	24.45	3.6
Hawaii & Pacific Islands	86.3	1.5	35.56	24.35	15.9
Canada	63.6	1.3	32.19	25.22	2.3
USA	66.5	1.2	34.46	28.53	N/A
Mexico	73.7	1.2	27.43	23.82	5.7
Central America	71.1	1:0	23.7	23.49	2.1
South America	71.6	1.4	26.42	19.05	6.4
Caribbean	60.9	1.6	44.16	28.30	5.4
Africa	74.7	1.3	33.93	25.47	4.3

a   Average annual room occupancy is the ratio of total occupied rooms to total available rooms.
b   Number of guests per room represents average double occupancy by dividing total numbers of guests by total number of occupied rooms.
c   Average room rate is room sales divided by the total number of occupied rooms.
d   Average rate per guest is room sales divided by the total number of guests.
e   Length of stay is the total number of guest days divided by the total number of registered guests.

Source: Worldwide Lodging Industry 1977

APPENDIX W

Leading Hotel Operators in Britain 1979

Rank	Organization	Hotels	Rooms	Notes
1	Trusthouse Forte	230	23,000	
2	Grand Metropolitan	54	8,500	London and County Hotels
3	Centre	21	4,500	Coral Leisure Group, excluding Butlins
4	Scottish & Newcastle	64	4,000	Thistle Hotels (31) plus Open House Inns (33)
5	Ladbroke	41	3,900	Dragonara, Mercury, Myddleton
6	Crest	54	3,800	Bass
7	British Transport	29	3,700	British Railways
8	Holiday Inns	13	2,900	Including Commonwealth Holiday Inns
9	Embassy	43	2,400	Allied Breweries
10	Imperial London	6	2,400	Private company
11	Rank	7	2,400	
12	Swallow	34	2,200	Vaux Breweries
13	Mount Charlotte	26	2,000	Nuthall and Ocean Hotels
14	Reo Stakis	27	2,000	
15	EMI	7	1,900	
16	Comfort	15	1,800	
17	Whitbread	100	1,800	Including tenanted and leased hotels
18	De Vere	16	1,700	
19	Norfolk Capital	17	1,700	
20	Metropole	5	1,650	
21	Hilton	3	1,400	London, Kensington, Stratford
22	G W Hotels	28	1,350	
23	C G Hotels	9	1,300	Formerly Casserley Group
24	Greenall Whitley	39	1,300	Compass Hotels & Red Rose Grills & Inns
25	North	11	1,300	Unlicensed
26	Anchor	36	1,250	Courage/Imperial
27	Lex	3	1,200	Carlton Tower, Gatwick Park, Heathrow
28	Sheraton	3	1,100	London and Heathrow (2)
29	Trafalgar House	4	1,100	Cunard Hotels and Ritz
30	Queen's Moat Houses	18	1,050	

The table is intended to provide a broad indication of bedroom capacity concentration and includes known operators with more than 1,000 bedrooms. Numbers of bedrooms are rounded. Both numbers of hotels and bedrooms have been compiled from various sources and are in some case estimates. Hotels and bedrooms outside Britain are excluded.

APPENDIX X

Leading World Hotel Operators 1978

Rank	Organization	Hotels	Rooms	Head Office	Notes
1	Holiday Inns	1,718	286,529	Memphis, USA	Franchise
2	Sheraton	402	102,019	Boston, USA	Int Tel & Tel Co
3	Ramada Inns	643	92,392	Phoenix, USA	
4	Trusthouse Forte	860	77,051	London, UK	
5	Hilton Corporation	175	62,972	Los Angeles, USA	See also No. 10
6	Howard Johnson	524	59,040	Braintree, USA	Imperial 1979
7	Day Inns of America	301	42,036	Atlanta, USA	
8	Quality Inns Intl	300	33,717	Silver Springs, USA	
9	Intercontinental	83	30,057	New York, USA	Pan Am Airways
10	Hilton International	76	28,034	New York, USA	Trans World Airlines
11	Club Mediterranee	98	27,168	Paris, France	
12	Western International	50	26,700	Seattle, USA	United Airlines
13	Hyatt	52	26,000	Chicago, USA	See also No. 30
14	Motel 6	254	25,473	Los Angeles, USA	City Investing Co
15	Novotel	192	23,140	Evry, France	Affiliates included
16	Balkan Tourist	251	20,492	Sofia, Bulgaria	State-owned
17	Intourist	64	18,347	Moscow, USSR	State-owned
18	Marriott	40	17,987	Washington, USA	
19	Rodeway Inns of America	147	17,986	Dallas, USA	Franchise
20	Red Carpet/Master Hosts	131	16,776	Daytona Beach, USA	
21	JAL Development	36	14,500	Tokyo, Japan	Japan Air Lines
22	Topeka Inn Management	74	12,410	Topeka, USA	Holiday Inn licensee
23	Commonwealth Hol Inns	58	12,254	London, Canada	Controlled by Scotts 1979
24	Hoteles Agrupados	22	12,000	Madrid, Spain	
25	Cedok	222	11,300	Prague, Czecho	State-owned
26	Grand Metropolitan	65	11,223	London, UK	
27	CP Hotels	31	10,375	Toronto, Canada	Canadian Pacific
28	Tokyu Hotel Chain	48	10,232	Tokyo, Japan	
29	Downtowner/Rowntowner	68	10,000	Memphis, USA	
30	Hyatt International	24	9,061	Chicago, USA	

The table is intended to provide a broad indication of bedroom capacity concentration and includes known operators with more than 10,000 bedrooms and Hyatt International (30) for comparison with Hyatt (13). Hotel consortia and referral chains are excluded.

Source: Based on *Service World International,* Vol. 13, No. 3, June 1979

APPENDIX Y

Membership of the Association of British Travel Agents[a]
1961-79

Year	Number of members	Number of recognized offices
1961	488	981
1962	525	1,037
1963	565	1,118
1964	599	1,202
1965	654	1,392
1966[b]	1,158	2,113
1967	1,489	2,629
1968	1,583	2,881
1969	1,642	3,067
1970	1,680	3,256
1971	1,735	3,497
1972	1,851	3,789
1973	1,963	4,106
1974	1,979	4,216
1975	1,915	4,144
1976	1,901	4,154
1977	1,919	4,164
1978	1,908	4,115
1979[c]	1,954	4,209

a   Until 1977, the count reflects the position at 30 June, but from 1978 it refers to 1 January;
b   Operation Stabilizer was introduced in October 1965;
c   As at 1 January 1979, there were 1,603 retail members, 147 tour operator members and 204 members both retail and tour operating.

Source: ABTA Annual Reports

APPENDIX Z1

British Statutory Tourist Boards
Principal Characteristics 1979

	British Tourist Authority
1 Geographical scope	Great Britain
2 Area	230,000 sq km
3 Population	55 million
4 Responsible to	Secretary of State for Trade
5 Functions	Overseas promotion Common activities Non-UK activities
6 Board membership	9 Chairman + 5 members + chairmen of 3 Boards
7 Main Committees	Marketing Infra-Structure Development Hotels and Restaurants British Heritage Camping and Caravan
8 Overseas offices/ regions	22
9 Management	Director General Deputy/Marketing Finance/Admin Services Strategic Planning Production Services Overseas Offices
10 Total staff	475 (302 home + 173 overseas)

Source: Annual Reports for the Year Ended 31 March 1979

English Tourist Board	*Scottish Tourist Board*	*Wales Tourist Board*
England	Scotland	Wales
130,000 sq km	79,000 sq km	21,000 sq km
47 million	5¼ million	2¾ million
Secretary of State for Trade	Secretary of State for Scotland	Secretary of State for Wales
UK promotion Development	UK promotion Development	UK promotion Development
7 Chairman + 6 members	7 Chairman + 6 members	7 Chairman + 6 members

	Scottish Tourist
	   Consultative Council
	Scottish Tourism
	   Manpower Advisory Cttee
	Scottish Working Group on
	   the Registration and
	   Classification of Tourist
	   Accommodation
		Caravan and Camping
		Tourist Attractions
		Farm Tourism
		Hotels
		Self-catering

12
Chief Executive
Development
Marketing
External Relations
Administration/Secretary
	9
	Chief Executive
	Secretary/Deputy
	Marketing
	Info and Regional Services
	External Relations
	Finance
	Research and Planning
		3
		Chief Executive
		Publicity
		Finance/Secretary
		Marketing
		Projects and Planning
		   Liaison
		Strategic Planning and
		   Research

160	127	93

APPENDIX Z2

British Statutory Tourist Boards
Operating and Development Expenditure and Income 1969-79

	1969/70 £000	1970/71 £000
British Tourist Authority (from 25.8.69)		
Operating expenditure and income		
Total expenditure and income	1,448	4,014
Less revenue	325	755
Net expenditure	1,123	3,259
Grant-in-aid	1,460	3,250
English Tourist Board (established 1.10.69)		
Operating expenditure and income		
Total expenditure	40	534
Less revenue	—	42
Net expenditure	40	492
Grant-in-aid	50	520
Development assistance		
Section 4 (grants and loans for tourist projects)	—	—
HDIS (hotel grants and loans	117	2,008
Scottish Tourist Board (established 1.10.69)		
Operating expenditure and income		
Total expenditure	120	265
Less revenue	37	57
Net expenditure	83	208
Grant-in-aid	80	220
Development assistance		
Section 4 (grants and and loans for tourist projects)	—	—
HDIS (hotel grants and loans)	—	387
Wales Tourist Board (established 1.10.69)		
Operating expenditure and incomes		
Total expenditure	85	179
Less revenue	25	14
Net expenditure	60	165
Grant-in-aid	65	175
Development assistance		
Section 4 (grants and loans for tourist projects)	—	—
HDIS (hotel grants and loans)	—	124
Total Authority and Boards		
Operating expenditure and income		
Total expenditure	1,693	4,992
Less revenue	387	868
Net expenditure	1,306	4,124
Grant-in-aid	1,655	4,165
Development assistance		
Section 4 (grants and loans for tourist projects)	—	—
HDIS (hotel grants and loans)	117	2,159

Source: Annual Reports

1971/72 £000	1972/73 £000	1973/74 £000	1974/75 £000	1975/76 £000	1976/76 £000	1977/78 £000	1978/79 £000
4,400	5,669	6,876	6,920	8,953	10,564	13,241	15,226
851	1,115	1,231	1,519	1,892	2,630	3,620	4,171
3,549	4,554	5,645	5,401	7,061	7,934	9,621	11,055
3,550	4,500	5,600	5,446	7,058	8,085	9,634	11,087
1,106	1,302	1,876	2,412	3,522	4,471	5,056	5,688
66	86	99	163	250	406	525	703
1,040	1,216	1,768	2,249	3,272	4,065	4,531	4,985
1,040	1,320	1,750	2,266	3,323	4,137	4,600	5,014
91	559	570	687	1,270	1,458	1,667	1,350
5,652	8,905	20,821	7,449	1,852	664	222	68
422	674	783	1,022	1,332	1,673	1,984	2,497
70	103	130	113	121	184	326	317
352	571	653	889	1,211	1,489	1,658	2,180
386	550	711	884	1,194	1,555	1,776	2,154
63	240	520	470	572	700	1,000	1,300
1,313	1,204	1,572	760	395	80	56	—
336	465	611	755	869	1,109	1,575	1,850
27	59	69	120	122	190	205	252
309	406	542	635	747	919	1,370	1,598
307	426	537	693	768	968	1,380	1,685
167	240	500	417	793	843	790	1,660
495	890	2,045	164	62	5	4	—
6,264	8,110	10,137	11,089	14,676	17.817	21,856	25,261
1,014	1,363	1,529	1,915	2,385	3,410	4,676	5,443
5,250	6,747	8,608	9,174	12,291	14,407	17,180	19,818
5,283	6,796	8,598	9,289	12,343	14,745	17,390	19,940
321	1,039	1,590	1,574	2,635	3,001	3,457	4,310
7,460	10,999	24,438	8,373	2,309	749	282	68

APPENDIX Z3

English Regional Tourist Boards Sources of Income 1971-80

Region	Source	71/72 £000	72/73 £000	73/74 £000	74/75 £000	75/76 £000	76/77 £000	77/78 £000	78/79 £000	79/80 £000
Cumbria	LAs[a]	18	19	24	36	36	25	31	35	38
(English Lakes)	ETB[b]	12	16	22	32	38	44	53	56	65
	Membership[c]	2	3	4	5	6	9	14	15	18
	Other[d]	9	11	19	19	18	22	42	49	58
	Total	40	49	68	92	97	100	139	155	179
East Anglia	LAs	4	8	13	24	41	48	50	32	36
	ETB	10	16	22	32	39	46	52	56	66
	Membership	—	—	5	7	8	8	11	14	16
	Other	—	3	17	24	35	56	91	131	151
	Total	14[e]	28	57	86	123	158	204	233	269
East Midlands	LAs	5	20	21	24	28	34	34	40	36
	ETB	10	16	22	34	40	47	52	56	72
	Membership	—	1	3	3	3	3	6	7	6
	Other	—	3	8	4	7	15	26	43	52
	Total	15[e]	40	52	66	78	99	118	136	166
Heart of England	LAs	7	21	22	42	44	49	47	53	59
(West Midlands)	ETB	12	21	24	34	40	47	52	56	67
	Membership	—	1	6	5	6	9	14	18	22
	Other	—	5	5	33	18	31	33	59	43
	Total	19[e]	48	57	115	108	135	146	186	191
London	LAs	75	85	105	120	140	154	165	180	220
	ETB	84	89	112	125	145	170	202	217	233
	Membership	20	26	35	42	57	70	96	117	147
	Other	35	52	63	62	87	151	212	301	337
	Total	213	253	314	349	429	545	675	815	937
Northumbria	LAs	32	38	45	59	77	89	95	101	113
	ETB	12	16	20	32	42	49	59	63	74
	Membership	2	3	3	4	6	6	6	7	7
	Other	7	6	8	11	10	27	46	31	29
	Total	52	63	76	106	135	171	204	202	223
North-West	LAs	18	22	27	32	38	43	43	52	57
	ETB	12	17	20	32	37	44	48	59	78
	Membership	—	1	3	3	2	4	4	7	9
	Other	—	5	7	6	8	18	22	27	42
	Total	30	44	57	72	86	109	117	145	186
South-East	LAs	14	16	21	27	28	29	27	37	49
	ETB	10	22	31	48	58	51	56	62	70
	Membership	—	2	4	5	6	9	13	18	29
	Other	6	10	15	15	13	25	33	38	44
	Total	30	48	71	94	105	113	129	155	192
Southern	LAs						23	27	29	35
	ETB						25	40	48	58
	Membership						3	6	7	13
	Other						13	31	70	111
	Total						64[e]	105	154	217
Thames & Chilterns	LAs	—	4	4	7	8	9	6	11	11
	ETB	2	20	20	27	33	39	46	49	59
	Membership	—	1	5	7	8	13	14	18	22
	Other	—	1	4	11	9	13	56	45	59
	Total	2[e]	26	33	51	58	74	123	123	151

Region	Source	71/72 £000	72/73 £000	73/74 £000	74/75 £000	75/76 £000	76/77 £000	77/78 £000	78/79 £000	79/80 £000
West Country	LAs	39	42	'45	50	55	56	57	61	68
	ETB	17	25	30	42	50	59	65	72	83
	Membership	1	2	4	4	4	8	13	18	20
	Other	7	15	37	38	50	65	77	96	107
	Total	64^e	84	116	135	159	188	212	247	278
Yorks & Humberside	LAs	9	12	22	50	78	88	97	101	113
	ETB	12	17	22	34	42	51	63	67	86
	Membership	—	2	4	4	11	12	14	16	24
	Other	10	23	23	36	36	38	76	80	89
	Total	31	55	72	123	167	189	249	264	312
Totals	LAs	220	288	349	471	572	646	679	732	835
	ETB	193	275	343	472	563	671	786	861	1,011
	Membership	24	41	77	87	118	154	212	262	333
	Other	75	133	204	258	291	473	744	970	1,122
	Total	511	736	974	1,288	1,545	1,946	2,421	2,825	3,301

Notes [a] Local Authorities
       [b] English Tourist Board
       [c] Membership subscriptions
       [d] E.g. guidebook sales

[e] Part year only
[f] Totals may not agree
   with sums of individual items
   because of rounding

Source: English Tourist Board, Annual Reports

Select Tourism Bibliography

This bibliography lists over two hundred works in tourism and related fields. It is confined in the main to publications in the English language and published in the United Kingdom. Articles in journals, publications in languages other than English or published outside the United Kingdom, and publications of local interest are, with some exceptions, excluded.

Readers interested particularly in publications on hotels and catering are advised to consult the bibliography of some two hundred sources in Medlik, S., *Profile of the Hotel and Catering Industry,* London, Heinemann, 1978.

Addison, W., *English Spas,* London, Batsford, 1951

Anderson, N., *Work and Leisure,* London, Routledge & Kegan Paul, 1961

Archer, B. H., *The Impact of Domestic Tourism,* Cardiff, University of Wales Press, 1973

Archer, B. H., *Demand Forecasting in Tourism,* Cardiff, University of Wales Press, 1975

Archer, B. H., *Tourism in the Bahamas and Bermuda: Two Case Studies,* Cardiff, University of Wales Press, 1977

Archer, B. H., *Tourism Multipliers: The State of the Art,* Bangor Occasional Papers in Economics, No. 11, Cardiff, University of Wales Press, 1977

Archer, B. H., *Tourism in the Third World: Some Economic Considerations,* Inaugural Lecture, Guildford, Surrey, 1979

Association Internationale d'Experts Scientifiques du Tourisme, *Manpower in Tourism,* Editions AIEST Vol. 20, Berne, 1979

Association of British Travel Agents, *Annual Report,* London, ABTA, annual

Association of British Travel Agents, *Education and Training Handbook,* London, ABTA, 1980

Baker, M. J.. *Marketing: An Introductory Text,* Macmillan, 1974

Bayliss, B. T., *European Transport,* London, Mason, 1965

Beazley, E., *Designed for Recreation,* London, Faber, 1970

Beeching Report, *The Reshaping of British Railways,* London, HMSO, 1963

Board of Trade, *Staggered Holidays,* London, HMSO, 1968

Boyd, H. W., and Massy, W. F., *Marketing Management,* New York, Harcourt Brace, 1972

British Airports Authority, *Annual Report and Accounts,* London, BAA, annual

British Airways, *Report and Accounts,* London, HMSO, annual

British Hotels, Restaurants and Caterers Association, *Annual Report,* London, BHRCA, annual

British Resorts Association, *Report of the Working Party on Traditional Resorts,* London, BRA, 1979

British Roads Federation, *Basic Roads Statistics,* London, BRF, annual

British Roads Federation, *Roads and Tourism,* London, BRF, 1970

British Roads Federation, *Conference on Roads and Leisure,* London, BRF, 1971

British Tourist Authority, *Annual Report,* London, BTA, annual

British Tourist Authority, *Digest of Tourist Statistics,* BTA, London, annual

British Tourist Authority, *British National Travel Survey,* London, BTA, annual

British Tourist Authority, *Survey of Mobile Caravanning and Camping 1970,* London, BTA, 1971

British Tourist Authority, *Tourism and the Environment,* London, BTA, 1972

British Tourist Authority, *The Measurement of Tourism,* London, BTA, 1974

British Tourist Authority, *Select Tourism Bibliography,* London, BTA

British Tourist Authority, *Tourism: A Leading Invisible Export,* London, BTA

British Tourist Authority, *Courses in Tourism and Related Subjects,* London, BTA, annual

British Tourist Authority, *International Tourism and Strategic Planning,* London, BTA, 1979

British Tourist Boards, *British Home Tourism Survey,* London, English Tourist Board, annual

British Tourist Boards, *Resorts and Spas in Britain,* British Tourist Authority, London, 1975

British Tourist Boards, *Tourism in Britain — The Broad Perspective,* London, British Tourist Authority, 1979

British Travel Association/University of Keele, *Pilot National Recreation Survey,* Reports No. 1 and 2, London, BTA, 1967 and 1969

British Waterways Board, *Leisure and the Waterways,* London, HMSO, 1967

Broadbent, S., *Spending Advertising Money,* 3rd edition, London, Business Books, 1979

Brunner, E., *Holiday Making and the Holiday Trades,* London, Oxford University Press, 1945

Bryden, J. M., *Tourism and Development: A Case Study in the Commonwealth Caribbean,* Cambridge, Cambridge University Press, 1973

Burkart, A. J., and Medlik, S. (editors), *The Management of Tourism,* London, Heinemann, 1975

Burton, T. L., *Recreation and Research Planning,* London, Allen & Unwin, 1970

Burton, T. L., and Wibberley, G. P., *Outdoor Recreation in the British Countryside,* Wye College, University of London, 1965

Business Statistics Office, *Business Monitor MQ6, Overseas Travel and Tourism,* London, HMSO, quarterly and annual

Central Statistical Office, *Annual Abstract of Statistics,* London, HMSO, annual

Central Statistical Office, *National Income and Expenditure,* London, HMSO, annual

Central Statistical Office, *Standard Industrial Classification,* Revised 1968, London, HMSO, 1968

Central Statistical Office, *Standard Industrial Classification,* Revised 1980, London, HMSO, 1979

Central Statistical Office, *Social Trends,* London, HMSO, annual

Chenery, R., *Comparative Study of Planning Considerations and Constraints Affecting Tourism Projects in the Principal European Capitals,* London, British Travel Educational Trust, 1979

Chisholm, M. (editor), *Resources for Britain's Future,* London, Penguin, 1972

Civil Aviation Authority, *Annual Report,* London, CAA, annual

Civil Aviation Authority, *Annual Statistics,* London, CAA, annual

Civil Aviation Authority, *Domestic Air Services (CAP 420),* London, CAA, 1979

Civil Aviation Authority, *European Air Fares; a discussion document (CAP 409) London, CAA, 1977*

Committee on Invisible Exports, *Britain's Invisible Earnings,* London, British National Export Council for the Financial Advisory Panel on Exports, 1967

Consultative Committee on Registration of Tourist Accommodation, *Report,* London, ETB 1979

Corbett, D. C., *Politics and the Airlines,* London, Allen & Unwin, 1965

Countryside Commission, *Coastal Recreation and Holidays,* London, HMSO, 1969

Countryside Commission, *Coastal Heritage,* London, HMSO, 1970

Countryside Commission, *The Planning of the Coastline,* London, HMSO, 1970

Dale, A., *Fashionable Brighton,* London, Oriel, 1967

Davies, E. T., *Tourism and the Cornish Farmer,* Exeter University Press, 1969

Deakin, B. M., and Seward, T., *Productivity in Transport,* Cambridge, Cambridge University Press, 1969

de Kadt, E., *Tourism — Passport to Development?* New York, Oxford University Press, 1979

Department of the Environment, *Passenger Transport in Great Britain,* London, HMSO, annual

Department of the Environment, *Highway Statistics,* London, HMSO, annual

Department of the Environment, *Local Government and the Development of Tourism,* DOE Circular 13/79, London, HMSO, 1979

Department of Industry, *International Passenger Survey — see* Business Statistics Office, *Business Monitor MQ6*

Department of Trade and Industry, *Civil Aviation Policy Guidance,* Cmnd 4890, London, HMSO, 1972

Department of Trade and Industry, *Future Civil Aviation Policy,* Cmnd 6400, London, HMSO, 1976

Dower, M., The *Challenge of Leisure,* London, Civic Trust, 1965

Dyos, H. J., and Aldcroft, D. H., *British Transport,* Leicester, Leicester University Press, 1969

Economic Commission for Europe, *The Planning and Development of Recreational Areas Including the Development of the Natural Environment,* London, United Nations, 1970

Economist Intelligence Unit, *The British Travel Industry, A Survey,* London, Association of British Travel Agents, 1968

Economist Intelligence Unit, *International Tourism,* London, EIU, 1970

Economist Intelligence Unit, *Economic and Social Impact of International Tourism on Developing Countries,* Special Report No. 60, London, EIU, 1979

Economist Intelligence Unit, *International Tourism Development Forecasts to 1990,* Special Report No. 62, London, EIU, 1979

English Tourist Board, *Annual Report,* London, ETB, annual

English Tourist Board, *Tourism Multipliers in Britain,* London, ETB, 1976

English Tourist Board, *Planning for Tourism in England,* London, ETB, 1978

English Tourist Board, *Forecasts of Tourism by British Residents 1985 to 1995,* London, ETB, 1980

English Tourist Board, *Development Guides DG2-DG31* (total 28 to end 1979), Development Advisory Services Unit, ETB, 1979

English Tourist Board, *Tourism Development Reports* (total 4 to er 1 1979), Development Advisory Services Unit, ETB, 1979

English Tourist Board, *Development Opportunity Portfolios* (total 12 to end 1979), Commercial Relations Department, ETB, 1979

English Tourist Board and Trades Union Congress, *Holidays: The Social Need,* London, ETB, 1976

English Tourist Board and others, *Tourism and Conservation,* London, ETB, 1974

European Travel Commission, *European Travel Market Study,* Geneva, ETC, 1972

European Travel Commission, *Freedom to Travel,* Dublin, ETC, 1969

European Travel Commission, *Implications on Tourism of the Boeing 747,* Geneva, ETC, 1972

European Travel Commission, *Papers Presented at a Seminar on Forecasting Tourist Movement held in London in January 1971,* British Tourist Authority, 1971

Foster, C. D., *The Transport Problem,* London, Blackie, 1963

Gilbert, E. W., *Brighton,* London, Methuen, 1954

Glasser, R., *Leisure: Penalty or Prize?* London, Macmillan, 1970

Goss, R. O., *Maritime Economics,* Cambridge University Press, 1970

Government Social Survey, *Planning for Leisure,* London, HMSO, 1969

Gray, H. P., *International Travel — International Trade,* Lexington, Heath Lexington Books, 1970

Greater London Council, *Tourism and Hotels in London,* London, GLC, 1971

Greater London Council, *Tourism — A Paper for Discussion,* GLC, 1978

Greater London Council, *Tourism — A Statement of Policies,* London, GLC, 1980

Hatch, A., *American Express,* New York, Doubleday, 1950

Heneghan, P., *Resource Allocation in Tourism Marketing,* London, Tourism International Press, 1976

Hern, A., *The Seaside Holiday,* London, Cresset, 1967

Higham, R., *Britain's Imperial Air Routes 1918-1939,* London, Foulis, 1960

Hollander, S., *Passenger Transportation,* East Lansing, Michigan State University, 1968

Home Office, *Immigration Statistics,* London, HMSO, annual

Horwath & Horwath International and Laventhol & Horwath, *Worldwide Lodging Industry,* New York, annual

Horwath & Horwath (UK) Ltd., *United Kingdom Lodging Industry,* London, annual

Horwath & Horwath (UK) Ltd., *Fiscal and Incentive Treatment of the Hotel Industry* in England, English Tourist Board, 1979

Hotels and Catering Economic Development Committee, *Hotels and Government Policy,* NEDO, 1974

Hotels and Catering Economic Development Committee, *Report to the NEDC, January 1977,* London, NEDO, 1977

Hotels and Catering Economic Development Committee, *Hotel Prospects to 1985, Research Findings,* London, NEDO, 1976

Hudson, E., *Vertical Integration in the Travel and Leisure Industry,* Paris, Institut du Transport Aerien, 1972

Hunziker, W., *Grundriss der Allgemeinen Fremdenverkehrslehre,* Zurich, Polygraphsscher Verlag AG, 1942

Hunziker, Z., *Social Tourism, Its Nature and Problems, Geneva,* Alliance Internationale de Tourisme, 1951

Hudson Davies, E., *Tourism in British Politics,* London, The Tourism Society, 1979

Industrial Welfare Society, *The Case for Staggered Holidays,* London, IWS, 1963

International Air Transport Association, *Importance of Civil Air Transport in the UK Economy,* Geneva, IATA, 1970

International Monetary Fund, Balance of Payments Manual, Washington, IMF, 1961

International Union of Official Travel Organizations, *Study on the Economic Impact of Tourism on National Economies and International Trade,* Geneva, IUOTO, 1966

International Union of Official Travel Organizations, *Economic Review of World Tourism,* Geneva, IUOTO, 1968, 1970, 1972, 1974

Jeffries, D. J., *The British Away From Home,* London, The Tourist Society, 1978

Johnson, P., *The Corpus of Knowledge in Hotel, Catering and Institutional Services,* 2 vols., London, Hotel, Catering and Institutional Management Association, 1977

Kaiser, C., and Helber, L. E., *Tourism Planning and Development,* Cahners, 1978 and Heinemann, 1978

Knight, J., and Parker, S., *A Bibliography of British Publications on Leisure* 1960-1977, London, Leisure Studies Association, 1978

Krippendorf, J., *Marketing et Tourisme,* Berne, Herbert Lang, 1971

Krippendorf, J., *Marketing im Fremdenverkehr,* Berne, Herbert Lang, 1971

Lambden, W., *Bus and Coach Operation,* London, Butterworth, 1969

Lawson, M., *Teaching Tourism,* London, Tourism International Press, 1974

Lewes, F. M. M., Culyer, A., and Brady, G. A., *Holiday Transport in Devon and Cornwall,* Exeter, University of Exeter, 1967

Lewes, F. M. M., *et al., The Holiday Industry of Devon and Cornwall,* London, Ministry of Housing and Local Government, HMSO, 1970

Lewes, F. M. M., Parker, S. R., and Lickorish, L. J., *Leisure and Tourism,* Reviews of United Kingdom Statistical Sources, Vol. IV, London, Heinemann Educational Books on behalf of the Royal Statistical Society and the Social Science Research Council, 1975

Lickorish, L. J., and Kershaw, A. G., *The Travel Trade,* London, Practical Press, 1958

Lindley, K., *Coastline,* London, Hutchinson, 1967

Mathias, P., *The First Industrial Nation,* London, Methuen, 1969

McIntosh, R. W., *Tourism: Principles, Practices, and Philosophies,* Columbus, Ohio, Grid, 1977

Medlik, S., *The British Hotel and Catering Industry,* London, Pitman, 1961

Medlik, S., *Higher Education and Research in Tourism in Western Europe,* London University of Surrey, 1966

Medlik, S., *Profile of the Hotel and Catering Industry,* London, Heinemann, 1978

Medlik, S., *The Business of Hotels,* London, Heinemann, 1980

Miles-Kelcey Ltd., *A Study of Tourist & Holiday Facilities in S.W. England,* London, British Tourist Authority, 1969

Medlik, S., *Britain — Workshop or Service Centre to the World?* University Lecture, University of Surrey, Guildford, 1977

Milne, A. M., and Laight, J. C., *The Economics of Inland Transport,* London, Pitman 1963

Middleton, V. T. C., *Tourism in Context,* British Tourist Authority, London, 1976

Middleton, V. T. C., *Managing Tourism Flows,* The Tourism Society, London, 1979

Ministry of Housing and Local Government, Coastal Preservation and Development, London, HMSO, 1963

Ministry of Land and Natural Resources, *Leisure in the Countryside: England and Wales,* London, HMSO, 1966

Ministry of Transport, *British Waterways,* London, HMSO, 1967

Munby, D. H., *Transport,* London, Penguin, 1968

Mutch, W. E. S., *Public Recreation in National Forests,* London, HMSO, 1968

Nature Conservancy, *The Countryside in 1970,* London, HMSO, 1964

Nicholson, M., *The Environmental Revolution,* London, Penguin, 1972

North, R., *The Butlin Story,* London, Jarrolds, 1962

Northern Ireland Tourist Board, *Annual Report,* Belfast, NITB, annual

Norval, A. J., *The Tourist Industry, A National and International Survey,* London, Pitman, 1936

Nightingale, M. A., *Tourism Occupations, Career Profiles and Knowledge,* London, The Tourism Society, 1980

Naylor, G. H., *The Contribution of Tourism to the Quality of Life,* London, The Tourism Society, 1980

O'Connor, W. E., *Economic Regulation of the World's Airlines,* New York, Praeger, 1971

Ogilvie, F. W., *The Tourist Movement,* London, Staples Press, 1933

O'Loughlin, C., *Economics of Sea Transport,* Oxford, Pergamon, 1967

Organization for Economic Co-operation and Development, *International Tourism and Tourism Policy in OECD Member Countries,* Paris, OECD, annual

Organization for European Economic Co-operation, *Tourism and European Recovery,* Paris, OECD, undated

Outdoor Recreation Resources Review Commission, *Outdoor Recreation for America,* Washington, ORRRC, 1962

Parker, S., *The Future of Work and Leisure,* London, MacGibbon & Kee, 1971

Patmore, J. A., *Land and Leisure,* London, Penguin, 1972

Peters, M., *International Tourism,* London, Hutchinson, 1969

Pickering, J. F., Greenwood, J. A., Hunt, Diana, *The Small Firm in the Hotel and Catering Industry,* London, HMSO, 1971

Pimlott, J. A. R., *The Englishman's Holiday,* London, Faber & Faber, 1947

Rae, J. B., *The Road and the Car in American Life,* Cambridge, Mass., Institute of Technology, 1971

Rae, W. F., *The Business of Travel,* London, Thos. Cook & Son, 1891

Reed, M. G. (editor), *Railways in the Victorian Economy,* London, David & Charles, 1969

Richards, G., *Tourism and the Economy,* Guildford, University of Surrey, 1972

Rivers, P., *The Restless Generation, A Crisis in Mobility,* London, Davis-Poynter, 1972

Roberts, K., *Leisure,* London, Longmans, 1970

Rochdale Committee, *Report of the Committee of Inquiry into Shipping,* London HMSO, 1970

Rosenberg, A., *Air Travel within Europe,* Stockholm, Ab Allmanna Forlaget, 1970

Rosenberg, A., *Air Travel Across the North Atlantic,* Stockholm, Ab Allmanna Forlaget, 1972

Rothwell, A. J., *The Small Firm and Co-operation in Tourism,* London, The Tourism Society, 1979

Robinson, H. A., *Geography of Tourism,* London, Macdonald and Evans, 1976

Savage, C. I., *Economic History of Transport,* London, Hutchinson, 1966

Schmoll, G. A., *Tourism Promotion,* London, Tourism International Press, 1977

Scottish Tourist Board, *Annual Report,* Edinburgh, STB, annual

Scottish Tourist Board, *Caravan Survey,* Edinburgh, STB, 1971

Scottish Tourist Board, *Tourism in Scotland,* Edinburgh, STB, 1969

Scottish Tourist Board, *Planning for Tourism in Scotland,* Edinburgh, STB, 1975 and 1977

Seekings, J. C., *The Changing Global Scene,* London, The Tourism Society, 1978

Sillitoe, K. K., *Planning for Leisure,* London, HMSO, 1970

Simpson, L., *Self-catering Trends in Europe,* London, British Travel Educational Trust, 1979

Smith, V. L. (editor), *Hosts and Guests: The Anthropology of Tourism,* Oxford, Blackwell, 1978

Stokes, H. G., *The Very First History of the English Seaside,* London, Sylvan Press, undated

Straszheim, M. R., *The International Airline Industry,* London, Allen & Unwin, 1969

Stratford, A., *Air Transport Economics in the Supersonic Era,* London, Macmillan, 1967

Thornton, R. H., *British Shipping,* Cambridge, Cambridge University Press, 1959

Thornton, R. L., *International Airlines and Politics,* East Lansing, University of Michigan, 1970

Tourism and Recreation Research Unit, *Scottish Tourism and Recreation Studies, Reports 1-7,* Scottish Tourist Board, 1975-1977

Travel Trade Directory, London and Folkestone, Travel Trade Gazette, annual

Travis, A. S., *Leisure, Recreation and Tourism,* London, The Tourism Society, 1978
Travis, A. S., *Strategic Appraisal of Scottish Tourism,* Edinburgh, Scottish Tourist Board, 1974
Turner, L., and Ash, J., *The Golden Hordes,* London, Constable, 1975

Underwood, E., *Brighton,* London, Batsford, 1978
United Nations, *Recommendations on International Travel and Tourism,* United Nations Conference on International Travel and Tourism, Rome, 1963

Wahab, S., *Tourism Management,* London, Tourism International Press, 1975
Wahab, S., Crampon, L. J., and Rothfield, L., *Tourism Marketing,* London, Tourism International Press, 1977
Wales Tourist Board, *Annual Report,* Cardiff, WTB, annual
Wales Tourist Board, *Tourism in Wales — A Plan for the Future,* Cardiff, WTB, 1976
Walwin, J., *Beside the Seaside: A Social History of the Popular Seaside Holiday,* London, Allen Lane, 1978
Wheatcroft, S. F., *Air Transport Policy,* London, Joseph, 1964
White, J., *History of Tourism,* London, Leisure Art, 1967
Williams, J. E. D., *The Operation of Airliners,* London, Hutchinson, 1964
Wimble, E. W., *European Recovery 1948-1951 and the Tourist Industry,* London, The British Travel Association, 1948
Wood, M., (editor), *Tourism Marketing for the Small Business,* London, English Tourist Board, 1980
Working Group of National Tourist Organizations of the EEC, *The Economic Significance of Tourism within the European Economic Community,* 1st Report 1975, 2nd Report 1977, 3rd Report 1978, London, British Tourist Authority
World Tourism Organization, *World Tourism Statistics,* Madrid, WTO, annual
World Tourism Organization, *Tourism Compendium,* Madrid, WTO 1975, 1977, 1979
World Tourism Organization, *Economic Review of World Tourism,* Madrid, WTO, 1976, 1978
World Tourism Organization, *Distribution Channels*, Madrid, WTO, undated

Young, G., *Tourism — Blessing or Blight?,* London, Pelican, 1973

Index

Index

The Geography of Travel and Tourism

B. Boniface

Bournemouth College of Technology

and C. P. Cooper

University of Surrey

Provides a comprehensive examination of the basic principles underlying the geography of tourist demand, supply and transportation, together with a broad survey of world tourism generating and destination regions. For students taking BTEC and SCOTBEC Diploma courses in both business studies and hotels and catering. It will also be of value to students studying geography of tourism for GCE A Level and those following vocational courses with the ITT, ABTA, and City & Guilds, and students of travel and tourism in other countries.

Contents: Organizational framework; Geography of tourist demand and tourism resources; Geographical elements of transport; Geography of transport operations; European scene setting; The UK and Eire – tourist demand and supply; Southern Europe and the Mediterranean; Northern Europe; Eastern Europe and the Soviet Union; North America; Latin America and the Caribbean; Africa and the Middle East; South and East Asia; Australasia and the Pacific Islands.

0 434 90166 0
280pp 246×189mm 33 maps
Paperback

Marketing in Travel and Tourism

Victor T. C. Middleton

University of Surrey

This book draws together concepts and principles derived from marketing theory and practice and applies them within the travel and tourism concept. It has been written to meet the needs of students and of practitioners in the tourism industry who are involved in marketing in both commercial and public sectors. Applications focus on areas as diverse as airlines, accommodation, tour operators and tourist organizations.

Contents: Marketing concept and orientation; Market factors; Behavioural focus of marketing; Segmentation; The marketing mix; Products in tourism; Pricing; Marketing planning; Market research; Implementing planned programmes; Marketing applications for carriers, tour operators and travel agents, national tourism organizations and town, resorts and regions; Prospects for marketing in tourism.

0 434 91254 9
240pp. 234×156mm
Paperback

The Holiday Makers

Understanding the impact of leisure and travel

Jost Krippendorf

University of Bern

This book – thought-provoking and profound in its analysis of the present and future patterns of work and leisure – will be as important for individual tourists as for hoteliers, tour operators and travel agents, and for many others who will reflect on their role in the world of leisure and travel of tomorrow. The different forms of tourism are analysed, the effects on the indigenous countries and their people examined, and positive steps to reconcile people's holiday requirements with the world's economic and social structures are outlined.

As director of the Institute of Tourism Research Jost Krippendorf has been able to draw on research supported by the Swiss Hotel Association and the Swiss Travel Savings Bank to write a compelling and challenging book.

0 434 91083 X
320pp 234×156mm diagrams and 48 photographs
Paperback